Athletic Training
Management
Concepts and Applications

Second Edition

Athletic Training Management
Concepts and Applications

James M. Rankin, PhD, ATC

Department of Kinesiology
University of Toledo
Toledo, Ohio

Christopher D. Ingersoll, PhD, ATC, FACSM

Athletic Training Department
Indiana State University
Terre Haute, Indiana

Boston   Burr Ridge, IL   Dubuque, IA   Madison, WI   New York   San Francisco   St. Louis
Bangkok   Bogotá   Caracas   Lisbon   London   Madrid
Mexico City   Milan   New Delhi   Seoul   Singapore   Sydney   Taipei   Toronto

McGraw-Hill Higher Education ⚡

A Division of The **McGraw-Hill** *Companies*

ATHLETIC TRAINING MANAGEMENT: CONCEPTS AND APPLICATIONS
SECOND EDITION

Published by McGraw-Hill, an imprint of The McGraw-Hill Companies, Inc., 1221 Avenue of the Americas, New York, NY 10020. Copyright © 2001, 1995 by The McGraw-Hill Companies, Inc. All rights reserved. No part of this publication may be reproduced or distributed in any form or by any means, or stored in a data base or retrieval system, without the prior written consent of The McGraw-Hill Companies, Inc., including, but not limited to, in any network or other electronic storage or transmission, or broadcast for distance learning.

Some ancillaries, including electronic and print components, may not be available to customers outside the United States.

This book is printed on acid-free paper.

1 2 3 4 5 6 7 8 9 0 QPF/QPF 0 9 8 7 6 5 4 3 2 1 0

ISBN 0-07-092143-1

Vice president and editor-in-chief: *Kevin T. Kane*
Executive editor: *Vicki Malinee*
Senior developmental editor: *Michelle Turenne*
Senior marketing manager: *Pamela S. Cooper*
Project manager: *Sheila M. Frank*
Senior production supervisor: *Sandra Hahn*
Coordinator of freelance design: *David W. Hash*
Freelance interior design: *Kristyn A. Kalnes*
Freelance cover design: *Rokusek Design*
Senior photo research coordinator: *Carrie K. Burger*
Compositor: *Interactive Composition Corporation*
Typeface: *10/12 Photina*
Printer: *Quebecor Printing Book Group/Fairfield, PA*

Library of Congress Cataloging-in-Publication Data

Rankin, James Michael.
    Athletic training management : concepts and applications / James M. Rankin,
  Christopher D. Ingersoll. — 2nd ed.
      p. cm.
    Includes bibliographical references and index.
    ISBN 0-07-092143-1 (alk. paper)
    1. Athletic trainers. I. Ingersoll, Christopher D. II. Title.

RC1210.R36 2001
617.1'027—dc21   00-035485
                                     CIP

www.mhhe.com

Brief Contents

Contents

Preface

Athletic Training Management: Concepts and Applications was conceived while preparing a self-study for the University of Toledo athletic training education program in 1988. We knew we had to have an organization and administration course in the curriculum. For years we haunted the book dealers' section in the exhibits at the NATA Annual Meeting and the District IV meeting asking if anyone had an organization/administration text specific to athletic training. Finally Vicki Malinee of Mosby said, "No one has. Would you be interested in writing one?" The rest, as they say, is history. The outline of the first edition closely followed the competencies in place at that time.

Since the first edition was completed, we felt there were areas that we could improve. The first chapter is one that we feel strongly needs to be looked at by athletic trainers, but the first attempt was difficult reading. Examples throughout seemed to be geared to the college athletic training environment, if there were athletic training examples at all. We have worked hard to improve situations like this throughout the text.

Much has happened in athletic training education (and in the athletic training profession, for that matter) in the intervening five years since the first edition. The NATA Education Council was formed in 1998. CAAHEP is now the accrediting body for entry-level athletic training education programs. The internship programs are being phased out, primarily due to the superiority of classroom instruction combined with clinical education in the accredited programs as demonstrated by significantly higher passing rates on the NATABOC certification examination.

The explosion in the clinical setting that began in the late 1980s continues to this day. Women are becoming a greater force with each passsing year. Our next NATA president is Julie Max from California State University-Fullerton in District 8. Women are becoming more of a presence in professional sports. Athletic trainers are working in increasing numbers in the industrial setting. We are becoming a major voice that cannot be denied any longer as key players in the health care of athletes and active people.

WHO IS IT WRITTEN FOR?

Athletic Training Management: Concepts and Applications is designed for the upper-division undergraduate or graduate athletic training student. Special care was taken to make the text a useful addition to the practicing athletic trainer's and sports medicine professional's library as well. Although a reasonably intimate knowledge of athletic training is assumed, other professionals who supervise athletic trainers will also find the book useful.

NEW TO THIS EDITION

The text has been arranged into the broad categories of Personnel Management, Facilities, Operations, Legal Issues, and Information Technology. Chapter 7, "Designing Athletic Training Facilities," has been brought forward in the text, giving students time to complete design projects in the semester before things get hectic in the last two weeks as they always do.

Practice Setting: Where Do We Work?

There has been a great expansion of the coverage of the various practice settings in chapters dealing with the sports medicine team (with a stronger emphasis on clinics, industrial settings, Olympics, and professional sports), facilities management, insurance, and legal issues.

How to Get a Job

In the first edition, chapter 4 covered recruiting the sports medicine team. It has now been divided into two chapters: chapter 3, "The Sports Medicine Team," and chapter 4, "How to Get a Job." There is a stronger hands-on emphasis now placed on developing the materials needed to apply for a job, and how to prepare for a job interview.

Legal Issues

Legal issues now comprise two chapters for the second edition. Chapter 15 covers legal issues and chapter 16 examines risk management. The legal issues section focuses on credentialing, standards of practice, and negligence. The whole issue of using standards of practice, either from state practice acts or from national or regional governing bodies, is explored with particular emphasis on using the standards to establish the duty to act. Athletic trainers must take care to work within the scope of practice permitted by their state credential and practice acts.

Chapter 16, "Risk Management," looks at the principles of risk management and explores some specific cases involving athletic trainers and tort law. These cases are all public domain information, published in either federal or state appeals court proceedings, and they show the scope of exposure that athletic trainers have in today's market. While names have been abbreviated to emphasize the case concepts, the correct citations are present with each case, enabling the student to go to the source material for more information. Students also need to understand that cases become part of case law through the appeals process. (If a case is only heard in a district court and ends there, that case is not published in law books. The case then becomes a file folder in the court's and attorney's records only.)

Insurance and Third-Party Reimbursement

A new chapter has been added on third-party reimbursement. Third-party reimbursement means athletic trainers must become familiar with CPT coding of therapeutic procedures and ICD-9 classifications for medical conditions. Nothing in the CPT codes restricts use by licensed healthcare professionals, including athletic trainers. As athletic training is credentialed in more states, more athletic trainers will bill for services as other licensed healthcare professionals do now.

Information Technology

Chapters have been added on hardware, software, and using the Internet and the Web to retrieve and use information. Modern recordkeeping, communications, and information storage all require the use of a computer. Various components of systems are discussed with an eye toward helping the reader evaluate his or her own needs and be able to make the best use of the resources available for computers.

Pedagogy

- *For Critical Thought* case studies are presented at the beginning of every chapter and include possible resolutions at the ends of the chapters.
- Bulleted summaries reinforce key concepts for test preparation.
- Websites are presented with each chapter to direct students to additional resources.

ORGANIZATION

Part One—Personnel Management

- Chapter 1, "Development of Management Theories," explores classical management theories and relates them to athletic training. Of particular note are the sections examining preferred work environment and preferred management style.

- Chapter 2, "Personnel Motivation and Evaluation," focuses on motivational theories and how they relate to athletic training. The second part of the chapter covers the evaluation of personnel. There has been extensive revision of the presentation of the motivational theorists from the first edition.
- Chapter 3, "The Sports Medicine Team," identifies those professionals who should be part of the sports medicine team in the various practice settings. Particular emphasis is given to the roles of athletic trainers in clinics, industrial athletic training, Olympics, and professional sports. Once it has been established who should be on the team, the focus of the chapter shifts to putting together a job description and searching for the right person for the team.
- Chapter 4, "How to Get a Job," gives students solid practical information to use to find where the jobs are, how to put together materials to apply for a job, keys to look for that identify the ideal job, and interview skills.
- Chapter 5, "Managing Change, Conflict, and Burnout," contains a review of group conflict, including an individual's response within a group context, organizational change, and the recognition and management of burnout.

Part Two—Facilities

- Chapter 6, "Athletic Training Facilities Management," examines facilities problems, including personnel assignments, the population served, hours of operation, and policies and procedures manuals. Particular emphasis is placed on the clinical education of student athletic trainers in the various practice settings.
- Chapter 7, "Designing Athletic Training Facilities," is a primer on the clinical focus areas found in athletic training rooms. Working with architects, concept plans, floor plans, and construction blueprints, as well as electrical, plumbing, and HVAC plans are discussed.

Part Three—Operations

- Chapter 8, "Medical Records," reviews record keeping in the various practice settings. The NATABOC Standard of Practice for record keeping is emphasized, along with expanded sections on SOAP notes and confidentiality.
- Chapter 9, "Insurance," covers athletic medical insurance in colleges and universities, and to a lasser extent in high school settings. Emphasis is placed on second-dollar insurance plans. Catastrophic insurance and liability insurance are also discussed.
- Chapter 10, "Third-Party Reimbursement," explores the relationship developing in the profession of athletic training with the managed health care industry. Utilization of CPT codes and ICD-9 codes are introduced, along with procedures for filing claims and handling denied claims. The importance of third-party reimbursement to athletic trainers is discussed.
- Chapter 11, "Financial Management," explores the world of budgeting for athletic trainers. How to set up a purchase plan, how to bid, and the differences between categories in a line-item athletic training budget are discussed.
- Chapter 12, "Emergency Care Planning," addresses standard operating procedures and emergency care. The importance of writing out the plan and practicing it monthly are emphasized.
- Chapter 13, "Organizing and Administering Preparticipation Physical Examinations," explores the components of a preparticipation examination with an emphasis on the areas to be covered and specificity for each sport. New to this chapter is an added emphasis on cardiovascular screening.
- Chapter 14, "Public Relations," discusses public relations and marketing as they relate to the profession of athletic training and the public consciousness. The concept document of the 1999 NATA Public Relations Plan is included as an appendix at the end of the chapter.

Part Four—Legal Issues

- Chapter 15, "Athletic Training Practice," concentrates on the credentialing of athletic trainers, bringing together various organizations' standards statements to establish a standard of practice, and negligence. Using standards to define duty to act enables state practice acts and national organizations' standards-of-practice statements to be the arbiters in court.
- Chapter 16, "Risk Management," explores the interrelationship of risk management strategies with court cases that demonstrate what happens when there is either a real or perceived breakdown in risk management.

Part Five—Information Technology

- Chapter 17, "Computer Hardware," looks at the common hardware platforms available for computers today. More emphasis is placed on the components of the system than on the specifics of the components.
- Chapter 18, "Computer Software," explores common computer applications such as word processing, spreadsheets, databases, virus checkers, record-keeping software, and web editing software.
- Chapter 19, "The Internet," explores the use of the Internet and the Web for communications via e-mail and discussion groups and for information retrieval.

PEDAGOGY

Chapter objectives and key terms are found at the beginning of each chapter; references are provided at the end of each chapter. These features help to reinforce the content and direct the reader to other relevant resources.

For Critical Thought. New to the second edition, this feature opens each chapter with a detailed case study. After reading the chapter content, an additional "For Critical Thought" section concludes the chapter and discusses some of the possible resolutions to the opening case study.

Summaries. New to the second edition, these appear at the end of each chapter to reinforce key concepts.

Glossary. A detailed glossary of all key terms is presented at the end of the book.

Applications for Consideration. At the end of each chapter, there are from one to three short problems that emphasize the key concepts of the chapter and challenge the reader to find solutions to the problems presented.

Websites. In this second edition, each chapter concludes with a list of one to eight websites. Every effort is made to insure that these are accurate. With so many web pages introduced and abandoned each week on the Web, some of these pages might not function. Government web pages are more likely to function over extended periods of time.

ACKNOWLEDGEMENTS

During the six years that the first edition of *Athletic Training Management: Concepts and Applications* was in development, many people assisted us. The staff at Mosby-Yearbook was both supportive and patient during the development stages of the book. In particular, we appreciated Vicki Malinee, who provided the initial support that gave us the courage to proceed, and Michelle Turenne, who made it happen.

With this second edition, now with McGraw-Hill, we began the process with a different creative team, but arrived with Michelle again, which made everything easy because she understands athletic training so well. She is also understanding of our "anal retentiveness."

With the first edition, several people openly shared their ideas and expertise, which shaped and improved the material during the earlier stages of development. We are very grateful to them. They included:

Bob Stahara, ATC, PT
Jefferson Hospital Sports Medicine
Pittsburgh, Pennsylvania

Greg Gamble, M.A., ATC
Insurance Consultant
Pebble Beach, California

Jim Busser, Ph.D.
University of Nevada, Las Vegas
Las Vegas, Nevada

Mary Ingersoll
Architectural Design Consultant
Terre Haute, Indiana

Cynthia McKnight, Ph.D., ATC
Azuza Pacific University
Azuza, California

Bruce Groves, Ph.D.
University of Toledo
Toledo, Ohio

John Drowatzky, Ph.D., J.D.
University of Toledo
Toledo, Ohio

For the second edition we must include the following people who made significant contributions to the overall project:

Marjorie Albohm, M.S., ATC
Orthopaedic Medicine of Indiana
Mooresville, Indiana

Mitchell L. Cordova, Ph.D., ATC
Indiana State University
Terre Haute, Indiana

Nikki Livecchi, ATC
Indiana State University
Terre Haute, Indiana

Mark A. Merrick, Ph.D., ATC
Indiana State University
Terre Haute, Indiana

Susan Norkus, M.S., ATC
University of Toledo
Toledo, Ohio

Jeff Otte, ATC
Indiana State University
Terre Haute, Indiana

Michelle A. Sandrey, Ph.D., ATC
Indiana State University
Terre Haute, Indiana

Catherine Stemmans, Ph.D., ATC
Indiana State University
Terre Haute, Indiana

Robert Sterner, M.S., ATC
University of Toledo
Toledo, Ohio

Erik Swartz, M.S., ATC
University of Toledo
Toledo, Ohio

We are also indebted to the staff at the NATA office, particularly Ellen Satlof, Susan Briggs, and Suzanne Cracraft, who were always willing to help us get important information.

From the first edition, many of our students read sections and offered suggestions. In addition, significant assistance came from many of our colleagues. This second edition also benefited from the generous help of others.

The publisher's reviewers provided excellent suggestions to help make this text more usable and comprehensive. Our sincere thanks to:

first edition

Robert Moss, Ph.D., ATC
Western Michigan University
Kalamazoo, Michigan

Gretchen Schlabach, Ph.D., ATC
Northern Illinois University
DeKalb, Illinois

Clint Thompson, M.A., ATC
Truman State University
Kirksville, Missouri

Karen Toburen, Ph.D., ATC
Southwest Missouri State University
Springfield, Missouri

Brian Toy, Ph.D., ATC
University of Southern Maine
Portland, Maine

Patricia Troesch, M.A., ATC
Miami University
Oxford, Ohio

Kenneth Wright, DA, ATC
University of Alabama
Tuscaloosa, Alabama

second edition

David Kaiser, Ed.D., ATC
Central Michigan University
Mount Pleasant, Michigan

Carla Baker, ATC
Eastern Washington University
Cheney, Washington

Lance McNamara, M.S., ATC
Southeast Missouri State University
Cape Girardeau, Missouri

Our families willingly surrendered numerous hours of time to support our efforts with this text. Our love and appreciation to Barbara, Joey, and Mary Rankin, and to Mary, Kayla, T.J., and Tommy Ingersoll.

James M. Rankin, Ph.D., ATC
Christopher D. Ingersoll, Ph.D., ATC

PART ONE

Personnel Management

CHAPTER 1

Development of Management Theories

After reading this chapter, you should be able to:

- Evaluate the type of leader you would be comfortable working with on the job.
- Describe the historical development of modern management theories.
- Identify contemporary management theories.
- Describe the difference among the historical theories and contemporary management theories.
- Evaluate the types of supervisors you work with and how each type affects working conditions.

Key Terms

scientific management
human relations management
leadership studies
zone of indifference
McGregor's Theory X and Theory Y
Management by Objectives
Leadership (Managerial) Grid
human resources management
Total Quality Management
situational leadership

FOR CRITICAL THOUGHT:
Leadership Styles

1. Absenteeism—Gregg, Melendez, Johnson
2. Equipment purchase for football athletic training room and Olympic sports athletic training room
3. Maintenance
4. Preseason physical exams—coordination with Megasports Clinic

The Monday morning staff meeting to review the previous week and plan the current week begins at three separate sites. The person in charge of the meeting proceeds through the agenda.

•

At the first site, the person in charge has devised a solution to be implemented by the employees. For the three employees who have problems being at work, either they will eliminate the problem by the end of the week or they will be seeking employment elsewhere. When discussing absenteeism, it also becomes apparent that someone has been following employees around to check on their time outside the athletic training room they were assigned to. Phone calls were made to other parts of the clinic to confirm that the athletic trainer actually went to that part of the building to perform a therapy technique requiring equipment only available there. No message, just checking up to see that the employee was not wasting company time. The manager also informs the staff that three new ultrasound units have been purchased for the football team, even though the athletic training room used for Olympic sports has none. One of the football team's ultrasound units will be moved over after the season is finished. It will be recalibrated if funds are available, or before the next football season. Preseason physical examinations for all fall and winter sports other than football, soccer, and volleyball are set for the Sunday of Labor Day weekend. That is the only time the football staff athletic trainers are available until November. They are simply too busy to schedule another time. That is the way it is in this authoritarian setting.

•

Another job site has the same meeting. The person in charge of this meeting goes over the same agenda, lists the problems of the week and informs the employees that management wants the problems to go away at once. Each area supervisor must take care of discipline on his/her own initiative. There is currently no company-wide policy. Management believes that each athletic training room can set its own requirements as long as the policy does not sabotage any other area and as long as that area does not bother top management with the mundane details. There is considerable anguish over whether football needs any more equipment when the other athletic training rooms have so little. The manager suggests that the two supervising athletic trainers from football and Olympic sports should go into another room and work out a solution. They should not come out until they have made up, and not tell management what they are going to do, just do it. There are no funds for maintenance, so do not ask. Take any money you need from another line in your budget, but do not bother the senior staff with the details. No corrections, suggestions, or help will be

forthcoming from management. The laissez-faire style of management appears very close to anarchy.

•

A third job site has the same meeting. The person in charge of this meeting goes over the same agenda and has prepared a short list of problems. The person then asks the workers if they have any additions. When the list is complete, the person in charge of the meeting requests input and solutions from the workers that will be considered by the group as a whole, modified with the input of the group, and implemented by the group that created the solutions with the guidance of management. Apparently all patients are being treated within acceptable time limits, and outcomes assessment has been positive. There does not appear to be a need to check up on workers, and the manager in charge praises the workers' diligence in patient care. Senior management requests information on absenteeism and discovers that two of the three employees have child care problems. One of the employees has inquired about the possibility of a six-month job sharing arrangement with another person, both being part-time, after which the employee would go back to full-time. Senior management approves such an arrangement and the clinic is no longer short-staffed for part of the day. The third staff member's spouse was involved in an automobile accident, and she requests an unpaid leave of absence until her spouse can take care of himself. Again, the request is granted, and part-time help is obtained from a graduate intern from a nearby university. A discussion of the reasons for the comprehensive nature of the athletic program is included so that everyone will understand that health care applies to all athletes, not just those in major money-making sports. Agreement is reached that one of the ultrasound units will go to the Olympic sports site, but that football can send *over athletes for treatment when all of their equipment is in use. Since almost all of the staff athletic trainers cover home football games, this also provides an opportunity for those staff members not assigned to football to become familiar with some of the athletes. This participatory approach works, because the athletic trainers make it work. They respect and support each other and the job they perform.*

The cultural setting of organizations and how the management style evolved is rarely studied in athletic training education programs. Corporate culture has been defined as a set of shared beliefs and values that the members of an organization have concerning the function and existence of the organization.[7] The significance is that corporate culture influences the behavior of everyone in the organization.

When people are looking for a job as an athletic trainer, one of the considerations needs to be the organizational culture and how the individual's personality will fit into that environment. To understand this concept, some study of the evolution of management theory is required. Bridges and Roquemore[4] stated that more than 98 percent of all first-time managers in all types of organizations obtain their first supervisory positions without first having any management training. Interestingly enough, when our students have been presented with the alternative styles from the case study, they almost universally choose to work in an agency with a democratic or participatory style of management. Yet when given an instrument that assesses their personal belief structure and what type of manager they would be, the overwhelming majority are closer to the authoritarian position. Few ever identify with the laissez-faire view. (See box 1-1.)

The word *management* is derived from the Italian *maneggiare* meaning to control or train.[12] Management and administration are not synonymous. Administration may be seen as the broader term, encompassing both policies and procedures, whereas management is specific and deals with accomplishing goals.

Administrative and leadership skills are needed for organizing people and processes to reach the goals of the organization.[32] There has long been confusion about whether the term *administration* refers to the attainment of desired goals or whether *leadership* is a better term. Lipham[21] states that administration means using existing procedures to complete the desired goals, whereas leadership involves using new policies and procedures to the same end.

Certo,[6] when identifying the difference between management and leadership, defines management as the broader term, encompassing behavioral as well as nonbehavioral issues. Leadership is defined as emphasizing only behavioral issues. The terms are not necessarily mutually exclusive. Current personnel administration and management approaches contain elements from many sources; therefore it is important to provide a historical overview of some principal theories.

SCIENTIFIC MANAGEMENT

Frederick Taylor

Modern management began in 1911 with the concept of **scientific management** developed by Frederick Taylor.[38] Taylor believed that management could use the scientific method to create a mathematical model in which money was the incentive to induce people to perform jobs.

In Taylor's scientific management, each worker became an impersonal cog in a machine. There was a strong emphasis on production through establishing a single "correct way" to perform a task that was taught to the workers. The workers were selected for their ability to follow the rules regardless of circumstances. The result was production at the expense of dehumanizing the workers. Scientific management did not allow for motivating factors such as recognition, prestige, power, self-esteem, or a sense of achievement.

If Taylor had been an athletic trainer, there would be only one way to tape an ankle or one protocol for performing joint mobilization on a

■ **What Kind of Organization Design Do You Want to Work for?**   *Box 1-1*

Do you have an idea of what type of organization you would like to work for? Most likely you have given it some thought, but your focus has probably been on the type of job or maybe its location. What about the personality of the organization? How much consideration have you given to the culture you would work best in? For this exercise, first complete the questions below and score them. Then, in your group, compare responses to the following questions: Are there group members who prefer to work in large bureaucratic organizations? Who prefer to work in smaller companies? Discuss with your group members why you feel that type of organization will best suit you. Also, imagine that you work in an organization whose culture is opposite your preference. How might that affect your work? Discuss with your class members.

For each of the following statements, circle the level of agreement or disagreement that you personally feel:

SA = Strongly agree   D = Disagree
A = Agree   SD = Strongly disagree
U = Uncertain

1. I like being part of a team and having my performance assessed in terms of my contribution to the team.   SA   A   U   D   SD
2. No person's needs should be compromised in order for a department to achieve its goals.   SA   A   U   D   SD
3. I prefer a job where my boss leaves me alone.   SA   A   U   D   SD
4. I like the thrill and excitement of taking risks.   SA   A   U   D   SD
5. People shouldn't break rules.   SA   A   U   D   SD
6. Seniority in an organization should be highly rewarded.   SA   A   U   D   SD
7. I respect authority.   SA   A   U   D   SD
8. If a person's job performance is inadequate, it's irrelevant how much effort he or she made.   SA   A   U   D   SD
9. I like things to be predictable.   SA   A   U   D   SD
10. I'd prefer my identity to come from my professional expertise rather than from the organization that employs me.   SA   A   U   D   SD

Scoring: For items 5, 6, 7, and 9, give yourself −2 for each SA, −1 for A, 0 for U, +1 for D, and +2 for SD. For items 1, 2, 3, 4, 8, and 10, reverse the scoring (+2 for SA, +1 for A, and so forth). Add up your total.

What the Assessment Means. Your score will fall somewhere between +20 and −20. The higher your score (positive), the higher your preference for small, innovative, flexible, team-oriented cultures, which are most likely to be found in research units, team-based structures, small businesses, or boundaryless organizations. Negative scores, on the other hand, indicate that you would be more comfortable in a stable, rule-oriented culture. This is synonymous with large companies and government agencies.

FUNDAMENTALS OF MANAGEMENT: ESSENTIAL CONCEPTS AND APPLICATIONS, 2/E by Robbins/DeCenzo, © 1995. Reprinted by permission of Prentice-Hall, Inc., Upper Saddle River, NJ.

shoulder. He would have assessed the "best" from all of the options and then trained his subordinates only in the method to be used. Individual variability would be forbidden. If the athletic trainers tried to do other versions of the basic pattern, either they would be replaced with athletic trainers who would do only what they were allowed, or the person's salary would be altered until the pay was enough incentive to do the job the way management intended.

The overall assumption of scientific management was that once the worker understood financial incentive (the only incentive that was effective according to Taylor), then his or her work output would automatically increase. Taylor is known for his emphasis on quantitative performance evaluation.

HUMAN RELATIONS MANAGEMENT

Human relations management was a reaction to scientific management that incorporated the behavioral sciences. Classic human relations values stress the superiority of feeling over thinking and promote an expanded interpersonal consciousness and spirit of openness. Organizations seem to be able to incorporate human relations values fairly easily, while systems values are more difficult.[19]

Mary Parker Follett

The most influential contributor to human relations management was Mary Parker Follett.[37] She completed a series of scholarly reports[25] that are the foundation of human relations management.

Follett believed that people in control of a particular function should deal directly with employees above and below them, rather than only with coworkers at the same level in some other area or department. Institutions that allow managers to work only within their peer level lose overall control of the organization. Managers from various departments must interact early, during the design of organizational strategy, rather than having each manager bring a completed plan for action to the initial meetings. If all participants have their own "finished" policies, they will strive to ensure that their policies are used, even at the expense of quality.

Follett believed that maintaining institutional balance is a continuing process, best exemplified by planning departments that continually reevaluate the circumstances surrounding a job. Planning allows both workers and management to be proactive rather than simply reacting after a problem presents itself.

Elton Mayo and the Hawthorne Studies

During the 1930s, businesses were unlikely to adopt the theories of a woman without overwhelming evidence of their feasibility. The data, which supported the management concepts of Follett, were provided by a group of Harvard University researchers led by Elton Mayo that became known as the Hawthorne Studies.[22] Mayo was seeking information on whether concern for employees would benefit performance rather than the traditional practice of scientific management with its emphasis on direction and monetary incentive.

The Hawthorne studies were conducted at the Western Electric Company's Hawthorne Plant in Cicero, Illinois, and involved a unit that assembled relays. After initial consultation with the workers, illumination at the plant was changed. When the amount of light increased, so did the productivity of the workers, which was expected. However, productivity also increased when lighting was reduced, which was totally unexpected. Equally unexpected was that the control group showed an increase in productivity, even though there were no changes to working conditions with this group.

Other studies followed that altered the working hours per day, workdays per week, rest periods, and other conditions. The workers were consulted before each change and were allowed to overrule management. Each change seemed to be met with an increase or no change in productivity, even though some of the changes were clearly negative.

Mayo concluded that group dynamics in the workplace was an important factor. The workers perceived that they were important to management, which created an attitude that their well-being and self-determination were of primary importance and their work was incidental.[22] These studies established that consideration for (and improved treatment of) workers was clearly in management's best interest.

Athletic trainers using Follett's theories would have the managers from a number of different departments where ankles were taped consult with each other to establish the best method. The workers would be asked to participate in the establishment of the overall process. In the end, however, should there be disagreements on the process, money would still be the final arbiter to establish what is correct.

The human relations approach was ultimately a failure. It challenged management was to devise financial incentives and good working conditions, but it did not recognize the importance of psychological variables.[11] Motivation to perform well involves much more than money, job security, and improved working conditions.

LEADERSHIP STUDIES

Iowa Studies

A number of **leadership studies** conducted in the 1930s and 1940s are significant to management and organization theory. The first of these, by Lippitt and White[20] at the University of Iowa, looked at the effects of leadership style on a group of variables including aggression and frustration in young boys. They tested three different types of leaders—authoritarian, democratic, and laissez-faire. The results suggested that boys strongly preferred the democratic style of leader when compared to the others, but also preferred the laissez-faire style to the authoritarian. When given tasks under the democratic style, the group's production was highest in quality and morale. Under the authoritarian style, quantity of production was highest, but it decreased as soon as the supervisor left the room. Under the laissez-faire style, a system rarely used today,[32] production actually increased when the leader left the room.

Ohio State Studies

Studies at Ohio State University[35] during the mid-1940s focused on situational variables and how these affected leadership rather than the traits of the leaders. Results suggested that there are two

dimensions of leadership, initiating structure and consideration. Initiating structure is a task- and goal-oriented variable related to the leader's ability to establish a structure and the group's response to the leader's attempts. Consideration is concerned with relationships and is related to personal factors such as trust, warmth, respect, and friendship.

University of Michigan Studies

Studies completed at the University of Michigan[18] by Renis Likert and others in the late 1940s found two dimensions of leader behavior that they labeled *employee oriented* and *production oriented*. These studies found that supervisors of high-producing departments received and gave general rather than close supervision, and were more employee oriented than task oriented. Employees had considerable latitude in establishing the process for doing work.

BEHAVIORAL SCIENCE

Chester Barnard

In the 1950s, human relations management was displaced by behavioral science theories that related the structures of scientific management to human relations. Chester Barnard was responsible for defining in a general way formal organizational structure, and using administration as a communications tool.[38]

Barnard[1] defined the terms *effectiveness* and *efficiency* in a new way. To Barnard, effectiveness referred to accomplishing objectives, that is, getting the job done, which was exemplified by scientific management. Athletic trainers who complete four patients per hour compared to those only completing three are more effective. He also saw efficiency as related to satisfying individual motives and maintaining morale, as exemplified by the human relations approach. To have an athletic trainer increase the number of patients completed in an hour requires incentive, which may be money but is more likely a complex mixture of variables.

Barnard believed that the test of effectiveness was completing goals, whereas the test of efficiency was instilling the motivation to participate.[1] Clearly, administration can be both effective and efficient, neither effective nor efficient, or only effective or efficient. Obviously the best solution is being able to complete tasks and instill the desire to be both an effective and efficient participant.

Another of Barnard's concepts is the **zone of indifference**.[1] He argued that there were only three responses possible to given dictates of management. Some orders are clearly unacceptable and will not be obeyed. When an athletic trainer is ordered by a coach to allow an athlete to participate against doctor's orders, the proper response is to disobey the order. Some orders are in a neutral zone, where they are barely acceptable or barely unacceptable. Athletic trainers in collegiate settings have routinely worked 70 to 80 hours a week while in-season for a major sport. While they know that management should hire additional athletic trainers, they also carry on grudgingly, since they know that the athletes are in need of professional care. In professional baseball at the minor league level, athletic trainers are often also traveling secretaries/business managers, which is not part of their athletic training education.

The rest of the orders are clearly acceptable. Athletic trainers in all job settings evaluate musculoskeletal injuries, initiate first aid, and communicate with appropriate medical personnel. Many job settings perform volunteer service for camps, weekend events, or special competitions. All employees are expected to volunteer for at least some of the events as a part of normal work expectations.

Just because the commands fall within the acceptance area does not imply that the workers would perform them without direction from management. Instead, the directives are what are expected by the workers from what they know of their organization. The workers are indifferent to these orders. When combined with Barnard's concepts of effectiveness and efficiency, it can be argued that the ability to administer is conferred from the lowest level in an organization, not decreed from the highest.

CONTEMPORARY MANAGEMENT

Management theory in the 1960s and 1970s was concerned with integrating personal needs with the completion of tasks. Management science and behavioral science were not mutually exclusive; they were considered complementary.

McGregor's Theory X and Theory Y

An early example of contemporary management is Douglas **McGregor's Theory X and Theory Y**.[23] Theory X resembles scientific management in its assumptions:

- The average person has an inherent dislike of work and will avoid it if he or she can.
- Because humans dislike work, most people must be coerced, controlled, directed, and threatened with punishment to put forth adequate effort toward the goals of the organization.
- The average human prefers to be directed, wishes to avoid responsibility, has relatively little ambition, and wants security above all else.[23]

Theory X is the authoritarian, condescending, punitive approach to management reminiscent of Taylor. There is no regard for the individual; once the workers are secure and free from having to make decisions, they are satisfied and productive. An example of Theory X is a sports medicine clinic that assigns fixed amounts of time for treatments such as joint mobilizations and then disciplines employees who fail to treat an appropriate number of patients per hour.

Theory Y generalizes from behavioral science the following assumptions:

- The expenditure of physical and mental effort in work is as natural as play or rest.
- The use of external control and threat of punishment are not the only way to make employees work toward organizational objectives. People will exercise self-direction and self-control in the service of objectives to which they are committed.
- Commitment to objectives is a function of the rewards associated with the achievement of those objectives.
- The average person learns under proper conditions not only to accept but to seek responsibility.
- The capacity to exercise a relatively high degree of imagination, ingenuity, and creativity in the solution of organizational problems is widely, not narrowly, distributed in the population.

- Under the conditions of modern industrial life, the intellectual potential of the average person is only partially utilized.[23]

The democratic approach, in which the needs of the organization for task completion are integrated with the personal needs of the worker, exemplifies Theory Y. Management is based on motivational values, only a small portion of which involve financial compensation. When staff athletic trainers can question each other on any professional problem, when personnel assignments can be varied with individual needs as long as athletic training room coverage is maintained, then a democratic outlook exists. Another example of Theory Y is when an athletic training staff ensures that the student athletic trainers understand injury evaluations as they are performed and answers fully and completely any questions. The Theory Y approach is much closer to Mary Parker Follett than to Taylor. McGregor was convinced that Theory Y was more accurate, but that traditional organizational structures, especially those of industry embodied Theory X.[32]

Management by Objectives

Another approach to integrating personnel needs with those of an organization has been called **Management by Objectives**.[31] In this system, performance objectives are established by the mutual decision of the workers and supervisors, progress toward the objectives is periodically reviewed, and rewards are allocated that reflect achievement of the objectives.

An MBO system contains four basic elements. These are goal specificity, participative decision making, a specific time period, and performance feedback.[31] During the planning stage, goals are mutually agreed on by both management and workers.[27] First, a mission statement is developed and both long-range and medium-range goals are identified. This is often done in sports medicine clinic settings, especially those affiliated with hospitals.

At the department level, objectives are defined to allow the organization to meet its stated purpose.[8] During departmental planning, both sides independently determine job task and methodology and afterward meet to agree on the goals for subordinates. The courses of action and job functions are very

structured. After obtaining the conceptual framework from both the athletic trainers and the supervising physicians, a plan of action is agreed upon to care for the patients served by the facility.

In theory, this system is very good at obtaining data to support the current structure or the need for change. The data, however, tend to be quantitative, rather than qualitative. Depending on the commitment from all levels of management, there is either great flexibility to change or there is little room for change except through the current definitions of the objectives.

Perhaps the greatest weakness is that MBO can be undermined at any level by a manager who does not adhere to the tenets of involving the employees in the decision-making process. A major problem in much of American industry is the presence of an adversarial relationship between the workers and management, which can sabotage the system to the extent that workers do only the minimum expected of them to collect their pay, but have no real commitment to improving the process or working conditions.

Deming[10] argued that setting specific objectives caused employees to focus on the criteria by which they would be rewarded (quantity which is measurable) rather than quality. Mistakes not seen as errors will be repeated to increase the quantity produced. Deming also felt that people viewed objectives as maximum standards rather than minimum. When employees reached the objectives, they tended to relax, decreasing the drive for continuous improvement.

Hersey and Blanchard[13] have stated that the greatest failure on the part of any organization is its inability to secure cooperation and understanding from its employees. Success or failure can be caused by leadership more than any other factor. Research starting with the Ohio State leadership studies suggested that initiating structure and consideration were the most important variables. Hersey and Blanchard suggested that initiating structure was equivalent to a concern for task and consideration was a concern for relationships.

Blake and Mouton's Managerial Grid

Robert Blake and Jane Mouton[2] developed an approach similar to Hersey and Blanchard's and called it the **Managerial Grid**. This has been further

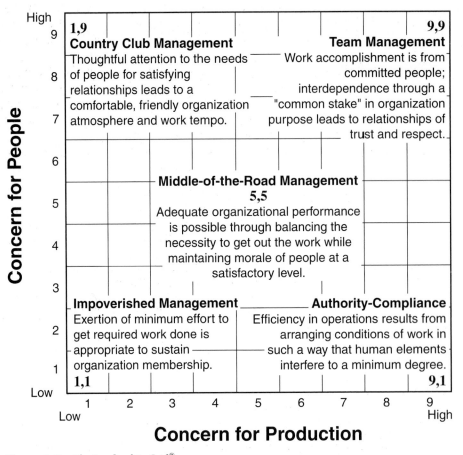

Figure 1-1 The Leadership Grid®
(The Leadership Grid® Figure from *Leadership Dilemmas—Grid Solutions* by Robert R. Blake and Anne Adams McCanse [formerly the Managerial Grid Figure by Robert R. Blake and Jane S. Mouton], Houston: Gulf Publishing Company, p. 29. Copyright © 1991, by Scientific Methods, Inc. Reproduced by permission of the owners.)

refined by Blake and McCanse as the **Leadership Grid**. (See figure 1-1.) The *x*-axis is labeled "Concern for Production" and the *y*-axis "Concern for People." Each axis is divided into nine sections, numbered from one to nine. Values are expressed as pairs of interdependent numbers; the first represents the *x*-axis and the second represents the *y*-axis. Of the eighty-one possible points, five are considered major stylistic differences and are explained on the grid. These differences are at points 1,9 (Country Club Management); 9,9 (Team Management); 5,5 (Middle-of-the-Road Management); 1,1 (Impoverished Management); and 9,1 (Authority-Compliance). In addition, two other refinements

have evolved: 9+9 Paternalistic Leadership and Opportunistic Leadership. In 9+9 Paternalistic Leadership, reward and approbation are accorded to people in return for loyalty and obedience, whereas failure to conform leads to punishment.[2] Managers who adopt any style that provides them with the greatest advantage are emblematic of Opportunistic Management.[2]

Reddin's 3-D Theory

From the work of Blake and Mouton, William Reddin proposed the 3-D Theory of Management Effectiveness[29] by incorporating managerial

1,1	**Impoverished Management**—Often referred to as laissez-faire leadership. Leaders in this position have little concern for people or productivity, avoid taking sides, and stay out of conflicts. They do just enough to get by.
1,9	**Country Club Management**—Managers in this position have great concern for people and little concern for production. They try to avoid conflicts and concentrate on being well liked. To them the task is less important than good interpersonal relations. Their goal is to keep people happy. (This is a soft Theory X approach and not a sound human relations approach.)
9,1	**Authority-Obedience**—Managers in this position have great concern for production and little concern for people. They desire tight control in order to get tasks done efficiently. They consider creativity and human relations to be unnecessary.
5,5	**Organization Man Management**—Often termed middle-of-the-road leadership. Leaders in this position have medium concern for people and production. They attempt to balance their concern for both people and production, but are not committed to either.
9+9	**Paternalistic, "Father Knows Best" Management**—A style in which reward is promised for compliance and punishment threatened for noncompliance.
Opp	**Opportunistic, "What's In It for Me" Management**—The style utilized depends on which style the leader feels will return him or her the greatest self-benefit.
9,9	**Team Management**—This style of leadership is considered to be ideal. Such managers have great concern for both people and production. They work to motivate employees to reach their highest levels of accomplishment. They are flexible and responsive to change, and they understand the need to change.

Figure 1-1   The Leadership Grid (*Continued*)
(Modified from Robert T. Blake and Jane S. Mouton, *The Managerial Grid III*, Houston: Gulf Publishing Company, Copyright © 1985. Reproduced by permission of the owners.)

TABLE 1-1   3-D Theory of Management

		Management Style	
Blake and Mouton Grid Location	**Management Type**	**Less Effective**	**More Effective**
9,9	Integrated	Compromiser	Executive
9,1	Dedicated	Autocrat	Benevolent Autocrat
1,9	Related	Missionary	Developer
1,1	Separated	Deserter	Bureaucrat

effectiveness, which he defined as the extent to which output requirements are met. The 3-D Theory incorporated four types of management: integrated, dedicated, related, and separated. These were derived from Blake and Mouton. Reddin then separated each style into a management style based on effectiveness. (See table 1-1.) Effective managers functioned in a way that fit the needs of both the organization and the workers. The less effective managers exhibited behavior that was not always appropriate to conditions of task or relationship. When the re-

sponse was appropriate to needs, management was considered effective. For example, a 1,1 score on the Leadership Grid could be earned either by someone who had a job that was very undemanding but necessary, such as making ice bags and ice cups, or by someone who was doing everything possible to not complete the necessary parts of a job. Likewise, just because a manager scores 9,9 does not guarantee that the manager is behaving in an appropriate way for a leader. The compromiser will sell his or her own mother to become a success.

Human Resources Management

In the 1970s, the concept of **human resources management** came into focus. Management finally realized that of human resources, capital resources, and physical resources, the only one that can synthesize, that is, produce an output greater than the sum of its components, is human resources.[30] Most large organizations, including healthcare facilities, have human resource departments today.

According to Miklovich and Boudreau,[26] human resource management is a series of decisions about the employment relationship that influence the effectiveness of employees and organizations. Human relations managers use a diagnostic model to assess conditions, set objectives, and evaluate the results.

Conditions are assessed in three areas. The first area is external conditions; these are economic, international, governmental, and union. The second is organizational conditions; these include the nature of the organization, its plans, and its finances. The final area is the characteristics of the employees, including attitudes, work experience, wages, and performance level.

Setting objectives involves maximizing the efficiency of the organization and being equitable to the workforce. To achieve both increased efficiency and fair treatment of the worker, management must blend methods, which requires planning. Human resources management activities can be broken into four areas: staffing, employee training and development, compensation, and employee or union relations. Finally, evaluation of the activities should note the changes in the organization's environment brought about by the setting of objectives and the choosing of human resource activities. Evaluation also means returning to step one and assessing conditions again or repeating the process. Athletic trainers working in clinical or industrial settings often find that when they are hired they have training sessions before they actually start work in the clinic. These sessions deal in policies and procedures, benefits, on-the-job requirements, and how the employee accesses the various programs available at the work site.

Total Quality Management

One of the recent theories to gain acceptance is that of **Total Quality Management (TQM)**, which is a collection of roles and practices that are oriented and that strive to always meet or exceed the needs and expectations of the consumer in an ongoing, planned system.[21] Who the customer is varies depending on the actual, immediate consumer of the goods. In athletic training settings, the customers are usually those receiving care. However, athletic trainers are also customers because they consume goods (expendable supplies, equipment) and services (staff time, calibration) in the delivery of athletic training to patients.

Implementation of a TQM system requires a great deal of planning and forethought. In the transformation of the traditional model (roughly management by objectives) to the new model, fundamentally new ways of thinking must be implemented. In the place of a hierarchical, control-focused, autocratic, capital-based organization must come a knowledge-based system utilizing networks, self-managed teams, and cross-functional employees.[16] The gap between these two positions is closed by empowerment at all levels in the organization and establishing an organizational climate that breeds trust and successful competition.

The three most important people in the quality management movement are W. Edwards Deming, Joseph M. Juran, and Philip B. Crosby. The most influential is Deming,[14] an American whose management concepts were broadly adopted by the Japanese during their post–World War II economic resurgence. Dr. Deming favored quality transformation at all levels of an organization based on assumptions that, among other things, state decisions must be based on facts, not supposition, the people who perform the work know it best, and teams can accomplish more than individuals. He developed this philosophy after encountering scientific management in the 1930s. In particular, Deming was upset with the concept of dividing the work between management and labor, with management taking the work for which they are better suited. Deming felt that this removed the worker from the responsibility for the quality of his or her work.[16] Quality became the work of inspectors, while workers who produced too many scrap pieces were fired. Deming's working thesis is embodied in fourteen points for managers to live by (see below). These have been applied in both business and service industries in recent years.

To implement total quality management, the concept that if better is possible, then good is never enough, must be followed.[24] Workers must be completely integrated into the decision-making process, which brings in aspects of human resource development. Many of the beliefs and practices, especially in selecting personnel and in staff development and training, are critical to total quality management.

Deming's fourteen points were developed for manufacturing settings, but with a little modification they can be set up to address the needs of medical service organizations. Batalden and Vorlicky[9] applied Deming's work to the medical arena by ini-

tially determining what constitutes service to patients, the patient population served, and standards of service for one year and five years into the future. Statistical evidence of quality of incoming materials, tasks performed at the facility by staff, and the costs of defective work on the efficiency of the operation must be determined. The competitive low-bid system often results in low quality, too. Deming[9] stated, "He that has a rule to give his business to the low bidder deserves to get rooked!"

One way to assess quality is through assessing patient satisfaction with the services received, possibly even asking them to measure the service against a performance standard. These outcomes assessments are utilized by health care agencies and governmental bodies to determine the effectiveness of a particular treatment protocol or even a profession.

Dr. Deming's fourteen points

1. Create, publish, and distribute to all employees a statement of the aims and purposes of the company or other organization. The management constantly must demonstrate their commitment to this statement.
2. Learn the new philosophy, top management, and the identity of all employees.
3. Understand the purpose of inspection—for improvement of processes and reduction of cost.
4. End the practice of awarding business on price tag alone.
5. Improve constantly and forever the system of production and service.
6. Institute training.
7. Teach and institute leadership.
8. Drive out fear. Create trust and a climate for innovation.
9. Optimize toward the aims and purposes of the company the efforts of teams, groups, and staff areas.
10. Eliminate exhortations to the workforce.
11a. Eliminate numerical quotas for production; instead, learn and institute methods for improvement.
11b. Eliminate Management by Objectives; instead, learn the capabilities of processes and how to improve them.
12. Remove barriers that rob people of pride of workmanship.
13. Encourage education and self-improvement for all persons.
14. Take action to accomplish the transformation.

Revised January 10, 1990. Originally published in *Out of the Crisis* by W. Edwards Deming. Published by MIT Center for Advanced Engineering Study, Cambridge, MA 02139. Copyright 1986 by W. Edwards Deming. Revised by W. Edwards Deming in January 1990. Reprinted by permission of MIT and The W. Edwards Deming Institute.

■ Your Preferred Leadership Style   *Box 1-2*

The following items describe aspects of leadership behavior. Respond to each item according to the way you would be most likely to act if you were the leader of a work group. Circle whether you would be likely to behave in the described way:

always (A), frequently (F), occasionally (0), seldom (S), or never (N).

If I were the leader of a work group . . .

A F 0 S N 1. I would most likely act as the spokesperson of the group.
A F 0 S N 2. I would encourage overtime work.
A F 0 S N 3. I would allow members complete freedom in their work.
A F 0 S N 4. I would encourage the use of uniform procedures.
A F 0 S N 5. I would permit the members to use their own judgment in solving problems.
A F 0 S N 6. I would stress being ahead of competing groups.
A F 0 S N 7. I would speak as a representative of the group.
A F 0 S N 8. I would needle members for greater effort.
A F 0 S N 9. I would try out my ideas in the group.
A F 0 S N 10. I would let the members do their work the way they think best.
A F 0 S N 11. I would be working hard for a promotion.
A F 0 S N 12. I would be able to tolerate postponement and uncertainty.
A F 0 S N 13. I would speak for the group when visitors were present.
A F 0 S N 14. I would keep the work moving at a rapid pace.
A F 0 S N 15. I would turn the members loose on a job and let them go to it.
A F 0 S N 16. I would settle conflicts when they occur in the group.
A F 0 S N 17. I would get swamped by details.
A F 0 S N 18. I would represent the group at outside meetings.
A F 0 S N 19. I would be reluctant to allow the members any freedom of action.
A F 0 S N 20. I would decide what would be done and how it would be done.
A F 0 S N 21. I would push for increased production.
A F 0 S N 22. I would let some members have authority that I could keep.
A F 0 S N 23. Things would usually turn out as I predict.
A F 0 S N 24. I would allow the group a high degree of initiative.
A F 0 S N 25. I would assign group members to particular tasks.
A F 0 S N 26. I would be willing to make changes.
A F 0 S N 27. I would ask the members to work harder.
A F 0 S N 28. I would trust the group members to exercise good judgment.
A F 0 S N 29. I would schedule the work to be done.
A F 0 S N 30. I would refuse to explain my actions.

■ Your Preferred Leadership Style   *Box 1-2 (Continued)*

A F O S N 31. I would persuade others that my ideas are to their advantage.
A F O S N 32. I would permit the group to set its own pace.
A F O S N 33. I would urge the group to beat its previous record.
A F O S N 34. I would act without consulting the group.
A F O S N 35. I would ask that group members follow standard rules and regulations.

Scoring: The scoring for this assessment may appear complex, but it isn't if you carefully follow these instructions. Circle statement numbers 8, 12, 17, 18, 19, 30, 34, and 35. If you checked S (seldom) or N (never) for any of those eight statements, place a 1 in the left margin next to the circled number. For the 27 statements not circled above, place a 1 in the left margin next to the statement number for each that you responded A (always) or F (frequently). You now have 1's to the left of many of the 35 statements. Circle the 1's you have written in front of the following statements: 3, 5, 8, 10, 15, 18, 19, 22, 24, 26, 28, 30, 32, 34, and 35. Count the number of circled 1's you have and place that number in box A. Count the number of 1's that are not circled for the remaining statements. Place that number in box B.

A	B

What the Assessment Means: Using the diagram below, place a mark on the people-centered scale that corresponds to your score in Box A. Likewise, using your score in Box B, place a mark on the task-centered scale. Draw a straight line connecting those two marks. The point at which this line intersects the leadership behavior scale indicates your leadership behavior.

Leadership Behavior

Task-Centered		People-Centered
20		20
	Laissez-faire	
15		15
10	Participative	10
5		5
	Autocratic	
0		0

Source: Adapted from J. W. Pfeiffer and J. E. Jones, eds., *A Handbook of Structural Experiences for Human Relations Training*, vol. I (San Diego: University Associates, 1974). © 1974 by the American Educational Research Assn. With permission.
From FUNDAMENTALS OF MANAGEMENT: ESSENTIAL CONCEPTS AND APPLICATIONS, 2/E by Robbins/DeCenzo, © 1995. Reprinted by permission of Prentice-Hall Inc., Upper Saddle River, NJ.

Breaking down class distinction between athletic trainers, physical therapists, and physicians is an important step. Encouraging personnel to move between related departments will spread understanding. In addition, rather than having numerical goals such as a specific number of patients treated per hour, highlight changes made in the system due to employee assistance in improving service delivery.[9]

Joseph Juran. Another theorist in TQM, Joseph Juran was concerned with a number of areas dealing with gathering information and using statistical interpretation. He believed that management had a large amount of data available, usually in computers, but did not know how to access the information (or refused to access it). He suggested that when products or services are of increasingly higher quality, costs may actually decrease. "Gold in the Mine" was the name Juran gave this principle.[16] If a sports medicine clinic is doing outcomes assessment of its patients, then it has data it can utilize. Those who follow Deming and Juran understand that managers needed to extract the meaning from the data available to them and use this information to change the process by which services are rendered.

Juran has suggested that the single greatest obstacle to management is lack of constancy of purpose[11] or management that does not remain totally committed to the plans and objectives that were agreed on at the outset of the process. Juran believed that when managers switch from company to company, continuity is lost.

Philip Crosby. Philip Crosby was not an academic, but a quality manager at Martin Marietta when he developed a quality standard called "zero defects."[16] He believed that this concept encouraged workers to turn out products that were perfect. Crosby defined quality as conforming to requirements, the system of quality as preventing problems, the standard against which everything is measured as zero defects, and the cost of quality as the price of nonconformance.[16] Athletic trainers who carelessly place EMS electrodes on a patient will in all probability find the treatment ineffective. The outcomes assessment will fail the quality standard.

Quality Circles. One of the early methods of implementing total quality management was the use of problem-solving teams known as quality circles. These teams consisted of eight to ten supervisors

and employees within a common area. The team would meet regularly to discuss specific problems, discover the sources of trouble from the workers performing the task, and formulate solutions for management to implement. These problems could be controlled and eliminated through the cooperation of management and workers, but only if management acted on the suggestions from the quality circle. Deming[10] stated that all too often quality circles were formed by management for employee involvement (EI), employee participation (EP), and quality of work life (QWL), but they failed soon after because management never took action on the suggestions for improvement. Quality circles are also employed in MBO with similar results.

In management, the bottom line is that institutions that are truly people-oriented survive by the efforts of the people who make up the organization. Ramifications of being people-oriented include such things as full employment, even in slow times; extraordinary amounts of training and retraining before it is desperately needed; and employees who are on an informal, personal level with one another.[28]

What TQM tries to achieve is a workplace where the employees perceive that they have a personal stake in the output. Workers seek to be measured against expectations that are achievable and that they have had a hand in setting. Performance is reviewed by peers and by managers who are active participants in the daily operation of the workplace. The Japanese Union of Scientists and Engineers began awarding the Deming Prize in 1950, the nation's highest quality award[37] (the first U.S. corporation to win it was a healthcare organization), and since the late 1980s the United States government has given the Malcolm Baldrige National Quality Award.[34]

TQM does not necessarily succeed. When TQM is a stand-alone program divorced from the total company, including the marketing, human resources, and upper management areas, it is incapable of dealing with the complexities of business life. When TQM programs are implemented too quickly without adequate planning, commitment, and development, they are doomed to fail. At times TQM programs fail because they are internal programs that do not focus on outcomes (customer satisfaction). Juran felt that TQM programs fail most often due to lack of participation by top-level management.[16]

Situational Leadership

Another style that blends elements of TQM and McGregor is Hersey and Blanchard's **situational leadership** model. This model contains elements from the leadership studies relating task-oriented and relationship-oriented variables. Situational leadership is a theory that concentrates on the behavior of the followers.[31] As Barnard utilized the *zone of indifference*, situational leadership looks at the response of the followers. Hersey and Blanchard thought that the correct leadership model was based on the willingness of the followers to complete a given task.

Hersey and Blanchard have identified four stages of follower readiness: being both unable and unwilling to do a job, being unable but willing to do a job, being able but unwilling to do a job, and being both willing and able to do the job.[33] The leadership styles consist of telling, selling, participating, and delegating. The readiness of followers is directly related to the appropriate style of leadership required. When an athletic trainer is willing to work long hours with a dangerous sport such as soccer, yet is prevented by lack of confidence from functioning to the level of his or her potential, then the most appropriate leadership response is a selling style.

Due to criticism, Blanchard has revised some of the terminology of the model, altering the four styles of leadership to directing, coaching, supporting, and delegating. Readiness is now a development level.

There are some major unanswered questions about this theory. Foremost is whether the theory can be proven to work.[15] It is highly questionable whether leaders can function best by adapting to fit any situation, or if they can actually function better by surrounding themselves with employees who think and act along lines of behavior similar to the management. (See box 1-2.)

Because nothing (not even effective problem-managing programs) lasts forever, new ideas to solve new problems must be encouraged, actively sought out, and developed. Most of these ideas will never work, but most of the anticipated problems will never arise, either. Carouthers[5] summarized the concept of management evolution as follows: "Managerial leadership consists of continuously knowing what is currently of value to customers, discovering what will be of increased value to the customers of its products/services, and creating, providing, and continuously improving strategic organizational suprasystems which, when used by the organizational members, ensure the creation of value for the customers of its products/services."

Summary

1. Frederick Taylor was the first proponent of scientific management, an authoritarian philosophy. Mary Parker Follett was a leader in the human relations management group, a humanistic response to Taylor. Her theories were confirmed by the Hawthorne Studies of Elton Mayo.

2. The Leadership Studies were a group of studies conducted at the University of Iowa, Ohio State University, and the University of Michigan that established democratic management as more effective than authoritarian management.

3. Chester Barnard described the zone of indifference, a situation in which workers perform a particular activity because they do not have a reason to prevent them from doing so, instead of being enthusiastic about completing the task.

4. Douglas McGregor identified Theory X and Theory Y as the descendents of Taylor and Follett. He believed that current management practice was closer to Theory X, but that Theory Y was closer to being correct.

5. Blake and McCanse developed the Leadership Grid, (refined from the Managerial Grid of Blake and Mouton) to describe the competing concerns for people and production.

6. Total Quality Management is a system in which customer satisfaction is the benchmark to successful practice. When the outcome conforms to customer expectations, then problems with satisfaction are eliminated.

7. Situational leadership is a system that seeks to motivate workers by discovering the behavior pattern of the workers before implementing a leadership style.

For Critical Thought

The three scenarios described in the beginning of the chapter have all happened to athletic trainers. The question that a student needs to address is how the style of leadership affects the dynamics of the clinic or athletic training room. Could students become employees who function at the top of their education, dedication, and practice if they work in settings that are opposed to their personalities or beliefs? This area of study is often ignored in athletic training education programs, but it should be examined with enough focus to ensure that a student athletic trainer's first job has some probability of success for both the employer and employee. By no means are we trying to present a business administration course in management, but to ignore this issue is risky.

Websites

Scientific Management:
http://www.lib.stevens-tech.edu/collections/taylor/guide/index.html

> A guide to the Frederick Taylor collection of materials on scientific management.

Development of Management Thought:
http://choo.fis.utoronto.ca/FIS/Courses/LIS1230/LIS1230sharma/history1.htm

> Development of Management Thought, an outline covering the major movements and people from scientific management to today.

Organizational Behavior:
http://www-bcf.usc.edu/~kxin/notes.html

> This site is the lecture outline for BUAD 304, Dr. Katherine Xin's class in Organizational Behavior at the University of Southern California.

The Deming Cooperative:
http://deming.edu/BA/BAMain.html

> This site contains the writings of W. Edwards Deming, one of the principal proponents of Total Quality Management.

Applications for Consideration

1. Michelle Garcia completed her undergraduate degree at a CAAHEP-accredited athletic training education program that leaned strongly toward Theory Y. She passed the NATA certification examination on her first attempt. She has been offered a job (her only offer) at a college in Central City, a city of 1.7 million people. The cost of living is high, as is the salary. Assuming that she has enough money to meet all of her living expenses, what things should she consider about the job itself, before deciding to accept or not? What if she had another offer in Middle City, a city of 450,000 people, same size college, and comparable salary? What things change in her decision process?

2. John Robert Ross works at a sports medicine clinic that has just adopted Total Quality Management. John has been asked by his supervisor to justify his position by establishing who the customers are for his services and what problems he experiences in delivering those services. Who would be the customers? Are they only athletes? Are there other personnel as well? Are there vendors? What types of problems may John have delivering services?

References

1 Barnard, CI. *The function of the executive.* Cambridge, MA: Harvard University Press, 1938.
2 Blake, RR, McCanse, AA. *Leadership dilemmas—Grid solutions.* Houston: Gulf Publishing Co., 1991.
3 Blake, RR, Mouton, JS. *The Managerial Grid III.* Houston: Gulf Publishing Co., 1985.
4 Bridges, FL, Roquemore, LL. *Management for athletic/sport administration.* Decatur, GA: ESM Books, 1992.

5 Carouthers, GH, Jr. Managing the managers of competitive strategic change: An exploratory study of variables of organizational context and individual managerial personnel in four American manufacturing business units. Knoxville: University of Tennessee; Doctoral Dissertation, 1989.

6 Certo, SC. *Modern management: Diversity, quality, ethics, and the global environment.* 6th ed. Boston: Allyn and Bacon, 1994.

7 Certo, SC, Peters, JP. *Strategic management concepts and applications.* New York: McGraw-Hill, 1991.

8 Deegan, AX II, O'Donovan, TR. *Management by objectives for hospitals.* 2nd ed. Rockville, MD: Aspen Systems Corporation, 1982.

9 Deming, WE. *Quality, productivity, and competitive position.* Cambridge: Massachusetts Institute of Technology Center for Advanced Engineering Study, 1982.

10 Deming, WE. *Out of crisis.* Cambridge: Massachusetts Institute of Technology Center for Advanced Engineering Study, 1986.

11 Edginton, CR, Williams, JG. *Productive management of leisure services organizations: A behavioral approach.* New York: John Wiley & Sons, 1978.

12 Grint, K. *Management: A sociological introduction.* Cambridge: Polity Press, 1995.

13 Hersey, P, Blanchard, H. *Management of organizational behavior: Utilization of human resources.* 2nd ed. Englewood Cliffs, NJ: Prentice Hall, 1972.

14 Horse, JE. Total quality management for school administrators. *Memo for the School Executive,* Spring: 5–6, 1992.

15 Ivancevich, JM, Matteson, MT. *Organizational behavior and management.* Boston: Irwin/McGraw-Hill, 1999.

16 Johnson, WC, Chvala, RJ. *Total quality in marketing.* Delray Beach, FL: St. Lucie Press, 1996.

17 Juran, JM. Quality problems, remedies, and nostrums. *Industrial Quality Control.* 22:641–653, 1966.

18 Katz, D, Maccoby, N, Morse, N. *Productivity, supervision, and morale in an office situation.* Ann Arbor: University of Michigan Survey Research Center, 1950.

19 Kelly, J, Kelly, L. *An existential-systems approach to managing organizations.* Westport, CT: Quorum Books, 1998.

20 Lewin, K, Lippitt, R, White, R. Patterns of aggressive behavior in experimentally created "social climates." *J Social Psych.* 10:271–299, 1939.

21 Lipham, JM. Leadership and administration. In: Griffiths DE, ed. *Behavioral science and educational administration.* Chicago: National Center for the Study of Education; 119–141, 1964.

22 Mayo, GE. *The human problems of an industrial civilization.* Boston: Graduate School of Business Administration, Harvard Business School, 1933.

23 McGregor, D. *The human side of enterprise.* New York: McGraw-Hill, 1960.

24 Meiss, R. *Total quality in the real world: From ideas to action.* R. Meiss; 1991.

25 Metcalf, HC, Urwick, L, eds. *Dynamic administration: The collected papers of Mary Parker Follett.* New York: Harper & Bros., 1940.

26 Miklovich, GT, Boudreau, JW. *Human resources management.* 6th ed. Homewood, Ill: Richard D. Irwin, 1991.

27 Odiorne, GS. *Management by objectives: A system of managerial leadership.* New York: Pitman Publishing Co., 1965.

28 Peters, TJ, Waterman, RH, Jr. *In search of excellence.* New York: Harper & Row, 1982.

29 Reddin, WS. *Managerial effectiveness.* New York: McGraw-Hill, 1970.

30 Riley, JJ. Human resource development: An overview. In: Kern JP, Riley, JJ, James, LN, eds. *Human resources management.* New York: Marcel Dekker, 1987.

31 Robbins, SP, DeCenzo, DA. *Fundamentals of management.* Upper Saddle River, NJ: Prentice-Hall, 1995.

32 Saxe, RW. *Educational administration today: An introduction.* Berkeley: McCutcheon Publishing, 1980.

33 Schermerhorn, JR, Jr. *Management.* New York: John Wiley & Sons, 1999.

34 Stahl, MJ, ed. *Perspectives in total quality management.* Maulden, MA: Blackwell Publishers, Inc. 1999.

35 Stogdill, RA, Cooms, AE, eds. *Leadership behavior: Its description and measurements.* Research Monograph No. 88. Columbus: Ohio State University Bureau of Business Research, 1957.

36 Taylor, FW. *The principles of scientific management.* New York: Harper & Bros., 1911.

37 Walton, M. *Deming management at work.* New York: Putnam, 1990.

38 Wolf, WP. *The basic Barnard: An introduction to Chester I Barnard and his theories of organization and management.* Ithaca: New York State School of Industrial and Labor Relations, Cornell University, 1974.

CHAPTER 2

Personnel Motivation and Evaluation

After reading this chapter, you should be able to:

- Identify major theories of personnel motivation.

- Evaluate personnel.

- Resolve conflicts within the organizational structure.

- Institute change in the organizational structure.

- Recognize the causes of stress and occupational burnout and develop effective means to combat them.

Key Terms

motivation
content theories
needs
intrinsic and extrinsic factors
process theories
operant conditioning
performance evaluation

FOR CRITICAL THOUGHT:
Job Evaluation Plan

Mary has just been appointed the head of athletic training services in Sports Medicine Clinic's (SMC) main therapy center. She discovers that the workers, while competent, are not highly motivated. They are mildly unhappy with the clinic. Mary's supervisor has asked her to develop a job enrichment plan to motivate the workers.

Mary's first task is to evaluate working conditions and staff benefits (including salary) and determine if any of these areas may be improved. All of the athletic trainers at SMC are part of a community outreach program that supplies athletic trainers to ten area high schools for twenty hours a week. Contractually they cover all home football, boys' and girls' basketball, and gymnastics events. The twenty hours does not include evening coverage of any other home contests, but the athletic trainers are encouraged to cover all home events.

The athletic trainers are paid $29,700 a year. Benefits include paid vacation, paid health insurance (traditional Blue Cross or an HMO), paid dental insurance, paid life insurance on the employee of 1.5 times the base rate of pay and, for an additional employee premium, $5,000 on the employee's spouse and children. While the employee pays into Social Security, the clinic also *contributes to a retirement plan through the McClelland Fund and is willing to set up a 401(k) plan through payroll deduction. There is no vision insurance. The clinic is located in a major metropolitan area with a cost index of $1.15 in the city, which drops to $0.94 in three suburbs about fifteen miles from the job site.*

What other aspects of working conditions does Mary need to assess? How would she begin to focus on employee needs in their clinical assignments? What value would there be in upgrading the salary and benefits package?

•

Annual Staff Evaluation

The college where Bill is employed has just instituted a new employee evaluation plan. Evaluations were completed by the athletic director and head athletic trainer, but the staff were never told any of the criteria on which they were to be evaluated. Bill has just received his copy of the evaluation of his job performance from his superior. He is bewildered to find that he has the same relative reward as his friend, Brian, told him he had received yesterday. Bill knew that Brian was moonlighting with the professional hockey team two nights a week and was habitually late the next morning each time. Brian told Bill that as long as he looked busy all the time, management did not really care if he was late once in a while. Yet, right there on Bill's evaluation was a notation that he had been late twice, which caused him to be in the second-highest group for merit, rather than the highest.

When Bill sought out his supervisor to go over his evaluation, he was told that the evaluations were final and there was no need to discuss them. Should Bill be concerned with his evaluation? What more should he find out about the evaluation? Does he have any recourse to what he believes to be errors in the evaluation?

People want to like their jobs. They want to be excited about the opportunities, the challenges that the job presents. Motivated people are always thinking about the task ahead and how to attack it. Since motivation is a combination process involving physiological, psychological, and sociological variables, the process of motivating each person is difficult. The easier and more productive way is to establish a motivating environment.

PERSONNEL MOTIVATION

The ultimate goal of management is to accomplish organizational objectives. If athletic trainers have the necessary skills and aptitude to complete the desired goals and are motivated to succeed, the organization will succeed. **Motivation** has been described as the forces that account for the level, direction, and persistence of effort expended to achieve a goal.[21] Direction involves the selection of one task when a number of possibilities exist. The level of motivation refers to the strength of a response once the direction has been chosen. Persistence alludes to the length of time a person will remain focused on the goal.[12]

To understand motivation, some basic fallacies must be recognized and avoided. The first fallacy is that attitudes produce behavior.[5] In reality, the converse (behavior produces attitude) is correct. People respond in given ways based on their environment and their life experiences. A second fallacy is that work is a process for which the worker receives either a reward or a punitive action, the so-called "carrot-and-stick theory." In fact, when the carrot is removed, the worker will no longer produce, whether or not there is a stick. The idea that fear or implied threat can be an effective motivator is the third fallacy. Negative motivation may institute some measurable increase in performance in the short term, but it is self-defeating. A fear of supervisors can lead employees to sabotage an entire operation by physically damaging the process or by convincing other workers that it is not worth the effort. A similar theory is that the attitudes of the workers can be molded to fit a preconceived idea of expectations. In reality, the ingrained attitudes of workers and management produce resultant behavior toward a task, not the other way around.

Motivation can be attributed to five basic factors: need, tension, drive, search behavior, and satisfied need. Robbins and DeCenzo[20] defined a need as an internal state that makes certain outcomes viable. Unfulfilled needs lead to increased tension, which causes people to strive to meet those needs. For search behavior to be successful, the fulfillment of a need must be within the person's grasp, or else the motivation to complete the task decreases greatly. Once the need is met, there is a reduction in tension.

Content Theories

The theories of motivation have come to be categorized as either *content theories* or *process theories.* **Content theories** derive from the internal characteristics of people. These theories focus internally on needs and how they can be satisfied.

Abraham Maslow and the Theory of Needs. Individual **needs** may be construed as missing elements that people seek to reach physical and mental stability. Water, food, sex, or warmth are basic examples of needs. Another is sensory privation, that is, sounds and sights of human involvement. Abraham Maslow[14] classified needs in a hierarchy with the most basic needs at the bottom. He based his theory on two underlying assumptions. First, the *deficit principle* holds that a satisfied need is not a motivator. Second, the *progression principle* holds that a need does not become activated until the next lower level is already satisfied.[14]

Maslow called the most basic needs physiological, and they included food, shelter, clothing, and the money to buy such things. Safety needs are the next level in the hierarchy. These include freedom from environmental threats of a physical, psychological, or economic nature (e.g., fringe benefits, job security). Physiological and safety needs can never be permanently satisfied, only met for the moment. These needs are followed by social and affiliation needs, esteem needs, and self-actualization needs. Social needs consist of friendship, love, affection, and acceptance by formal or informal groups, either at work or socially. Esteem needs involve self-respect, titles, status symbols, power, prestige, and promotion. Self-actualization needs encompass learning, competence, achievement, creativity, and success.

The hierarchy is arranged with survival needs at the bottom and self-actualization needs at the top. In theory, as each level of need is met, beginning at the bottom level, new needs in the hierarchy surface and seek to be satisfied. The reality is that individual differences exist with respect to these wants and needs. People put a different time priority and intensity priority on their needs. They may choose to satisfy lesser needs when satisfying higher needs is possible but riskier. They may also try to satisfy higher-order needs before some lower-order needs have been met. (e.g., for the most part athletic training is an underpaid profession with long hours and high pressures in the college/university or professional settings, yet people employed there often derive satisfaction that they do not receive in other venues.) At the higher levels, needs are rarely met, whereas at the lower levels they are only met temporarily. People are in constant need of positive reinforcement as they strive to meet their needs.

Maslow's assumption that people try to fulfill their needs in a fixed order has been modified by other researchers. Wonderly[25] found that Maslow's order held up only with a low level of expectation. He found that cultural forces involved with parenting (e.g., mothers sacrificing for their children) and social recognition (e.g., artists sacrificing for their art) also become significant factors.

David McClelland. The concept that workers are motivated by needs that are acquired or developed as a result of individual life experiences is embodied in the work of David McClelland.[15] McClelland stated that there are three basic needs that all people have learned to one degree or another. These are the need for achievement, the need for power, and the need for affiliation.

Those with a high need for achievement will seek jobs having individual responsibility for results, challenging but attainable goals for themselves, and feedback on their performance. They have a need to excel and will seek out situations where there is an element of risk or even the possibility of failure. These people would seek athletic training jobs in professional athletics, Division I college or university athletics, or jobs as directors of sports medicine clinics. Without the need to overcome obstacles that might cause failure, there is no challenge for these people. They place a high degree of importance on receiving feedback on their performance.

The acquisition and exercise of power motivates others. While they enjoy being "in charge," they place more importance on making others conform to their expectations and on gaining public recognition than they do in competence at a particular task. According to McClelland and Burnham,[16] the need to influence others' behavior for the good of the organization predominates. They see a distinction between *personal* power and *social* power. Personal power is exploitive and can lead to authoritarianism (e.g., an athletic trainer who keeps athletes and student athletic trainers "in line" by humiliating them in front of their peers). Therefore it must be tempered by maturity and self-control. Those who covet social power use it in a socially responsible way, directed toward organizational objectives. McClelland and Burnham believe that contrary to popular belief, good managers are not people-oriented, nor do they covet personal success; rather, they like power.

People with a high need for affiliation are motivated by the need for close interpersonal relationships, companionship, and social approval in the workplace. They are more interested in the morale of their patients or assistants than in completing a task on time. Often they will seek to avoid confrontation rather than make an unpopular decision. People rating affiliation needs highly value the respect of their subordinates. Athletic trainers with high affiliation needs will work in settings with strong one-on-one relationships that can be nurtured over time, such as sports medicine clinics.

The work of McClelland has several implications for those involved in management. The first is that the bridge must be good between the employees' psychological needs and the demands of the job. The greater the interaction of job and needs, the more committed the employee will be to the job. Another implication is that tasks must be delegated to workers who find them stimulating and fulfilling. Workers with high affiliation needs should be given duties with a high potential for recognition. Workers with high achievement needs should have responsibilities requiring them to achieve well-defined tasks. Finally, employers must assess a potential employee's psychological need for achievement, power, or affiliation

during the hiring process. The job must be evaluated periodically to determine how well it conforms to the employee's needs. One way to assess job fit is to look at the quality of the work produced. If the work is consistently good, then the assumption that the employee and the job are right for each other has merit.

Kuhl[6] expanded on McClelland's work, suggesting that the three areas be redefined as the three Fs of motivation: flirt—sex and affiliation; flow—achievement and hunger; and fight—aggression and power.[6] In addition, Erez[6] found that further work by McClelland documented that there was a physiological response to activating the three areas. When people who were high on autonomy and power were shown incentives that increased their power, their norepinephrine levels increased. People with high affiliation needs who were shown romantic movies had increased dopamine levels in their blood.

Frederick Herzberg's Two-Factor Theory. Intrinsic and extrinsic factors that influence motivation levels were the focus of the work of Frederick Herzberg.[11] Most researchers thought that if increased money, responsibility, and supplies led to increased job satisfaction, the opposite of these would lead to job dissatisfaction. Herzberg built on the work of Maslow and challenged the concept of a continuum for job satisfaction from good to bad.

Herzberg and his associates conducted interviews with 200 engineers and accountants from a firm near Pittsburgh. These workers were asked to define what factors related to their current or any previous job made them happy, and what factors made them unhappy. Herzberg found that the job factors that made workers happy had to do with the nature of the job itself. These factors, called intrinsic factors (or motivators or satisfiers, depending on who is doing the analysis[12]), include achievement, recognition, the work itself, responsibility, advancement, and the possibility for growth. If these were all present at adequate levels, job satisfaction increased. If they were absent, however, there was only mild dissatisfaction.

The extrinsic factors (or hygienes or disatisfiers), which were identified as things relating to the work setting, were what made these workers unhappy. These factors include supervision, company policy and administration, working conditions, relationships with supervisors, peers, and subordinates, salary, status, job security, and personal life. If these were all present, the employee was simply neutral about the job. However, if they were absent in any degree, the employee was dissatisfied with the job. A schematic example of intrinsic and extrinsic rewards is shown in Figure 2-1.

Herzberg's hygienes and motivators work well with Maslow's hierarchy.[10] The hygienes correspond to Maslow's lower three levels: physiological, security, and social needs. The motivators correspond to Maslow's esteem and self-actualization needs. If the hygiene needs are not being met, they become the employee's focus. When they are met, job dissatisfaction is removed and the motivators become the employee's focus. Although the employee initially may view a task from an intrinsic point of view, the focus can be shifted to extrinsic by inappropriate rewards.[18] When subjects obtain rewards they were not seeking for work that they consider interesting, they may lose interest in the work when compared with others who obtained no reward.

Herzberg's work has led many employers to add "job enrichment" activities to the workplace. The implication is that if an employer will provide additional opportunities for advancement, growth, and more responsibility, then the worker will be motivated. Employers must remember that offering programs aimed at the extrinsic factors will only result in a neutral reaction by the employees at best. Employers need to remove extrinsic factor problems and concentrate on the intrinsic factors to improve the job climate. Athletic trainers have long complained about low salaries and long hours, but if the salary is adequate to meet minimal needs, then the athletic trainer looks at the work itself, and growth and responsibility become the things that drive continued high performance.

These opportunities should provide what Herzberg referred to as "vertical load" rather than "horizontal load." Horizontal loading is to assign more work at the same level of responsibility, such as adding coverage of additional sports to an athletic trainer's job description. Vertical loading increases the range, role, and challenge of the job, such as adding teaching or athletic administration.

Finally, Herzberg's research leads to the conclusion that when the objectives make sense to the worker, they will be completed. When delegating tasks to workers, supervisors must be sure to explain why the objective is important as well as what is to be done. Yet even better, have the employees participate in the formulation of the objectives to solve problems that affect both management and workers.

Edward Deci.   Edward Deci believed that the pursuit of competence is a powerful motivator. Deci defined Herzberg's intrinsic factors as those things that are rewards in themselves. Simply the act of striving motivates people. Athletic trainers who want to maintain their certification must continue to pursue educational competence by continuing education units earned over the term of their employment. Those who do not remain current in their profession may actually be detrimental to their athletes (e.g., consider how salt tablets or water deprivation were used thirty years ago versus today).

Deci hypothesized that most people need and seek stimulation in their external environment. If it is not present, their internal environment creates the illusion of an external environment; this condition has been seen in prisoners of war who were kept in conditions of sensory deprivation. In the healthcare field, the only stimulation for many employees is the work itself, because recognition from peers, superiors, and patients is lacking. An athletic trainer once related that in thirty-five years of working Division I football, only one ex-athlete ever came in to show his family where he was cared for when he was injured as a player. It is easy to see that an environment where athletic trainers give quality health care, when nobody cares about them, can produce resentment, lack of motivation, and various coping behaviors.[13]

Deci thought that people can be overstimulated. When the work continues to increase, no matter how competent the output, a saturation point may be reached with a corresponding decrease in motivation and even in commitment to doing the job at all. Athletic trainers who do not learn to set limits on the number of hours they will be available may find themselves in demand from 6:00 A.M. to 11:00 P.M. every day and may soon see a marked decrease in their desire to work.

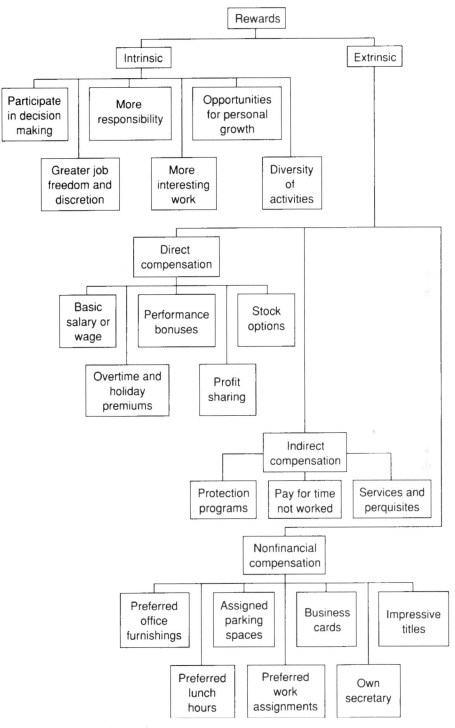

Figure 2-1   Types of rewards

(From Stephen P. Robbins, Organizational Behavior: Concepts, Controversies, and Applications, *ed 6.
© 1993, p. 582. Reprinted by permission of Prentice-Hall, Englewood Cliffs, NJ.)*

Process Theories

Theories that describe the motivation process as an explanation for human behavior have been developed along with the content theories. **Process theories** look at how individual behavior is directed and maintained.

J. Stacey Adams's Equity Theory.   The equity theory of J. Stacey Adams[1] posits that workers compare their efforts and rewards with a sample of others who are in a similar situation. This theory is based on the assumption that people wish to be treated equitably at work. To that end, each person establishes a ratio of what they input into a job (e.g., skills, experience, learning, hours on the job) with what they receive from that job (e.g., salary, benefits, recognition). They then compare their ratio of output/input with others.

Workers who perceive an inequity can respond in any of several ways. They can change inputs, change outputs, change the reference sample, or change jobs. There was an athletic trainer in a university setting who, on external review of the athletic department by a government agency, was found to have a salary that was 30 percent less than a peer in the same job classification. The athletic trainer sought to rectify the inequity by applying for a raise, which was granted.

Vroom's Expectancy Theory.   Victor Vroom's Expectancy Theory[24] is a comprehensive description of the motivation process. The expectancy theory is built around three factors: expectancy, instrumentality, and valance. Vroom defined *expectancy* as the belief that a person will actually achieve a specific outcome; *instrumentality* as the belief that rewards and other outcomes will occur as a result of successful performance; and *valance* as the value a person assigns to specific outcomes.

Vroom defined expectancy theory variables in terms of three areas: effort-performance linkage, performance-reward linkage, and attractiveness. Effort-performance linkage is defined as the perception of how hard the achievement of a behavior will be (such as passing the NATA certification examination) and the probability of actually achieving the behavior. If a student athletic trainer is willing to consistently value competence and knowledge during didactic course work along with compelling effort in the clinical setting, then the probability of success is good. Those students willing to spend additional time preparing for the examination, whether in group settings, practice tests, or other types of work, perceive they are better prepared when they take the examination.

Performance-reward linkage is the belief that taking action will get the desired results. The relationship is between "what you do" and "what you get."[6] An athletic trainer who wants to work in a sports medicine clinic may seek to perform volunteer hours in such a clinic, go to an educational program with clinic placements, or complete another degree such as physical therapy to increase the likelihood of employment in the desired setting. Athletic trainers who perform well have clear performance goals that they are sure can be achieved. They perceive a strong relationship between performing their jobs well and obtaining rewards that they value.

Attractiveness is the importance a worker places on a preferred outcome that the worker does not yet have but wants. The reward may be a promotion, more money, a lateral transfer, or even a change in jobs or career. The question is whether attaining the goal is possible.[6] It is up to each person to decide if the costs of obtaining a goal are worth the effort. The athletic trainer who wants to work in professional sports and achieves the goal may discover that once there, the demands from coaches, players, management, and family are so incompatible that they leave the athletic trainer feeling unhappy. The athletic trainer has discovered that the attainment is not worth the effort. Another athletic trainer in the same situation, with a supportive family and working relationships marked by respect and appreciation, might feel that the attainment was worth the effort.

Robbins and DeCenzo[19] suggested an interpretation of Vroom in a classroom setting. The class is ATHT 4650, "Organization and Administration of Athletic Training Programs," a senior capstone course at Middle States University. An athletic training student, mostly an A/B student, takes the first examination five weeks into the semester. To date the class has been enjoyable, and the student athletic trainer is learning a great deal. The student studied hard for this examination and has consistently scored A's and B's in athletic training classes when studying with similar effort. Good grades are important, to the student, to the student's family, and as a means of obtaining a graduate assistantship at the graduate school of choice. Then the exam is returned, and the student has scored 54. The class average was 76. The student is visibly upset. How could this have happened? As a result of the outcome of the test, the student starts missing classes. Where there were pages of notes daily, the student now takes fewer class notes and creates more art work that is not class related.

In terms of expectancy theory it could be said that studying (effort) results in correct answers (performance), which will produce a high grade and the final step needed for graduate school. The attractiveness of the outcome, a good grade, is high. The performance-reward linkage is directly related to your perception of the fairness of the test. Perhaps too much weight is given to questions the student perceives as unimportant, or the student believes the instructor is biased in grading the paper. Another possibility is the effort-performance linkage. While all of the students have taken all of the didactic classes in the program before the capstone, not all clinical experiences were alike. Some students may have had only high school experience that, while valuable, did not include opportunities for interaction with physicians, for observing surgeries, or for addressing specific incidents or injuries that are common knowledge to those within the collegiate athletic training rooms. These students may perceive that there was a reliance on the college clinical setting in designing questions that negated experience in high school or clinical settings, unfairly penalizing those out of the college setting. Whatever the reason, the result is that the student now places a lower importance on the class and proceeds to fulfill the lowered expectation.

EVALUATION

In the preceding section, motivation and different theories of motivation were discussed. Behavior was found to be substantially a function of consequences. What people do is determined by their perceptions of the rewards offered for doing it. Most people want to be competent and master their work environment.

Performance appraisal traditionally has been viewed as a measurement problem, but it is probably better expressed as a communications problem. Athletic trainers, and people in general, need to know what is expected of them, how their achievement is going to be measured, and the extent to which they are meeting these expectations. Once they know the standards for being rewarded, they will behave in ways that will maximize their rewards.

B. F. Skinner and Operant Conditioning

B. F. Skinner[22] theorized that an organism operates in the environment and will respond when encountering a stimulus. If the stimulus is reinforcing, the rewarded behavior will be repeated, whereas a behavior with aversive consequences will probably not be repeated. He termed the process **operant conditioning**, which can be thought of as a sequence in which a stimulus elicits a response with the consequences of that response modifying future responses to the same stimulation. The concept may be represented with four variables. These are positive reinforcement, extinction, punishment, and avoidance learning.

Positive reinforcement is a reward that satisfies an organism in some way. Positive reinforcement increases or strengthens the behavior that it follows. The reinforcer may be money, appreciation, status, or anything else that is similar to Herzberg's motivators and can be applied either continuously or intermittently. In a clinical setting, those student athletic trainers who display competency and a good work ethic will generally be given sport assignments that are high profile, both within the athletic department and within the student athletic trainer corps.

Extinction refers to a procedure in which behavior previously reinforced is no longer supported. One way to cause extinction is to ignore the individual rather than directly sanctioning the behavior. Student athletic trainers may be invited to help in coverage of athletic contests, or volunteer in a clinic to help in special event coverage. Those who may have problems being at their clinical assignment on time or getting along with patients may discover that

Classroom instruction is the prelude to clinical site demonstration of competency.

they are no longer invited. As the previously rewarded behavior is no longer reinforced, over time the lack of desired outcome will lead to a decrease and finally elimination of the undesired behavior.

Punishment is the use of an aversive stimulus designed to inflict enough hardship to cause the behavior to stop. Punishment can include a decrease in responsibility or rank, denial of privileges, or criticism. Those students who display substandard behavior will not receive team assignments or will be assigned as assistants to other student athletic trainers who may have even less experience.

Skinner did not approve of the use of aversive stimuli, because punishment does not eliminate most behaviors, it only suppresses them temporarily. Punishment commonly results in negative feelings directed at the punisher. In some instances punishment is mainly in the mind-set of the receiver (e.g., when the athletic administration will not give resources deemed necessary by the athletic trainers to complete their jobs).

When an aversive stimulus is removed as a behavior is completed, then the likelihood is that the behavior will be repeated. This process is called negative reinforcement. The question that arises is: is the return of a positive stimulus the reason a behavior is reinforced, or is the removal of the aversive stimulus the reason? Will a student athletic trainer who is habitually late respond favorably when given a good placement for being on time? If they do, is it due to the withdrawal of the aversive stimulus, or the application of the positive one?

Behavior modification is a therapy technique based on Skinner's work in which a behavior is extinguished by the removal of the reinforcing variable and replacement of the behavior by reinforcement. Avoidance learning is a form of behavior modification in which people learn how to avoid being punished. When presented with a stimulus that requires action, failure to act brings punishment. People will then decide between accepting punishment or completing a desired response.

W. Clay Hammer

W. Clay Hammer[9] identified six rules that can be used to expand on Skinner's work. First, do not reward uniformly. Failure to discriminate when appropriate reinforces the minimal amount of work necessary to complete the lowest level of acceptable output (i.e., mediocrity). Second, failing to respond to employees' behavior is a negative response, not a neutral one. Failure to give positive reinforcement when it is due may result in decreases in performance over time. Third, people must be made aware of what they need to do to be rewarded. Fourth, people need to know when they are doing things wrong. To reduce errors, the correction should happen during the activity rather than waiting until after it is completed. In fact, the longer the delay between the action and the punishment, the less effect the punishment has toward extinguishing the behavior.[3] Fifth, never punish a subordinate in front of others. Public punishment equals public humiliation, a situation that may even lead other workers to come to the defense of the person who was reprimanded. Finally, be fair. The consequences of a behavior should be suitable to the achievement. Overrewarding undeserving performance is as detrimental as underrewarding a deserving performance.

Workers respond better to an administrator who is "employee oriented" than to one who is "task oriented." A pioneering study conducted by Sasser and Leonard[20] at the Prudential Insurance Company in Newark, New Jersey, revealed that when comparing matched groups of employees, the supervisors' age, experience, education, or salary had no relationship to their effectiveness as supervisors. Instead, the employee groups with high levels of productivity had administrators who talked with their employees and appeared interested in what the workers were achieving. They gave general rather than highly specific directions to the workers, allowing the workers to bring their own point of view to the problems to be conquered.

Historical Background of Evaluations

As far back as the third century, the Wei Dynasty in China used a royal evaluator.[8] The first industrial application of merit rating scales was by Robert Owen at his cotton mills in Scotland in the early 1800s. Each employee found a colored block when they arrived at work, letting them know how they performed the previous day. Around World War I, Frederick Taylor (scientific management) used statistics to judge business effectiveness. Time management studies were used to evaluate the speed at which workers performed their assignments. In the 1920s, graphic scales from poor to excellent were in general use. Human relations theorists emphasized the need to evaluate job personality and trait variables. By the 1950s, Management by Objectives had an impact on evaluation. The first MBO corporation was General Electric in 1952.[23]

The Equal Pay Act of 1963 prohibits pay differences between men and women performing the same work. Title VII of the Civil Rights Act of 1964 makes it illegal to discriminate in employment on the basis of race, color, religion, sex, or national origin. With the passage of these acts and the issuance of guidelines by the Equal Employment Opportunity Commission (EEOC) in 1966 and 1970, the courts became involved in evaluation decisions. In *Griggs v. Duke Power Company* (1970) the United States Supreme Court ruled that any testing procedure through which a person is hired or promoted must relate directly to duties of the job to be performed.[23] The decision made it illegal to use any test of mental ability for purposes of selection or promotion if no correlation can be established between the test and job performance. The EEOC also mandated that all criteria used in hiring, firing, and promotion must be related directly to the job. Thus, it would be acceptable to ask an athletic trainer what he or she would do in a particular situation, but it would be illegal to ask them to write an essay on the merits of assisted suicide.

Management must be able to document that any evaluation tool used is reliably predictive and significantly correlated with substantial components of the work. In *Brito v. Zia* (1973) the Tenth Circuit Court of Appeals ruled that employee evaluations are in fact tests and therefore are subject to EEOC regulation.[17] In *Albemarle Paper Company v. Moody* (1975) the United States Supreme Court declared that the accuracy and validity of tests could be assessed. With these two cases, it was established that performance appraisals are subject to court consideration in two areas: (1) the accuracy and validity of evaluations to predict future performance and promotion, and (2) the accuracy and validity of evaluations to demonstrate past performance. Interpretations of the Age Discrimination in Employment Act in 1981 also established that any criteria by which maximum age limits are enforced are subject to justification by business necessity or public safety.[17]

In 1990, the Americans with Disabilities Act (PL 101-336 as amended by PL 104-59) (ADA) was passed. The law is designed to eliminate discrimination against persons with disabilities. An important facet of this law is that when a disabled employee is adequately performing his or her job, employee evaluations may not be used to eliminate the disabled from the workforce. The Americans with Disabilities Act has led to further defining of the criteria that can be applied to the ability to perform a job. Employers should determine, before they encounter an ADA claim, what are the essential functions of a job.[4] This starts with two considerations:

- Does the employer actually require employees in the position to perform the function?
- Would removing the function fundamentally alter the job?

This allows an employer to complete a written job description as long as it reflects the duties actually performed (see chapter 3). Employers establish the qualifications that make up a particular job, including knowledge and skills, experience, education, certification, licenses, and other job-related criteria.

Based on the historical background of **performance evaluation**, it is possible to reach several conclusions:

- Any performance evaluation needs to cover the entire organization.

- Employees need to know what is expected of them and when and how the criteria will be assessed.
- Mutual trust between those doing the evaluation and those being evaluated generates the most effective evaluations.
- Rewards must be given to those who meet the performance criteria.

The basic purpose of performance evaluations is to obtain information about a person's job performance. This provides a basis for resource allocation, including raises, promotions, transfers, and layoffs.[12] Performance evaluation also evaluates the employer's selection procedures.

Effective Performance Evaluation

Veninga[23] suggests four prerequisites to successful performance evaluation. The first is that all employees are evaluated. The implication is that each level of an organization will be subject to periodic review. No area will be left out due to status or power standing.

Second is that employees must know the criteria they will be evaluated by, who will perform the evaluation, and when the evaluation will occur. The criteria for the evaluation are of particular importance. These criteria are enhanced or diminished by the type of instrument used in the evaluation. The *essay technique* is a written description of worker strengths and weaknesses. The output tends to be the impression of the writer rather than an objective appraisal; however, explanations are allowed that are not possible in other methods. *Rating scales* usually involve the application of a set of responses ranging from superior to unsatisfactory to performance-based criteria. *Checklists* usually require only yes or no answers, which make the criteria quite clear. Yet these instruments also eliminate degrees of satisfaction by management. In addition, they are difficult to construct. Validity (does the instrument measure the required criteria) and reliability (will the instrument measure the same thing each time it is used) are both legal constructs that must be addressed. The *field review* method involves several supervisors rating one employee. Supervising athletic trainers in college or university settings

Staff evaluation of a student athletic trainer's performance should take place in private.
(*University of Toledo Sports Information.*)

often evaluate student athletic trainers via the field review method. The advantage is that group evaluations tend to eliminate the likes and dislikes of the evaluators. The major disadvantage is the time it takes to review the performance of a large group of employees. The *comparison* method ranks employees within their peer group or job category. The advantage is that the employee knows exactly where he or she stands within the group. The disadvantage is that comparisons of individual effectiveness become more difficult when employees must be rated against each other. Finally, the *face-to-face* method involves a direct interview. These interviews take place at any and all times during the year as needed to reinforce desirable behaviors or eliminate unwanted behaviors. Interviews are often difficult due to being centered on personality and how the employee fits in with the other workers rather than on

the criteria for successful completion of employer goals.[2]

Other managers prefer a more formal evaluation procedure at set times during the year. The evaluation produces a written document that can be used later in promotion or discipline. One method of initiating a formal interview is to write a paper covering the quality of job performance, the utilization of resources, the competencies demonstrated by the employee, and the problems to be resolved. The quality and quantity of work involve reviewing the objectives that apply to a certain job or employee and determining if these were suitably completed and done on time. Utilization of resources encompasses both human and material resources expended to meet the work objectives. The employee's interaction with his or her peers with regard to using the expertise of others, delegating tasks, and giving others assistance when warranted are good criteria. Demonstrating competencies is listing strengths of the employee point by point. Lastly, problems associated with an employee should be written as clearly and expeditiously as possible. The evaluator needs to be aware that interpersonal relationships should not be assessed during evaluations unless they have a direct impact on job performance. The central issue is whether the job is being completed. A major disadvantage to the once-a-year evaluation is that most employer goals have shorter durations. Some may be over only a week or a month. Waiting for a year to pass before discussing the results of completing these goals leads to the discussion becoming a mere formality conducted on an untimely basis, covering things that are difficult to remember, no longer of immediate concern, and properly discussed only when they happen.[2]

The formal interview based on written documentation needs to let the employee know the reasons for the evaluation. The discussion should be focused on the employee's accomplishments. The employee should be allowed to question and discuss the evaluation as it proceeds. From the discussion, the employee should be able to understand the management's perspective of the strengths and weaknesses he or she brings to the job.

Veninga's third point is that there must be trust between the evaluator and the person being evaluated. Trust is built when the employee believes that the evaluation is objective and that the major outcome of the evaluation is to help the employee to reach his or her potential. There are four errors that will cause a breach of that trust:

- leniency error
- halo error
- similarity error
- low differentiation error

Leniency error exists when evaluators consistently rate all performances too high or too low (negative leniency). This inflation by a particular department may then affect other variables, such as resource allocation. Halo error occurs when one trait influences the ratings of other traits. For example, an athletic trainer who is always in the athletic training room and always appears to be busy may be perceived as a competent worker who meets performance objectives when the person actually knows and does little, and fellow employees may cover the lack of output or substandard output to protect their own positions. Conversely, an abrasive personality may be perceived negatively in a way that negates the employee's positive accomplishments. In similarity error, an evaluator may see in himself or herself the personal qualities to be an excellent athletic trainer and then rate the employees on how closely they resemble them, rather than on the competencies required for the job. When all of the employees receive essentially the same evaluation, low differentiation error is the result. When the job is perceived as more uniform than it is, evaluators tend to ignore differences in performance. Workers know who is performing his or her job and who is not. If they perceive that their evaluations are too similar to those of the slack employees, trust and belief in the process will be compromised.

Veninga's final point is to give adequate rewards for high performance. It is important to remember that people do things for their own reasons, not reasons that supervisors want. The rewards that are earned affect the performance given to earn them. Herzberg's intrinsic and extrinsic rewards become solid motivators. Extrinsic rewards are related to employee dissatisfaction. Once these are met, the employee is neutral about the job at hand. The intrinsic rewards are related to employee satisfaction and will enhance job productivity.

Summary

1. Motivation has been described as the forces that account for the level, direction, and persistence of effort expended to achieve a goal.

2. Abraham Maslow defined motivation as fulfilling a series of needs from physiologic to self-actualization.

3. David McClelland identified the need for achievement, power, and affiliation.
4. Frederick Herzberg defined the principles of intrinsic and extrinsic motivating factors.
5. Edward Deci believed the pursuit of competence was a powerful motivating factor.
6. J. Stacey Adams defined the equity theory, where employees compare rewards and use the comparison to determine if what they receive when compared with what they invest in a job is worth the effort.
7. Victor Vroom's expectancy theory identifies the effort-performance linkage, the performance-reward linkage, and attractiveness as motivators.
8. The purpose of performance evaluation is to let people know what is expected of them, how their achievement is going to be measured, and the extent to which they are meeting these expectations.
9. B. F. Skinner's theory of operant conditioning helps to explain employee behavior in the workplace.
10. W. Clay Hammer refined Skinner's work, especially in regard to negative reinforcement.
11. *Griggs v. Duke Power Company, Brito v. Zia*, and *Albemarle Paper Company v. Moody* are major Supreme Court decisions that helped define the parameters of employee evaluation.
12. The Americans with Disabilities Act helped to open the workplace to disabled people.
13. All employees should be evaluated.
14. Employees must know the criteria they are evaluated on.
15. There must be trust between the employee and evaluator.
16. Adequate rewards must be given for superior performance.

For Critical Thought

Job Evaluation Plan. After establishing an accurate job description that encompasses all aspects of the job, it is possible to define those activities and rewards that will improve job performance. Mary must make sure that the enrichment program does not simply horizontally load the athletic trainers with more assignments. She needs to evaluate the work relationships at the external site that the athletic trainers must deal with and provide support and help in dealing with problems. She should arrange for the clinic to trade hours worked in evening coverage with morning hours in the clinic to insure a forty-hour week. Mary could offer her athletic trainers part of the responsibility for planning and execution of the coverage of local charity events while counting this time as work time. If there is a company newsletter or employee bulletin board, notice should be placed of jobs well done. What other things could Mary do? Would it help to improve the extrinsic rewards (such as benefits)? How about intrinsic rewards?

Annual Staff Evaluation. Bill has a number of avenues for recourse. He should approach the next higher supervisor and request information on his evaluation. He has the moral right to know the criteria for the evaluation and to confront and discuss the biases for the evaluators. He could challenge the validity of the evaluation in court should he feel strongly enough. What else should he consider?

Websites

Abraham Maslow:
http://www.wynja.com/personality/maslow.html

This site contains information on Abraham Maslow and the theory of needs.

Motivation articles:
http://www.accel-team.com/default.html

A commercial site with articles on the work of McClelland, Maslow, Herzberg, Mayo, and McGregor.

Victor Vroom:
http://www.geocities.com/Athens/Forum/1650/htmlexpectancy.html

A site explaining the expectancy theory.

B. F. Skinner:
http://www.psych.nwu.edu/~garea/skinner.html

This site contains an outline of B. F. Skinner's theory of operant conditioning.

U.S. Department of Justice ADA Home Page:
http://www.usdoj.gov/crt/ada/ada-home.html

This is an outstanding site covering legal issues and ADA.

Applications for Consideration

1. Miguel Santos has been an athletic trainer at Eastern Sports Medicine Services for the past three years. His performance has never been evaluated to his knowledge by his supervisors or his peers. When the clinic is bought by a conglomerate in New Jersey, a new head athletic trainer is hired. The new clinic owners try to implement New Jersey's athletic trainer practice act, limiting what athletic trainers have done in the past. When Miguel goes beyond in the performance of his duties that which his employers desire, his competency is challenged and he is forced to resign. Does Miguel have any recourse? Would documented performance evaluations have been to his advantage over the term of his employment? Why or why not, in this case?

2. Tonya Scott has been evaluated by her direct supervisor each year of her employment in the Metro Sports Medicine Clinic via an essay technique. She only had one evaluator, whereas others in her department are evaluated by a team of three evaluators using a checklist. What are the possible advantages and disadvantages for Tonya? Is it fair? Will she trust the outcome? Will the other employees trust the outcome?

3. Thomas Washington's employer, a large western sports medicine hospital, has decided that there is an unacceptable level of employee turnover. They decide they need to provide a job enhancement program. The new program includes: (1) designated parking spaces, (2) additional vacation time each year, (3) an improved benefits package, and (4) a family summer camp. Will the package work? Why or why not?

References

1 Adams, JS. Toward an understanding of inequity. *Journal of Abnormal and Social Psychology*, 67:422–436, 1963.
2 Bannon, JJ. *911 management*. Champaign, IL: Sagamore Press, 1999.
3 Beck, RC. *Motivation: Theories and principles*. 3rd ed. Englewood Cliffs, NJ: Prentice-Hall, 1990.
4 Cameron, D, Sharp, TF, eds. *A sourcebook on the Americans with Disabilities Act*. Columbus: Ohio Rehabilitative Services Commission, 1996.
5 Edginton, CR, Williams, JG. *Productive management of leisure services organizations: A behavioral approach*. New York: John Wiley & Sons, 1978.
6 Erez, M. *Culture, self-identity, and work*. New York: Oxford University Press, 1993.
7 Green, TB. *Performance and motivation strategies for today's workforce: A guide to expectancy theory applications*. Westport, Conn: Quorum Books, 1992.
8 Haar, LP, Hicks, JH. Performance appraisal: Derivation of effective assessment tools. *Journal of Nursing Administration* 6(7):20–29, 1976.
9 Hammer, WC. Reinforcement theory and contingency management in organizational settings. In: Tosis, HL, Hammer, WC, eds. *Organizational behavior and management: A contingency approach*. Chicago: St. Clair Press, 1974.
10 Hersey, P, Blanchard, H. *Management of organizational behavior: Utilization of human resources*. 2nd ed. Englewood Cliffs, NJ: Prentice-Hall, 1972.
11 Herzberg, F, Mausner, B, Snyderman, B. *The motivation to work*. New York: John Wiley & Sons, 1959.
12 Ivancevich, JM, Matteson, MT. *Organizational behavior and management*. Boston: Irwin/McGraw-Hill, 1999.
13 Mackay, L. *Conflicts in care*. London: Chapman & Hall, 1993.
14 Maslow, AH. *Motivation and the personality*. New York: Harper & Row, 1954.

15 McClelland, DC. *The achieving society.* New York: Van Nostrand Reinhold, 1961.

16 McClelland, DC, Burnham, DH. Power is the great motivator. *Harvard Business Review,* 54(2):100–110, 1976.

17 Murphy, KR, Cleveland, JN. *Performance appraisal: An organizational perspective.* Boston: Allyn & Bacon, 1991.

18 Pittman, TS, Boggiano, AK, Main, DS. Intrinsic and extrinsic motivational orientations in peer interactions. In: Boggiano, AK, Pittman, TS, eds. *Achievement and Motivation.* New York: Cambridge University Press, 1992.

19 Robbins, SP, DeCenzo, DA. *Fundamentals of management.* Upper Saddle River, NJ: Prentice-Hall, 1995.

20 Sasser, WE, Leonard, FS. Let first-level supervisors do their job. *Harvard Business Review.* 58(2):113–121, 1980.

21 Schermerhorn, JR, Jr. *Management.* New York: John Wiley & Sons, 1999.

22 Skinner, BF. *Science and human behavior.* New York: The Free Press, 1953.

23 Veninga, RL. *The human side of health care administration.* Englewood Cliffs, NJ: Prentice-Hall, 1982.

24 Vroom, VH. *Work and motivation.* New York: John Wiley & Sons, 1964.

25 Wonderly, DM. *Motivation, behavior, and emotional health: An everyman's interpretation.* Lanham, MD: University Press of America, 1991.

CHAPTER 3

The Sports Medicine Team

After reading this chapter, you should be able to:

- Identify individuals who can contribute to the sports medicine team.

- Identify the differences between formal and informal contracts.

- Identify the differences in the sports medicine team by practice setting.

- Conduct a search for sports medicine team members.

- Screen candidates for positions on the sports medicine team.

- Select individuals from a pool of candidates who can best serve an organization.

Key Terms

allied health professionals
contract
practice setting
job description
Americans with Disabilities Act
recruiting
screening
interviewing

FOR CRITICAL THOUGHT:
Creating a Sports Medicine Team

Maria has accepted a position as a health teacher and athletic trainer at a suburban high school of 1300 students on the outskirts of a major metropolitan area. She is the first athletic trainer the school has employed. The practice act in her state specifies that she may only see patients under referral from a licensed healthcare provider. Maria must establish a relationship with a team physician. Does she need formal relationships with other healthcare professionals? Who does she need to work with to establish an effective emergency care plan? What possible problems could Maria face if the school has an on-site school nurse, and how should Maria address the situation before there is a problem?

●

Robert has accepted a position at a Division II college in a nearby state. The team physician has just retired. The previous athletic trainer now is employed in town in the local branch of a multistate healthcare system. Robert has to establish a team physician and affiliations consistent with a collegiate athletic training program. What medical areas does Robert have to consider in his decision? Does he need to establish links to all of the local hospitals? Who should Robert work with first to establish a team?

●

Jim was hired at Work-Fit, an industrial athletic training site at a family-owned foundry in the western part of the country. There is a plant physician on call at all times and a first aid station staffed by a nurse twenty-four hours a day. What working relationships are different in this setting than in other athletic training sites? What rules or laws apply to the practice of athletic training in this setting that do not have the same effect in other settings?

Sports medicine is, without doubt, a team effort. Herbert[4] proposes the following definition for sports medicine:

> The provision, primarily, of medical or allied health care to athletes, exercisers, recreational enthusiasts and others in the delivery of preventive, primary or rehabilitative care related to the prevention, treatment or rehabilitation of injuries and conditions related to sport, exercise or recreational activity, as well as the rendition of service and advice for fitness and training purposes to individuals who desire to engage in the aforementioned activities, related services or products to those who are interested or involved in sport, exercise or recreation even though in this latter sense, the term 'medicine' may be inherently inappropriate.

Many different providers are now involved in the delivery of sports medicine services. No single person on the sports medicine team can provide comprehensive health care for the athlete. Identifying people who should be on the sports medicine team, searching, screening, and selecting members requires careful planning and consideration.

WHO SHOULD BE ON THE TEAM?

Many medical and other **allied health professionals** can serve as members of a sports medicine team. The team is directed by a physician. There are two types of physicians, a doctor of medicine (M.D.) and a doctor of osteopathy (D.O.). While both types of physicians may use all approved treatment methods including drugs and surgery, D.O.s generally emphasize musculoskeletal intervention, while M.D.s will generally use more drug therapy.[6]

In small programs, the members may consist of a physician (of any number of specialities) and an athletic trainer. In larger programs, the list will expand to include physician's assistants, physical therapists, sport psychologists, chiropractors, podiatrists, dentists, nutritionists or dieticians, and fitness or strength training personnel.[4] Their involvement may range from consultant to primary caregiver, and their compensation may range from unpaid consultant to full-time employee under contract. Table 3-1 gives a list of potential members and outlines their responsibilities. Terms of employment, potential team members, available resources, and site considerations are all factors when assembling the sports medicine team.

Contracts

There are two basic types of agreements by which athletic trainers and other sports medicine professionals are hired: contract agreements and handshake agreements. A **contract** is a written document that binds an employee to an employer. This type of agreement is favored in high schools and college and university settings, is used by about one-half of professional teams, and is rarely used in sports medicine clinic settings. Some contracts are quite detailed, outlining the responsibilities of an employee. Terms are set forth concerning job performance requirements, salary, benefits, and so forth. Alternatively, a contract may be a generic agreement that specifies only that the athletic trainer is employed for a certain length of time and a specific salary. All job requirements, benefits, and so forth are specified in the facility's policies and procedures manual.

Staff athletic trainers may be considered faculty, unclassified staff, or classified staff in a college or university setting. They may belong to an employee union, depending on institutional policy. They may be limited to being paid for only forty hours a week

■ **TABLE 3-1**   Sports Medicine Team Members and Their Responsibilities

Profession	Responsibilities
Athletic trainer	The leader of the sports medicine team. Delivers daily health care for athletes and coordinates services provided by other healthcare professionals (staff or consultant).
Team physician	Primary medical authority on the sports medicine team; makes the final decision regarding the health care of the athlete.
Family physician	Primary care physician, particularly for the high school athlete. May serve as team physician.
Internist	Provides evaluation of internal injuries, supervises treatment, performs surgery, and may serve as team physician.
Orthopedic surgeon	Provides evaluation of orthopedic injuries, supervises treatment, performs surgery, and may serve as team physician.
Neurologist	Handles neurological injuries; may serve as team physician.
Radiologist	Reads and interprets diagnostic photographs.
Physician's assistant	Supports physicians by participating in medical history taking, patient examination, ordering of various tests, and treating minor injuries.
Orthodontist or Dentist	Handles dental injuries.
Ophthalmologist	Handles eye injury and surgery.
Optometrist	Handles eye testing and supplies immediate eyewear needs.
Ear, nose, and throat specialist	Handles ear, nose, and throat problems.
Podiatrist	Provides diagnosis and treatment (including medications, tests, and surgeries) to injuries to the foot and ankle.
Athletic training educator	May serve as a staff athletic trainer, coordinate student athletic trainer help, or serve as a consultant to the sports medicine team.
Psychologist	May assist the sports medicine team by counseling athletes who are experiencing problems performing or are having difficulty coping with injury.
Emergency medical technician/Paramedic	Provides emergency medical care for severe or life-threatening injuries.
School nurse	May provide immediate care during periods of nonparticipation in sports or serve as a liaison in the high school setting.
Physical therapist	Through patient education, exercise, and therapeutic modalities, physical therapists treat musculoskeletal disorders, including pain. There are nineteen recognized APTA Specialty Sections, including Sports Physical Therapy.
Physical therapist assistant	Administer physical therapy care under the supervision of a physical therapist. Does not perform evaluation.
Occupational therapist	Provides therapeutic services related to the restoration of activities for daily living.
Nutritionist	Plans nutritional programs for prevention and performance.
Coach	In high school, college, and university settings, participates in prevention of athletic injuries.
	In some states with licensure the physician is the legal leader of the sports medicine team, and the athletic trainer is the physician's agent. Athletic trainers operate only by referral (or standing orders).

for the work year, even though they work more than the forty-hour limit during football season. In this case they receive leave time for the overtime hours.

The college or university will have an institutional policies and procedures manual for its employees (both faculty and staff) that covers many, if not all, facets of employment. It incorporates employee rights and responsibilities, and it lays out due process procedures for grievances by or against an employee. This may affect what can be included in the athletic training room policies and procedures.

In high school settings, the athletic training contract is usually a supplemental contract, the same as coaches' and other extracurricular activity supervisors' contracts. Often the athletic trainer will have a separate contract for each sport season: fall, winter, and spring. The duties are in addition to teaching, or they are a separate, part-time, or full-time position. Athletic training positions, similar to other extracurricular activity supervision positions, are governed by the teacher's union contract with the school board. Some high school athletic trainers are full-time employees of the school (or school district) with no teaching responsibilities.

Sports medicine clinics may give written contracts to physicians, athletic trainers, and physical therapists. Sometimes the contracts will specify initial employment criteria; these contracts automatically roll over at maturity. In this arrangement, salary and benefits are often subject to yearly negotiation, whereas other conditions of employment are as specified in the original document. Sports medicine clinics may have split shifts. Clinics, especially those with outreach contracts with high schools, may have specific times of year when the athletic trainer will work in excess of forty hours a week, banking the excess to use as paid leave at a later time. Usually, clinics allow athletic trainers in this situation to take one or two days off a month to compensate for overtime. The athletic trainer in this situation must be careful that the hours worked can be compensated for by this release time, as some locations may forget to credit their employees accrued time off.

A "handshake" agreement is a verbal agreement that addresses the same basic issues as written contracts but is not in writing. This type of contract is just as binding, in theory, as a written one. It is much more open to interpretation and more difficult to prove in a court of law than is a written agreement. With no written job description, the athletic trainer has little or no protection against claims that he or she is operating outside the job description. Handshake agreements are frequent in clinic and professional team settings.

There are advantages and disadvantages to both types of contracts. In the written agreement, salary, benefits, and work requirements are explained in writing. Having a defined task helps the employee to understand management's evaluation of job performance. By meeting all of the expectations of the contract, the employee may reasonably presume the contract will be continued. There is some job security in this arrangement. Handshake agreements, when honored by employers and employees, are more flexible for organizing daily, weekly, or monthly schedules. However, because the contract terms are only verbal, when disagreements arise there is only the word of the employee against the word of the employer. There is less job security because the means of evaluating job performance are not always made known to employees and may be changed without notice.

Many specialized physicians, such as neurologists and ophthalmologists, tend to serve the team as consultants, regardless of setting. Searching, screening, and selecting consultants generally follows a different format than that used for contracted professionals.

Setting

The **practice setting** largely determines who will be on a sports medicine team. Many factors can influence who will be considered for team membership. The following settings are those most commonly seen in the United States; however, there are other types of athletic training facilities that are not directly addressed here.

High School. The sports medicine team in a high school environment generally is not as extensive as that in collegiate or professional sports, for a variety of reasons. One reason is that most student athletes have a family physician. Parents may prefer to have their son or daughter seen by their family physician when they are injured or ill. This makes effective healthcare delivery difficult for athletic trainers because of the sheer number of physicians from diverse specialties and backgrounds with whom athletic trainers must work. Another reason for limited team membership is that high schools may or may not have a team physician. Those who do can provide more comprehensive and cooperative health care for their athletes. The Joint Advisory Committee of the Ohio State Medical Association, the Ohio High School Athletic Association, and the Ohio Athletic Trainers' Association has produced a comprehensive guide to the role of physicians in the high school setting.[5]

The high school setting also introduces the legal ramifications of providing medical treatment to minors. It is necessary to obtain permission from parents before administering health care to high school athletes who are minors. This can be accomplished through a permission-to-treat form distributed to parents at the first team meeting or through the school administration at the beginning of the academic year. Hopefully the parents can be convinced of the value of a team physician. Many of the problems of dealing with multiple physicians can be reduced or eliminated if a team physician can be appointed.

In those states with licensure, a team physician is a mandatory part of the team. While a team physician may not always treat every athletic injury or illness that happens, the physician must supervise the provision of athletic training at the site, including countersigning injury evaluation forms and treatment plans.

On average, the athletic training facilities and resources available are less lavish in the high school setting than in the college or university, professional, or clinical settings. Athletic trainers must be frugal with their minimal budgets. Large retainer fees for physicians or funds for consultants are not usually available. In terms of health care, it is best to find a physician who is interested in sports medicine and who parents feel comfortable with and are willing to identify as the team physician.

There are high school settings that have very comprehensive sports medicine teams. In fact, some high schools have sports medicine teams that are more comprehensive than those of some college or university or clinical settings.

College or University.   The resources available to college or university sports medicine teams are generally superior to those at the high school level. Yet there are still very large differences in the available resources within the college or university setting.[9] Compared with high schools, the colleges have better facilities, better finances, greater availability and cooperation of support staff, and possible involvement in academic programs. These factors, along with the prestige of being involved with high-profile athletic programs, attract highly qualified professionals. There are often far more athletic trainers preparing for jobs in the college/university setting than there are jobs available in this sector.

While the NCAA does not require the employment of a certified athletic trainer at each practice and competition site, it does require the presence of a person qualified and delegated to render emergency care to stricken individuals.[8] For competition, this person may be a physician, but at most practices this person is an athletic trainer. Physicians in the college setting may be volunteer or compensated.

Clinic.   Sports medicine team members in a clinical setting vary according to the location and logistics of the clinic. If the clinic is privately owned, a primary consideration is whether the clinic is physician owned, ATC/PT owned, or physical therapist owned. Clinics may also be located in hospitals and may have the support staff and financial resources available to such a setting.

Athletic trainers in the clinical setting perform a variety of functions.[3] Some athletic trainers are administrators who are in charge of the day-to-day operation of the facility. Other athletic trainers work in marketing efforts aimed at both the medical community and the public. Still others work as staff athletic trainers at the clinic.

The majority of clinics that employ athletic trainers have outreach programs with local high schools, colleges, agencies, and professional teams. In some regions, the overwhelming majority of high school athletic trainers are from outreach programs from local clinics. In some instances, the clinic provides the services of the athletic trainer without charge for public relations. Often, however, clinics will use the outreach program to attract new clients. With managed care now such a large part of the healthcare arena, clinics need to assess the viability of this approach before they enter a market that may not return what is expected. In various parts of the country, clinics that were once heavily involved with outreach programs have reassessed their positions and even consolidated or eliminated programs.

When a clinic contracts with a physician to provide medical service and referral to clinic staff, the specialty of the physician on call may dictate the course of action. The physicians associated with clinics can be as varied as the specialties that are allied with sports medicine, including (but not limited to) orthopedics, family medicine, pediatrics, internal medicine, and podiatry. Physicians under contract may be either part-time or full-time employees.

Professional.   Athletic trainers working in professional sports settings find employment in a variety of ways. In professional baseball, athletic trainers begin in the minor leagues. Usually a first job is either in rookie league or short-season Single A baseball, and the position is little more than a part-time job, since it only covers June 1 to August 31. When management has an opening at the next higher level, athletic trainers will move up into more long-term positions. To be full-time, the athletic trainer may have to work with a major league team's athletes in South America during the off-season in North America.

In the NFL, most athletic trainers are hired from among the teams' summer camp intern athletic trainers or from college programs that have had players make it to the pros. The summer camp interns are invariably drawn from athletic training programs from which players have graduated to the NFL. The NFL does not have the time for young athletic trainers to overcome a sense of awe, so having worked with NFL-caliber players before is an important qualification.

In professional basketball, most athletic trainers come from college/university positions. Even so, professional basketball is the epitome of "who you know." Many supremely qualified athletic trainers are never interviewed for positions in the NBA or WNBA because they do not have the necessary contacts.

In professional hockey, at the NHL level, networking through the Canadian Athletic Therapists'

Association has been a major factor in employment. At minor league levels, athletic trainers come from college programs, and some are contracted through sports medicine clinics.

Until the formation of the WNBA, professional team sports in the USA at the major league level was dominated by males. There are many highly qualified women still waiting for a chance to prove themselves in professional sports. At the minor league level there have been women working in professional ice hockey for a number of years. At one point a few years ago, over half of the athletic trainers in the Continental Basketball League were women, many contracted from clinics. There have been a few women in minor league professional baseball, and some have worked in NFL summer camps.

In addition to professional team sports, athletic trainers are employed by professional tennis and golf. There are also professional leagues (basketball, volleyball, soccer) in Europe and other parts of the world that employ NATA-certified athletic trainers.

Physicians in professional athletics are almost always paid a stipend as team physician, and some still may bill the team for services rendered to athletes away from the athletic training room. The specialists or consultants are on referral from the team physician and always bill the team for services rendered. In baseball and ice hockey, where there are functioning minor leagues developing players, there are usually local team physicians. In addition, the parent organization may have a system-wide team physician or referral specialist whom they want to have superintending control the local physicians for their athletes.

Olympics.   Those athletic trainers who wish to work with U.S. national teams and the Olympics must understand that there are few paid staff positions in this setting. Athletic trainers and physicians are almost all volunteers who become involved by volunteering two or more weeks a year at one of the Olympic training centers (Colorado Springs, Lake Placid, Chula Vista, CA, and an education center at Northern Michigan University in Marquette, MI). Volunteers must be certified or licensed in their areas and provide their own transportation to the training center. The center will provide dormitory-type housing and meals. Athletic trainers, physical therapists, and physicians who travel with teams to international competition (Olympics, Pan-American Games, World Championships, World University Games, etc.) are selected from this group of volunteers.

Industrial. In some states athletic trainers practice in an industrial setting when employees become injured at work. These employees are engaged in physically active jobs. The Saginaw Division of General Motors was the first to employ an athletic trainer in its facility.

In traditional athletic training, the athletic trainer is the intermediary between the athlete, the coach, and the team physician. In the industrial setting, the athletic trainer is still the intermediary, this time between the worker, the supervisor, and the company physician. In traditional athletic training, a large percentage of injuries suffered are to the musculoskeletal system. In the industrial setting, OSHA has identified sprains/strains as 45 percent of injuries, fractures as 13 percent of injuries, and wounds and contusions each as 10 percent. With 70 to 80 percent of all injuries in the industrial setting in these areas, athletic trainers have a role to fill in this setting.

Salaries in the industrial setting are competitive with those of other athletic training settings. In addition, there may be other benefits not found in other areas, such as a consistent work schedule and possibly even paid leave between Christmas and New Year's Day, in addition to other traditional vacations. Athletic trainers are employed in heavy manufacturing facilities (steel mills, foundries), light manufacturing facilities (assembly operations in many different industries), and even prisons, where they work with the staff (rarely if ever with inmates).

In addition to traditional athletic training skills, those within the industrial setting may become involved with ergonomics, work readiness conditioning, biomechanics, and job-specific training, to name a few. One advantage of workers compensation law is that management may specify which medical professionals injured workers will see for a specified number of visits if the medical care is to be paid for by workers compensation. This allows the

therapy and rehabilitation to be directed to the in-house athletic trainer.

This type of athletic training position is not authorized by practice acts in all states, and in some states it may be forbidden.

JOB DESCRIPTIONS

Job descriptions define the expected, allowed, and disallowed duties of employees. They should be included in the policies and procedures for both full-time and part-time employees. The first step in providing job descriptions for the staff is to simply list all persons who are directly involved in the sports medicine program. Members of the team can vary widely with the setting, as discussed earlier. Additional input in a college or university setting may come from an athletic training educator.

Consultants who are affiliated with the program should be listed in the athletic training room policies and procedures manual. They may be assigned through the head athletic trainer, the team physician, or the medical director. They often include such specialists as a family medicine physician, orthopedic surgeon, internist, physical therapist, neurologist, orthodontist, radiologist, ophthalmologist, psychologist, or podiatrist.

Another connection that must be established is a relationship with emergency medical technicians (EMTs) or paramedics to assist in emergency transportation. These professionals are employed by emergency medical services, including the fire department rescue squad and ambulance companies. This association is a necessary part of the emergency care plan of an athletic training facility. Care and communication are critical if EMTs and paramedics have a different protocol for certain serious head and neck injuries from that which is employed by athletic trainers. In many jurisdictions, once the EMT has been summoned to take over an emergency, then he or she has final authority over procedures to be used.

A detailed description of the duties of each professional on the sports medicine team will reduce confusion about responsibilities and make the operation run more smoothly. In addition, a detailed description protects athletic trainers from legal

■ **Job Description for a Head Athletic Trainer**   *Box 3-1*

- Direct the program for prevention, treatment, and rehabilitation of athletic-related injuries for all men and women athletes.
- Supervise full-time certified trainers.
- Administer emergency care and make medical referrals.
- Supervise the student athletic trainer's clinical experience in the training room and assist the program director with the assignment of student trainers to specific responsibilities.
- Teach courses assigned by the Department of Exercise Science.
- Maintain a system of injury records on all athletes with guaranteed confidentiality.
- Arrange for the purchase of medical supplies and therapy equipment.
- Control and maintain therapeutic equipment in the training room.
- Coordinate a corps of team physicians who perform the duties of prescriptions, referrals, and examinations.
- Comply with and establish a line of communication among parent, physician, athlete, and coach.
- Coordinate with food service all special feedings, such as preseason football and special events.
- Educate and counsel coaching staff, athletes, students, physicians, and coworkers.
- Supervise student athletic trainers' coverage of training rooms, practices, games, and summer sports camps.
- Other responsibilities as assigned by the athletic director.

■ **Job Description for an Assistant Athletic Trainer**   *Box 3-2*

- Assist in the care, prevention, treatment, and rehabilitation of athletic-related injuries.
- Assist with the day-to-day operation of the training room.
- Organize and maintain daily medical records.
- Assist in ordering and maintaining inventory for all pharmaceuticals and supplies.
- Help coordinate and supervise the student athletic trainer program.
- Supervise and monitor athletic insurance program to include policy and rate changes.
- Coordinate the provision of a trainer for all female (or male) varsity sports using the assistance of the other certified trainers and student trainers.
- Other duties as assigned by the athletic director.

complications that may occur during the performance of their jobs. Without a written job description, an athletic department wanting to distance itself from potential legal action could decline to help the athletic trainer by stating that the athletic trainer acted outside the scope of his or her assigned duties. We questioned twenty athletic trainers in the college or university setting in various parts of the country and found only two with a written job description. Boxes 3-1 and 3-2 detail job descriptions for college/university head and assistant athletic trainers.

POSITION ANNOUNCEMENTS

When the primary and consulting members of the sports medicine team have been identified, the primary members must be hired and the consultants identified and contracted. When hiring an athletic trainer to work in either the high school, college or university, or clinic environments, a job description is the starting point in creating the position.

Job Description

The term *job description* also defines the advertisement for a position. This should accurately portray the position in question. There should be anywhere from seven to nine areas addressed in the description. These include a brief description of the position, starting date, job responsibilities, unit housing the job, job qualifications, salary, description of the institution, community information, and application procedures, including a closing date.

Description of the Position. The brief description of the position should include the job title, basic information about the responsibilities, the nature of the employment agreement (e.g., full-time or part-time, teacher or athletic trainer, tenure-track position, nontenure-track position, clinic-only position, clinic with high school coverage, etc.), and the proposed rank associated with the position. Because this is the first entry in the job description, it is important to provide enough information so that the reader can determine if he or she would be interested in the position and if he or she has the qualifications to be a viable candidate.

Starting Date. The date the position starts should be identified in the opening section. This tells the potential candidate when he or she must be on the job site to begin work. If the starting date is flexible, it should be noted on the announcement.

Job Responsibilities. Job responsibilities should be as complete as possible, but not so involved that the reader loses interest in reading the rest of the job description. The job description will most likely be mixed in with a number of others, so it needs to stand out. All important information about the position, positive or negative, needs to be included. The responsibilities will be different in each job setting, so sell the unique features. Failure to communicate a clear picture of the position may attract candidates who will immediately lose interest in the position when the omitted information is provided. This may result in a large number of qualified applicants who consent to an on-site interview but will turn down the job when it is offered. This can be a waste of time for both the candidate and the institution. In addition, an inaccurate job responsibilities section is a major source of legal exposure should someone who meets the stated responsibilities not be offered the job in favor of someone apparently less qualified, but who is actually better suited to the job.

Description of the Position Location. A brief description of the department or unit in which the position is located allows the candidate to gauge the types of people he or she will work with if hired. It also provides information about who will be the immediate supervisor of the candidate. For example, in a college or university environment, positions housed in an academic unit may be supervised by a department chair or dean, whereas positions housed in an athletic department will generally be supervised by the athletic director. In clinics, physicians will be direct medical supervisors and may also set basic policy if they are part of the management group. Where physicians are employees rather than owners, employee supervision may be split into different areas (fiscal, work hours, locations, medical).

Job Qualifications. The stated job qualifications identify the type of individual the institution is interested in. Most athletic training positions require NATABOC—Certified Athletic Trainer status, many require a master's degree, and some may also require a physical therapy license. The amount of job experience required of the candidate should also be spelled out in this section. If the position requires three years of experience in a sports medicine clinic, that needs to be made clear in this section. If the job is for a women's basketball athletic trainer for a university and requires experience working with women's basketball, then that requirement must be stated in the job qualifications.

If applicants must have certain qualifications, it is important to indicate which ones are essential.

In states with licensure or other credentialing of athletic trainers, eligibility for the credential is a necessity. Some states already require any newly licensed athletic trainer to be a graduate of a CAAHEP-accredited athletic training education program. The NATABOC has made it a requirement to graduate from a CAAHEP-accredited education program after January 1, 2004 to be eligible to sit for the NATABOC certification examination.

It is also common practice to identify certain qualifications as desirable. This means that certain qualifications are desired but not required for the job. Candidates must be considered for the job only on the basis of possessing the *required* credentials; separation within the job pool may be done with the aid of the desired credential.

Salary. Salary information should be identified, although most institutions prefer to use general language when describing salary (e.g., "Commensurate with experience").

Description of the Institution and the Community. Institution and community information is provided for the benefit of the potential applicants. Because geographic relocation is often necessary when taking a position or changing jobs, any information that can be provided about the institution or community will help the applicant get a feel for the environment outside the job.

Application Procedures. Application information is provided to explain exactly what is necessary to officially apply for the position. This should include a closing date for applications if one is to be used. If a date is specified, then from a legal standpoint it must be honored with late applications not considered. This problem can be avoided by adding the phrase "or until the position is filled" after the closing date.

Certain documents may be required to evaluate candidates. Resumes, transcripts, and letters of recommendation are commonly requested materials. These materials should be used by the search committee to determine if a candidate is qualified for the position, to determine a candidate's past performance, to judge strengths and weaknesses, and so forth. It is legally required that the contents of these documents remain confidential.

A sample job description is presented in Figure 3-1.

SEARCHING

Simply identifying the type of professional desired on the sports medicine team is not adequate; he or she must be sought out. This is accomplished by knowing where to look, recruiting the type of professional needed, and advertising the position in question.

Where to Look

Where to look for sports medicine professionals will depend on the type of professional needed. Where to look depends on the role the person will play on the team (e.g., staff member vs. consultant). A permanent staff member is more likely to be found through a national search. If a consultant is desired, local or regional sources may be sufficient. Table 3-2 provides some likely places to find sports medicine professionals. In addition, physicians, physical therapists, and athletic trainers may be found by contracting with an agency that recruits professionals to meet the job description.

Advertising Positions

After identifying the type of professional desired for the sports medicine team, you must decide where to advertise to reach the desired pool of applicants. Before trying to advertise, some institutions may require that the job description is cleared with an affirmative action office. Once the job is approved by the affirmative action office, you can study potential advertising media.

Equal Opportunity/Affirmative Action. Observing equal opportunity and affirmative action (EO/AA) guidelines involves several processes. The general purpose of EO/AA is to prevent discrimination on any basis other than job qualifications. Open recruitment is the cornerstone of EO/AA. Anyone who is a minority in this field and meets the qualifications set forth in a job description may be eligible for a direct hire. This means that the search can be discontinued and that person can be offered the

Midwestern State University,
Lake City, Midwest 48602

POSITION:	Athletic Trainer

DATE OF OPENING: August 1, 2000

RESPONSIBILITIES: Under the direction of the head athletic trainer: supervise health care of intercollegiate athletics including prevention, emergency care, evaluation, and rehabilitation of athletic injuries with primary responsibility for men's basketball; teach one course a year in the CAAHEP-accredited Undergraduate Athletic Training Education Program; supervise clinical experience of student athletic trainers.

THE DEPARTMENT: The Department of Intercollegiate Athletics is home to 22 men's and women's varsity athletic teams. We are members of NCAA Division II and the Inland Lakes Conference.

QUALIFICATIONS: Master's degree, NATABOC certification, 3 years experience supervising student athletic trainers required, college teaching experience desirable

SALARY: Commensurate with experience

THE UNIVERSITY: Midwestern State University, founded in 1865, has programs from the undergraduate through doctoral levels in the College of Arts and Sciences; College of Business; College of Education and Allied Professions; and School of Health, Physical Education, and Recreation.

LOCATION: Lake City is a community of 60,000 and serves as a major retailing area for west central Midwest and east central Anotherstate. It has two private colleges in addition to the University and is 70 miles from Anytown and 180 miles from Chicago.

APPLICATIONS: Send a letter of application, resume, and at least three letters of reference to:
David Jones, ATC
Chair, Athletic Training Search Committee
Midwestern State University
Department of Intercollegiate Athletics
Lake City, Midwest 48602

CLOSING DATE: Applications received after December 15, 2000 cannot be guaranteed full consideration.

MIDWESTERN STATE UNIVERSITY IS AN AFFIRMATIVE ACTION/EQUAL OPPORTUNITY EMPLOYER

Figure 3-1 Sample job description

■ **TABLE 3-2**   Where to Find Sports Medicine Team Members

Profession	Where to Look
Athletic trainer	Colleges or universities that have athletic training curricula; other institutions
Team physician	American College of Sports Medicine Career Services Bulletin, NCAA News, American Orthopedic Society for Sports Medicine, American Academy of Family Practitioners or American Academy of Pediatrics journals, local medical society, nearby university medical center
Physical therapist	Colleges or universities that have physical therapy curricula, sports medicine clinics, private practices, hospitals
Family physician	Sports medicine clinics, private practice, hospitals
Internist	Sports medicine clinics, private practice, hospitals
Orthopedic surgeon	Sports medicine clinics, private practice, hospitals, university medical centers
Neurologist	Private practice, hospitals
Radiologist	Private practice, hospitals
Orthodontist (or dentist)	Sports medicine clinics, private practice, hospitals
Ophthalmologist (or optometrist)	Private practice, hospitals
Psychologist	Colleges or universities, sports medicine clinics, private practice, hospitals
Emergency medical technician	Ambulance services, hospital emergency rooms, volunteer fire departments

position. Minority individuals provide unique insights and experiences that cannot be obtained elsewhere. This is especially so in athletic training and sports medicine, where a large percentage of the athletes are minorities but the support staff historically is not.

Americans with Disabilities Act.   In 1990, the **Americans with Disabilities Act** (PL 101-336 as amended by PL 104-59) was passed. The law is designed to eliminate discrimination against persons with disabilities. Its purpose is to mainstream persons with disabilities into the economic and social aspects of American life. The major thrust of this law is to provide equal access and equal services to persons with disabilities. An approach of equal but separate is unacceptable.

Determining the essential functions of a job allows an employer to complete a written job description, as long as it reflects the duties actually performed. Employers establish the qualifications that make up a particular job, including knowledge and skills, experience, education, certification, licenses, and other job-related criteria. A person with a disability must have these qualifications for ADA to apply.[1] An applicant with a disability cannot be excluded because he or she cannot perform a periph-

eral function. Should it be possible to transfer such a function to remaining employees and transfer some of their work to the disabled person, then the switch must be made. There are dwarf athletic trainers, diabetic athletic trainers, and at least one blind athletic trainer.

This law does not require that persons incapable of performing the job without doing harm to others be allowed to do so. An otherwise qualified blind person may not use the courts to enter medical school; however, someone who uses a wheelchair probably will be found competent to perform, even in a field such as emergency medicine, if some routine changes in working conditions are made. For more information about this legislation, contact: U.S. Department of Justice, Civil Rights Division, Coordination and Review Section, P.O. Box 66118, Washington, DC 20035-6118.

Where to Advertise.   There are relatively few sources to consider when advertising for an athletic trainer. For college or university (both faculty and staff), high school, clinic (both clinic and high school outreach), industrial, professional, and graduate assistant positions, advertisements will reach athletic trainers seeking employment, if they are placed on the National Athletic Trainers' Association (NATA) Placement Vacancies board (a computer bulletin board of job openings available from the NATA web page [the job list is also available in hard copy from the NATA and by fax from the NATA Fax on Demand Service and by phoning the NATA for a taped version]), or if they are listed in *ATHTRN-L* (an e-mail group for those interested in athletic training), *NATA News, NCAA News, PT Forum, The Chronicle of Higher Education, Update,* and *Career Services Bulletin* of the American College of Sports Medicine. In addition to these sources, job descriptions can be sent to directors of CAAHEP-accredited athletic training education programs or other institutions that prepare athletic trainers. For college or university or high school positions, sources traditionally used in other professions, such as local newspapers, are not necessary unless required for affirmative action reasons. For clinic settings, newspaper advertising is more common. Be aware, however, that fewer than 15 percent of all jobs are found in newspaper classifieds.

Another source for job posting is at NATA national and district meetings. At the 1993 NATA Annual Meeting and Clinical Symposium, the placement desk handled 6500 resumes for almost 300 job seekers.[10] There were 294 jobs posted, and 236 employers accepted resumes. Sixty-six employers conducted more than 600 interviews at the convention site.

Professional sports athletic training positions are found most often through knowing someone, by interning with a team, or by having professional or personal friends, relatives, and/or former employers working in the professional sports environment. Professional baseball teams will hire athletic trainers for the low minor leagues from among people who write to the director of minor league operations at a particular team and have appropriate credentials and references. Athletic trainers at higher levels of professional baseball have obtained their positions by advancing from the low minors. It is unfortunate yet true that professional team sports in the United States have not yet hired a female athletic trainer.

Recruiting

Recruiting can refer to one of two different processes. One is actively recruiting professionals for a full-time or part-time position at an institution. This position can also be advertised, perhaps nationally, but certain people who are uniquely qualified may be encouraged to apply for the position. The other process involves recruiting people to serve as volunteers or consultants. This recruiting process is generally restricted to a limited geographic region. To secure a consultant, it is helpful to be located in the same general area if the person is to work hands-on with the athletes. This allows immediate access and allows the necessary consultation in a reasonable period of time. If the consulting services can be rendered over the telephone or consultation is only periodic, geographic proximity may not be necessary.

If one person has not been specified for recruitment, a more general approach may be used. A potential source for identifying candidates to recruit is academicians in the specified discipline. They may have recent graduates who are looking for jobs or may be in contact with past graduates who might be interested in the position available. Vita banks, such as those kept by the NCAA, the American College of Sports Medicine, college alumni associations, or local medical societies may have a mechanism for identifying those who fit the job description.

SCREENING

Once a pool of qualified professionals is identified, it becomes necessary to develop a **screening** process. This is usually accomplished with an interview. Prior to the interview, it is necessary to identify candidates who should be interviewed.

Who Is Involved?

In sports medicine clinics, interviews are usually conducted by a small group, including the medical director, the athletic training supervisor/administrator, staff athletic trainers, and/or physical therapists. Should the clinic be hiring an athletic trainer for an outreach position, a representative of the high school may be invited to participate, although it is not required. When hiring a medical director for a clinic, representatives of all the professions that work in that clinic should be involved in the selection. Depending on the reason for the departure of the present medical director, input from that person could be helpful as well.

In a college or university athletic training facility, deciding who will be involved in the screening process is simply a question of forming a search committee. Determining who should be included on the search committee is left to personal preference and/or institutional policy. It is a good idea to include representatives of the following interests: the candidate's immediate supervisor (team physician and/or head athletic trainer), a peer (assistant athletic trainer), a representative of a cooperating department (student health center, physical therapist, or physical education representative), an outside representative (many times the coach with whom the athletic trainer works most closely), and the department or division supervisor (athletic director or team physician).

In most other athletic training settings (high school, professional sports, industrial settings), hiring is done by a principal, an athletic director, or a personnel director. The interview may be done by this person or by a team of people with whom the athletic trainer will work. Rarely is the team approach a group meeting—more often it is a number of individual meetings. Most other aspects of the hiring process are similar to the college or university model.

Interviewing

Selecting the right candidate for a job is a difficult task. Different people have different styles of conducting interviews. No matter what style of **interviewing** is used, certain information will help determine what a candidate can contribute to the organization. Productive interviews should include an orientation or expectations-setting phase, an experiential presentation, and an organization sell.[2]

During the orientation phase, explain how the interview will proceed, describe the organization and the open position, and allow candidates to review their background. The experiential presentation gives candidates the opportunity to relate their strengths and weaknesses to the position and gives time for follow-up questions. During the organizational sell, point out the advantages of the organization and the open position. Four specific points to be addressed during the "sell" are the interest level in the work, security, mentoring, and socialization.[2] It

is imperative that the interviewer gauge from the interview how well answers to probing questions will identify on-the-job behavior. Often questions are asked about how an applicant feels about a certain aspect of the job. That information is not really useful; however, if the next question is why the applicant thinks that, more practical information can be gained. By going beyond simple answers to reach reasons for wanting to work in a specific setting, the interviewer gains more valuable information than by getting answers that give no insight into how the interviewee will perform on the job. A well-organized interview should be beneficial to both the candidate and the organization.

Questions: Legal and Illegal. Obviously it is advantageous to learn as much as possible about a candidate during an interview. The questions asked will reveal the candidate's career objectives, strengths and weaknesses, suitability for the position, and so forth. It is also necessary to protect the applicant from discrimination based on any factors not relating to his or her ability to perform the job. We suggest contacting the organization's affirmative action office about institutional policies for interviewing before making any inadvertent errors. In some institutions there is a mandatory training session for all interviewers about legal and illegal questions and suggestions. It is important to be aware that certain laws, such as the Civil Rights Act of 1964, protect candidates' equal opportunity. Table 3-3 outlines lawful and unlawful questions that may be asked during an interview.

Who to Interview. Chosing persons to interview is largely an individual decision. Clearly, the organization is interested in hiring someone who can best benefit the sports medicine team. A first step in deciding who to interview is to refer to the job description. If an applicant does not meet the qualifications set forth in the job description, that person should be eliminated from the pool of potential interviewees. Hiring someone who does not meet the qualifications when other applicants do can lead to litigation.

After unqualified applicants are eliminated, other criteria must be established to narrow the field. An often-overlooked ability in athletic trainers is good communications skills. Athletic trainers must interact with athletes, coaches, physicians,

■ TABLE 3-3   Lawful and Unlawful Interview Questions

Inquiry	Lawful	Unlawful
Name	Name	Inquiry into any title that indicates race, color, religion, sex, national origin, or ancestry
Address	Inquiry into place and length of current and previous address	Specific inquiry into foreign addresses that would indicate national origin
Age	a. Request proof of age in form of work permit issued by school authorities b. Require proof of age by birth certificate after hiring	Require birth certificate or baptismal record before hiring
Birthplace or national origin		a. Any inquiry into place of birth b. Any inquiry into place of birth of parents, grandparents, or spouse c. Any other inquiry into national origin
Race or color		Any inquiry that would indicate race or color
Gender		Any inquiry that would indicate sex
Religion or creed		a. Any inquiry to indicate or identify denomination or customs b. May not be told this is a Protestant (Catholic or Jewish) organization c. Request pastor's recommendation or reference
Family status		Inquiry about marital status, pregnancy, number of small children at home, availability of baby sitters, or other personal family matters
Disability	Inquiry into ability to perform the essential tasks required of job	Inquiry into individual's disability (physical or mental impairment) or the nature or severity of a disability
Citizenship	a. Whether a U.S. citizen b. If not, whether one intends to become one c. If U.S. residence is legal d. If spouse is citizen e. Require proof of citizenship after being hired	a. If native-born or naturalized b. Proof of citizenship before hiring c. Whether parents or spouse are native-born or naturalized
Photographs	May be required after hiring for identification purposes	Request photograph before hiring
Education	a. Inquiry into what academic, professional, or vocational schools attended b. Inquiry into language skills, such as reading and writing of foreign language	a. Any inquiry asking specifically the nationality, racial, or religious affiliation of a school b. Inquiry as to what is native language or how foreign language ability was acquired, unless necessary for the job

■ **TABLE 3-3** Lawful and Unlawful Interview Questions (*continued*)

Inquiry	Lawful	Unlawful
Relatives	Inquiry into name, relationship, and address of person to be notified In case of emergency	Any inquiry about a relative that is unlawful
Organization	a. Inquiry into organization memberships, excluding any organization for which the name or character indicates the race, color, religion, sex, national origin, or ancestry of its members b. what offices are held, if any	Inquiry into all clubs and organizations where membership is held
Military service	a. Inquiry into service in U.S. Armed Forces b. Rank attained c. Which branch of service d. Require military discharge certificate after being hired	a. Inquiry into military service in armed service of any country but United States b. Request military service records
Work schedule	Inquire into willingness to work required work schedule	Any inquiry into willingness to work any particular religious holiday
Other qualifications	Any question that has direct reflection on the job	Any non–job-related inquiry that may present information permitting unlawful discrimination
References	General personal and work references not relating to race, color, religion, sex, national origin, or ancestry	Request references specifically from clergymen or any other persons who might reflect race, color, religion, sex, national origin, or ancestry of applicant

other allied health personnel, and athletes' families on a daily basis. Being able to inform, respond, reinforce, and calm is a valuable skill that all athletic trainers should have.

In a college or university setting, if the position is to have primary responsibility in a specific sport, the next factor may be experience in that sport. Those with the most experience in that sport would remain in consideration, whereas those who have little or no experience in that sport can be removed from consideration. In sports medicine clinic settings, previous experience in a similar job setting may be a factor. In professional sports, experience dealing with professional-caliber athletes while in the collegiate setting may also be a factor. In high schools, a variety of athletic training experiences combined with a teaching credential in an open

teaching position may be the limiting factors. There are always other factors that may be used to limit the field to a manageable number. Generally, the number of applicants in the final cut is between two and five. It is wise to delay nonacceptance letters to applicants in the last two or three cuts in case none of the finalists can be hired. This avoids the embarrassment of rescinding a rejection.

Selecting

After identifying two to five finalists during the screening process, it is time to select a person to whom the position can be offered. In the ideal situation, a unanimous choice is made by the search committee or the interview team. If there is not a consensus, some other method must be established to identify the person who will be offered the position. This is usually accomplished by offering the job to the candidate with the support of a majority of the search committee.

In some situations, the search committee's charge is to provide counsel to the committee chair. If this is the case, the ultimate decision may be made by the committee chair. In almost all situations, the charge of the committee is to recommend a candidate to the supervising administrator (e.g., athletic director, department chair, dean). Therefore, final decisions are made by the supervising administrator. In cases where a single candidate cannot be identified,

several candidates can be forwarded to the supervising administrator. In fact, forwarding more than one candidate is standard procedure at some institutions.

In clinics and high schools, the interview process will usually bring one or more candidates to the top of the group. The personnel director (or principal or athletic director) will need to make a decision based on input from those who have interacted with the candidate. Whether in a college or university, clinic, or high school setting, the person who is most compatible with the person having the final hiring decision will usually get the job.[7]

Summary

1. Sports medicine is a team concept.
2. A variety of medical and allied medical professionals can participate on the team.
3. Some team members have written contracts, others handshake agreements.
4. Consultants do not always have formal contracts.
5. Job setting plays a large role in who is on a sports medicine team.
6. Job settings are discussed for high school, college/university, clinic, professional, Olympic, and industrial sites.
7. Job description refers to a written list of duties and responsibilities, often found in the institution's policies and procedures manual.
8. The term *job description* can also refer to a position vacancy notice with a number of specific subheadings.
9. Items found in a job description include description of the position, starting date, job responsibilities, description of the position location, job qualifications, salary, description of the institution and community, and application procedures, including closing date.
10. Advertising positions requires some preliminary work, with EO/AA guidelines and ADA taken into account.
11. Positions are advertised in a variety of locations.
12. Once a job pool is identified, a screening committee must be formed.
13. The screening committee selects those to interview.
14. Care must be exercised during the interview not to violate anyone's civil rights through inappropriate interview questions.

For Critical Thought

After Maria, Jim, and Robert completed reading this chapter, Maria and Jim are satisfied with their new positions. Robert, however, has encountered resistance from athletes and coaches who favored the old athletic trainer and team physician, who had different approaches to a wide variety of things. Should Robert (could Robert) have asked more questions at his interview that would have alerted him to this situation? Was his desire to work in the college environment at all costs blinding him to the realities of the setting as well? What should he do now?

 **Websites**

NCAA Home Page that links to the Sports Medicine Handbook:
http://www.ncaa.org

U.S. Olympic Committee Sports Medicine Page:
http://www.olympic-usa.org/inside/ in_1_3_5_9.html

Applications for Consideration

1. Northern States Sports Medicine recently opened sites throughout five northern states and wants to establish outreach relationships with local high schools at each of the sites. They need to hire athletic trainers and an athletic training administrator and contract with additional medical staff to serve as team physicians. Create a job description for an athletic trainer in a clinic/outreach position. Where would you post such a job?

2. Back to Work, an industrial athletic training site in Illinois, has contracted with four manufacturing facilities to set up clinics and staff them eighty hours a week. How many athletic trainers does Back to Work need? Do you have enough information? What additional information would be helpful? How does practicing athletic training in this setting compare to a college/university setting?

References

1 Cameron, D. Sharp, TF. eds. *A sourcebook on the Americans with disabilities act.* Columbus: Ohio Rehabilitative Services Commission, 1996.

2 Casey, TF. Making the most of a selection interview. *Personnel,* 67(9):41–43, 1990.

3 Gray, RS. The role of the clinical athletic trainer. In *Clinical athletic training.* Thorofare, NJ: SLACK Incorporated, 1997.

4 Herbert, DL. *Legal aspects of sports medicine.* 2nd ed. Canton, OH: PRC Publishing, Inc., 1995.

5 Joint Advisory Committee on Sports Medicine of the Ohio State Medical Association, Ohio High School Athletic Association, and the Ohio Athletic Trainers' Association. *Role and responsibilities of the team physician.* Columbus: Ohio State Medical Society, 1983.

6 Konin, JG. The roles of health care providers. In: *Clinical athletic training.* Thorofare, NJ: SLACK Incorporated, 1997.

7 Kopke, K. Poole, R. Job placement procedures. Presented to the 1994 District IV (GLATA) annual meeting, March 10, 1994, Detroit.

8 *NCAA Sports Medicine Handbook.* Indianapolis: NCAA Publications, 1999.

9 Rankin, JR. Financial resources for conducting athletic training programs in the collegiate and high school settings. *Journal of Athletic Training,* 27:344–349, 1992.

10 Tsuchiya, M. Q & A on employment: Another successful year at the annual meeting. *NATA News,* 1993; August: 21.

CHAPTER 4

How to Get a Job

After reading this chapter, you should be able to:

- Search for a job in athletic training.

- Prepare a résumé.

- Prepare a cover letter.

- Prepare for a job interview.

- Determine the suitability of a job.

- Understand and be able to ask for job benefits.

Key Terms

searching
résumé
cover letter
interview
benefits
networking

FOR CRITICAL THOUGHT:
Deciding on the Appropriate Job

Sara Jackson, a certified athletic trainer, recently completed her master's degree at the University of the East. She identified twelve jobs that interested her on the NATA Placement Vacancy Notices on the NATA's home page. The jobs were equally divided among college, high school, and clinical settings. She prepared résumés for each job setting and a cover letter specific for each job. She was invited to a personal interview for three of the positions. One was a clinic with high school outreach in a large metropolitan area, one was at a small college that has never had an athletic trainer, and the last was a full-time clinic position in a large university hospital. Where else could Sara have looked for job announcements? What kind of information could Sara have put in her résumé and cover letter that would have made her a viable candidate for these positions? How should she prepare for an interview for each of these job opportunities? What are some important issues for her to consider if she is offered a position at any of these institutions?

After interviews are completed, Sara receives not one, but two job offers (both of the clinics) in the same week. She informs each clinic that she will discuss the offer with her family and respond in two days.

The first offer is from the clinic in the large hospital. The salary offer is $27,500 for a twelve-month contract. Benefits include paid vacation, paid health insurance (either traditional Blue Cross, an HMO, or a hospital-run PPO), paid dental insurance, paid vision insurance, life insurance on the employee of 2.5 times the base rate of pay, and at no extra charge life insurance of $10,000 on the employee's spouse and $5,000 on each child, credit union on site, and state retirement system rather than Social Security. The university will set up a 401(k) account if desired. The state retirement system will allow the employee to buy in up to five years' service credit in teaching/athletic training and will include time as a graduate assistant in the buy-in. The relative cost of living index in the university community is $1.03 compared to a national norm of $1.00. The area is subject to substantial snow in the winter, making it ideal for outdoor winter activity. This also means high heating costs during late fall through early spring. Air conditioning costs in the summer are modest.

The other job offer comes from the clinic with the high school outreach in a large metropolitan area in the southern part of the country. The salary offered is $27,000 for a twelve-month contract. This salary would include a bonus ($1,000 per credit hour) should Sara elect to teach classes in the athletic training education program at the nearby college where the clinic has an affiliation agreement. Benefits include paid vacation, paid health insurance (traditional Blue Cross or an HMO), paid dental insurance, paid life insurance on the employee of 1.5 times the base rate of pay and, for an additional employee premium, $5,000 on the employee's spouse and children. While the employee pays into Social Security, the clinic contributes to a retirement plan through the Magellan Fund and is willing to set up a 401(k) plan through payroll deduction. The clinic has a day care center on site that is free for employees and has a modest charge ($10/day) for patient use. There is no vision insurance. The clinic is located in a major metropolitan area with a cost index of $1.15 in the city which drops to $0.94 in three suburbs about 20 miles away from the job site. The area has a moderate climate in winter (snow every third year staying for about one hour) with minimal heating costs, but substantial air conditioning costs in the late spring through early fall.

Which job should Sara accept and why? Do you have enough information to reach a viable answer? What other factors go into the decision?

There are four essential steps in obtaining employment: (1) search all potential sources for a vacancy, (2) prepare a résumé, (3) write a cover letter, and (4) present oneself well in an interview. If these steps are carefully followed, the chances of obtaining the ideal job will be significantly improved. Even the most qualified applicant can lose a job opportunity by not presenting him or herself properly.

SEARCHING FOR A JOB

Finding a job to apply for is the first task. This is done by **searching** the publications that advertise athletic training jobs (see the "Websites" section at the end of the chapter for a list of some job listing sources). Athletic training positions are available in a variety of settings, and locating a job of interest is an important first step. Reviewing job listings in local newspapers and other print resources, as well as using the placement service at state meetings, NATA district meetings, and the NATA national meeting, will help to narrow the choices. An important source that should never be overlooked is networking. The NATA Placement Committee's web publication, *Athletic Training Placement Issues Handbook and Guide,* identifies networking as the means by which most athletic trainers secure new employment.[11] Once the jobs of interest have been identified, it is important to contact the organizations offering the jobs to express this interest. This typically involves sending a résumé and a cover letter seeking an interview for the advertised position.

Résumé

The résumé allows a person to present oneself to a potential employer in a structured and controlled format. Presenting a good résumé is essential, because most reviewers will spend about thirty seconds deciding whether someone is a viable candidate for the job. Likewise, each applicant has about thirty seconds to eliminate himself or herself from contention. A well-constructed résumé allows a presentation of previous education, work experience, and career objectives to the potential employer.[2]

The purpose of a **résumé** is to allow for initial contact when first applying for a job, and to serve as a point of reference during an interview. A potential employer is also given an opportunity to learn about each candidate and to determine if one of the candidates is the right person for the job. This is why it is important to write a good résumé, one that will grab the readers' attention and maintain their interest[2] (see box 4-1).

It is best to develop a résumé systematically. The first step is to *target* the résumé. Identify the type of job that is of interest and tailor the résumé to reflect the requirements for that job. Secondly, honestly assess individual strengths and weaknesses, and highlight the strengths for the potential employer. Finally, decide on résumé format.

There are several formats to choose from. The most common and most universally accepted is a chronological format. This format lists education, work experience, etc., in reverse chronological order. Employers prefer that the most recent educational and work experiences are listed first, followed by previous experiences.[11] This format is especially recommended for inexperienced candidates. The second format is termed *functional.* Functional résumés emphasize skills and exclude or de-emphasize dates.

■ **Some Basic Do's and Don'ts When Preparing Your Résumé** *Box 4-1*

Do:
- Make your résumé clean, clear, and perfectly typed and proofread.
- Start at the top of the document with your name, address(es), and telephone number(s).
- Include career objectives.
- Tell enough about yourself to interest the potential employer in learning more about you. The résumé should get you the interview. The rest is up to you.
- Take the time to prepare a résumé that sells your skills for the job market.

Don't:
- Use colored paper; white or cream is best.
- Use odd-sized paper. The standard $8\frac{1}{2}'' \times 11''$ is best.
- Send a hard-to-read original typed on a faint ribbon or a poorly reproduced copy. Always send a clean original or a very clean copy. If you prepare your résumé on a computer, use a laser printer, not a dot matrix printer.
- Cross anything out. A surprising number of applicants cross out their addresses to write in a new one.

The final format is a combination of the previous two. It presents chronological information, but also allows for elaboration on specific skills and/or abilities.

Common headings used in résumés include identifying information, education, work experience, publications and presentations, honors and awards, extracurricular activities, memberships, and references. It may be beneficial to have multiple versions of a résumé. Each should be arranged to optimally present background for the specific type of job. When students are searching for their first athletic training job, keep the résumé to one page in length, not including references.

Identifying Information.   Place the name first at the top of the page, not the word *résumé.* Include present and permanent addresses, telephone number(s), and e-mail address(es). As an alternative, either a home address, telephone number, and e-mail address and/or a work address, telephone number, and e-mail address can be included. A social security number should not be included on a résumé. A name and social security number obtained from a résumé seen on someone's desk, can lead to identity theft, which can cause untold problems.

Career Objectives.   A focused, concise career objective is important, because it conveys an individual's ideal employment. A description of the type and level of employment desired and additional long- or short-term goals may also be added to the résumé. This section can be tailored to a specific job one is applying for.

Education.   For recent graduates, educational information should precede work experience. List the degree(s) earned in the reverse order of obtaining them, major and minor areas of study, and schools attended. List the most recent educational experiences first (reverse chronological order). Certifications and/or licenses should also be listed in the order they were obtained, after the degrees. If an ATC credential was obtained before a PT credential, then the correct order is ATC, PT. Many employers are also interested in grade point average. A good rule of thumb is to include your grade point average if it is above a 3.0 (on a scale of 4), but omit it if it is below 3.0. Additionally, any courses taken in a specialized area and any military or specialized schools attended should be listed. It is not necessary to list high school information.

Work Experience.   This section should emphasize responsibilities and achievements in positions held, including specific examples. Any type of cooperative educational experiences, internships, or student teaching assignments should be listed here. You may also list volunteer experiences in this section. It is especially important to use phrases, not sentences. Use action-packed verbs such as "developed," "maintained," or "implemented." It is unnecessary to include unrelated employment experiences, e.g., "I ran a Kool Aid stand when I was seven years old."

Publications and Presentations.   Any published papers, articles, or presentations should be included in this section. Entries should include papers published in refereed or non-refereed journals; presentations made at local, state, regional, or national meetings; presentations made to community groups; or any other publication or presentation that demonstrates a commitment to advancing athletic training.

Honors and Awards.   Include any awards received in this section. College honors or awards, scholarships, nominations to *Who's Who* or other listings, community or employment awards, and military citations should be mentioned. Be careful of credentials that are obtained by buying a book that includes the names of individuals who buy it. Employers know the value of such credentials.

Extracurricular Activities.   List any involvement in school clubs or associations. Any offices or positions held in the organizations should be indicated. Involvement in extracurricular activities is a sign of leadership and responsibility.

Memberships.   Involvement in professional associations demonstrates a commitment to the profession. List involvement in any professional, student, community, recreational, or service groups. It is wise not to include organizations that may be considered controversial.

References.   The sentence, "References provided upon request," or words to that effect, are not necessary. Employers assume that references will be provided if requested.[8] If it is decided to include information about references, such as addresses or telephone numbers, clear it with the references first.

Most colleges and universities have a career planning and placement office that can offer free services such as workshops, pamphlets, handouts, and samples of successful résumés to help students to create viable documents. Many of these offices also organize job fairs, especially teaching job fairs with recruiters from a number of states and school districts looking for teachers. Some of these positions may be teacher/athletic trainer. If these services are available, make use of them.

An example résumé is provided in figure 4-1.

JOHN Q. PUBLIC

Local Address: Work Address:
123 Elm Street   Department of Athletics
Lake City, MW   Midwestern State University
48603   Lake City, MW 48602
(517) 555-7890   (517) 555-0987

CAREER OBJECTIVE:

To secure employment as an athletic trainer in a college or university setting with clinical and teaching responsibilities.

EDUCATION:

M.S.   Midwestern State University
        Major: Athletic Training, conferred August 15, 1996
        Grade Point Average: 3.76, Magna Cum Laude
B.S.   University of Evergreen
        Major: Exercise Science/Athletic Training, conferred May 16, 1995
        Grade Point Average: 3.43, Cum Laude

ATHLETIC TRAINING EXPERIENCE:

Assistant Athletic Trainer, Midwestern State University, Lake City, MW, August 1996 to present. Responsibilities include providing athletic training services for NCAA Division II football program and clinical supervision of undergraduate student athletic trainers.
Graduate Assistant Athletic Trainer, Midwestern State University, July 1995 to June 1996. Responsibilities included providing athletic training services to Lake City Senior High School and teaching Introduction to Clinical Athletic Training, and Advanced Taping Skills in the Department of Kinesiology to students in the athletic training education program.

PUBLICATIONS AND PRESENTATIONS:

Public JQ, Jefferson L: Data from my masters thesis, *Journal of Athletic Training* 34:1–2, 1992.

HONORS AND AWARDS:

Outstanding Student Athletic Trainer, University of Evergreen, 1995

EXTRACURRICULAR ACTIVITIES:

President, Eta Sigma Gamma, Health Honorary, University of Evergreen
Delta Psi Kappa, Physical Education Honorary, Midwestern State University

MEMBERSHIPS:

National Athletic Trainers' Association, Certified Member (8/96), Certification Number 041234566
Great Lakes Athletic Trainers' Association
Midwest Athletic Trainers' Association
American College of Sports Medicine
Fellowship of Christian Athletes

Figure 4-1   An example résumé

REFERENCES:

David Jones, ATC
Head Athletic Trainer
Department of Intercollegiate Athletics
Midwestern State University
Lake City, MW 48602

John Chen, M.D.
Somewhere Orthopedic Hospital
755 Medical Center Plaza
Lake City, MW 48603

Jerry Washington, ATC
Head Athletic Trainer
Department of Athletics
University of Evergreen
Evergreen, NS 43560

Figure 4-1   An example résumé (*Continued*)

Cover Letters

When making initial contact with a potential employer, a good cover letter is essential (box 4-2). Simply sending a résumé will most likely result in being removed from consideration. A **cover letter** is sent to convey important information about qualifications, attitudes, and character.[6] A cover letter can tell the employer why the applicant became involved in particular activities or what has been gained from previous experiences. More importantly, it conveys to the employer the applicant's reason for writing and identifies any special attributes or experiences the employer should take notice of when reading the résumé. It is not advisable for the candidate to draw negative attention to the application by having spelling errors, grammatical mistakes, and/or typographical errors in the cover letter or résumé. Also, anything that may make an application less appealing, such as drawing attention to a low GPA, lack of job experience, or sporadic work experience, should be avoided.[5]

Types of Cover Letters. There are two different approaches to cover letter writing. The first is to write a detailed application letter. Supporters of this method argue that the job applicant must show a genuine interest in working for an organization. This method allows applicants to emphasize or verify important parts of their résumé and allows the potential employer to evaluate how well the applicant will fit in their organization. The second advantage is that it gets right to the point and requests an interview.[6] Since securing an interview is the purpose of the cover letter, why not get to the point?

Flattery is inappropriate in a cover letter. Remember the old Chinese proverb:

He who praises me on all occasions is a fool who despises me, or a knave who wishes to cheat me.

Asking too many questions in a cover letter or trying to impress the reader with vocabulary or writing style should be avoided. Applicants should be blunt and to the point and explain the most important parts of their résumé.

The second method of cover letter writing is the AIDA method. This type of letter is divided into four sections: *Attention, Interest, Desire,* and *Action.* One way a job candidate can catch a potential employer's

---

■ **Writing an Effective Cover Letter**
Box 4-2

- Write to the advertisement. If they ask for a certain skill, make sure they know you have it.
- Use a high-quality grade of paper in white, ivory, buff, or gray. Use the same paper as your résumé.
- Never send a handwritten cover letter.
- Send correspondence to a specific contact person. Take the time to call and get their name.
- Be sure to follow up with a phone call.
- Proofread everything before it goes out for grammar, punctuation, and spelling errors.
- Avoid using clichés.

---

attention is to point out what he or she can do for their organization. It is helpful to make the employer feel as though the organization is important, and that what is occurring in the organization is of interest to the candidate. Applicants who emphasize personal gain in the cover letter will see few positive results.

Once the attention of the reviewer is obtained, it is vital for the job seeker to get the employer interested in him or her. In this part of the letter, the goal is to motivate the reader to look at the résumé. This can be done by drawing information from the résumé and using key phrases, such as, "As you will note from my résumé." Strengths that have been identified on the résumé should also be highlighted at this time.

The next step is to create desire. If the résumé is organized properly and the cover letter was used to identify the important parts of the résumé, the employer may be interested in pursuing the applicant.

Finally, the letter must end appropriately. Rambling on will cause the reader to lose interest. Simply end the letter by telling the potential employer that a call will follow the application in order to verify receipt of application materials. Doing this makes sure that some type of correspondence will follow the receipt of the letter.

Writing a Cover Letter.   Regardless of the type of cover letter used, there are certain suggestions that will help in writing an effective cover letter. It is a good idea to start off emphasizing the skills one has that match those requested in the job description. It is also a good idea to be sure to address the letter to the person who will screen and evaluate candidates, not "To whom it may concern," or to "Director of Personnel." It demonstrates in a positive way the level of interest in the job, and that the applicant has made inquiries so the application gets to the right people. Remember, it is often the cover letter that sets up the interview. Without a letter that captures the employer's interest, potential employers may not even look at the résumé. Therefore, it is important to take the time to write a great letter. An example cover letter is presented in figure 4-2.

INTERVIEWING

After sending out a cover letter and résumé, it is time to prepare for an interview. The interview represents the culmination of the job search process. If a successful job search is desired, it is important to know what is involved in the process.

Types of Interviews

There are three types of **interviews**: (1) the mass interview, (2) the preliminary interview, and (3) the on-site interview. The mass interview is what might occur at NATA district or national conventions. This type of interview serves as a screening process to determine if a candidate meets the basic qualifications of the position and the organization. If this meeting is positive, a more in-depth interview may be arranged.

The preliminary interview is used to determine a possible match between the candidate and the prospective employer. Basically, it is the same as the mass interview except there is only one person being interviewed. This type of interview may take place at a mutually agreed upon location, at the job site, or over the telephone.

If all goes well in a mass interview or preliminary interview, the on-site interview may be requested.

While the interview will be conducted in much the same manner as the preliminary interview, this interview involves meeting more people, and it lasts longer than the others. This interview will also tend to be more formal than the other types.

A commonly asked question about the interview is, "Who is going to pay for traveling expenses?" The policies for the on-site interviewing vary greatly. Some employers reimburse completely, while others may reimburse partially or not at all. Consequently, it is important to know the reimbursement policies before committing to an on-site interview. For the most part, college and university positions and professional positions will pay expenses. Some clinic or industrial positions will reimburse costs, while others will not. High schools rarely will pay interview expenses. In most cases, applicants are advised in writing of the institution's policies for reimbursement. If nothing is provided, it is wise to ask.

If expenses are covered by the employer, there are a few things to be aware of:

- Receipts: Make sure to keep all receipts that are related to the interview, such as travel costs (mileage, tolls, parking, air fare, ground transportation), hotel accommodations, and food.
- Transportation: It is appropriate to select the most convenient and economical means of transportation (if candidates decide to drive their own vehicles, the route and mileage should be indicated). Local transportation (taxis, shuttles, etc.) and baggage costs should also be documented.
- Meals: This should cover food costs on a day-to-day basis and include taxes and tips (these expenses are highly variable).
- Most organizations know the average cost for an interview, therefore costs should not be inflated or exaggerated. Doing so usually reflects negatively on the applicant.

There are a few items not usually considered travel expenses. These are entertainment, travel insurance, personal phone calls, hotel stopovers on the way to the site, and expenses for others accompanying the applicant on the interview. If there are any questions about what will be covered, it is better to ask ahead of time rather than being left with unexpected bills.

November 8, 1999

John Q. Public, ATC
Chair, Athletic Training Search Committee
Your University
Department of Athletic Training
Yourtown, YS 12345

Dear Mr. Public:

This letter is in response to your advertisement for a head athletic trainer/assistant professor in the Department of Athletic Training. Please accept this letter as my official application for consideration in this position.

My interests in and contributions to athletic training have been in the areas of athletic training administration and student preparation. I am currently serving as assistant athletic trainer with primary duties in football coverage. I am also involved in teaching in our CAHEA-accredited athletic training education program. I am also interested in scholarly activity. I have published several articles and made numerous professional presentations, primarily in the area of preparing student athletic trainers for careers as football athletic trainers.

Athletic training administration and student preparation are the areas I feel I have the most expertise. I am interested in contributing my knowledge and experience to the Your University Athletic Training Program. I will be contacting you soon to ensure that you have received all of my materials. Thank you for your consideration.

Sincerely,

Job Applicant, ATC
Department of Athletics
University of Another City
Another City, AS 54321

Figure 4-2   An example cover letter

Interviewing

Once a candidate has made it to an on-site interview, it is vital to concentrate on making a good impression (box 4-3). Remember, first impressions are lasting impressions. Some helpful hints on making a good impression follow.

First, visualize the entrance. It is important to know how, and when, to move in an interview. If this is not a preplanned event, the candidate will be forced to react rather than choosing how to act in advance. Second, give a good handshake when meeting the interviewer. This is not only proper etiquette, but people are more likely to like and hear one another when they shake hands. Third, sit eye-to-eye with the interviewer. This makes the interviewer look to the applicant more as an equal or colleague. People tend to equate power with height. Slouching in a chair or sitting in a lower chair allows the interviewer to look down on the interviewee. If talking to someone in a wheelchair, candidates should react to them on that level. If it is necessary to make an important remark during the interview, stand up and say it. Fourth, move slowly. Quick, jerky movements seem wooden and less credible. Fifth, candidates benefit from being aware of the space they take. Leaders tend to take up more space than others. Make sure to sit straight, and do not hold your arms to the side or on your lap. Instead, it is better to lean forward with arms spread. Finally, candidates should be natural and be themselves—attitude will influence the interviewer's evaluation. Candidates benefit by emphasizing strong points and remembering that the interviewer is looking for inherent personal energy and enthusiasm. It is important to dwell on the positive and ask questions when they are indicated.[1] The interview will allow the candidate time to "sell" him or herself to a potential employer.

It is also important to be aware of body language. Certain nonverbal signals are involuntary. Sometimes a person's body language provides a truer indication of what they are thinking or feeling than verbal cues. During interviews, your actions may appear to either verify and validate or negate what you are saying. Body language is not universal. It is influenced by culture, geographical differences, family traditions, economic position, and social

---

■ **How to Sell Yourself During an Interview**   *Box 4-3*

- Understand the job market and keep up with the competition through thought and preparation.
- Prepare for the interview with an honest self-evaluation of goals, work style, and financial needs.
- Research the institution.
- Dress appropriately for the interview.
- Project the right attitude by being positive and confident.
- Relax, but remain sharp.
- Answer questions in a confident, honest, and straightforward manner.
- Answer all the questions that are posed, remembering that tough questions, even ones that are discriminatory, offer additional opportunities to reinforce competence and desire for the job.
- Communicate strengths and goals.
- Ask questions to elicit vital information about the job and to demonstrate energy and active participation in the interview process.
- End the interview on a positive note.
- Follow up the interview with a letter.

---

class. Each person has a unique body language. People should learn to identify those elements of their own body language that occur most often. Avoid using body language that may be difficult to interpret or may be misconstrued. Body language should confirm verbal responses. The most important factor is the behavior exhibited in the early minutes of the interview. Be aware of breathing patterns, eye contact and movement, hand and arm motions, and torso movement and position.[7]

Successful interviewees generally share the characteristics of resourcefulness, good written credentials, ability to support their arguments, desirable social attributes, and positive demeanor and style. Knowing this, make sure that all of these qualities come through when interviewing. Often it is helpful to practice an interview in front of a mirror or participate in "mock" interviews.

"Mock" Interviews

Participating in a "mock" interview before an actual interview is a useful preparation tool. Granted, an actual interview will be more stressful, but any practice will help individuals present themselves positively. Anticipating questions that may be asked of you and preparing appropriate answers will prevent your having to fumble for words when first meeting a potential employer (box 4-4 and box 4-5).

■ **Some Questions that Employers Will Almost Certainly Ask**[15] *Box 4-4*

- Why do you want to work for our (university, high school, clinic, etc.)?
- What duties does your present job include?
- What do you like to do in your leisure time?
- How do you feel about working with minority or disabled coworkers or patients?
- Why should this (university, high school, clinic, etc.) hire you?
- What can you tell me about yourself?
- What do you expect to be doing five years from now?
- What do you like and dislike about your present job?
- What are your salary requirements?
- What is your greatest professional accomplishment?
- How often do you work overtime at your present job?
- What is your work history?
- What are your strengths and weaknesses?
- What can you contribute to this (university, high school, clinic, etc.)?
- What would you do if . . . ? (hypothetical situations)
- Do you have any questions?

■ **Questions to Ask to Determine that a Position Is Worth Pursuing** *Box 4-5*

- Ask about the turnover rate for the position. A high turnover rate suggests that the job cannot be adequately performed as structured.
- If it is a new position, determine if it has been well thought out.
- Ask the interviewer how the hiring supervisor is perceived in the organization; if the supervisor is in danger of being terminated, the job responsibilities might change with new management.
- Remember that working for an institution in transition can be just as risky as working for one in trouble.
- Verify the management philosophy of the supervisor with others in the institution.
- Make sure that the job is possible to do as described.
- Pay attention to intuitive feelings that something is wrong.
- Ask if there are internal candidates (those currently employed by that institution in some other capacity); such people may be involved in the interviewing of external candidates, which may allow them to promote their own candidacies. In addition, external interviews may only be for the purpose of satisfying affirmative action guidelines, while the position has already been awarded to the internal candidate.

Watch for "Red Flags"

Athletic training job candidates may be extremely naive when interviewing for a new position. They are focused on selling themselves to the employer, but may fail to identify that a job is not worth the effort. In some situations, there is a high turnover because the athletic trainer cannot function in the job as he or she was trained to do, or the salary may not cover even basic expenses. Another situation arises when the position may currently be filled by someone who will be fired if the new hire is adequate. This may lead to present staff undermining the efforts of the new athletic trainer, to that person's detriment. If a situation does not "feel" right, then asking questions of current employees and even of local competitors may help to identify what is wrong and decide whether it can be corrected. If any of these situations exist, think very seriously about whether or not the position is worth the potential problems that may arise. Choosing an impossible-to-do or uncertain job can be a very frustrating experience. Looking for these clues may save job seekers from a frustrating experience.

Negotiating for Salaries/Benefits/Perks

It is difficult to determine an exact salary to secure. Geographic location, setting, experience, and many other factors influence your potential salary. In order to get a ballpark figure, candidates can talk to others who are not involved with the position applied for. Possible salary ranges can be discussed with peers, former professors, or current coworkers. When determining individual value, the athletic trainer must do an honest appraisal of him or herself and estimate what their worth is to the organization. Athletic trainers have historically underestimated their worth and have often accepted positions for salaries that nearly qualified them for welfare.[10] Accepting absurdly low salaries (e.g., $20,000 for a twelve-month, full-time job that requires a master's degree) is damaging to the athletic training profession. Employers can keep salaries artificially low because young athletic trainers new to the job market will take extremely low salaries. Certified athletic trainers should not be afraid to hold out for what they are worth!

Many athletic trainers are not aware of the **benefits** that are available when considering a job. Standard benefits in a traditional setting include paid vacation, various health options, retirement, personal leave days, and options such as parking, credit union membership, and tuition remission for employees and dependents (box 4-6). Some institutions will set up federal 125 plan accounts (dependent child care and health expense accounts). Excluding retirement (which may or may not be offered), these benefits cost approximately 14 to 15 percent of the base salary in the traditional setting. The greatest variability among institutions is in health insurance. There are single coverage, family coverage, traditional plans such as Blue Cross and

---

■ **Standard Full-Time Employment Benefits**   *Box 4-6*

- Paid vacation
- Health insurance
- Prescription drug insurance
- Life insurance
- Long-term disability insurance
- Dental insurance
- Vision insurance
- Retirement
- Tuition remission for the employee and/or dependents
- Credit union membership
- Parking
- Profit sharing
- Sign-on bonus
- Personal leave days off
- Christmas bonus
- Discount on purchases
- Automobile allowance
- Meal allowance
- Moving expenses
- Child care

Aetna, health maintenance organizations (HMO), and preferred provider options (PPO).

In the clinic setting additional benefits may include profit sharing, sign-on bonuses, moving expenses, child care, holiday bonuses, and mileage and meals when going to satellite clinical settings. Many clinics will offer at least partial tuition toward a master's degree. Some clinics also offer a "comp time" benefit, allowing athletic trainers to stockpile hours during football and winter sports to be paid at a later time when the employee may work reduced hours or even no hours in a pay period. Standard benefits packages in the private sector constitute a larger percentage of the base salary, as much as 25 to 35 percent.

"Cafeteria plan" benefits packages are also available at some institutions. These plans offer each benefit with an assigned dollar value and let the employee select benefits most desired up to a fixed dollar value. For example, comprehensive health insurance for an employee may cost $100 a month, while full family coverage may cost $350 a month. Dental insurance with orthodontic coverage may cost $50 a month, while the same insurance without orthodontic coverage may cost $15. When the total of selected benefits reaches a maximum, such as $6,000, then any additional benefits desired must be paid for by the employee at the full rate.

These benefits are seen by personnel managers as separate from the "perks" that go with an athletic training position, such as season tickets, company car, uniforms (all in your school colors, of course), and training table meals. Most part-time athletic trainers, team physicians, and sports medicine team consultants receive no benefits.

In addition to traditional benefits and perks, there are some attractive nonstandard benefits that may be available to the athletic trainer. Some examples include paying professional dues (NATA, APTA, ACSM, etc.), travel expenses to symposia and conventions, and malpractice insurance. Other benefits may also be available or negotiable. Individuals in the job market may find value in exploring all benefits that may be available in a job they are considering. Athletic trainers should not be afraid to use benefits as a bargaining point when discussing whether to take a certain position or not. For the employer, it is advantageous to sell the benefits and perks the organization has to offer.

In these days of economic hard times, it is becoming harder for athletic trainers to negotiate their share of fringe benefits. Perks, benefits, and incentive bonuses are more likely to be negotiable in clinical settings. This is not to say that benefits and bonuses are not available in more traditional athletic training sites, but they tend to be standardized in these settings. Before a job interview, a prospective candidate should understand the market value of an athletic trainer in terms of salary and compensation packages for the particular setting and geographic region. Ideally, candidates should know what is standard at an institution before asking for what they want.[9] Many institutions use a combination of salary and benefits along with incentive arrangements to attract and keep talented workers. Remember, if these issues are not negotiated for, it is hard to get them!

Follow Up!

After completing the interview, be sure to follow up with any requested materials. Also, a brief typewritten letter of appreciation should follow within forty-eight hours of the interview.

THE IMPORTANCE OF NETWORKING

Once the résumé is complete, spend time assessing the strengths, weaknesses, and the particular role a candidate can play in an organization. It is also beneficial to determine how to meet people who can facilitate getting an interview. At this point the question becomes, how to meet people that can help get the interviews that lead to a job? Many allied health professions, especially athletic training, are close-knit, and often getting an interview depends more on *who* the applicant knows than on *what* he or she knows. The group of people candidates currently know may or may not be able to give leads on a particular job. They may, however, be able to introduce the candidate to other people who can get them an interview or a job.

By creating and maintaining relationships with people, a career network is being developed. One author[14] defines **networking** as ". . . a tight chain of contacts threading itself through virtually every crevice of an industry, top to bottom." This means that students shouldn't be afraid to introduce themselves to others in the profession. Develop alliances with other students, both from the same program and from other programs. Get to know the faculty and clinical instructors as well as team physicians, and any other member of the sports medicine team. Students should introduce themselves to leaders in the profession at meetings. Networks provide the means to meet professionals—ones that can open doors for a potential career.

Building a network takes time and effort, but if done with honesty and integrity the network will last a lifetime. How does one build a network? Students should first begin by making a list of all the people they know. This includes other athletic trainers, physicians, educators, family members, friends, and employers. This list becomes the starting point. These people may or may not be able to get the student athletic trainer a job, but they will be able to introduce the student to others in their field or related fields.

How to meet people? Begin small. Students of athletic training should start by introducing themselves to other certified athletic trainers when travelling on the road with sports teams. Athletic training students should act professionally and confident at all times. Remember, actions speak louder than words. Students should become members of professional associations such as the NATA or district and state associations. Additionally, those who learn about the history of the profession and how it has grown have accomplished a major first step to becoming an athletic training professional. Attendance at local and regional athletic training meetings will help also. All of these activities provide the athletic training student opportunities to meet people.

When meeting other professionals, remember these three things: (1) professionalism, (2) honesty, and (3) confidence. Always act professionally. Professionals and students alike never know when or where they will meet another person in the profession who may be able to provide a career opportunity for them in the future. Be honest. People who have been in the profession awhile have good people skills and will usually know when someone is telling the truth and giving a real representation of himself or herself. Finally, speak with confidence. Remember, it has been hard work to make a place in this field; be proud of accomplishments made without sounding conceited.

Networking is about helping peers and the profession. As one grows in the athletic training field, it is important to maintain the contacts made, and to make new ones. Remember that person who may have led the student to the interview and helped them to get that job, may need the help of a colleague (or former student) someday.

There are no sure-fire secrets to searching for a job. What may work for one person may not work for another. A complete cover letter, well-constructed résumé, and good networking skills will help to get a foot in the door. How well one does in an interview will depend on planning, preparation, and how one is able to handle himself or herself. By following the examples provided in this chapter, students will not only make themselves more marketable, but also will be able to carry out the process with much less stress.

Summary

1. There are many ways to locate and review job listings for athletic training positions.
2. The résumé is a way for job seekers to present themselves to a potential employer in a controlled and structured format.
3. Résumés should contain the applicant's name, address(es), career objectives, education, work experience, publications and presentations, honors and awards, extracurricular activities, memberships, and references.
4. A cover letter conveys important information about the job applicant to the potential employer. A good cover letter brings attention to

the candidate's strengths, qualifications, attitudes, and character.

5. The job interview is the culmination of a long process. Three types of interviews include the mass interview, the preliminary interview, and the on-site interview.

6. The interview allows the candidate to make a good impression with the potential employer. Successful interviewees share the characteristics of resourcefulness, good written credentials, support for arguments, desirable social attributes, a good demeanor, and style.

7. Athletic trainers should fully investigate any position that is offered to them, including salary, benefit packages, and vacation time. Any "red flags" should be taken seriously.

8. After an interview, applicants should follow up with a letter of appreciation.

9. Networking prior to and during the job search can prove to be invaluable.

For Critical Thought

Sara really needs more information than was provided in the opening scenario. She also needs to be able to compare the management style of the two clinics. Sara thrives when she has a decision-making role in an organization. Participative management is the closest style to hers. Upon making inquiries and by asking appropriate questions during the interview process, Sara was able to establish that in the clinic outreach position she would have freedom to implement her own policies at the high school and to participate in decision-making meetings in the clinic. The hospital, while paying slightly more and having a slightly better benefits package, operates with a more authoritarian style of management. All decisions that affect working conditions come down from upper management. Worker consultation is minimal. The job has had three athletic trainers in the last twenty-seven months.

With this additional information, Sara and her family elect to accept the clinic-outreach position.

Websites

NATA Placement Vacancy Notice:
http://www.nata.org/Departments/membership/placemen.htm

You must be an NATA member and have the access code (available in *NATA News* each month).

NATA Placement Committee:
http://family.med.und.nodak.edu/nata/placement/handbook/

Tsuchiya M., ed. *Athletic Training Employment Issues Handbook and Guide*

ACSM Career Services Online:
http://www.wwilkins.com/classifieds/ADS/ACSMJOBS.HTM

Includes jobs in a variety of areas within sports medicine.

Chronicle of Higher Education Career Network:
http://chronicle.com/free/jobs/

Includes jobs in all areas of academe. Free listings are one week old. To access current listings, you must subscribe to the *Chronicle*.

NCAA News: The Market:
http://www.ncaa.org/market/ads/athletic_trainer/

Listing of athletic training positions in collegiate settings.

NFHS News: The Market:
http://www.ncaa.org/nfhs/market/ads/athletic_trainer/

Listing of athletic training positions in the high school setting.

Applications for Consideration

1. Mary C. Martin, having searched a variety of jobs databases, finds three athletic training jobs that she wishes to apply for. The first is in a sports medicine clinic. The second is as a full-time athletic trainer in a high school. The third is working at a state prison in southeastern Kentucky, treating the staff (not prisoners). When she begins to write, does she use the same letter for each position? What about the résumé? Does she tailor the résumé to the job she is applying for?

2. Jon Jefferson is an assistant athletic trainer at a large university. The head athletic trainer died suddenly last month. Jon expresses his lack of interest in assuming the head athletic trainer position, so a search committee is assembled to do an external search to fill the head athletic trainer position. One member of the search committee wants to advertise the position in the NATA Placement Vacancy Notices and the *NATA News*. Another wants to contract with a private employment agency. A third wants to recruit a specific individual from another university. They ask for Jon's opinion. What information would Jon need to have before deciding what to do? How would Jon use this information?

References

1 Anderson, K. Making a good first impression. *Nursing*, 21:145–146, 1991.

2 Barnum, CM. Writing resumes that sell: Quick—you've got 30 seconds to explain why you're the best person for the job. *Management World*, 16:10–11, 1987.

3 Bassett, J. 12 techniques for selling yourself at a job interview. *Legal Assistant Today*, 9(3): 40–46, 1992.

4 Casey, TF. Making the most of a selection interview. *Personnel*, 67(9):41–43, 1990.

5 Clabes, JG. Cutesy cover letters are like bricks: Write them and prepare to sink. *The Quill*, 76:20–21, 1988.

6 Dulek, RE, Suchan, JA. Application letters: A neglected area in the job search. *Business Horizons*, 31:70–75, 1988.

7 Fleischmann, ST. The messages of body language in job interviews. *Employment Relations Today*, 18(2):161–166, 1991.

8 Harcourt, J, Krizan, AC. A comparison of resume content preferences of Fortune 500 personnel administrators and business communication instructors. *Journal of Business Communication*, 26:177–190, 1989.

9 Harris, AS. Benefits: Let's make a deal. *Black Enterprise*, 21(7):117–123, 1991.

10 Rankin, JR. Financial resources for conducting athletic training programs in the collegiate and high school settings. *Journal of Athletic Training*, 27:344–349, 1992.

11 Tsuchiya, M, ed. *Athletic Training Employment Issues Handbook and Guide*. http://family.med.und.nodak.edu/nata/placement/handbook/ 1998.

12 Tyler, L. Watch out for "red flags" on a job interview. *Hospitals* 64(14):46.

13 Ugbah, SD, Majors, RE. Influential communication factors in employment interviews. *Journal of Business Communication*, 29(2):145–159, 1992.

14 Weinstein B. *Resumes don't get jobs: The realities and myth of job hunting*. New York: McGraw-Hill, Inc. 1993.

15 Weis, D. 10 questions recruiters will ask. *Nursing*, 20:116–118, 1990 (Mar).

CHAPTER 5

Managing Change, Conflict, and Burnout

After reading this chapter, you should be able to:

- Institute change in the organizational structure.

- Recognize the causes of and responses to conflict.

- Resolve conflicts within the organizational structure.

- Recognize the causes of stress and occupational burnout, and develop effective ways to combat them.

Key Terms

strategies for change
conflict
role definition
feedback
conflict resolution
coalitions
negotiation
intergroup conflict
mediation
burnout

FOR CRITICAL THOUGHT:
Managing Yourself as Your Job Is Consolidated

LaDonna, like the other staff members at St. Pius Hospital, had heard the rumors for months. The hospital was going to cut back all medical employees and contract with individuals, rather than staff departments as they had done in the past. Now, November 15, here she was in the first full-building staff meeting the hospital had ever called.

The hospital's chief administrator was explaining that in an effort to cut costs and save the hospital corporation, they were changing the way they conducted business with their staff. They were no longer going to have staff physicians, nurses, or allied professionals. Instead, they were going to contract with individual physicians to provide medical services. The physicians would be self-employed contractors who would provide medical services to the hospital for a fee, but all taxes, insurance, benefits, and retirement expenses would be the responsibility of the physician. All allied health professionals that the physicians worked with would now be employees of the physicians, and their presence in the hospital would be a part of the contract the physician negotiated with the hospital. The hospital would have to pay the physicians a little more than they did now as hospital employees, but the hospital would have no benefit costs, resulting in savings of 30 percent per employee.

Those medical personnel who worked at the hospital's four outpatient ambulatory care centers would purchase their equipment, including office equipment and the buildings, and hire their own allied personnel. The hospital personnel department would be helping physicians in this transition by having financial counselors, loan officers from various local banks, and other support staff available to the physicians and allied personnel daily over the next three months. The transition would be completed by May 1.

No one could explain to LaDonna what would happen to her and the other athletic trainers and physical therapists that worked in the hospital and satellite sites. She knew that CARF standards specified certain staffing levels in hospitals, both for physicians and allied professionals. What was not clear was how the financial arrangements had to be handled. What would happen to her 401(k) plan, health insurance, dental insurance, paid vacation, liability insurance, and other benefits? Would she even have a job after May 1? What should she be doing to insure her family's financial well-being?

ORGANIZATIONAL CHANGE

The starting point for any discussion of organizational change must be that change is the *only* constant. Managers will either participate and use change to focus and/or redirect the organization or else risk losing their competitive position in the marketplace. More changes have happened in medical and related fields in the last decade than ever before.[19] There is competition from a wide variety of healthcare providers, with the result being reduced revenues.

Many factors influence the need for change, with social expectation being the primary factor. People are demanding quality at the lowest possible cost. Traditional healthcare settings (hospitals) are having their purpose blurred with the introduction of wellness programs, patient education programs, outpatient settings, populations that are living longer and are in need of more long-term care, and more community-based programs in mental health, chronic disease conditions, and other areas.

To change the focus of a healthcare organization, the administration must rethink its mission in light of today's competition. Additionally, organizations must recruit and retain talented assistants who view change as a problem to solve, not a barrier. Kriegel[18] asserted that once change is in motion, it has to be encouraged to flame brightly, rather than allowing it to wither in a sea of "Yeah, but . . .," "Things will get back to normal when . . .," or "Let's wait and see if. . . ."

Strategies for Change

There are several **strategies for change**[29] that should be understood. The first is the use of *rational-empirical* strategies. The basis for this approach is that people are rational, and once they understand what is in their best self-interest they will proceed in that direction. The strength of the rational-empirical method is its foundation in the scientific method. The weaknesses of this method include not having time to implement the scientific method before change must take place, and the fact that people are seldom rational about change. Reactions to change vary from resistance, denial, fear, and sabotage, to belief and acceptance.

One of the problems that can be solved by this method is seen in today's sports medicine clinics that have hired certified athletic trainers to place in local high schools. Many clinics based in large metropolitan areas entered into the high school market with the expectation of receiving a steady patient influx on referral from the athletic trainer. Often, parents have preferred to take their children to the family physician and to a rehabilitation facility that the physician prefers. Beginning in early 1994, a number of large city sports medicine clinics reassessed their mission and decided to leave the high school market. A corollary issue involves the high schools; what will they have to do to continue receiving the athletic training services to which they have become accustomed? Some high schools even fear lawsuits based on the claim that after providing athletic training services in the past, failing to provide an athletic trainer will be considered negligence.

Another set of tactics is the use of *normative-reeducative* strategies. These presuppose that people are motivated by unsatisfied needs. Assumptions include the idea that organizational problems might not be solved rationally and that change needs to be based on interpersonal communications, conflict resolution strategies, negotiations, and sensitivity training. Intervention methods are needed to convince the workers to accept and implement change.

A third method of change includes *power-coercive* strategies, which can be seen in all levels of government. If the president of the United States issues an order restricting the flow of information in healthcare settings or decreasing the allocated funds available, then his or her orders are followed. If the governor of Ohio mandates a give-back in funds allocated for education spending, reductions are made. If the athletic director at the University of Central States decides to reallocate 10 percent of the athletic training budget to the new handball team or to buy new turf shoes for the football team, then the budget transfer takes place. There is little that can be done in a direct defensive stance to a power-coercive strategy. Power-coercive orders can be challenged by department heads, but at some risk. The two major ways are to threaten to resign (there is, of course, the risk that management will accept the resignation) or to threaten to inform the media. Some politicians obtain undated letters of resignation from all appointed subordinates when they take office and use them if they become displeased with the subordinate's work. Economic and political sanctions are the tools used to reach management's goals.

Organizational Development and Systematic Change

Veninga[29] proposes four steps to implement organizational development and change. The first step is *awareness*. Management assesses the life cycle of the organization, the interest of management toward change, and the environment within the organization to accept and implement change.

Greiner[16] listed five crises of management in organization life cycle assessment that must be overcome to effectively implement change. These are leadership, autonomy, control, red tape, and "psychological saturation." In other words, crises of leadership are solved by finding new leadership acceptable to current leadership. Crises of autonomy are resolved by delegating authority. Crises of control are settled by delegating with superintending control. Crises of red tape (rules to control) are reconciled by growth through collaboration, which involves eliminating some rules and increasing communication. Crisis of burnout is an ongoing problem without any quick answers. The suggestion has been made that change does not happen when organizational forces are in balance. Only when employees perceive that something is out of balance is change possible. Even then, the organization must be flexible enough to change.

Veninga's second step is *diagnosis*. Whereas the awareness phase is basically subjective, diagnosis is concerned with obtaining objective evidence that can be used to produce change. Management collects data that can reduce haphazardness, show employees that others are thinking along similar lines, and serve as the initial step of change. Information is collected through a variety of means, including survey questionnaires, interviews, stratified sampling of affected areas, and self-generated scales. Follow-up patient satisfaction surveys are a form of data that management can use. In addition, the exit interview and three-to five-year follow-up of the graduates of a CAAHEP-accredited (Commission on Accreditation of Allied Health Education Programs) or NATA-approved athletic trainer education program can be used. These data are used to reevaluate the direction of a program relative to its professed objectives.

The third step is *intervention*. Those components of an organization that are changing, if not the entire organization, and what the anticipated changes mean must be clearly understood. There will certainly be resistance due either to uncertainty or to a decrease in authority or power. The studies by Coch and French[6] show that resistance to change can be decreased by having workers participate in the formulation of the problem, the potential solutions, and implementation of the best alternatives. Objective evidence of the success or failure of a new solution must be obtained and used to continue or modify the proposed solutions. Newly implemented solutions that are having good results then need to be reinforced. If a sports medicine clinic sees other clinics getting out of the high school market, that clinic must evaluate its own response in light of its mission statement, its profit-loss statement, and the public relations impact. Making a change only because of another clinic's actions is foolish, but a clinic that fails to evaluate its own position and act accordingly is equally unwise.

The last step is *evaluation*. Veninga suggests that the history of change has involved enthusiastic support by proponents of the new way of doing things with little empirical evidence to justify the change. Two questions must be answered to evaluate change. The first is whether the change resolved the problems identified in the diagnosis. If the change did not accomplish the goals, and assuming the organization really desired change, then either the diagnosis or the intervention was faulty. The second question is whether the change resulted in any new problems that need action. A way to look at this problem is to remember that during the Civil War, surgeons operated to save lives, but they did so with knives they wiped on their aprons. We now know the knives must be sterile, but the surgery must still be performed to save lives. The knowledge of bloodborne pathogens, however, cannot deter us from seeking still better ways to protect patients. We cannot be overwhelmed by the responsibility for the conditions that result from our changes, or change will not occur at all.

CONFLICT ADJUSTMENT

Conflict can be defined as a type of competition in which the parties to the conflict are aware of the directly opposite (or conflicting) nature of their positions and in which each side wishes to continue to hold its position. Conflict is a special frustration in which one or more goals is blocked by competing goals.[2] Time and energy spent in improper competition (e.g., turf wars) is time and energy that is not available to complete the goals of the organization. As a starting point, conflict is endemic to most institutions and literally permeates athletic training settings. Group conflict is a natural consequence of joining a group, and, in fact, may be as common as group harmony.

Some preliminary statements about conflict need to be understood before trying to remove all conflict. The first statement is that conflict is not necessarily negative to growth. When conflict occurs, people have to reassess their positions, which is a good thing. Some people think that the stability of a group cannot increase until conflict has surfaced, been confronted, and been resolved. The second statement is that conflict is usually personal. The statement, "Don't take this personally, but . . ." is not reasonable, because people engage in conflicts specifically because they do take them personally.[26] The third statement is that disruptive conflict may sabotage an organization. People have a finite amount of energy to invest at work. When the psychological energy that should be directed at the job at hand is instead spent on plotting and exacting retribution for public and private grievances, the organization suffers. People begin to use energy to protect their turf in a self-defeating fashion.

Causes of and Responses to Conflict

There are many explanations for conflicts groups such as communication difficulties, organizational structures, and other psychological and social factors. Forsythe[10] contends that all of these are interrelated and that a complete list of causes is impossible to make. He claims that there are three mechanisms that can cause disagreements to become open conflicts: competition for scarce resources, the use of threatening, antagonistic power strategies, and the personal characteristics of the group members.

Competition invariably means that for someone to succeed, someone else must fail.[9] In contrast, cooperation, or individual success that leads to group success, decreases the potential for conflict. Among the methods for exerting influence, some are more contentious than others. Threats, punishments, and bullying are all contentious methods, because they are direct, nonrational, and unilateral.[9] Such tactics usually increase hostility, counteractions, and unwillingness to compromise. In fact, the ability to threaten sets up a potential conflict, and the use of threats increases the conflict. The interpersonal dynamics focus on the differences between competitors and cooperators. *Competitors* attack conflict with the attitude that they must win at all costs, whereas *cooperators* attack conflict by being concerned that everyone in the group comes out of the conflict with something. Competitors often win because they do not care what is thought of them as long as they win. In response, the cooperators sometimes will withdraw from the group rather than face repeated losses.

Many of the responses are tinged with aggression. Depending on the setting, one or more of the parties may not see a particular act as aggressive. Socially justified acts are not viewed as aggressive (e.g., defensive war), but unjustified acts are.[2] *Negative reciprocity* is a social norm that allows a person to retaliate for harm done. *Equity* is a social norm that says "an eye for an eye" is acceptable, but no more than that.[2]

Veninga[29] asserts that within an organization, roles must be clearly defined if the group is to function effectively. **Role definition** reduces competition. Roles can be divided into three types. The first roles are *mandatory*; these are the roles that are basic to employment. A person hired to be an athletic trainer must function as an athletic trainer. The second roles are *allowable*; these are the roles that are not a required part of the job but that a worker chooses to do. For example, a clinic athletic trainer may begin to solicit contracts with high schools or to organize and conduct data-based research. Finally, the last roles are *disallowed*; these are the actions that may not be done. In jurisdictions with licensure of athletic trainers, practicing without a license or outside the state practice act is a disallowed role that could subject both the athletic trainer and the employer to legal sanctions.

Many institutions have rules governing employee behavior in the workplace. Some institutions forbid employees to hold outside jobs or elective office while employed, to date or marry fellow employees, or to take another job in the immediate area within a specified time after voluntarily leaving employment. To minimize conflict, the role description (actual job role) and the role prescription (what the athletic trainer believes he or she was hired to do) must be similar.

Defensive employees are not secure in their roles and they cause management to take a lot of time to reassure them. Defensiveness is caused by a perceived threat to personal territory, such as an evaluation process that makes an employee feel that his or her speech or behavioral mannerisms are being used to categorize him or her. A wary, guarded response may also be provoked by control, especially hidden control, or the feeling that one is being used. There are also a number of problems in work settings that cannot be discussed and therefore increase fear. Highest on the list is management practice.[26] Neutrality of management leads to employees who do not know where they stand. Sometimes defensiveness can be triggered by a supervisor who lets an employee know that management is "better" than the employees. The attitude can also be caused by a feeling of certainty on the part of the employees. Workers who consider themselves superior to their peers, not needing to learn new facts or to share knowledge with the other workers, will engender a defensive attitude.

Defensiveness can be lessened in a number of ways. First the management must assess the causes of the defensive behavior. For each of the defensive climates just discussed, there is a management position that will help to diminish the defensiveness. When the employees fear evaluation, changing the process to one focused on solving problems with the employee's input will often get the message across in a more positive light. If the employees perceive that the messages they are receiving are designed to control their behavior or impose solutions, a problem-oriented approach from management may change the climate. The sender of the message will ask the receiver to help define a mutual problem, which implies that there is no predetermined agenda or solution to impose.

When employees perceive that management is neutral to their performance, empathy is a rebuttal. The supervisor who conveys sensitivity for the feelings and worth of the employees will be perceived as supportive and will reduce anxiety. Equality and provisionalism are the responses to counter superiority and certainty. Equality implies that the speaker is willing to work in mutual planning in a climate of respect and trust. Provisionalism implies that the sender is researching possible alternatives and wants the receiver's input rather than taking sides on an issue.

Another recommendation to diminish defensive behavior is to remember that defensive people do not listen well and have a need to express frustration and anger.[29] Athletes have used athletic trainers as a confidential outlet for their anger and frustrations for many years. By being a good listener, the athletic trainer may begin to understand why the person feels threatened. Responses to hostility must be minimal. You must allow a hostile person to come to a conclusion in his or her own mind before seeking input. If he or she is not ready to listen, it may be appropriate to put concerns and recommendations in writing, allowing the person to read and consider the response at a later time.

A final recommendation is for athletic trainers to control their own defensive feelings when with defensive people. The more calm and collected they can be, the more likely that good listeners will be able to find constructive alternatives. Little good comes from having a defensive person respond in kind to another defensive person's complaints.

Contentment and Feedback

In chapter 2, Abraham Maslow and his hierarchy of needs was reviewed. These needs are insatiable. Because constant attention to satisfying needs is a natural condition, administrators may question how they can help to meet the needs. Superficially the administration may keep workers informed about where they stand and what the future may hold. Veninga[29] suggests that feedback is a critical part of meeting needs. In management terms, there are three types of **feedback**: positive, negative, and problem-centered. Positive feedback is the act of reinforcing desired behaviors, that is, making employees feel that their work and presence are valued. Negative feedback is offering a negative opinion about a behavior without offering any constructive suggestions. Problem-centered feedback also attacks negative problems; however, it offers constructive opportunities for both parties to meet and discuss possible solutions.

An example of the use of the three types of feedback might be seen in a situation where student athletic trainers wish to have personal (i.e., dating) relationships with athletes. In the positive feedback setting, student athletic trainers who sponsored gatherings that excluded athletes would be encouraged. In the negative feedback setting, the practice of dating athletes would be forbidden. In the problem-centered feedback setting, the staff could point out the difficulty of remaining impartial in healthcare decisions when athletic trainers date the athletes they care for; however, they may allow students to date athletes on teams they do not work with.

There are a number of tangible benefits from using feedback. For example, there is an increased respect between the administrator and the worker. Supervisors who become involved are much more highly valued than those who let their workers go without direction. Another benefit is that misunderstandings decrease. With proper feedback there will be less distortion of the intent of directions given; with no feedback, the receiver of the directions can change them in a way that is most favorable to the receiver. A third benefit of feedback is that open communication from a supervisor has been shown to increase a subordinate's self-concept.[29]

There are costs, however, to implementing a feedback program. As a supervisor becomes more involved, it takes time away from other administrative duties. Additional management personnel may be needed, and management may find out some things (e.g., workers' opinions of management policies, supervisors, or products) that they do not wish to know (even though for the well-being of the organization they need to know them). The administration may even discover that the workers perceive management as ineffective or counterproductive. Directions that supervisors thought were perfectly clear may have been unclear to the receivers.

Resolving Conflicts

An early theorist in conflict resolution was Mary Parker Follett. She believed **conflict resolution** could be simplified to three positions: win-lose, lose-lose, or win-win. Another name for win-lose could well be domination. If one side has the power, they win and the weaker side loses. An example is the result of political elections where, if the winners had not been the incumbents, all the patronage position holders would lose their jobs in favor of people from the winning side. Lose-lose situations are the result of compromise. Neither party is happy because both had to give something up to get part of what they want. Win-win situations result in integration. These are found by looking at the wants and needs of both parties and arriving at a solution that gives each side what they want without giving up their position. The primary goal is finding a solution that has high quality and high acceptability to those affected by it. Win-win orientations are facilitated by managers who use a confronting style in managing interpersonal problems, who give time and effort to helping both workers and bosses clarify what they mean when they speak on an issue, and who use problem-solving methods.[29]

An example of these three points of view could be seen in a sports medicine clinic that originally identified a market to employ athletic trainers but now is having trouble providing enough work for them. The win-lose answer (dominance) could be to either lay off one of the athletic trainers or to reassign one of them as an aide in another department. The lose-lose answer (compromise) could be for the athletic trainer to take less pay and the clinic to accept that all athletic trainers would continue at full benefits but at reduced hours. The win-win answer (integration) could be to institute a marketing campaign stressing the need for athletic trainers, sponsoring community projects (e.g., fun runs), and actively seeking outreach contracts with local area high schools. These would all increase the visibility of athletic trainers and the demand for their services.

Beck[2] identified four types of personal conflict based on Miller's gradient theory. These are approach-approach, avoidance-avoidance, approach-avoidance, and double approach-avoidance. The approach-approach condition assumes two possible alternatives; as one is approached, the likelihood of reaching it increases while the likelihood of reaching the other decreases. Many athletic trainers want to work in the college or university setting for a variety of reasons, including the age of the athletes, medical control, and travel. Other athletic trainers choose to work in a setting with higher salaries and stable, forty- to fifty-hour work weeks, as in a sports medicine clinic. These minor conflicts are easily resolved.

The avoidance-avoidance position is a problem with two alternatives in which moving away from one possibility means getting closer to the other. Movement in the opposite direction results, even as the final position is in sight. This is considered being "caught between a rock and a hard place." The response may be to leave the field, either physically by quitting or mentally through sleep, drugs, amnesia, or suicide.

The approach-avoidance situation occurs when a goal is both desirable and hostile. When a person works as a head athletic trainer in a major college setting, he or she may find that the hours necessary to be successful in that setting cause major friction in marriage and home life. As the goal is neared, the pain from the problems that the achievement created cause a reevaluation of the desirability of reaching the goal. There is a temporary shift in the relative strengths of the approach motive and the avoidance motive.

The last condition is the double approach-avoidance condition where two goals may be mutually exclusive. As one goal is approached, the other goal is lost as a practical reality. An example would be an athletic trainer desiring to work in a sports medicine clinic and as a teacher or athletic trainer in a school setting. If the athletic trainer takes a clinic position, the teaching credential may expire. If he or she takes the teaching position, the access to clinic resources may disappear, and because advanced-level rehabilitation skills are practiced less often in the high school setting than in the clinic, the opportunity to work in the clinic at a later date may be diminished.

A problem that may change the effectiveness of a solution is the building of **coalitions** by the parties involved. Even though the problem may have started just between two people, when each side calls on friendships and favors owed to establish its position as the correct one, many others are soon involved. Coalition members disagree on many things, but they choose to ignore their differences to achieve a goal desired by the coalition. An example seen in government is when Senator A supports Senator B's favorite pork-barrel project in return for favorable consideration of his or her pet project.[17] Coalitions tend to be temporary as members strive to get more power elsewhere.

Forsythe[10] stated that coalitions usually operate on the "cheapest winning solution" theory that occurs when no single group can control the outcome. For example, this occurs when there are thirteen possible votes on the athletic board at Northern State College. There are various factions on the board (those close to football coaches, friends of the associate athletic director in charge of women's basketball and nonrevenue sports, business people who like to brag at their club that they control Northern State College finances, etc.). At least seven votes are needed to win a position, and there are blocs of six, five, one, and one votes. A coalition of six votes and one vote is most likely. Although a coalition of the six group and the five group is possible, the five group also represents the greatest threat to the six group because a coalition of the five group and any one are equal to the six group, and the five group and both ones will win. By being on the inside with the six group, the five group has knowledge ahead of time of the six group's arguments and can counter them. The best interests of the six-vote group are served by remaining in a coalition that is as small as possible.

Common methods of resolving interpersonal conflicts include imposition, withdrawal, inaction, yielding, compromise, and problem solving. Imposition (which could be called win-lose) forces one side to accept the position of the other side. The result may lead to withdrawal, a response in which the losing side leaves the group rather than accept the winning side's position. Inaction (avoidance) is a condition whereby one or both sides ignore the problem and hope that it will go away. Yielding (smoothing or conceding) involves one side retracting its demands rather than having a confrontation that it may lose. Compromise (lose-lose) finds a solution in the area between the two each sides' positions, requiring each side to yield something in order to get something. Problem solving (win-win, confrontation) is agreeing on the problem and then agreeing on a solution that is satisfactory to both sides.

Negotiation is a process of communication in which all competing sides to a disagreement exam-

ine the issues, give their positions, and exchange proposals and counterproposals. There are three approaches to negotiation:[10] the soft negotiator, the hard negotiator, and the principled negotiator. Soft negotiators have a goal of achieving an agreement; they tend to be soft on both people and problems. Hard negotiators have a goal of victory and are hard on both people and problems. Principled negotiators have a goal of reaching a wise outcome and tend to be soft on people and hard on problems.

Sometimes negotiation breaks down, and third-party intervention is necessary. Third parties are outside the entanglements surrounding the problems being negotiated. They facilitate resolution by allowing the parties to present their arguments in a nonargumentative atmosphere. Arbitrators permit solutions to be proposed and accepted while also allowing the parties to "save face" by blaming the third party for the suggestions (which they ultimately accept, but would not have offered as their solution). Finally, negotiators can interpret misunderstandings for each side, preventing further alienation. The success of third-party intervention is tied to their power in relation to the other parties. Judges and go-betweens are both third-party interveners, but they are different in terms of the power they exert. The success of a third party is related to how well the intermediary serves to end the disputes separating the parties.

Intergroup Conflict

Conflict between groups is endemic in all levels of social organization. The causes of **intergroup conflict** may begin with competition. When two groups are in competition for a prize and only one can win, the other must lose. In a society that devalues losers, these groups are now enemies to each other, to be overcome by any and all means. The *realistic conflict theory* maintains that the competition is over limited resources.[10] These resources are things people value, such as food, wealth, power, territory, energy, and respect. These are in such short supply that when one group gains, another loses. Everyone wants to be part of the group that possesses the desirable objects. Because control equals success, groups take steps to both reach their goals and prevent other groups from reaching their goals.

Another cause of conflict has to do with social grouping. Membership in a particular group can, even in the absence of competition, produce intergroup conflict. In college or university environments, many academics have an us-versus-them outlook on the athletic department. For the athletic trainer on a dual appointment (a clinician who also teaches and has faculty rank), members of both the faculty and the athletic department want to know if the athletic trainer is "with us" or "with them" when the groups are in conflict. The question for the athletic trainer is whether he or she belongs to "my group" or another group. The notion of being in two different groups is enough to activate intergroup discrimination favoring "my group." Even minimal contact, such as belonging to an alumni association, may lead to favoring unknown peers over perhaps more appropriate outsiders.

Forsythe[10] has suggested that preference for group may be explained, at least in part, by the *social-identity theory*. There are three assumptions at work in this theory. First, because individuals are categorized, someone can be distinguished as being *in* "our group" or *out* of "our group." Second, people try to maintain a positive social standing. Third, a great deal of social identity comes from group identity. These three assumptions suggest that members of one's own group are favored to maintain social identity. Having a group identity can be a confusing position for athletic trainers at times. They are not coaches, nor are they athletes. The athletic trainer, then, is neither part of management nor part of labor, yet is working for the common goals of the group.

A final source of conflict is belligerent and quarrelsome use of language and physical threats over sometimes relatively minor points. The behavior includes insults, swearing, verbal assault, and finally physical assault. Such actions intensify the intragroup solidarity against outsiders and may precipitate activity that destroys the framework of order.

Mediation

One way to **mediate** conflicts before they get beyond reason is to have each group separately prepare three lists.[29] The first is a list of the qualities that best describe a group. The second is a list of the qualities that best describe another group. The last list is the qualities that members of each group think the other group would give to them. A third party compiles composite lists and then the groups meet and discuss what they have found.

Intergroup contact leads to intergroup cooperation through the setting of superordinate goals. These are goals that cannot be achieved by either group working alone, but can only be reached by the two groups working together. Establishing a common enemy, which forms a new quasi-group allowing common achievement, is a useful tactic that also provides an outlet for frustrations that will not be directed at members of the new group.

STRESS AND BURNOUT

The word *stress* comes from the Latin word *strictus*, which means "tight," and the French word *stringo*, which means "to draw together."[8] The term refers to the responses that occur in the body as a result of a stressor (i.e., stimulus). Everyone experiences stress. However, too much stress, especially if it is prolonged and unrelieved for a long period of time, can result in mental or physical illness.

The modern concept of psychological stress was defined by Hans Selye[27] as a nonspecific response of the body to any demand made upon it. Stressors may be physical, social, or psychological, and they may also be negative or positive.

Selye differentiated the responses to positive stressors (eustress) and negative stressors (distress). Eustress is considered "good stress" and is felt to be beneficial, while distress is considered "bad stress" and responses to it are detrimental. Both kinds of stress result in physiological responses in the body, although stress should not just be considered a nonspecific physiological response. Currently, the stress response is an interrelated process that includes the presence of a stressor, the circumstances in which the stressor occurs, the interpretation of the situation by the person, his or her typical reaction, and the resources available to deal with the stress.[23] For example, one athletic trainer may look forward to his or her daily meeting with the coach. This meeting can be viewed as an opportunity to communicate and work together to achieve the safest environment and situation for the athletes. Another athletic trainer may interpret his or her daily meetings as nerve-racking and anxiety producing. The second athletic trainer sees the meetings as a source of distress, while the first sees the meetings as eustress.

Response to Stress

The body will respond to stress both psychologically and physiologically. These two responses, however, are not independent of each other. They occur simultaneously and are interrelated.

With the presence of a stressor, the stress process begins, psychological processes "kick in," and the manner in which the stressor is perceived is determined. Stress may cause arousal and anxiety. The arousal results from the body's increased awareness to the presence of a stressor. Arousal causes signals to be sent to the brain to produce a response (a physiological action). Feelings of tension, apprehension, and worry describe anxiety. The extent to which a person psychologically responds to a situation or stressor largely depends on how the situation is interpreted and how ready the person feels to handle the situation. Athletic trainers must respond and react to many situations and potential stressors throughout each day. Certified athletic trainers who are prone to stress will make extreme, universal, outright judgments and engage in psychological misrepresentations in which they overemphasize all of the negatives of a given situation.[23] An example of this occurs where athletic trainers teach state-required first aid and emergency care courses for secondary-school program directors (coaches, club advisors, etc.). Some feel that those athletic trainers are "selling out" and compromising the potential job market in the secondary school setting.

Physiologically, every system in the body is affected by the stress response, with the nervous and endocrine systems primarily regulating the responses. The nervous system causes many involuntary physiological responses to occur when a stressor is encountered, such as changes in heart rate, blood pressure, and/or respiration rate, among others. The endocrine system secretes hormones to prepare the body to deal with the stressor.[15] Since the hormones may remain in the blood for days to weeks, and the nervous system response is usually short-lived, the endocrine system may cause the long-term negative effects associated with stress and disease.[23]

Selye[27] labeled the body's physiological response to stress the *general adaptation syndrome (GAS)*. In GAS, there is a three-part response to stressors: alarm, resistance, and exhaustion. Selye believed that when stress was applied, an animal first went into a stage of alarm (fight or flight), followed by a stage of resistance or adaptation, if appropriate time was allowed for the body to recover. In this stage, the body adjusts to the stress and may appear to return to normal balance. If insufficient time is available, or if the stress is too great, instead of resistance, there follows a stage of exhaustion. In this stage, the body is less able to resist an illness, and even death may result.

Occupational Stress

Occupational stress is the stress experienced by a person at work. Both occupational stress and burnout are problems that affect athletic trainers in all settings. Greenberg[15] describes five determinants of stress in the workplace: factors intrinsic to a job, role in the organization, career development, relationships at work, and organizational structures and climate. Factors associated with work deal for the most part with quantitative and qualitative overload. Quantitative overload is having too much work to do; qualitative overload is having work that is too hard. A classical study by Russek and Zohman[25] found that in a study of 100 coronary patients, 25 percent had been working two jobs, and an additional 45 percent had been working in excess of sixty hours a week. They also found that prolonged emotional stress was present in 91 percent of the cases. The effects of quantitative and qualitative overload include physical symptoms and visible effects such as job dissatisfaction, lower self-esteem, escapist activity, and low motivation.[30] Vaughn[28] found certain survival responses were characteristic of adults who grew up in high-stress environments. These were carried over into their jobs and eventually contributed to burnout. These characteristics include tenacity, diminished self-worth, preoccupation, lost sense of normalcy, intensity, responsibility, fear of loss and abandonment, and denial.

Role within an organization refers to role ambiguity, role conflict, and role responsibilities. Role ambiguity exists when athletic trainers do not know what is expected of them. An example of role ambiguity occurs when an athletic trainer has no written job description but is attacked by one of the groups that think the athletic trainer should cater to them. The athletic trainer is in a vulnerable position if either the coaches or athletes are unhappy and his or her supervisor thinks that he or she acted outside the job description. Role conflict exists when athletic trainers are caught between the demands of two different groups, such as coaches and athletes. Consider someone with limited pain tolerance who drops out of practice every time there is a minor ache or pain. The next time the athlete is injured, the coach's response may be "Get him back in three minutes or he is done for the week!" However, the athlete is really hurt and needs attention in the emergency room before returning to practice. Role responsibilities refer to those obligations that come with the job. Efforts have been made to separate responsibility for "things" from responsibility for "people."[29] The general consensus is that having responsibility for people is far more stressful than dealing with things.

Career development can be broken into two areas. The first deals with job security and the second with job status. Job security has not been a major issue in athletic training until recently, when a number of football coaches have changed jobs and brought along their own athletic trainers, causing the current athletic trainers to be let go. Because the college/university and professional job market is essentially stagnant in terms of job growth, and displaced head athletic trainers find an equivalent position hard to get, it is fortunate that this practice is still somewhat rare.

For athletic trainers, job status is a definite problem. For many athletic trainers there is a ceiling on their job opportunities due to the nature of their job and location. Rarely do athletic trainers move on to athletic administration or healthcare

administration. The title of head athletic trainer is the peak position in the college or university setting. Professional sports athletic trainers all strive to reach the "major leagues" where the pay and benefits are appropriate to qualifications.

Reaching this goal is even more difficult for women. In major football schools, women are still the minority, with few holding the position of head athletic trainer. In professional team sports in the United States, women have even less chance. With many preeminently qualified women looking at the lack of gender opportunity in football, basketball, baseball, and ice hockey, athletic training must appear at times to be a closed shop dominated by "good old boys." As of 1999, women who want to work in professional team sports have available at the major league level only the Women's NBA. Women have been working at the minor league level in ice hockey and basketball for a number of years. There have been a few women in minor league baseball, but none have risen to the level of AAA baseball. Others must go to Europe to work in the women's professional leagues in basketball and volleyball. In Europe, the female athletic trainer has another set of frustrations to deal with—the healthcare system there is even more heavily dominated by male physicians. Some European coaches prefer to seek assistance from a male physician and ignore the team's female athletic trainer.

In a clinic setting, athletic trainers may be dealing with either a cooperative or a superiority-conscious supervisor, depending on the state they work in, the physical therapy practice act, and the athletic training practice act, if any. In some jurisdictions athletic trainers may not work independently but must function under the direct supervision of a physical therapist. In those states, athletic trainers without the dual credential of physical therapist have no opportunity to advance in the clinical setting. Researchers[7] have found that good mental health correlates with opportunities for advancement in the workplace.

Positive relationships at work refer to having coworkers who are supportive and understanding of what is expected of the athletic trainer's position. These coworkers are critical to an athletic trainer's success. Good working conditions are a major variable for individual health and well-being. At worst, the workplace can be an untenable place when coworkers try to sabotage the athletic trainer's standing with employers, supervisors, or athletes.

Finally, organizational structure and climate refers to the employee's ability to participate in the decision-making process that controls his or her job role. When there is participation, employees feel greater job satisfaction and self-esteem. When participation is negligible, all manner of escapist behavior comes to the fore.

Occupational stress is a complex issue. Not only are the previous five types of work stressors involved, but also each individual's personal characteristics play a part in determining the amount of stress. Characteristics such as anxiety levels, neuroticism, tolerance of ambiguity, Type A behavior patterns, and others will affect stress in the workplace. Stresses from outside the job and the worker are also involved. Family problems, life crises, financial situations, and environmental factors also influence occupational stress. Work stressors, individual characteristics, and extraneous factors may not all be evenly weighted. Different settings have different levels of intrinsic job stressors and career development stressors. Different employees have differing levels of anxiety and tolerance and will be experiencing different external factors. For example, an athletic trainer in a college setting may be experiencing stress from outside the workplace because he or she is not spending much time at home due to a long workday and work week. An athletic trainer in a clinical setting may experience stressors because his or her role in the organization is unclear.

Signs of Stress and Disease

People under stress will display identifiable signs and symptoms. Selye[27] listed twenty-seven detectable signs that result from negative stress. The signs include both physical and emotional responses. There is some evidence supporting a relationship between occupational stress and disease or illness. There is evidence of both physiological effects of occupational stress and disease states associated with occupational stress.[15]

Burnout

Too much work or frequent frustration at work can lead to a syndrome of physical and emotional exhaustion called burnout. The term **burnout** was first used in literature by Herbert Freudenberger[11] in 1974 when he defined burnout as an individual becoming inoperative for all intents and purposes. Christina Maslach,[20] another major theorist, has defined burnout as a syndrome encompassing emotional exhaustion, depersonalization, and reduced personal accomplishment that can happen to people involved in dealing with other people. In an allied healthcare profession, causes of burnout can include disillusionment (differences between qualifications and what the professional is allowed to do), helplessness (being faced with situations that defy solutions), work setting (being in control when everyone else is losing their composure and blaming it on the athletic trainer), status (not being compensated commensurate with ability and education), and funding (not provided with adequate resources to do the job).[31] People who are labeled workaholics or are idealists who are overcommitted to the time pressures of a job are susceptible to burnout. Women who combine the added stress of homemaking with a healthcare career are also at higher risk of burnout.[21] In addition, children who grow up in high-stress environments eventually tend to seek out high-stress jobs.[23] Yuen[32] determined that much research has been done on the problem of burnout in the healthcare professions, but that the pressures causing burnout in students during field work have been virtually ignored.

Symptoms of burnout include fatigue, illnesses, migraines, ulcers, feelings of helplessness and resignation, irritability, sleeplessness, withdrawal, depression, high blood pressure, smoking, drinking, illicit drug use, distancing, paranoia, and inflexibility of thinking.[3,20,22,28,29,31]

The nature of athletic training is one of caring about and serving the athlete. When the emotional demands of the job overcome an athletic trainer's ability to cope, burnout ensues. Too many athletes to serve, coaches' expectations, chronic injuries that heal slowly, and personality conflicts with administrators, coaches, or athletes can all cause the athletic trainer to feel both physically and emotionally drained at the end of each day. Athletic trainers receive few rewards for their efforts, experience role conflict, lack autonomy, and may have a feeling of powerlessness to deal with on top of all of these problems. The certified athletic trainer can easily be in a constant state of high emotional arousal and anxiety during the day, and therefore is prone to experience burnout.[1]

Stages of Burnout

Five stages have been proposed in the progression of burnout.[30] The first stage is job contentment, sometimes called the honeymoon. During this period the employee is enthusiastic and willing to accept the stresses that go with a new position and learning new skills. The second stage is job disappointment. The realization of what the job actually is has begun to set in at this stage. The first symptoms of burnout may begin to appear here. The third stage, job disillusionment, follows. Job disillusionment is differentiated from job disappointment by the appearance of overt anger and resentment. There may also be a conscious attempt to put distance between the workers and the client. The fourth stage is job despair. The operative feeling is being trapped by circumstances, finances, or other factors that make escape impossible. The final stage is work redefined. The workers will change their working lives by changing jobs, resigning due to health problems, or possibly leaving the profession. Many of those who simply change jobs will repeat the cycle of burnout again.

Preventing Stress and Burnout

To counter stress and burnout, an athletic trainer must be proactive. Gieck[11] has offered the following steps toward managing stress: First, athletic trainers need to acknowledge when they are under stress. Physical exercise is important, because it helps an athletic trainer better withstand fatigue and develop self-discipline and self-esteem. Exercise also

contributes to a more healthy lifestyle. Diet goes hand-in-hand with exercise in fostering a healthy lifestyle by cutting down sugar, alcohol, and caffeine. Athletic trainers must acknowledge that the workday has a definite end. When the day is over, athletic trainers must leave and not wait around in case someone should need them. The solution to being indispensable at work is to have interests outside of work, even if these interests are simply playing tennis and watching old movies.

Time management, which means creating a logical order for the day's tasks, may be one of the most important ways to prevent burnout and manage stress. In the college, high school, and professional settings, a certified athletic trainer must be able to manage his or her time appropriately so that all the necessary tasks can be accomplished during the course of the day. For example, daily activities can include treatment for injuries, overseeing or implementing rehabilitation programs, clinical supervision of student athletic trainers, meetings with coaches and administrators, documentation and record keeping, coverage of practice and events, and communication with team physician(s), just to name a few. The athletic trainer who is able to use his or her time wisely will succeed in preventing the negative effects of stress.

Other authors have suggested setting challenging, yet realistic, goals, developing social support systems, taking vacations,[29] and doing the same things but doing them differently and taking them less personally.[20] Vaughn,[28] in an article directed toward nurses, suggested being able to separate what they are from what they do. Being a perfectionist does not change feelings of low self-esteem. Doing exceedingly more (in a quantitative sense) is not so important as doing the same things the job has always demanded but doing them better (in a qualitative sense).

Extent of the Problem

Gieck[13,14] suggested in the early 1980s that athletic trainers suffered a high frequency of burnout. His conclusions were supported by a study done by Campbell, Miller, and Robinson[3] in 1984 at the NATA 35th Annual Meeting and Clinical Symposium in

Nashville, where 221 conference participants completed a survey form. The results indicated that only 34.9 percent of the respondents were symptom-free. The remainder suffered anywhere from one to eight medical conditions that were related to job stress. Those who considered themselves burned out were found to be seven times more likely to have considered changing jobs within the last six months. In addition, 70 percent of married respondents who were not burned out considered themselves happily married, whereas only 30 percent of those who were burned out felt the same.

In contrast, Susan Capel[4] conducted a detailed study of athletic trainer burnout. She developed an Athletic Trainers Questionnaire from the Maslach Burnout Inventory (MBI), a role conflict and role ambiguity scale, a locus of control scale, and a demographic scale. The questionnaire was administered to 332 ATCs. Capel found relatively low scores for role conflict and role ambiguity. Athletic trainers were also found as a group to have an internal locus of control. When analyzing the burnout subscales of the MBI, she determined that personal accomplishment was the strongest negative finding—99 percent of athletic trainers scored at either moderate or

high levels. Burnout intensity followed, as 83 percent scored at the moderate level. In contrast, 55 percent of athletic trainers scored in the low range for emotional exhaustion and 78 percent scored in the low range for depersonalization, with 100 percent in both categories at low or moderate. The research concluded that 34 percent of athletic trainers scored low for total burnout and 66 percent scored moderate, whereas no one scored high on the MBI. Capel inferred that athletic trainers had generally less burnout than other healthcare and human services workers.[4] Capel found previous work by other researchers in the athletic training literature to be primarily anecdotal, rather than empirical research.[4]

Capel[5] also assessed why athletic trainers left the profession and found that only 21 percent left due to the negative factors that induce stress (salary too low, limited opportunities, or long hours) in the workplace. Although long hours were cited by 37 percent of the respondents as a negative aspect of the profession, it was cited as the reason for leaving the profession by only 4 percent of those who left. A far larger number left to enter physical therapy practice or to return to graduate school.

Summary

1. Change is a constant in organizations. Strategies for change include rational-empirical strategies, normative-reeducative strategies, and power-coercive strategies.
2. Four steps for implementing change include awareness, diagnosis, intervention, and evaluation.
3. Conflict is a type of competition in which each party wants what the other party does not. Conflict does not have to be negative, but it is personal, and if disruptive, it can destroy an organization.
4. There are many causes of and responses to conflict within groups.
5. Three types of feedback include positive, negative, and problem-centered.
6. Three possibilities in conflict resolution includes win-lose, lose-lose, and win-win.

7. Four types of personal conflict are approach-approach, avoidance-avoidance, approach-avoidance, and double approach-avoidance.
8. Coalitions are a way to solve conflicts.
9. Negotiation involves communication between all competing sides in order to examine the issues, give positions, and exchange proposals for change.
10. Intergroup conflict usually results from competition.
11. Stress is a nonspecific response of the body to any demand made upon it. Stressors may be physical, social, or psychological and may also be negative or positive.
12. The body will respond to stress both psychologically and physiologically; these responses occur simultaneously and are interrelated.

13. Selye described the body's physiological response to stress as the general adaptation syndrome, which is characterized by a three-step response to stressors: alarm, resistance, and exhaustion.

14. Both occupational stress and burnout are problems that affect athletic trainers in all settings.

15. Five determinants of stress in the workplace are factors intrinsic to a job, role in the organization, career development, relationships at work, and organizational structures and climate.

16. Individuals under stress will display identifiable signs and symptoms.

17. Too much work or frequent frustration at work can lead to a syndrome of physical and emotional exhaustion called burnout.

18. Symptoms of burnout include fatigue, illnesses, migraines, ulcers, feelings of helplessness and resignation, irritability, sleeplessness, withdrawal, depression, high blood pressure, smoking, drinking, illicit drug use, distancing, paranoia, and inflexibility of thinking.

19. To counter stress and burnout an athletic trainer must be proactive.

20. Time management, which means creating a logical order for the day's tasks, may be one of the most important ways to prevent burnout and manage stress.

For Critical Thought

Now that LaDonna has had a week to think about the situation, she has begun to make inquiries. First she consulted with the orthopedic surgeon whom she had been working with. Her practice could support four athletic trainers working in conjunction with three physical therapists, the surgeon stated. She wanted LaDonna to be one of the athletic trainers. Next LaDonna spoke with the personnel department and assessed her benefit package and how to go about keeping the benefits that were most important to her. She spoke with the retirement plan administrator, who told her how to convert the plan to a personal plan with no tax liability. She then consulted with the other athletic trainers and they discussed what their possible outcomes were. Two had begun to search for another job in another area of the country. The other eight decided to stay where they were for the present and see how the situation resolved. The orthopedic surgeons from the hospital could all use athletic trainers, so none of them would be without a job. Salaries under the new arrangement were still to be negotiated. While not completely comfortable, LaDonna was confident that everyone was working toward a common goal, full employment for all current employees, and she was heartened by that.

Websites

http://www.queendom.com/burnout.html

A burnout inventory.

http://www.stress.org.uk

Stress UK. Home page for an organization that discusses both personal and occupational stress.

http://www.lenski.com

Lenski and Associates. A consultation firm for colleges and universities, specializing in improving organizational life through effective conflict and change.

Applications for Consideration

1. Patricia Burns works for Eastern College, an NCAA Division II institution in the midwest. She is the only certified athletic trainer for 32 sports, 16 male and 16 female, and has to supervise care for 495 athletes of her school's 800 students. Practices are any time between 6:00 A.M. and

9:00 P.M. every day throughout the school year, depending on the sports that are in season. Pat is feeling stress but loves her job. (She was formerly a computer programmer for the federal government for fifteen years, but left for what she thought would be better working conditions, better job security, and more money.) Suggest a burnout prevention program to keep Pat in her job for the foreseeable future.

2. Lucy Ramirez is an athletic trainer (who is subcontracted to a high school) in a sports medicine clinic where there are a lot of interoffice politics.

There are rumors daily that the clinic is getting a contract to run the athletic training program at North Central State University, that they are going to expand their high school outreach program, or that they are going to abandon the outreach program altogether and have all of the athletic trainers working as physical therapy aides. Coalitions are forming. What are the dangers to Lucy's position in these changing scenarios? What considerations does she need to think about? Is her job safe?

References

1 Arnheim, DD, and Prentice, WE. *Principles of athletic training*. 10th ed. Dubuque, IA: WCB McGraw-Hill Publishers, 2000.

2 Beck, RC, *Motivation: Theories and principles*. 3rd ed. Englewood Cliffs, NJ: Prentice-Hall, 1990.

3 Campbell, D, Miller, MH, Robinson, WW. The prevalence of burnout among athletic trainers. *Athletic Training*, 20:110–113, 148, 1985.

4 Capel, S. Psychological and organizational factors related to burnout in athletic trainers. *Athletic Training*, 21:322–327, 1986.

5 Capel, S. Attrition of athletic trainers. *Athletic Training*, 25:34–39, 1990.

6 Coch, L, French, J. Overcoming resistance to change. *Human Relations*, 1:512–532, 1948.

7 Cooper, CL, Marshall, J. Sources of managerial and white collar stress. In: Cooper, CL, Payne, R, eds. *Stress and Work*. New York: John Wiley & Sons, 1978.

8 Dirckx, JH. ed. *Stedman's concise medical dictionary for the health professions*. 3rd ed. Baltimore, MD: Williams & Wilkins Publishing, 1997.

9 Deutsch, M. A theory of cooperation and competition. *Human Relations*, 2:129–152, 1949.

10 Forsythe, DR. *Group dynamics*. 2nd ed. Pacific Grove, CA: Brooks/Cole Publishing Co., 1990.

11 Freudenberger, HJ. Staff burn-out. *Journal of Social Issues*, 30:159–165, 1974.

12 Gieck, J. Stress management and the athletic trainer. *Athletic Training*, 19:115–119, 1984.

13 Gieck, J. Athletic training burnout: A case study. *Athletic Training*, 21:43, 1986.

14 Gieck, J, Brown, RS, Shank, RH. The burnout syndrome among athletic trainers. *Athletic Training*, 17:36–40, 1982.

15 Greenberg, JS. *Comprehensive stress management*. 2nd ed. Dubuque, IA: WCB Publishers, 1987.

16 Greiner, LE. Evolution and revolution as organizations grow. *Harvard Business Review*, 50(4):37–46, 1972.

17 Jellison, JM. *Overcoming resistance*. New York: Simon & Schuster, 1993.

18 Kriegel, RJ. *If it ain't broke, BREAK IT*. New York: Warner Books, 1991.

19 Marszalek-Gaucher, E, Coffey, RJ. *Transforming healthcare organizations: How to achieve and sustain organizational excellence*. San Francisco: Jossey-Bass, 1990.

20 Maslach, C. *Burnout: The cost of caring*. Englewood Cliffs, NJ: Prentice-Hall, 1982.

21 Moss, VA. Burnout. *AORN Journal* 50:1071–1072, 1074–1076, 1989.

22 Plant, ML, Plant, MA, Foster, J. Stress, alcohol, tobacco, and illicit drug use amongst nurses: A Scottish study. *Journal of Advanced Nursing*, 17:1057–1067, 1982.

23 Prentice, WE. *Fitness and wellness for life*. 6th ed. Dubuque, IA: WCB McGraw-Hill Publishers, 1999.

24 Robinson, BE. *Work addiction: Hidden legacies of adult children*. Deerfield Beach, FL: Health Communications, Inc., 1989.

25 Russek, HI, Zohman, BL. Relative significance of hereditary diet and occupational stress in CHD of young adults. *American Journal of Medicine*, 235:266–276, 1958.

26 Ryan, KD, Oestrich, DK. *Driving fear out of the workplace*. San Francisco: Jossey-Bass, 1991.

27 Selye, H. A syndrome produced by diverse nocuous agents. *Nature* (London), 138:32, 1936.

28 Vaughn, G. Workaholism. *AORN Journal*, 56:873–877, 1992.

29 Veninga, RL. *The human side of health care administration*. Englewood Cliffs, NJ: Prentice-Hall, 1982.

30 Veninga, RL, Spradley, JP. *The work/stress connection: How to cope with job burnout*. Boston: Little, Brown, 1981.

31 Welch, ID, Medeiros, DC, Tate, GA. *Beyond burnout*. Englewood Cliffs, NJ: Prentice-Hall 1982.

32 Yuen, HK: Fieldwork students under stress. *American Journal of Occupational Therapy*, 44:80–81, 1990.

PART TWO

Facilities

CHAPTER 6

Athletic Training Facilities Management

After reading this chapter, you should be able to:

- Identify the policies and procedures necessary to conduct athletic training room business.

- Identify various ways that personnel are used in an athletic training room.

- Identify how personnel are used in athletic training education programs.

- Describe various ways to communicate among sites that must be covered by the sports medicine program.

- Set up and run a student athletic trainer club.

Key Terms

policies
procedures
chain of command
clinical evaluation
personnel scheduling
multisite communication
student athletic trainer organizations

FOR CRITICAL THOUGHT:
Becoming a Facility Manager

Elizabeth has been a clinical athletic trainer for fourteen years in three different sites, both outreach in a high school and working only in the clinic. She has just been hired as the director of therapy at the largest sports medicine clinic in Metropolis. She is to be the director of operations, overseeing fourteen athletic trainers, twenty-three physical therapists, four occupational therapists, ten clinical exercise physiologists who work primarily with cardiac rehabilitation patients, and six recreation therapists. She is to coordinate with other hospital departments, particularly social work and nutrition. When she arrives on the job, she immediately recognizes some major problems that were covered up during the interview. First, there is no assignment of patients to the specialists that they need; instead, whoever is available at the moment sees the patient. There is a great deal of crossover among the athletic trainers, physical therapists, and occupational therapists. Often athletic trainers are assigned Medicare or worker's compensation cases if they are not as busy as the physical therapists at any particular moment. This is a clear violation of the law. Physical therapists are performing rehabilitation of severe ankle sprains and knee injuries that occurred in athletic participation that was covered on-site by clinic staff athletic trainers. Additionally, there is crossover between the occupational therapists and the recreation therapists.

Beth has to make some decisions quickly. First, she needs to assess exactly what the mission of her department is and what resources she has to complete the task at hand. Next, she needs a patient assessment to see whether the type of patient load the department sees is covered by adequate staffing. She notes that there is a strong outreach program with ten local high schools and two professional teams. Only two of the athletic trainers work a full shift in the clinic. She also notes that the twelve affiliate sites create only enough referrals to justify five positions. The hospital board believes that the outreach program is good public relations, however, and the program stays at current levels.

What does Beth have to do now? Should she compartmentalize the functions and only assign therapists to particular patient areas? Should she encourage some of the athletic trainers to obtain additional qualifications? Two of the athletic trainers have approached Beth about the possibility of billing athletic training services. What does she have to do to set this in motion?

The smooth operation of an athletic training facility requires a knowledge of management theory and personnel development (see chapters 1 and 2). The basic skills and knowledge to be applied will vary greatly with the setting, but the foundation is caring for patients. Sports medicine is the provision of health care to athletes and those engaged in physical activity, especially as it relates to returning to competition and to the activities of daily living that may be temporarily compromised after an injury and

during rehabilitation. Budgets may establish the parameters within which a sports medicine team may operate, but an adequate standard of health care is always the outcome that must be realized.

Facility managers must control the resources at their disposal, both people and things. Establishing policies and procedures, personnel scheduling, budgeting, and communications are among the topics that must be addressed. The purpose of this chapter is to identify the necessary components of athletic training facility management in a systematic way that enables an athletic trainer to wisely use his or her resources.

POLICIES AND PROCEDURES

One of the most important aspects of facility management is establishing the policies and procedures for operating the facility. **Policies** are the basic framework of principles and rules used to govern and expedite decision making.[8] Clear and accurate written statements of the policies for operating the athletic training facility are essential for communications. Administrators often use these operating statements to evaluate the functioning of the athletic training room. **Procedures** describe the process by which something is done.[8] There may well be some overlap in the written definitions of the what and why (policy) and the how (procedure). While policies and procedures create stability, it is important to realize that too many specific rules can also be restrictive to the point of stifling individual creativity.[3]

A facility's policies and procedures should address the following issues: (1) population to be served, (2) appropriate use of the facilities, (3) job descriptions for the staff (see chapter 3), (4) chain of command, and (5) supervision.

Population Served

The first issue to be resolved for any athletic training facility is to establish the patient population that will be served. The type of patient seen in different athletic training facilities varies with the setting and the institution. Sports medicine clinics will treat anyone who is referred to the clinic by a licensed

Having adequate supplies at outdoor locations is part of facilities management.
(*University of Toledo Sports Information.*)

practitioner. Referring medical practitioners often will make the first appointment for a patient, and may even participate in the initial interview to establish treatment goals and parameters. Walk-in patients are often covered by standing orders from the clinic's medical director or staff in the jurisdictions that allow them. In other jurisdictions, clinics set up specific times of the day or week for triage of walk-in patients to obtain physician input and direct orders for treatment. In some states, (e.g., where there is no state credentialing of athletic trainers) direct referral is not required by law.

Some university athletic training facilities treat only varsity athletes, whereas others treat cheerleaders, marching band members, club sports participants, and even intramural sports participants. Most universities will provide some coverage to visiting athletes if arrangements are made in advance and the team is traveling without a certified athletic trainer.

In some conferences it is a policy that care must be provided to visiting teams as needed. In certain legal jurisdictions, the athletic training staff of a university must treat the entire university community.

High schools provide a special set of problems dealing with the treatment of minors (see chapter 16). Consent to treat must be obtained before any care can be given. Most schools have the parents complete a form that authorizes the school to provide emergency care for students who have been injured. Parents are free to reject the provision of treatment until they have been notified of the situation. Athletic trainers need to have copies of the school permission-to-treat form or have their own form signed and kept on file to allow treatment to take place. Athletic trainers in a high school setting will usually treat only athletes from the school teams, but may also treat members of the student body, faculty, or administration.

In industrial settings, the company physician refers the patient to the athletic trainer in the rehabilitation site that has been established at the workplace. In most state worker's compensation jurisdictions, the company can direct the injured worker for a specific number of visits to see a designated medical practitioner.

It is important to be aware of the legal responsibilities to the population served and to the employing institution (see chapter 16). The population served must be consistent with institutional policies and procedures. Should an athletic trainer perform services on a person outside the defined population the athletic training room serves, the institution's liability insurance would probably not cover the athletic trainer for any injury that may result. In addition, if an institution excludes a population such as club sports and an athletic trainer assists a club sport athlete, that athletic trainer may be responsible to the institution for the cost of the supplies used on the athlete. Regardless of who is to be treated in the athletic training facility, it is crucial to be aware of the responsibilities that come with these patients.

Facility Usage

An athletic training room is a healthcare facility before it is anything else. There are certain principles for operating a healthcare facility that must be adhered to, most of which involve common sense.

- Strict confidentiality is a must.
- Sterile procedures must be carried out.
- Respect is required for the patients served.
- No problem is to be ignored or mishandled due to the personal feelings of the staff toward the patient.

This is by no means a complete list, but it should start the facility administrators considering all of the ramifications of maintaining the same standards as a physician's office or a department in a hospital. At the same time, the patients must respect the nature of the facility and the professionals who staff it. Vulgarity, sexism, harassment, theft, and the use of tobacco, drugs, or alcohol must not be tolerated.

The athletic training room is the main site in which athletic training is practiced in colleges or universities, high schools, and professional athletics.

The services provided by athletic trainers include the prevention of athletic injuries, evaluation and recognition of athletic injuries, and medical referral, first aid and emergency care, rehabilitation and reconditioning, organization and administration, counseling and guidance, and education.[7]

At some institutions the athletic training room is to be used only for services to varsity athletes. At others the athletic training room may be used as a clinical teaching laboratory, by the student athletic trainers club, or by outside groups such as continuing education classes (e.g., massage). The availability of the athletic training room for these purposes must be defined in the policies and procedures. It is wise to identify both days and times for these outside activities. Any use not approved in the policies and procedures should not be considered. Generally sports medicine clinics are not available for outside uses, but they may be used as sites for in-service programs.

Most college or university athletic training facilities will post some general rules of conduct within the athletic training room. Some sample rules (with translations) regarding athletic training room use (all taken from actual athletic training rooms) include:

- The athletic training room is not a student union, please don't use it as one! (We want to encourage only those who are in the athletic training room for healthcare reasons to be there.)
- The athletic training room is not an appropriate place to study. (Studying during treatments is one thing, but using the athletic training room as a study lounge is inappropriate.)
- Persons who are not patients or athletic training room personnel are not permitted in the athletic training room without permission from the head athletic trainer. (Please wait for your friends outside, as your presence is disruptive to good traffic flow and takes up space.)
- Please leave cleated shoes at the door. (They cut up the carpet and track in dirt.)
- No form of tobacco is allowed in the athletic training room at any time. (This is unsanitary.)
- Ice is to be used for therapy and not for consumption. (If too many people eat the ice there may not be enough at the end of the day.)

Job Descriptions

Job descriptions of facility personnel should be included in the policies and procedures for both full-time and part-time employees. For a detailed discussion of job descriptions, see chapter 3, "The Sports Medicine Team."

Chain of Command

Identification of the person responsible for the health care of patients and the order of subordinates establishes the **chain of command** and is essential for the smooth operation of an athletic training facility. It should be clear who has the ultimate responsibility for medical decisions at a facility (physician), who is designated to implement those decisions in a particular situation (supervising athletic trainer), and the persons whom the supervisor may designate as the agents to complete the tasks (athletic trainers). The physician is responsible for clearing a patient for return to participation, not the athletic trainer and not the coach.

In the college or university setting, the team physician has the final say in medical matters, and athletic directors may have the final say in administrative and organizational matters. The head athletic trainer acts as a mediator between the two and supervises the rest of the athletic training staff. This often leads to conflict; for example, unpopular decisions of the team physicians can be blamed on the athletic trainers and can adversely affect performance evaluations and possibly continued employment.

The ideal administrative situation for an athletic trainer may be where the athletic trainer is employed by the sports medicine department (hospital, clinic, private practice, etc.) that furnishes medical coverage to a college or university athletic department. When athletic trainers are employed by the team physicians they work under rather than the athletic director, there is a clear-cut chain of command in medical decisions.

In a high school setting, the chain of command is much more open as the athletic trainer deals with a team physician and, in addition, many family physicians about medical matters, and the school

athletic director, principal, or even superintendent of schools about administration. When dealing with multiple physicians, the high school athletic trainer needs to keep in mind that physicians' written orders govern to what extent and how soon the athlete may be returned to activity and competition. With so many different physicians, the athletic trainer may find that what physician A prescribes, physician B categorically rejects.

In the professional setting, especially in baseball and ice hockey where there are minor leagues, there may be a local team physician and the affiliated major league organization may have its own team physician. For injuries that are not career threatening, the organization may rely on the local physician; however, when the injury may be career ending or when the organization has a great deal of money invested in an athlete, then the parent organization may send in its physician to take superintending control.

In the sports medicine clinic setting, the administrative structure is varied, depending on where the clinic is housed. At some point there is a medical director in control of implementing medical policy, which is made by the director or by a board of directors.

SUPERVISION OF STUDENT ATHLETIC TRAINERS

Athletic training education is in a state of transition and will continue to be so for the next few years. As of January 1, 2004, only graduates of CAAHEP-accredited athletic training education programs will be eligible to take the NATABOC Certification Examination and acquire the credential of Certified Athletic Trainer. Students in internship education programs must have an accepted exam application before January 1, 2004, to be eligible to take the examination. Allowing four years to complete a bachelor's degree program, those students who entered college in the Fall of 1999 were the last class that will be given a full four years to complete the education program.

Student athletic trainers need clinical sites and clinical supervisors to practice and implement the knowledge and skills that they have learned in the classroom. The most common traditional site is a college or university athletic training room. Additional sites are now found in high schools, professional team facilities, hospitals, clinics, industrial sites, and health clubs.

There are three organizations that affect the educational setting, content, and evaluation of student athletic trainers. These are the NATA Board of Certification (NATABOC), the Joint Review Committee—Athletic Training (representing CAAHEP), and the NATA Education Council.

NATA Board of Certification

The NATA Board of Certification determines the qualifications of entry-level athletic trainers and administers a certification examination to those who meet the qualifications. The NATABOC publishes the Role Delineation Study,[4] which is used to construct the NATABOC Certification Examination. The mission of the NATA Board of Certification is:

> ". . . to certify athletic trainers and to identify for the public, quality healthcare professionals through a system of certification, adjudication, standards of practice and continuing competency programs."[5]

The NATABOC (which is accredited by the National Commission for Certifying Agencies, a branch of the National Organization for Competency Assurance) is the only accredited certification program for athletic trainers in the United States. The NATABOC has established fifteen Standards of Professional Practice for Athletic Training (see chapter 15). The NATABOC statement on supervising athletic trainers is as follows:

> "Certified athletic trainers who are supervising athletic training students' educational experiences shall afford supervision adequate to assure (following stated written and verbal direction) that the student performs his or her tasks in a manner consistent with the Standards of Practice of the Profession of Athletic Training. Certified athletic trainers who are supervising athletic training students must be recognized as an athletic trainer at the setting where the athletic training students are obtaining athletic

trainer experience hours to satisfy the eligibility requirements."[5]

The interaction between the student and supervising athletic trainer involves daily personal contact at the site of the supervision. In addition, the certified athletic trainer must be in close enough proximity to intervene if necessary to protect the patient being treated. At the time of application for the certification examination, the student must verify that at least 25 percent of the required experience hours were obtained covering practices and/or games involving the sports of football, soccer, wrestling, basketball, gymnastics, lacrosse, volleyball, rugby, and rodeo.[5]

Joint Review Committee—Athletic Training

The second organization is the Joint Review Committee—Athletic Training, a branch of the Commission for the Accreditation of Allied Health Education Programs. The JRC—AT administers the *Standards and Guidelines for an Accredited Education Program for the Athletic Trainer.*[1] The *Standards and Guidelines* specify that accredited education programs must provide classroom instruction in thirteen key content areas.[1] Regarding clinical education, the Standard is that the education program has to include opportunities for clinical experiences under the direct supervision of a qualified clinical instructor in an acceptable clinical setting.[1] The Guidelines suggest that the education program should be designed to develop the psychomotor competencies from *Athletic Training Educational Competencies,*[6] yet allow further development of the cognitive and affective domains as well. Primary clinical sites should include athletic training rooms, practices and competitions in (but not limited to) a variety of high-risk activities previously mentioned. To increase the student's clinical experience, educational programs are encouraged to establish formal affiliations with other institutions in the immediate area and to expose students to community-based facilities such as sports medicine clinics, physical therapy clinics, health centers, hospital emergency rooms, industrial sites, and physician's offices.

As with the NATABOC guidelines, the *Standards and Guidelines* specify that clinical experiences involve daily personal contact at the clinical site between the supervisor and the student. The Guidelines also specify that clinical instructors need to be available to students, and to insure that availability, a ratio of students to clinical staff is recommended at eight to one.[1] The Standards specify that clinical instructors must be NATA Certified Athletic Trainers (or equivalent qualification), and should have at least one year of experience after certification.

NATA Education Council

The third group that affects clinical education is the NATA Education Council, which publishes *Athletic Training Educational Competencies*.[6,7] The third edition is in effect September 2001. The competencies and clinical proficiencies identify the skills and knowledge required of an entry-level athletic trainer. The Joint Review Committee—Athletic Training requires these competencies to form the basis for accredited education programs. The second edition of competencies identifies six practice domains.[7] The third edition expands the domains to twelve major subject areas.[6] These include:

- Risk management and injury prevention
- Pathology of injuries and illnesses
- Assessment and evaluation
- Acute care of injury and illness
- Pharmacology
- Therapeutic modalities
- Therapeutic exercise
- General medical conditions and disabilities
- Nutritional aspects of injury and illness
- Psychosocial intervention and referral
- Health care administration
- Professional development and responsibilities

The NATA Education Council is moving to require that clinical education experiences be offered using academic courses or academic credit. The clinical experience has to be at least two academic years. In addition, those clinical instructors who assess competencies and proficiencies will have the additional qualification of "approved clinical instructor."

During the clinical experience, interaction at the site of supervision is required between student athletic trainer and clinical instructor.

Clinical Evaluation

Clinical evaluation of student athletic trainers needs to follow a formal education model, including objectives to be demonstrated and reinforced in psychomotor and affective domains for the major tasks a student has completed in the classroom. Lack of formal emphasis has led to situations of haphazard learning[9] or, worse, to student athletic trainers being used as underpaid (or unpaid) staff rather than students who are still learning their profession. Where competencies and clinical proficiencies are the basis of clinical education, instruction can complete the task of implementing the knowledge and skills that make up the core of the profession of athletic training. There are a variety of ways to reinforce behaviors in the clinical setting, including case study, simulations, and demonstrations.[9]

Evaluation should be given both in a *formative* (nonjudgmental) and *summative* (judgmental) sense.[10] Formative evaluation is given either verbally or in writing, preferably as soon after an experience as possible so that the issues are still fresh. If there is a threat to safety, then evaluation is immediate. This type of evaluation should be directly related to standards of practice.[10] Summative evaluation is usually a written evaluation at the conclusion of the clinical rotation. It includes information about conformity to the norms established for practice, or for this clinical site or instructor. If the rotation is a full semester, a midterm evaluation would allow the student and the instructor to orchestrate change in proficiency and behavior consistent with the level of competence at the site.

The clinical instructors must be completely aware of the level of knowledge each student possesses when he or she enters the clinical rotation. What is an everyday experience to a seasoned clinician may still be very new to students. Clinical instructors usually behave similarly to those who were their mentors. Good clinicians seem to be able to take the best qualities of their peers and pass them on to their students.[2]

PERSONNEL SCHEDULING

Personnel scheduling is one of the cornerstones of a well-organized sports medicine program. Proper use of human resources will ensure an efficient, effective, and pleasant working environment. Several factors must be considered when establishing a working schedule, including the purpose of the facility, hours of operation, personnel available, and the extent of coverage necessary for proper medical care.

Purpose of the Facility

A clear understanding of the mission of the athletic training facility is required to adequately assign personnel. Is the facility a service site or a teaching site? Is it a combination of the two? Does the athletic trainer work in a closed practice site such as a factory or prison? Does the athletic trainer cover a specific team or does he or she work out of an athletic training room covering all athletes who come in the door, regardless of which team they play on? Does the athletic trainer work in a clinic setting with physically active patients who do not have the daily benefit of the facilities a college or university may have for the exclusive and free use of its patients? The atmosphere found on the practice field, where the responsibility of the athletic trainer is broadly defined and specialized in acute evaluation and care, is very different from that found in a sports medicine clinic, where the emphasis is on postacute care, chronic care, and rehabilitation, and where the focus is tightly controlled.

In some instances, athletic trainers may find that they are responsible for being in many different settings in the course of any given day. These could include practice or game coverage at a field, rehabilitation and reevaluation in a sports medicine clinic, prepractice or pregame preparation in the athletic training room, a rehabilitation setting away from the main athletic training room or clinic, supervision of graduate students placed in high schools, or even a satellite clinic or a research center located off campus.

There will be less medical supervision and less backup assistance at field sites than in clinic sites.

Providing athletic training services to high-risk sports requires qualified athletic trainers who can operate with minimal direct supervision and can also correctly activate the emergency medical system and/or team physician involvement in healthcare decisions.

In an industrial setting, the athletic trainer will use the same knowledge and skill that more traditional practice sites require. Workers who expend physical effort are injured just as athletes are. Primarily, the injuries are musculoskeletal, require acute evaluation and care, and are followed by referral to the plant physician and/or rehabilitation. The work hours match the shift times at the industrial site, some facilities being open twenty-four hours a day while others are only open for eight hours.

Although attendance at each site involves caring for patients, each setting has its own constraints. Only after a careful and comprehensive evaluation of these issues can a functioning, efficient schedule be developed.

Hours of Operation

An athletic training facility must be open a sufficient number of hours to adequately cover the healthcare needs of the patients. This will vary based on the site and the focus of the coverage. Hours in a clinic setting will usually be more predictable than practice or game coverage hours. Defining the hours of operation allows for the development of a flexible schedule that ensures that the facility is properly staffed and allows athletic trainers to vary their working times as needed. In some cases, the schedule may be different for weekdays and weekends or for morning versus afternoon coverage. By analyzing the needs of the site and by accurately tracking the patient or workflow, one can get a more specific idea of how many people will be needed to efficiently carry out the necessary duties.

The setting often dictates the hours of operation. A private clinic or an industrial site is a more structured operation, with set schedules and defined hours. Many clinics are open about ten to twelve hours during the day, with an early morning shift to accommodate patients before they go to work and an afternoon shift to accommodate patients on their way home from work or to recreation activities. In addition, many clinics subcontract services to high schools, with the athletic trainer working in the clinic in the morning and in the high school in the afternoon. Some of these clinics may also use part-time athletic trainers in the high school settings. Some clinics will be open on Saturdays for evaluation and treatment of injuries that occur during Friday night high school contests covered by clinic staff. A few of these clinics will also see patients from other teams, even though there is no contract for these services with the school.

A high school athletic training room during the fall and winter sports seasons may have athletes coming and going throughout the course of the day. If the athletic trainer is not a teacher in the school, it is possible to have the athletic training room open for therapy during a student's study hall and/or lunch hour. If the athletic trainer also teaches in the school, the hours available to work with students during the day may be greatly reduced.

The extent to which the facilities are used will help to determine the schedule. Most athletic trainers in a high school setting do not remain in the athletic training room until the final athlete or coach has left the building. This may be as late as 9:30 P.M. during the week. Games involving varsity, junior varsity, or freshman teams may mean having games scheduled every day at one time or another during the year. During the fall this could mean three football games, two volleyball games, two or more soccer games, two or more cross country meets, and two tennis matches at home, all during one week. A decision must be made about the need for an athletic trainer at each of these events.

In a college or university setting, most athletic trainers usually work with specific teams. When the team practices or performs, the athletic trainer is there. In addition, most athletic trainers also have assigned hours in the athletic training room to provide therapy and rehabilitation services for injured athletes. Student athletic trainers are assigned to work with clinical instructors, and participate in team coverage, athletic training room coverage, or a combination of both. Usually the upper-class students have completed more didactic course work and are given more responsibility, possibly being as-

signed a specific team and therapy time, whereas first and/or second-year students will work with a clinical instructor practicing more basic skills and are assigned coverage in a specific athletic training room.

The hours of operation of the main athletic training room are usually 7:00 A.M. to 7:00 P.M. or until the last athlete has left that day. This may vary with practice times set by the coaches of the various sports. Satellite athletic training rooms may be open similar hours or they may be closed except for the times that teams are working in the vicinity. Many college or university settings have only one athletic training room open for therapy and rehabilitation in the mornings and then all sites open in the afternoon for team coverage. Regardless, the hours of operation must be consistent with the scope of the program.

Often in professional athletics, the athletic training room hours are dictated by management. The athletic training room is open for therapy, rehabilitation, and practice or games. At the conclusion of each day, administrative tasks must be completed, such as written reports made for different levels of management, coaches, and general managers. Athletic trainers in the professional setting may work fourteen to eighteen hours per day during their competitive season. In addition, after the season is over, the athletic training room may remain open on a more limited basis to complete the rehabilitation of injuries from the competitive season. These include injuries that kept the athlete out of competition and injuries with which the athlete continued to play.

Personnel Considerations

Staff responsibilities vary greatly between full-time certified athletic trainers, part-time and graduate student certified athletic trainers, other therapists, and professional consultants. Team and athletic training room assignments must be made within the experience and qualifications of the individual.

Full-Time Certified Athletic Trainers. In college or university and high school settings, the full-time staff will generally be assigned to collision, contact, and other high-risk sports (e.g., gymnastics). Usually there is not sufficient staff to cover all of these sports, and part-time staff and certified graduate assistants fill in where needed.

The head athletic trainer has the responsibility of coordinating staff assignments and delegating such duties as he or she deems necessary. Many times the head athletic trainer's only team assignment is football. Responsibility for setting and implementing the budget, controlling inventories, coordinating physician involvement in the sports medicine program, possibly organizing travel, including packing of athletic training supplies and equipment, and even nutritional programming falls within the head athletic trainer's realm. Many of these obligations are delegated to assistant athletic trainers, part-time staff, and graduate assistants.

Assistant athletic trainers are full-time employees who provide athletic training services to specific teams, supervise athletic training rooms, and help to supervise the remainder of the clinical staff, both part-time and student. Whereas the head athletic trainer is assigned only to football, the assistant athletic trainers are responsible for supervising the delivery of athletic training services to all remaining teams by full-time and part-time staff, graduate assistants, and student athletic trainers. Assistant athletic trainers are also responsible for assignments delegated by the head athletic trainer in other areas of program administration, such as inventory, insurance, travel planning, and so forth.

Some athletic trainers may have faculty and/or administrative responsibilities in addition to athletic training coverage. These athletic trainers with split appointments may only be available for a certain season or for certain times during the day. When this type of appointment is in a college where teaching and service to athletics are the main responsibilities, then the assignment is viable. In institutions where faculty must produce research and publications, a split assignment is a liability to the athletic trainer. It is very difficult to serve two separate jobs, each demanding full-time hours and responsibilities. Usually, all full-time athletic training staff members serve as clinical instructors, supervising student athletic trainers' acquisition of required clinical proficiencies to be eligible to take the NATA certification examination.

Full-time athletic trainers in sports medicine clinics will perform rehabilitation, therapy, and reevaluation as deemed appropriate by the medical director. They may also be involved in the prevention of injury through conditioning, taping, bracing, and/or padding, among other areas. The duties and responsibilities of an athletic trainer in a clinic setting may be more closely related to the state practice act for athletic training than would be the case in high school, college or university, and professional settings.

Slightly more than one-half of the athletic trainers employed in the clinic setting will provide athletic training services to a third party (usually a high school, but also possibly professional, junior high school, college, or university). Those athletic trainers will be present at that site as contracted, which may be anywhere from only game coverage to complete practice and game coverage, although it is usually somewhere in between. A typical contractual arrangement will be for 20 hours a week, practice and game coverage. When multiple games in a week take the hours over the 20-hour contract, the athletic trainer will usually receive remission from morning clinic time.

Part-Time Athletic Trainers. Part-time athletic trainers usually have responsibility for one sport or athletic training room during a given portion of the day. In the college or university setting, many athletic trainers have a full-time position with a split appointment between teaching responsibilities in the allied health, physical education (or other) department and the athletic department. Split appointments may lead to conflict between the academic arena and the athletic training arena. The coaches want the athletic trainer present for more and more hours, while the academic position may be demanding greater research and scholarly productivity to be tenured and/or promoted. Part-time athletic trainers may also be employed in high schools or some small colleges (without a teaching contract or a clinic affiliation) for either a specific sport season, such as football, or for an entire school year. In addition, sports medicine clinics may hire part-time athletic trainers to cover high schools or to cover high-traffic times in the clinic.

Graduate Assistant Athletic Trainers. Most college or university athletic training programs employ from one to six or seven graduate assistants,

Staff athletic trainers demonstrate techniques for students as needed in clinical instruction.
(*University of Toledo Sports Information.*)

usually certified athletic trainers, to provide services to intercollegiate athletics at the school. These athletic trainers will usually be given team coverage for more high-risk activities than undergraduate students will be given. They may be counted as clinical supervisors in an athletic training education program after they have been certified for one year. For the athletic trainer seeking employment in the college or university setting, a graduate assistant placement is almost a required credential in today's market.

Many college or university programs also contract with area high schools to provide athletic training services with graduate assistant certified athletic trainers. This provides the graduate student with additional opportunities, the athletic training program with the means to fund graduate assistants, and additional exposure in the community. For those

students wanting employment in a high school setting, this is a highly desirable experience.

Team versus Athletic Training Room Coverage

A final consideration for staff assignments is whether the athletic trainer will be assigned individual team coverage or assigned to work out of a particular site. There are advantages and disadvantages to both methods. The major advantage to being assigned team coverage is that the athletic trainer is familiar with all of the athletes, their personalities, injuries, prognoses, therapy, and rehabilitation records. The disadvantages are that the demands of travel and practice coverage are constant.

The time load may be lessened by assigning a group of athletic trainers to a single site. Travel assignments and field responsibilities can then be rotated among the group. With a number of teams working out of a single athletic training room, athletic trainer A will go with the first team to travel, athletic trainer B will go with the next team, and so forth until all of the certified athletic trainers have traveled and the cycle can begin again. There is greater variety but less familiarity with particular athletes, their psychological reaction to injury, their faithfulness at therapy and rehabilitation, and their coaches' expectations of the athletic trainer. This arrangement may also enable athletic trainers with young children to keep their jobs while not traveling for a period of time. While both systems are used in athletic training rooms throughout the country, team assignments are the predominant form of coverage.

FUND-RAISING

The ability to raise monies outside the normal budgeting process (fund-raising) is an increasingly important part of an athletic trainer's ability to obtain new facilities and equipment. Many college and university athletic training programs actively solicit funds from area physicians, especially those who are referral physicians for the athletic medicine program. Some companies sponsor research and will donate much of the equipment necessary to the athletic training program to conduct the research. Other income may be generated by performing contract services for hospitals, physicians, summer sports camps run by athletic departments or private for-profit companies, and organized competitions that use the athletic department facilities, such as state high school tournaments and national and international competitions.

Funding to remodel an existing athletic training facility, especially if it is not part of an overall building renovation, most often depends on the athletic training staff's ability to raise money. Working with team physicians or graduates of the athletic training education program is one way to acquire funds. We are aware of one university that sells plaques to the families of athletes naming a piece of equipment or a table after the athlete. This is a very successful fund-raising activity for the short term.

Often at the college or university level, a piece of equipment is needed for rehabilitation programs but is too expensive to be included in the budget. Most athletic departments have a fund for monies from donors that is used for special projects, to supplement underfunded budgets, or to go to postseason tournaments. This type of fund is a good source for the purchase of an isokinetic device or a new high-volt electric stimulator. Another source of funds for athletic training equipment is the specific sport budget within the athletic department. Because football is the only major sport that routinely uses prophylactic knee braces on some athletes, these braces are often bought from the football budget rather than the athletic training budget. Neoprene knee sleeves with patellar supports could be purchased by the sports budgets for teams such as basketball and volleyball.

In a high school setting, an athletic trainer should never underestimate the ability of the school's athletic booster club to provide monies or, more likely, in-kind services such as construction of tables, donation of a refrigerator or freezer, donation of shirts and hats for student athletic trainers, or any number of other needed services. Athletic trainers need to assess how committed the club is and make the club aware of the athletic training room's needs. Replacing older-looking, fully functional equipment may not be in the athletic trainer's best interest; purchasing a new TENS, Russian Stim, or EMS unit may be better. Until asked, these organizations may not be aware of how they could help. They may end up being a lucrative, untapped source.

MULTISITE COMMUNICATION

Institutions with multiple athletic training facilities must establish fast, reliable means of **multisite communication** between locations. The ability to contact an athletic trainer on the field or at a distant site may be crucial in proper injury management. There are a number of methods of communicating between a home base and athletic trainers in the field. Three of the more popular methods include cellular phones, two-way radios, and beepers.

Telephones

Cellular telephones are an extremely popular method of direct communication from disparate sites, possibly miles apart. The use of cell phones is pervasive today due to superior electronics and low cost of operation. No longer are cumbersome battery packs required for their use. Cell phones cost little more than traditional service, if handled properly. Caution must be observed concerning confidentiality. Unless the phones are encrypted (both sending and receiving), then anyone with a scanner can intercept the frequency and listen to the conversation. There is also an unanswered health question at this time about the safety of microwave antennas being closely aligned with the head. There are some models that point the antenna away from the head, with no loss of signal, and decreased microwave exposure.

The traditional telephone is an effective means of communication between two or more athletic training facilities. Simply calling someone on the telephone is one of the easiest and most familiar forms of communication. The telephone is limited, however, to sites with phone jacks installed. A major problem with traditional telephones can occur when the only phone is located in an area that is locked up when the school administration leaves for the day. Alternative access, whether a key for the phone room or the installation of additional telephones, is a must.

Two-Way Radios

Two-way radios are portable, handheld units that provide great freedom of movement in the field. Unfortunately, a disadvantage to this type of communication is that anyone who has a receiver tuned to the same frequency can monitor the conversation. If privacy is important, a regular telephone should be used. Because the radio is for emergency communications, casual conversations should not be allowed. A clear channel should be available to contact the emergency medical service, team physician, and so forth.

Two-way radios transmit a signal directly to another portable radio over short distances or by relaying the signal through a transmitter to another radio from a greater distance. To do both requires a two-channel unit. Radio-to-radio transmissions are usually used for communications between sports medicine team members in the immediate area. Radio-transmitter-radio transmissions are used to contact other personnel who are located at a distant site, such as ambulance services or the police.

Beepers

The use of beepers or pagers has become popular in many professions where instant communication is a necessity, especially when the person who must be reached is mobile. A beeper can either relay a voice message, display alphanumeric or numeric codes (e.g., the phone number of the person trying to contact the athletic trainer), or even receive e-mail and the World Wide Web.

The use of beepers is a relatively inexpensive way to maintain contact with many facilities at once. This is an excellent tool for athletic trainers who are required to cover a number of sports but cannot physically be present at each one.

STUDENT ATHLETIC TRAINER ORGANIZATIONS

Student athletic trainer organizations are an excellent adjunct to an athletic training education program. Many students, particularly first-year students, are intimidated by the number of people with whom they are involved in the athletic training room. There may be anywhere from 20 to 90 first-year student athletic trainers and only 30 to 40 upper-class student athletic trainers. It seems that all of these upper-class student athletic trainers know the athletes, the athletic training staff, physicians, coaches, and administrators who may be in the athletic training room. The new students are not familiar with any of these people, and if they are left alone, many will drop out because they cannot relate to the environment. A student athletic trainer club is a good way to bridge the gap and allow for positive interaction between new and upper-class students.

The club promotes peer relationships in social and educational settings. To be successful, the agenda of the club must be student driven. If the club has good senior leadership, and good underclass participation, it can perpetuate the success year-in and year-out. There needs to be a faculty advisor who is supportive and attends all meetings, yet does not try to force an agenda on the club. Ideally, the advisor helps the club to plan activities, helps eliminate red tape, oversees the financial operations, and encourages student involvement. When students feel they have a stake in the club and how well it functions, they are empowered to continue the programs already in place.

An excellent activity for student athletic trainer clubs is promotion of a "Parent's Day" activity. All too often, parents know about as much as the general public about where athletic trainers work and who they work with. A Parent's Day allows tours of the facilities, opportunities to meet with intercollegiate staff and education program staff, have a meal, and possibly attend a competition.

One major function of some student athletic trainer organizations is to promote participation in state, NATA district and NATA national meetings. To get started, a group of four to six students needs to attend a professional meeting and then report to their peers what they accomplished at the meeting. One student is not enough. By going to the meetings, students are beginning to develop a network of peers and other athletic trainers, which may be important in the job market in the future. All such meetings include educational programs geared toward students.

A student athletic trainer club is an excellent location for in-service education programs with outside speakers, such as physicians instructing about evaluation techniques, healthcare problems, or other issues, and for employed athletic trainers to give students first-hand exposure to job settings, working conditions, program requirements, and to answer student questions. Care must be exercised to give first-year students in-service opportunities that allow them to learn and increase their interest and commitment, while not discouraging them by having a program with too high a required background. In all probability, separating first year student in-service programs from upper-class student programs is appropriate on the basis of each specific topic. If the in-service is part of the club meeting, at the conclusion of each education session, the students could unite to conduct club business.

Student athletic trainer clubs are good groups for fund-raising. Many clubs have sold clothing to the members to promote unity. Students often can find a local restaurant that will allow the club to exchange service for donations. Some clubs sell programs or work concessions at varsity games. Student government may be an untapped source of funds, as well as college student activity funds. Clubs have held outside fund-raising activities to pay for rooms, registration fees, and even transportation to NATA national and district conventions. These monies should be available to all students who wish to go to the meeting, not just the officers or upper-class students.

Of critical importance to the success of a student athletic trainer club is that the organization be founded by the students. Once it is in place and is an ongoing entity, the club will be self-sustaining. If, however, this is one more thing the staff forces onto the students, participation will be marginal at best.

Most student athletic trainer clubs are recognized student organizations at their college or university. Recognized student organizations usually can use campus meeting rooms at no charge, advertise meetings at no charge, and have access to other services. To accomplish this usually means working with campus student government and/or the office of the dean of student affairs. In all probability a constitution, by-laws, and election of officers will be required, along with some form of dues, as there may be filing fees to become a student organization. Many institutions prohibit potential organizations from collecting dues, until their status has been approved.

Summary

1. Facility management is management of people and things.
2. Policies are principles that govern operations.
3. Procedures are the processes for implementing policy.
4. Who is served in a facility must be established.

5. What activities may take place in a facility must be established.
6. Who is responsible for decision making on day-to-day operations, on healthcare decisions, and on financial decisions must be established.

7. Supervision of student athletic trainers is influenced by the NATABOC, JRC—AT, and the NATA Education Council.

8. Student athletic trainer clinical education should be based on competencies and proficiencies with clear, written objectives.

9. Personnel scheduling at particular locations depends on whether teams are covered or on clinical sites.

10. Hours of operation are variable with setting.

11. Full-time certified athletic trainers, part-time certified athletic trainers, and graduate assis-tant certified athletic trainers have different responsibilities, depending on status and setting.

12. Fund-raising activities are often needed to re-model facilities or purchase equipment.

13. Two-way communications are a must. Cellular phones are the most popular method at this time.

14. Student athletic trainer organizations promote unity within the student group, integrating first-year students with established student athletic trainers.

For Critical Thought

Now that Beth has had a meeting with her section head and been given the green light to move as she sees fit, she calls a staff meeting. At the meeting, she announces that she will be assigning flexible depart-ment boundaries. Space will be allocated on the basis of patient load over the last two years, and new hires will be in the areas that can support the posi-tions. She has been in contact with the state medical board, state licensure board, and Medicare concern-ing athletic trainers billing for athletic training ser-vices. As long as athletic trainers do not bill Medicare, they may work in sites where others work with Medicare patients. A recent opinion of the AMA and the state licensure board has held that li-censed professionals can bill for services using the CPT codes for physical medicine. Armed with the NATA outcomes research, she has gone to her mar-keting department and begun an aggressive cam-paign to let the public know that licensed athletic trainers are employed in her facility to treat the problems they experience from physical activity. She is continuing to push for greater interaction with the HMOs in town and has a meeting set with both Blue Cross and with Aetna for the next week. She never realized the complexity of healthcare adminis-tration, or how athletic training was becoming a part of the environment. At this time, she is excited about the department's future, concerned and always striving to increase her opportunities for success.

Websites

NATA Board of Certification:
http://www.natiaboc.org/

Commission on Accreditation of Allied Health Education Programs:

http://www.caahep.org

NATA Education Council, JRC-AT:
http://www.cewl.org

Applications for Consideration

1. After a job market analysis and student interest profiles showed that an athletic training edu-cation program is quite viable, Northwestern States University has begun the process of seek-ing CAAHEP accreditation. They have hired Dr. Erik Donovan as program director and located the education program in the College of Health Sciences. The new program director needs to meet with the athletic training staff and assess the current clinical education setting. With the expansion of competencies from past competency documents and clinical instruction

standards, Erik must approach the head athletic trainer, Bill McMillan, tactfully and convey that each needs the other to be successful. What points should Erik cover? Should the meeting include the other full-time staff athletic trainers? How should he discuss clinical education requirements, especially the need for clinical courses, with syllabi and objectives that will have to be taught by the staff athletic trainers?

2. Donald Washington is the head athletic trainer at Western State University, a small NCAA Division IA institution. He has one full-time assistant athletic trainer and two ATC graduate assistants to cover eighteen sports, including football, men's and women's basketball, cross country, track, swimming, lacrosse, tennis, baseball, softball, wrestling, field hockey, and volleyball. Which sports would Don assign to his ATCs and which ones could be covered by student athletic trainers under the supervision of a staff athletic trainer? Why would he make these choices?

3. Margaret Marcos has just accepted a position with Work-Trak, an industrial athletic training site at the Daimler-Chrysler plant in Youngstown. She will be the second athletic trainer at the facility and work second shift. The plant physician is only present first shift until noon and is then on call. There is a first aid station staffed by a registered nurse twenty-four hours a day. Who does Margaret have to establish working relationships with? When should this be done?

References

1 Commission of Accreditation of Allied Health Education Programs. *Standards and guidelines for an accredited educational program for the athletic trainer,* 1998.

2 Koehneke, P. Educating student clinicians versus student technicians. *Athletic Therapy Today,* 2(2):52–53, 1997.

3 Konin, JG. Administrative policy and procedure. In Konin, JG. ed. *Clinical athletic training.* Thorofare, NJ: SLACK Incorporated, 1997.

4 National Athletic Trainers' Association Board of Certification. Certification. In *Credentialing information and professional practice and discipline standards for the practice of athletic training.* Omaha, NE: National Athletic Trainers' Association Board of Certification. Inc., 1998.

5 National Athletic Trainers' Association Board of Certification. *NATABOC role delineation study.* 4th ed., 1999.

6 National Athletic Trainers' Association. *Athletic training educational competencies.* 3rd ed. Dallas: National Athletic Trainers' Association, Inc., 1999.

7 National Athletic Trainers' Association, Professional Education Committee. *Competencies in athletic training.* 2nd ed. Dallas: National Athletic Trainers' Association Inc., 1992.

8 Walker, B, Muenchen, J. Policies and procedures are necessary in the training room. *Athletic Training.* 13:211, 1978.

9 Weidner, TG, August, JA. The athletic therapist as clinical instructor. *Athletic Therapy Today,* 2(1):49–52, 1997.

10 Weidner, TG, August, JA, Welles, R. Pelletier, D. Evaluating clinical skills in athletic therapy. *Athletic Therapy Today.* 3(3):26–30, 1998.

CHAPTER 7

Designing Athletic Training Facilities

After reading this chapter, you should be able to:

- Describe the components of athletic training room design that use space in an efficient, safe, and functional manner.

- Communicate to architects the needs of the different areas in an athletic training room.

- Describe traffic flow, electric, water, light, space, color, floor coverings, and storage needs in an athletic training room.

- Describe the types of equipment that are needed in a functional athletic training room and the amounts of space and other resources this equipment will use.

- Explain from architectural drawings the components of an athletic training room as they will exist when finished.

- Identify problems to be avoided in designing an athletic training room.

Key Terms

concept planning document
space allocation
program areas
floor plans

FOR CRITICAL THOUGHT:
From Storage Room to Athletic Training Facility

Upon arriving for her new job as head athletic trainer at East Anglia High School, Marsha Brady-Smith was informed that she would have the use of an old utility room for her athletic training room. She received $12,500 to equip the room. The dimensions of the room were twelve by twenty-four feet. The room had no doors, electrical outlets, or plumbing fixtures. She was asked to draw a simple floor plan to show the location of doors, electrical outlets, fixtures, and where equipment would be placed. She was also asked to identify any special considerations for the room.

This drawing was to be sent to the architect to develop plans. The architect developed a full set of plans for the renovation. The plans were sent to Marsha to review. Marsha reviewed the plans and noticed that the doors she requested going into the men's and women's locker rooms were changed to provide access to the outside of the building instead. She called a meeting with the architect to discuss the change in door location. The architect said that fire code required that outside access to the room must be available.

Marsha understood this need, but she also wanted to have doors to the locker rooms. In order to achieve this, she would need three doors rather than two. This would increase the cost of construction, and the space allowance for the addition of the third door would take up valuable floor space. No additional funds are available to fund this additional door. Marsha must find an appropriate compromise between what she thinks she needs and what she can actually have in her athletic training facility.

She considers transferring some of the money for capital equipment to fund this extra door. She considers relocating the second door to a foyer area between the two locker rooms rather than in one or the other. She also considers going into the athletic director's office to demand that extra funds be applied to this project, because the requested compromise will hinder her ability to perform her job. What would you do? Are there other options Marsha has not considered?

This chapter is designed to help the athletic trainer become a useful and informed consultant when a new athletic training facility is created. We will discuss preliminary considerations that are helpful in the planning phase, the development of a concept planning document, program area construction considerations, common symbols used for architectural floor plans, strategies for communicating with the architect, and ideas for remodeling existing facilities.

PRELIMINARY CONSIDERATIONS

Before meeting with an architect, athletic trainers must spend some time thinking about what will be needed in a new athletic training facility. They should be careful not to allow themselves to be closed in by what they perceive to be the parameters within which they can work.

Designing the ideal facility is important for the athletic training program's needs. This includes exhaustive consideration of not only what is needed to function today and tomorrow but also ten years from now.

CONCEPT PLANNING DOCUMENT

The **concept planning document** includes the philosophy of the facility and intended space allocation.[1-3] Developing a facility philosophy and specific space allocation should be considered.

Facility Philosophy

After preliminary considerations, a facility philosophy must be developed. The administration's philosophy must be determined first, then a philosophy for the athletic training facility can be fashioned. Finally, specific space allocation must be considered.

The Administration's Philosophy. Information that should be extracted from the administration's philosophy of the facility should include the type of sports (intercollegiate, intramural, public) to be served, the number of athletes who will use the facility, the hours of use, and any other functions the facility must serve. Each of these considerations may factor into the size of the facility, its location, its security, and its floor plan. If intramural sports must be served as well as intercollegiate sports, a larger facility may be necessary. The layout of the facility may also be affected by a need to keep traffic from intramural and intercollegiate sports separate. Likewise, if the athletic training facility space is to be used for instructional purposes, space for a classroom should be allocated.

Athletic Training Facility Philosophy. The guiding philosophy of the athletic training facility must fit within the position taken by the administration for the building. Points to be included in the athletic training facility philosophy are: proposed uses of the facility, placement of the facility within the building, facility access, operational hours, the number of staff members who will occupy the space, the estimated number of athletes who will use the facility, and typical traffic flow patterns of the facility.

When describing the intended uses of the athletic training room, all possibilities must be considered. Is the facility to be available only to student athletes? Will areas be provided for student athletic trainers to study? Will classes meet in the facility that require laboratory space for therapeutic modalities or injury evaluation? The number of potential uses are determined by the people involved, but athletic trainers must make sure their needs are known.

If the athletic training room is to be established in a new building, placement is important. An exit to the outside, proximity to locker rooms, and other considerations are some points worth considering. One important point regarding facility placement is access. Athletes should be able to easily access the athletic training facility. Entrances from locker rooms, both male and female, make it easy for athletes to enter the facility for treatment.

Emergency access is also vital, both into and out of the athletic training facility. If an emergency occurs on the field and the athlete needs to be transported into the athletic training facility, then stretchers, wheelchairs, and assorted equipment must be able to easily fit through the entrance. Likewise, if an accident occurs in the training room, easy access for paramedical personnel is essential.

Operational hours of the facility must also be factored into the philosophy of the facility. Consider not only opening and closing times, but also peak load times. These factors may influence personnel decisions as well as facility size.

Who will be using the facility? Identify the type and number of staff members who might occupy the facility. Athletic training rooms will employ some of the following professionals: athletic trainers, physicians, physical therapists, student athletic trainers, a secretary, a dentist, a psychologist, and a nutritionist.

The people using the facility will, of course, have many activities to perform. Make a list of all the activities that are to occur. The following are some possibilities:

- Taping
- Injury assessment
- Injury treatment
- Rehabilitation

- General office and record keeping
- Drug screening collection
- Physician's examination room

Estimate (or, better yet, use data collected from the current athletic training facility) the number of athletes or patients who will use the new athletic training room. Include the total number of athletes served, as well as the number of athletes in the facility during peak hours.

Traffic flow in the proposed facility should be predicted. Where will the athletes enter the facility? Where will they go once they enter? Where will they exit the facility? It is important to think about heavy traffic areas and to try to allot extra space to prevent overcrowding. The athletic trainer will also need to consider keeping high-traffic areas away from entrances and exits.

Specific Space Allocation

Space allocation is the assignment of available square footage in an athletic training room to various tasks. Athletic trainers need to start with a list of specific program areas. When the list is complete, the functions or tasks performed in each area must be specified. The type of equipment needed to perform various functions and/or tasks and the number of people using the area during peak loads will help determine the square footage necessary. The area occupied by the equipment, as well as sufficient area for supervisors, spotters, and so forth, should be determined.

To calculate needed square footage during peak loads, allow two to three square feet per person. Remember to subtract square footage occupied by equipment from this estimate. Secor[6] suggests the following formula to calculate necessary square footage:

(number of athletes at peak time/20 tables per day) $\times$ 100 sq ft.

This formula does not address square footage taken up by equipment. Try both methods, or others if available, and make a determination on necessary square footage for the athletic training facility. If it is not possible to get a feel for the room available, try using the method suggested in the second Applications for Consideration question at the end of this chapter.

Remember, athletes or patients are not the only people occupying space during peak loads. Athletic trainers, students, physicians, and/or parents may also occupy space. Take these additional bodies into account during the design phase and try to make room for all of them.

During the planning phase, specific construction needs will have to be considered. Although they are not experts in architecture or construction, athletic trainers should think about any special needs they may have for the following:

- Electrical (e.g., ground fault interrupters in wet areas [see IEEE Recommended Practice for Electric Systems in Health Care Facilities[4]])
- Plumbing
- Telephone, computer, communications systems (a separate data line is helpful if the computer has a fax or modem)
- Computer network connections
- Ventilation (the hydrotherapy area needs extra ventilation)
- Flooring type (nonslip tile in wet areas)
- Wall covering
- Ceiling type and height (extra high ceilings, such as ten feet, are helpful when there are seven-foot basketball players)
- Door width (wide enough for stretchers) and height (remember the tall athletes)
- Cabinetry, including possible computer workstations
- Lighting

Also, be as specific as necessary, but concise, in the room's requirements. Lengthy wording will cause contractors to overbid, possibly causing your request to be denied. If it sounds difficult, contractors will pad the bid to accommodate anticipated complexities.

Application of Title III of the Americans with Disabilities Act

Public facilities must remove architectural barriers in existing facilities or provide appropriate accommodations in new construction. Considerations for barrier removal include:

- Installing ramps
- Making curb cuts in sidewalks and entrances
- Repositioning telephones
- Adding raised markings on elevator control buttons
- Installing flashing alarm lights
- Widening doors
- Installing accessible door hardware
- Installing grab bars in toilet stalls
- Rearranging toilet partitions to increase maneuvering space
- Repositioning paper towel dispenser in a bathroom
- Installing an accessible paper cup dispenser at water fountains
- Removing high-pile, low-density carpeting

PROGRAM AREA CONSTRUCTION CONSIDERATIONS

There are several **program areas** that will appear in most athletic training facilities. These areas are for the specific functions that take place in the athletic training room. Resources will largely determine which areas are currently available and which areas cannot be supported. Before addressing program area considerations, we will look at several general facility considerations. Specific program areas that may be included are: taping, treatment, rehabilitation, hydrotherapy, office, private examination room, dental, storage, specialty pad and orthotic work area, locker room, lavatory, and shower area, janitorial closet, conference room or athletic training library, rehabilitation pool, and X-ray room.

General Facility Considerations

Before planning specific program areas, a number of general considerations should be addressed. Some of these items will exist in specific program areas, while others will be included in all program areas. Regardless, the following are several things to consider relative to the whole facility:

- Flooring
- Ceiling height and materials
- Lighting
- Stereo system
- Location and size of entry and exit doors
- Telephone location

- Drinking fountains
- Bulletin boards, chalkboards
- Colors

Flooring. There are two primary choices for flooring in an athletic training facility: carpet or tile. Carpet works well in rehabilitation areas, but not in hydrotherapy areas. Carpeting is not slippery and it is quiet.[1] An industrial-grade carpet is usually adequate. An industrial tile is also acceptable. Make sure the tile is the nonslip type in wet areas. Industrial-grade carpeting is cheaper and easier to maintain, but not as durable as tile.

Ceiling Height. An eight-foot ceiling is not functional in an athletic training facility. Tall athletes cannot perform overhead exercises in a room with eight-foot ceilings. Consider a ten-foot ceiling, at least in areas where athletes will be exercising. In addition, consideration must be given to the sound absorption qualities of the ceiling. Fiberglass drop panels are excellent sound absorption devices. If the ceiling is left as unfinished concrete or metal, there will be a great deal of reflection of sound, making concentration difficult.

Lighting. An athletic training facility should be bright. Fluorescent lighting is usually best. Lighting should provide 20 to 50 foot-candles of illumination four feet above the floor for activities of high visual contrast or large size, such as taping, reading, supervising, or performing rehabilitation.[1] For routine physical examinations where skin coloration and facial expressions are observed, between 50 and 100 foot-candles are recommended.

Windows in an athletic training facility allow natural sunlight to mix with artificial light. Ideally, windows should allow visual contact with both the sky and ground activities.[2] Natural sunlight has been shown to have a more calming effect on a person's psyche than artificial light.[1] It should be possible to adjust artificial lighting to maintain available light at an adequate range for the tasks completed in the area.

Stereo System. Music in the training room can be soothing or motivational. At the very least, music appears to be a harmless ergogenic aid. The stereo system should be located in a secure area to prevent theft. If the controls to the stereo are placed in a restricted area, others will have difficulty changing the station or turning up the volume.

Entry Door Location and Size. The location of the entry door is vital to effective traffic control in an athletic training facility. Easy access to any part of the training room can be expedited with well-planned placement. Make sure it is wide enough to permit passage of all potential users of the facility, including emergency medical technicians.

Doors also help to ensure privacy and provide climate control. It has been shown that when there is an air temperature difference greater than 1°C, that air will flow from one room to the next.[1] To stop the airflow that may change temperatures, doors must remain closed. It is desirable to have a separate entry and exit into an athletic training facility to promote smooth traffic flow.

Telephone Location. Telephones should be located where they can be easily reached. If multiple phones are possible in an athletic training room, one should be placed in the office area and one in the rehabilitation area. These are the two places an athletic trainer will most likely be found. Talking on the phone in a taping area is too chaotic. If the phone rings while an athletic trainer is in the taping area, it is best to go to a quieter area (e.g., office area) to talk.

Drinking Fountains. If athletes are expected to exert themselves during rehabilitation, be prepared to rehydrate them. Place drinking fountains in easily accessible areas in the athletic training facility, preferably near the rehabilitation area and away from examination or treatment areas.

Bulletin Boards and Chalkboards. Bulletin boards are helpful for posting announcements. Chalkboards are useful for instructional purposes for both athletes or patients and student athletic trainers.

Colors. Many athletic training facilities are adorned in school or institutional colors. Remember that colors can induce moods. Here are some emotions evoked by selected colors:

- Reds: exciting, stimulating, tension, danger. Strong reds and greens in large areas can create unpleasant tensions.
- Oranges: similar to reds, but not to as great an extent.
- Yellows: cheerfulness, humor, less tension than reds and oranges. Tints (creams and beiges) are safe colors.

- Greens: calm, restful, peaceful, constructive. Imparts serenity when used with small amounts of red or orange.
- Blues: rest, repose, calm, but overuse can generate depression.
- Violets: convey uncertainty, also convey depression and tension.
- Neutrals (grays, browns, tans): Grays make good background colors, best when mixed with other colors. Browns and tans are homelike in milder tones and masculine in heavier tones.
- White: safe, associated with cleanliness; sanitary.
- Black: strong accent color, should be used in small quantities.[5]

Colors in any healthcare facility should be calming, but not depressing. If stimulating colors (e.g., reds) are used, put them in areas where emotions invoked can aid in the rehabilitation process. For example, exciting colors in the exercise area may be desirable, but calming colors should be in treatment or hydrotherapy areas.

Taping Area

The taping area can be the busiest area in the athletic training facility during peak hours; therefore it is necessary to determine the greatest population of athletes and staff during peak loads. Enough space should be allotted to this area so that traffic flow for the taping area does not interfere with other areas. Ideally the taping area should be close to the entrance so athletes can be attended to without disrupting other athletic training facility activities.

To determine the physical space needed to accommodate the taping area, consider the space needed for taping tables and benches, a counter area with sink, adequate waste receptacles, and all of the people who may be in the area.

Treatment Area

The treatment area will generally consist of treatment tables and modalities carts. The following should be considered when planning the treatment area:

- Size and number of treatment tables, including privacy curtains

- Placement of electrical outlets
- Size and number of modalities
- Sight supervision for staff
- Availability of sink and cabinets

Rehabilitation Area

The rehabilitation room will house large equipment items (depending on the capital equipment budget), so careful attention should be directed toward allowing adequate room in this area. Of particular concern is allowing adequate space for patients to exercise. In general, the following should be addressed when planning the rehabilitation area:

- Type, number, and size of equipment
- Placement of electrical outlets
- Carpet for exercises on floor
- Sight supervision for staff

Hydrotherapy Area

The hydrotherapy area usually consists of whirlpools, ice machines, hot and cold water supply, and sink. In addition to determining adequate area size, special plumbing and ventilation concerns need to be addressed. To determine the appropriate size of the area, consider the following:

- Type, number, and size of whirlpools
- Size and capacity of ice machine
- Storage for coolers, water bottles, and so forth Other concerns include:
- Ventilation
- Ground fault interrupters (GFI) for electrical outlets[4]
- Location for whirlpool controls
- Electrical outlets that are high on walls
- Sink and spigot for filling coolers
- Special plumbing needs (i.e., floor drains)
- Nonslip tile flooring
- Proximity to exit
- Sight supervision for staff

Enclosing the hydrotherapy area with glass will seal in humidity and noise while allowing sight supervision. This will also require adequate ventilation to remove the excess humidity.

A treatment area supervised by an office with continuous visual contact.

Office Area

The type and number of chairs, type and number of files, supply storage, electrical outlet placement, and computer connection should be included in planning the office area. Strategic placement of windows to allow sight supervision of all areas of the athletic training facility is strongly recommended. A separate office for each staff athletic trainer will allow maximum work with minimum interruptions. The windows should also have curtains or blinds to allow for privacy when warranted, such as during counseling and education sessions.

Physical Exam Area

The physical exam area will generally have several people occupying space at one time. Athletes, physicians, athletic trainers, and student athletic trainers may all be in the area at once. It is necessary to plan for that many people.

The placement, type, and size of items in the exam area should also be considered. Many physical exam areas include the following items:

- Desk
- Telephone
- Exam table
- X-ray view boxes
- Counter and sink
- Storage cabinet
- Chalk or grease board

If one examination room is to be used as a suture room by the team physicians, higher levels of lighting than previously discussed are warranted. This can be provided by a specific lamp or room lighting equivalent to 100 to 200 foot-candles.[1] The placement of electrical outlets and the availability of

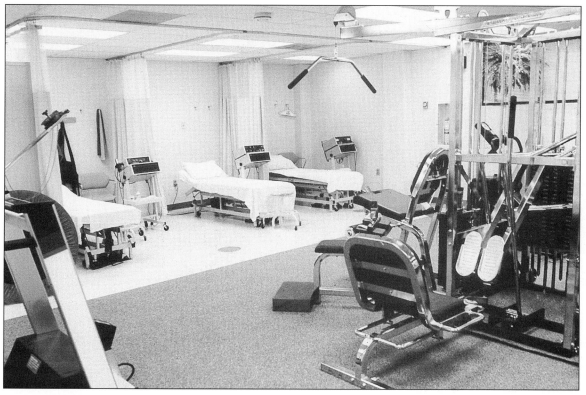

The treatment area in a clinic.
(*Courtesy of the Toledo Hospital PR staff.*)

privacy should also be included in planning the physical exam area.

Pharmacy Area

Pharmacy law is becoming the standard of practice in many athletic training rooms. A separate room within the athletic training area for storing and dispensing prescription medications is a necessity. This room is often set up with the health center pharmacy department (which has the only keys). One of the pharmacists from the health center can be sent to the athletic training room daily to dispense prescribed medications to the athletes.

Dental Area

If a dental area can be accommodated within the athletic training room, the type and size of equipment will need to be determined for space planning. The following construction needs must be considered:

- Counter and cabinets
- Sink
- Electrical outlets
- Plaster trap

Storage Area

Considerations for planning a storage area include:

- Type, number, and size of items to be stored
- How much will be stored in the facility and how much will be stored elsewhere
- Shelving
- Ventilation
- Future storage needs

Depending on the climate in the local area, individual climate control for the storage room may be a

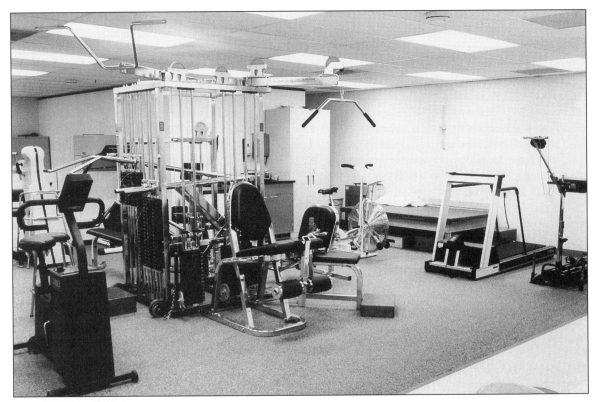

The rehabilitation area in a hospital-based sports medicine clinic.
(*Courtesy of the Toledo Hospital PR staff.*)

necessity. Many of the expendable supplies will deteriorate quickly if exposed to excessive heat. This can occur in the northern states during the summer as well as in the South.

Specialty Pad and Orthotic Work Area

If specialty pads and/or orthotics are routinely made, space for these tasks must be assigned. Considerations are as follows:

- Type and size of equipment needed
- Activities to be performed
- Storage needed
- Counter space
- Electrical outlet placement
- Plaster trap, if casting will be performed

Locker Room, Lavatory, and Shower

If a locker room, lavatory, and/or shower are to be included within the athletic training facility, the following items should be considered:

- Who will use the area?
- Size and number of lockers
- Ventilation
- Electrical needs
- Flooring
- Plumbing

Some secondary considerations are important as well, such as persons with limited strength should be able to operate the showers, hooks for clothing and towels need to be in the immediate area, yet

The hydrotherapy area should have individual mixing valves for whirlpools and ground-fault interrupters to connect to the electric supply.

outside the spray area of the shower, and the toilet paper dispenser should be within easy reach of people who are positioned on the toilet seat.

Janitorial Storage and Closet

A janitorial storage closet, no matter how small, is handy for minor cleaning chores. This area ideally includes a sink, some shelving, and hooks or racks for cleaning implements.

Conference Room or Athletic Training Library

A space dedicated for conferences and athletic training resources is an asset to staff and student athletic trainers. When determining needed space for this

area, consider the types of meetings to be held in the area, the number of books and journals to be stored, and other activities to be performed in the area. In addition, some athletic training rooms have an audiovisual area allowing videotape viewing and/or CD-ROM use.

Rehabilitation Pool

If a pool specifically designed for rehabilitation can be justified in an athletic training room budget, the following items need to be considered:

- Access for people with disabilities
- Graduated depth, up to seven feet
- Deck area should have nonslip surface
- Temperature needs for water

- Separate room for filter system and maintenance equipment
- Windows for sight supervision

X-Ray Room

An X-ray room has several specific requirements, such as lead shielding for walls. It is also necessary to ensure that adequate space is provided for the type of pictures that will be taken. When deciding on square footage for an X-ray room, be sure to consider the type and size of equipment needed (including plumbing, space for the processing unit, and a silver trap for reclamation of photographic silver), special electrical needs, and space for file cabinets.

CONSTRUCTION DOCUMENTS

Construction documents are divided into as many as twenty-two sheets (box 7-1). Of all these documents, the athletic trainer will be primarily concerned with the **floor plans** (known as architectural plans), mechanical plans (plumbing, electrical, HVAC) and with the finish schedules (table 7-1), which will

■ **List of Construction Documents**   *Box 7-1*

Sheet Number	Title
1	Title sheet
2	Index, abbreviations, and symbols
3	Location
4	Site layout and survey control
5	Grading and drainage
6	Utilities (may be two, three, or four sheets with electricity and communications, water, and sewer on separate sheets)
7	Roads, parking, etc.
8	Interior pedestrian circulation (traffic flow)
9	Planting plan
10	Planting details
11	Irrigation plan
12	Irrigation details (pressure reducers, controllers, valves)
13	Site details (walks, drinking fountains, walls, drain inlets, etc.)
14	Lighting details (light fixtures, pull boxes, etc.)
15	Sign layout
16	Sign details (may include office or room signs)
17	Architectural plans (floor plans)
18	Architectural detail (sections and elevations)
19	Mechanical layout (electrical and HVAC plans)
20	Mechanical details (sections and elevations)
21	Plumbing
22	Finish schedules (finish materials list)

■ **TABLE 7-1** Interior Finish Schedule

Room	Floor			Base			Walls			Ceiling			Area	Remarks
	Carpet	Ceramic tile		Wood	Vinyl	Coved	5/8" Sheetrock	Conc. Block		Ceiling Ht.	5/8" Sheetrock	Acoustical tile	Sq. Feet	
Office	8			8			8			9'-0"	8			
Hydrotherapy		8				8		8		10'-0"		8		Nonslip floor tile
Locker Rooms		8				8		8		10'-0"		8		
Treatment Area	8				8			8		10'-0"		8		

detail materials used on various surfaces. Athletic trainers should also look over interior elevations, or, if possible, have the architect or designer produce a virtual walk-through on computer. This will give the athletic trainer a chance to experience the training room before it is built. This may be very helpful in discovering errors before construction begins. The athletic trainer needs to be familiar with architectural symbols used in plans (box 7-2). Figure 7-1 provides an example of a floor plan for a small high school athletic training facility, and figure 7-2 is an example of a college athletic training facility.

COMMUNICATING WITH THE ARCHITECT

When athletic trainers can effectively communicate with architects, they are more likely to get what they want. This section presents some basic terminology and processes that will help athletic trainers communicate to architects what the facility should include.

Concept Plans

Concept plans communicate what the proposed facility should provide. This should be shared with

■ **Architectural Symbols**   *Box 7-2*

Symbol	Description	Location
	Wood frame wall	Floor plan
	Masonry wall	Floor plan
	Steel frame wall	Floor plan
	Interior door	Floor plan
	Exterior door (with sill)	Floor plan
	Fixed window	Floor plan
	Casement window	Floor plan
	Sink	Floor plan
	Refrigerator	Floor plan
	Lavatory	Floor plan
	Toilet	Floor plan
	Urinal	Floor plan
	Wall switch	Electrical plan
	3-way switch	Electrical plan
	Duplex outlet (wall plug)	Electrical plan
	Waterproof outlet	Electrical plan
	220V outlet	Electrical plan
	Floor outlet	Electrical plan
	Strip outlet	Electrical plan
	Ceiling box for light fixture	Electrical plan
	Wall box for light fixture	Electrical plan
	Fluorescent fixture	Electrical plan
	Telephone jack	Electrical plan
	Fan	Electrical plan
	Thermostat	Electrical plan
	Smoke detector	Electrical plan

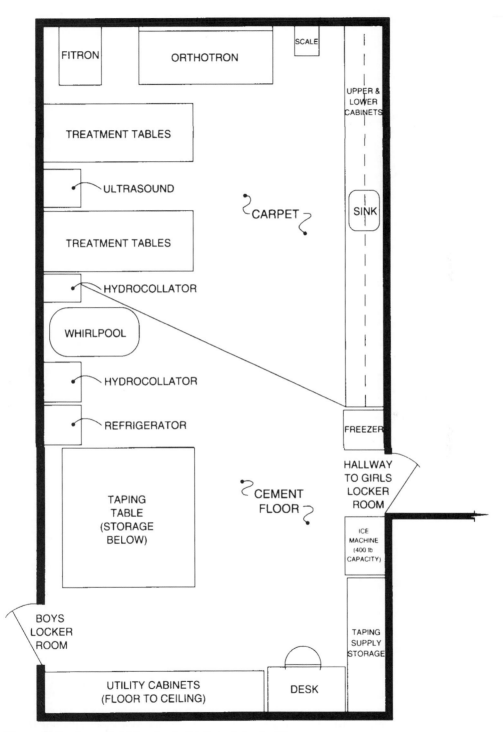

Figure 7-1   A sample high school athletic training facility
(*Courtesy of Mary Ingersoll.*)

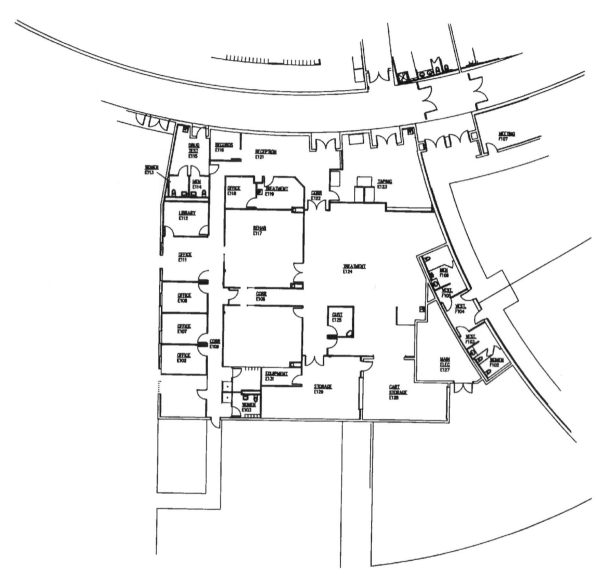

Figure 7-2   A college athletic training facility

the architect before any drawings are started. A concept plan can simply involve an oral walk-through of the facility to the architect. Tell the architect what has to happen in the proposed facility, how it will "feel" when athletic trainers are in there, the program areas that must be represented, and so forth. Spend some time with the concept plan. Do not provide this information without a great deal of serious contemplation of the details that happen in an athletic training room daily. It is important to remember that the architect may or may not be familiar with what athletic trainers need. If important aspects of the proposed facility are not addressed in the concept plan, chances are that they will not appear in preliminary drawings. Inclusion of desired facilities in the very early stages is less expensive and more efficient than trying to add them later in the process.

Equipment is usually not represented on floor plans unless it is part of the job. If you want to see

■ **Floor Plan Checklist**   *Box 7-3*

Walls
- correct room size(s)
- half walls are noted

Doors
- correctly placed
- correct swing
- correct size

Steps
- riser height
- tread width
- necessary ramps

Cabinets
- sufficient number
- correctly placed
- correct size

Equipment
- correctly placed
- correctly scaled

Floor slopes at wet areas
- whirlpool area
- shower area

Lighting
- correct placement

- correct fixture type
- correct fixture size
- correct switch type (i.e., dimmer vs. on/off)

Convenience outlets (wall plugs)
- correct placement
- correct number
- GFI where necessary

Telephone and network outlets
- correct placement
- correct number

Elevations
- correct ceiling heights
- correct counter heights
- correct half wall heights

Door, window, and finish schedules
- nonslip tile appropriately noted
- correct door width
- all floor, wall, and ceiling finishes are what you want

HVAC (Heating, ventilation and cooling)
- correct thermostat placement
- correct ventilation in hydrotherapy area

how equipment will look on the floor plan, ask the architect to create an overlay for you.

Preliminary Drawing

The preliminary drawings should represent items communicated in the concept plan. It is important that preliminary drawings are carefully reviewed. Using a checklist will ensure that you do not forget to check each important aspect of the facility (for example, see box 7-3). The following are aspects that warrant special scrutiny:

- Review for space allocation
- Review for traffic flow

- Point out special considerations
  Electrical
  Plumbing
  Lighting
  Ventilation
  Heating and cooling
  Walls and floors
  Approve placement of doors and direction of swing

Some things requested in the concept plan are probably missing; some of those requests were mandatory, whereas some were clearly wishes. Make sure that the most important items were not omitted.

Final Drawing

When the final drawings are received, they should be reviewed again for space allocation and approval of each aspect of construction detail. This will be the last chance to change any aspect of construction. If something needs to be changed, added, or eliminated, it must be done now! Major revisions during this phase are frowned upon and are usually the result of poor initial planning (and may also cause increases in architect fees). This is the time for the virtual walk-through, if available.

REMODELING AN EXISTING FACILITY

If remodeling an existing facility is contemplated, the athletic administration needs to make sure that new construction would not be cheaper or more useful. Often, extensive renovations are more costly than new construction.

Remodeling an existing facility will follow the same general rules as facility construction, except that the costs, ramifications, feasibility, and so forth of removing walls, doors, and other items in the facility must now be included. There is also a loss of flexibility in terms of square footage, plumbing fixtures, electrical circuits, and so forth. Accessibility for people with disabilities will become an issue as well. That is, steps will need comparable ramps, and rest rooms, showers, and program areas will need to be accessible to those in wheelchairs.

If the facility intended for renovation is quite old, more headaches will be encountered than the facility is probably worth. However, athletic trainers may have no choice in the matter. If the facility must be remodeled, give renovation as much attention as new construction would receive. The facility will still have to service the athletic trainer's needs.

Summary

1. Preliminary considerations include assessing needs for both the short and the long term.
2. The expectations of the administration will define some of the parameters of the athletic training room's design.
3. Athletic training facilities must consider proposed uses, placement of the facility within the building, facility access, operational hours, number of staff, number of athletes, and typical traffic flow patterns.
4. Space is allocated based on how equipment is used in a program area and how much the area is used.
5. General facility considerations include electrical, plumbing, telephone, computer, communications systems, computer network connections, heating/ventilation/air conditioning, flooring type, wall covering, ceiling type and height, door width and height, cabinetry, lighting, and color.
6. Title III of the Americans with Disabilities Act affects both new construction and remodeling.
7. Program areas that have special needs include the taping area, treatment area, rehabilitation area, hydrotherapy area, physical exam area, dental area, storage area, specialty pad and orthotic area, rehabilitation pool, and office area.
8. Reading construction documents requires some basic knowledge of blueprints.
9. Concept plans give the architect information about what the athletic trainer believes must be in the finished athletic training area.
10. Preliminary drawings represent the items from the concept plan. They need to be checked for completeness and accuracy.
11. Final drawings are the plans that will be given to contractors. These must be rechecked for all parameters before construction begins. This is the last chance to make any changes.

For Critical Thought

Now that Marsha has had time to reflect, she has decided that the best alternative that will cost the least will be for the second door to be installed in the foyer between the entry doors to the boys' and girls' locker rooms. She considered going to the booster club to try to raise money for the door, but thought that saving the booster club for permanent equipment was a wiser choice.

Marsha also noted that the architect's plans did not include any differences in floor coverings between the taping area, rehabilitation area, and the hydrotherapy area. This could lead to serious problems with slipping on the floor or getting the carpeted area wet. Finally, she noted that there were no ventilation ducts over the hydrotherapy area, allowing an accumulation of dampness and mold. These things were easily remedied in meetings with the architect and school representatives.

 **Websites**

Americans with Disabilities Act Considerations:
http://janweb.icdi.wvu.edu/kinder/

> Americans with Disabilities Act Document Center: ADA statute, regulations, ADAAG (Americans with Disabilities Act Accessibility Guidelines), Federally reviewed tech sheets, and other assistance documents.

Technical accessability requirements:
http://www.adaproject.org/adaag.htm

> Contains scoping and technical requirements for accessibility to buildings and facilities by people with disabilities under the Americans with Disabilities Act (ADA) of 1990.

Electrical safety:
http://www.medinaec.org/FAQ%20Safety.html

> Information about electrical safety and ground fault interrupt.

Websites with photographic tours of athletic training facilities:
http://www.utoledo.edu/~sportsmed/

http://web.indstate.edu/athtrn/ newpage5.htm

http://www.wellesley.edu/Athletics/facilities/ medtrain.html

http://waynesburg.edu/~sportmed/ facility.htm

Homes Design Plus:
http://designsplus.com/info/read.html

> How to read floor plans. Specific to private residences but still gives good information.

Applications for Consideration

1. Alana Smith has just taken a position as the athletic trainer at South Central High School. The bond issue passed a week later to give South Central a new building. As a preliminary task to planning a new athletic training facility, Alana needs to establish what she has now in the way of space, traffic flow, equipment location, and so forth. Alana has decided to use your help to plan and draw a floor plan for an athletic training facility, so she contacts the instructor of the Organization and Administration class, Michael Samuelson, to match the size of her proposed athletic training room to the one in your current institution. Do the same thing for an athletic training room that you are familiar with.

2. Michael Samuelson wanted to assess whether the preliminary plans Alana Smith developed would make an acceptable athletic training room. He took the student athletic trainers, a 100-foot tape measure, and some masking

tape into the gymnasium. Using the floor plan he obtained from Alana, Michael had the students plot out the floor plan on the gymnasium floor with the masking tape. After finishing the layout, everyone went inside the "athletic training facility" and tried to determine if there was adequate space, how traffic patterns might flow, efficiency of design, and so forth. Do the same as a class project. Make recommendations on how the plan can be improved.

References

1 Beck, WC, Meyer, RH. *Health care environment: The user's viewpoint.* Boca Raton, FL: CRC Press, Inc., 1982.

2 Carpman, JR, Grant, MA, Simmons, DA. *Design that cares.* Chicago: American Hospital Publishing, Inc., 1986.

3 Helwig, D. Designing athletic training facilities. Presented at the 41st Annual National Athletic Trainers' Association, Inc. Clinical Symposium and Workshop, Indianapolis, IN, June 11, 1990.

4 IEEE Industry Applications Society. *IEEE recommended practice for electric systems in health care facilities.* New York: The Institute of Electrical and Electronics Engineers, Inc., 1986.

5 Pile, JF. *Interior design,* Englewood Cliffs, NJ: Prentice Hall, 249–250, 1988.

6 Secor, MR. Designing athletic training facilities or "where do you want the outlets?" *Athletic Training, JNATA.* 19:19–21, 211, 1984.

7 LaRue, RJ. Designing for inclusion: The Americans with Disabilities Act and Architectural Barriers Act. In Sawyer, TH. ed. *Facilities planning for physical activity and sport,* Dubuque, IA: Kendall/Hunt Publishing Co., 1999.

PART THREE

Operations

CHAPTER 8

Medical Records

After reading this chapter, you should be able to:

- Identify the components of medical histories, preparticipation physical examinations, and injury record forms.

- Identify other medical records or release forms and why they must be kept.

- Identify components of the medical record from other sources in the form of reports, diagnoses, test results, and so forth.

- Explain confidentiality as it applies to medical records.

- Describe the SOAP format for medical records.

- Describe documentation standards and how they apply to medical records.

Key Terms

medical record
statute of limitations
communication
legal (use of records)
research
documentation for reimbursement
SOAP
medical record software

FOR CRITICAL THOUGHT:
The Importance of Documentation

Darren Sadukas is the starting sweeper for the University of Western Pennsylvania soccer team. In the final minutes of the second half, he twists his knee while making a cut on the turf and immediately goes down. The team's athletic trainer, Sonya, comes onto the field and assesses the injury. Her first impression, due to the mechanism and positive results in the Lachman and pivot shift tests, is an ACL tear. After transporting the athlete off the field, Sonya applies ice and compression to Darren's knee. She removes a blank evaluation form from her kit and fills out all the necessary information regarding the details of the injury. After the game, Sonya takes Darren into the athletic training room and performs another evaluation to confirm some of her original suspicions. Again, she records all tests performed and their results on the original evaluation form under a separate follow-up entry. Sonya then arranges an appointment for the following morning with the team physician. While Darren is finishing his ice treatment, Sonya fills out the university's referral form and makes a copy of her injury evaluation form for Darren to take to the doctor in the morning. Darren is given written instructions for the night, is fitted for crutches and, after arranging for transportation to the doctor's office, goes home. Sonya places the records and copies of the referral and take-home instructions in Darren's file.

With the referral form and injury evaluation form in hand, Darren arrives at the doctor's office at 8:30 A.M. He's feeling a little better but the swelling has increased considerably, despite the efforts to control it following the game. The receptionist has Darren fill out a patient information form and makes a photocopy of his insurance card and other paperwork. Before seeing the doctor, they have already arranged for him to receive an X ray in the adjacent radiology facility to rule out a fracture. Darren makes the short trip to the radiology department and fills out another personal information/insurance form. The X rays do not take very long, and Darren is soon on his way back to the doctor's office with the X rays in hand.

The X rays prove negative for fracture after the review by Dr. Wright, the radiologist who reports his findings to Dr. Thompson, the team physician. Dr. Thompson performs an orthopedic evaluation and records all findings on the evaluation form. Dr. Thompson diagnoses Darren with an ACL rupture and possible meniscal involvement. He instructs the receptionist to schedule an MRI and prescribes some NSAID's and painkillers. Darren is taken to the school's pharmacy and hands the pharmacist his prescription. In a little less optimistic mood, Darren returns to the athletic training room and gives Sonya the diagnosis/treatment sheet from the doctor's office. Sonya makes copies of all the forms from the doctor's office places them in the athlete's file.

Four weeks later, surgery is performed at the University of Pincon medical center. Five days later, Darren returns to the athletic training room to begin the rehabilitation program the orthopedic surgeon has ordered. Over the next few weeks, Darren gets discouraged and only comes to 60 percent of the scheduled therapy appointments. Each treatment and each missed appointment is noted on his therapy record. When he comes to a therapy appointment, Sonya is careful to do a follow-up examination and note the results in the progress notes for this injury.

While his healing is much slower than he anticipated, he begins to play pickup basketball in the student recreation center in violation of the surgeon's and the athletic trainer's orders. He reinjures the same knee, requiring additional surgery. After the surgery he files suit against the athletic trainer, the university, and the orthopedic surgeon, alleging that his reinjury was caused by the defendants' failure to complete his therapy program in a timely fashion.

At discovery his lawyer is presented with copies of his therapy record with the missed appointments, copies of his progress notes, and physician's reports.

Record keeping in medical settings involves the storage and retrieval of information from a specific location containing personal, financial, and medical data.[2] Personal data consist of information such as name, address, birth date, sex, personal physician, who to notify in an emergency, and any other data to identify the patient. Financial data address who will pay the bill (or how the bill will be paid) and include employer, insurance information and policy numbers, parents' employers, parents' insurance and policy numbers, or a statement of no insurance coverage. Medical data are written in a comprehensive clinical record that gives a continuously updated history of the treatment rendered, reasons for the treatment, physician of record for each incident, physical examinations, medical histories, X-ray reports, laboratory findings, consultation reports, progress notes, and signed consent forms, among other information. In some states, the law defines what should be in the hospital **medical record**. In most other states, the regulatory agency for hospitals issues rules and regulations specifying medical record content. For example, in Illinois the regulation reads:

> For each patient there shall be an adequate, accurate, timely, and complete medical record. Minimum requirements for medical record content are as follows: patient identification and admission information; history of patient as to chief complaints, present illness and pertinent past history, family history, and social history; physical examination report; provisional diagnosis; diagnostic and therapeutic reports on laboratory test results, X-ray findings, any surgical procedure performed, any pathological examination, any consultation, and any other diagnostic or therapeutic procedure performed; orders and progress notes made by the attending physician and when applicable by other members of the medical staff and allied health personnel; observation notes and vital sign charting made by nursing personnel; and conclusions as to the primary and any associated diagnosis, brief clinical resume, disposition at discharge to include instructions and/or medications and any autopsy findings on a hospital death. (Illinois Hospital Licensing Requirements §12-1.2[b] [1979])

The National Athletic Trainers' Association Board of Certification has established fifteen Standards of Professional Practice.[12] Standard 3 deals with documentation and states that documentation must include:

1. Athlete's name and any other identifying information.
2. Referral source (doctor, dentist).
3. Date; initial assessment, results and database.
4. Program plan and estimated length.
5. Program methods, results and revisions.
6. Date of discontinuation and summary.
7. Athletic trainer's signature.[12]

The length of time the records must be retained is most often determined by the length of time a patient has to file a claim for negligence governed by the statute of limitations in that state. A **statute of limitations** is a state law that gives the length of time in years (between one and eight, depending on the state) that a person has to file a claim. The statute is subject to a number of conditions for when the time frame starts (time of accrual of action) and when it can be interrupted (tolling) (see chapter 16 for a discussion of negligence and malpractice). In some states, the time frame does not begin until the discovery of the malpractice, so an action could be initiated fifteen or twenty years after the actual harm. The safest length of time for retaining medical records in these states is the statute time after the patient's death. For minors, it is worth remembering that the statute of limitations may not begin until the patient legally becomes an adult. Files of athletes who have gone on to professional athletics should be kept for the duration of the professional career for the purpose of documenting any possible workman's compensation claims.[11] To destroy obsolete records there may also be state statutes that specifying burning, shredding, or other methods to maintain confidentiality.[2]

NECESSITY OF RECORDS

The extent to which athletic trainers in college or university, high school, and professional practice must conform to the hospital standard for medical records is unclear in a legal sense. Certainly those athletic trainers who work in clinics affiliated with hospitals are already participating in the full scope of these requirements. In private clinics, record keeping follows the same standards. The greatest departure from the hospital standard of the medical record-keeping process in athletic training has been in the college or university and high school athletic training rooms. Records in these settings vary from complete and updated per hospital standards to almost nonexistent. This may be due in part to athletic trainers in these settings viewing each new injury as a separate incident, almost as if it were a new patient. Each injury begins a new evaluation form, and subsequent treatments and procedures are entered on the record of the particular injury. Copies of these forms may be appended to the physician's continuous record as needed. Recent court decisions have shown that having proper treatment records is a major factor in the outcome of sports injury cases.[11]

Primary Reasons for Records

There are two primary uses for records and several secondary considerations. The first primary use is **communication**. Communication is necessary for the planning and execution of patient care. Because athletic trainers are always governed by the wishes of their physician supervisors, written orders eliminate confusion as to the diagnosis and expected treatment.

Communication is often considered either *formal*, that which requires a written notation, or *informal*, that which is spoken. Most of the communication in a sports medicine context is of sufficient importance to be considered formal. Every physician, athletic trainer, and therapist should document everything—recommendations, discussions, evaluations, and the like—as a daily part of the job.[7] Making record keeping part of the daily routine will help establish the foundation of clear communication and documentation.

Having clear written communications between the athletic training staff and the physician giving primary care treatment to an athlete is vastly preferable to oral communication, which can be misconstrued. One method suggested for this important avenue of communication is an interactive form, requiring the signature of the person receiving the form, a copy of which is then returned to the sender. Herbert[7] suggested that evaluation forms sent with an athlete to a physician should even be countersigned by the athlete, acknowledging the initial impression of the injury to be presented to the physician.

Written records help the people involved with the case to know what each has done, which adds continuity to the case. Often, treatments are administered by different people. If the treatments are not recorded, no one will know what the others are doing. The efforts of each person will be isolated rather than part of a coordinated whole. This often leads to confusion on the part of the athlete, especially if each person is giving the athlete different advice about what should be done to supplement the formal treatments. Failure to obtain a written plan would mean that different athletic trainers could easily perform different procedures, which could inhibit the consistency and efficiency of treatment.

The other primary reason for keeping records is a **legal** one. It is necessary to provide a complete, specific, and accurate record describing the procedures used to provide injury care to a patient. This is especially important when defending against negligence and other liability actions. Memories fade when time passes, and failure to put treatments and evaluations in writing is often interpreted to mean the treatments and evaluations have never been done. Many cases claim the defendants failed to provide adequate information, diagnosis, reporting, and so forth, between the consulting and the primary healthcare provider.[3] When an athletic trainer testifies from the written record, "Darnell was scheduled for therapy six days that week, but only came on Tuesday and Friday," it has greater impact in favor of the athletic trainer, as opposed to not being able to recall when or how many times the patient reported for therapy.

Secondary Reasons for Records

Secondary reasons for keeping records include **research** efforts, **documentation for reimbursement**, and traffic flow patterns. Research is aided by precise and accurate record keeping. Most athletic trainers would not consider themselves researchers, but some of them are. Consider the following: A few years ago the athletic training staff at the University of Nevada–Las Vegas had a varsity athlete who was a heart transplant patient. The case report was published in *Athletic Training* (1989; 24:224–25), enabling other athletic trainers to evaluate and utilize the information if and when they are faced with a similar situation. Another area of debate is the rehabilitation of ACL injuries, which is constantly changing, with much controversy over open-chain versus closed-chain methods. Those who advocate closed-chain rehabilitation protocols have experienced difficulty providing objective, quantifiable data in support of their approach as the methods to acquire this data through research have been inherently open-chain. Methods of treatment and rehabilitation can be improved if athletic trainers record what they do and then periodically evaluate their records.

Documentation supporting an athlete's interaction with the healthcare system is required before insurance companies will reimburse caregivers for services rendered. With almost all collegiate athletic programs utilizing "second dollar" insurance plans (see chapter 9), accurate records allow the "first dollar" carrier to reimburse to the extent of coverage in a timely fashion, allowing the athletic department plan to cover any remaining charges within the allowable time frame (usually one year from the date of injury). In addition, as athletic training gains its rightful place in the various states as a credentialed medical profession, the profession will be legally entitled to use Physicians' Current Procedural Terminology (CPT) codes. This will enable athletic training to become a covered service in health insurance plans, and athletic trainers will be able to bill for services rendered as athletic trainers instead of the current practice of billing as an aide to another allied health care professional.

The CPT codes are the codes used for third-party reimbursement. They establish the procedure performed at various medical and allied medical facilities. They are five-digit numbers in which the first two digits represent a class of actions. For example, 97128 is the code for ultrasound, with the stipulation that a physician or therapist must be in constant attendance during the treatment. For billing purposes with insurance carriers, these codes must be transmitted along with the International Diagnostic Code (ICD.9.CM), which establishes the exact diagnosis for which the procedure from the CPT codes was performed.

Records provide the only means of establishing daily, weekly, monthly, and yearly traffic patterns in the athletic training room. Records can verify to administration the need for additional equipment, facilities and/or staff, or justify cuts in the program. From records it is possible to demonstrate increases or decreases in the volume of work handled in the athletic training room. Although it may seem tedious, keeping records of all treatments, including tape applications and ice bags, helps to give a true representation of the traffic patterns in the athletic training room.

CONSTRUCTING THE WRITTEN RECORD

Written records in a medical setting can use a wide variety of writing styles. In therapeutic documentation, the most common styles are narrative, problem-oriented, anecdotal, and SOAP note format.[1] Narrative involves documenting the patient's problems with an essay technique. Narrative allows the writer to explain why things are happening. A major disadvantage to narrative is the amount of words a new reader must read to understand the situation. In problem-oriented styles, the problem is prioritized and all information about the problem is grouped into appropriate subheadings. This type of note is seen in clinical settings where a number of athletic trainers and physical therapists are documenting the same group of problems with a patient.[1] Anecdotal style uses preprinted forms with minimal narrative information entered into spaces on forms. The information is quickly available, although the construction of these types of forms is tedious and time-consuming. SOAP is the most popular and will be discussed later in this chapter.

With records, there are some commonsense principles that must be followed at all times. First, records must be maintained in more than one location.[7] What would happen if there was only one copy and a fire destroyed the records area? The physician report confirming the injury evaluation form should be placed in the athlete's personal file, in the athletic training room's master file logging all physician contacts, and in a computer file, should the system be computerized. The use of carbonless, multiple-copy forms is one way to implement a system of cross-filing of records at multiple locations.[7]

The patient's name must be at the top of every piece of paper in the file. In addition, the person making the notes must indicate the time and date of each entry and sign the entry in ink (including professional title). The language should be specific, objective, concise, and complete in all details. When in doubt, the note should be written on the record. It is important to document the why as well as the what when describing treatments, and to document any untoward events (adverse reactions to treatment, falls, etc.), as well as steps taken.

Knowledge of medical terminology in record writing and reading is vital. Due to both the number of health care professionals an athlete will typically deal with and the enormous amount of information that is acquired and relayed through medical records during the course of an injury, practitioners need to understand the medical terminology used. Most terms in medicine have Latin-based prefixes, suffixes, or roots. Understanding the commonly used prefixes, suffixes, and roots can help you to understand the terms.[8] Only standard English and universally recognized medical abbreviations should be included. (See box 8-1.)

All entries must be made in a timely fashion and must be accurate and legible. Complex procedures need to be committed to hard copy within twenty-four hours so that details are not lost in memory or translation. The timeliness of entering documentation into the medical record is a legal issue as well. In cases where there is a negative outcome to a patient that may be subject to litigation, if the record is not completed until days before the plaintiff's lawyer obtains copies of the record, there is a substantial question about covering up information.

Contradictions are a potential disaster. To correct an inaccurate record, care must be taken that the error is still completely legible, and the reasons for the change must be stated in writing. Never obliterate any part of a record. Liquid paper, cross-outs, or any other damage to the record will allow the plaintiff's attorney to claim that the destroyed material clearly implicates the defendants in a conspiracy to cover up the errors. Records that have been disposed of or are missing also may be interpreted as an attempt to cover up an error. The defendants will not be able to disprove these types of assertions. Tampering with records after copies are in the hands of the plaintiffs, or would be accessible to them from another location, is indefensible.

There is a fundamental difference between clinic record keeping and traditional athletic training room record keeping. In hospitals, physician's offices, and medical clinics, records are set up so that each contact is written into the record immediately after the previous contact, with no space left between the visits. Notation is made in the record as to additional reports, summaries, and so forth that apply to a specific incident and follow immediately in the record. Evaluation forms, patient orders, and the like are inserted into the record at the appropriate locations. This continuous record method can be used in athletic training rooms if the athletic trainer pays scrupulous attention to detail and enters data in complete form immediately. However, with the variety of people involved in delivering treatment and rehabilitation in the athletic training room, it may be difficult to do this. Some high schools and colleges try to simulate a continuous record with the use of an individual daily log-in sheet for each athlete that is kept in their medical file. This form gives the reason for each visit, the treatment received, and the administering athletic trainer. More often in college, university, or high school athletic training rooms each visit generates a separate initial injury evaluation, and all follow-up care is noted relative to this separate incident. A new injury starts the cycle over again.

SOAP Note Format

SOAP is an acronym describing a progress-note documentation format for medical records.[8] It is a format that was developed by Dr. Lawrence Reed as a part of a system of organizing the medical record (called the *problem-oriented medical record*) in order to help standardize note taking.[8]

SOAP is an acronym for *subjective, objective, assessment,* and *plan.* It also has developed some variations such as SOAPE, SOAPIE, and SOAPIER, with *e, i,* and *r* representing evaluation, intervention, and response, respectively.[10] The SOAP note format may be used for all general initial and progress injury documents. Some athletic training facilities and clinics also have developed SOAP note documents for specific joints or areas of the body.

Subjective information is gathered from the patient and is relevant to the patient's present condition. It includes the patient's complaints, what family, observers, and friends may explain about the injury and/or past injuries, and the note writer's observation of the patient. Other more specific information, which would be appropriate for the subjective part of the SOAP note, may include:[8]

- relevant medical history
- how the patient describes the mechanism of the injury or illness
- if the patient heard any noises at the time of the injury
- if the patient reports a loss of function
- descriptive terms of any pain or sensations associated with the injury or illness

■ **Standard Medical Abbreviations**   *Box 8-1*

AROM	active range of motion	PMH	past medical history
AC	acromioclavicular	PROM	passive range of motion
ADL	activities of daily living	PT	physical therapy
AT	athletic training	Pt./pt.	patient
ASIS	anterior superior iliac spine	PWB	partial weight bearing
		qd	once daily
bid	twice a day	qid	four times a day
CP	cold pack	R/O	rule out
CPR	cardiopulmonary resuscitation	RROM	resistive range of motion
		Rx	prescription, including therapy and treatment
CWI	crutch walking instruction	SLR	straight leg raises
D/C	discharge	SOAP	subjective, objective, assessment, plan
DTR	deep tendon reflex		
DVT	deep vein thrombosis	TENS	transcutaneous electrical nerve stimulation
Dx	diagnosis		
ES	electrical stimulation	tid	three times a day
FWB	full weight bearing	TTWB	toe touch weight bearing
FH	family history	UE	upper extremity
Fx	fracture	US	ultrasound
HP	hot pack	WBAT	weight bearing as tolerated
HTN	hypertension	WNL	within normal limits
Hx	history	Whp	whirlpool
LBP	low back pain	Y/O	years old
LE	lower extremity	Δ	change
MEDS	medications	<	less than
MMT	manual muscle testing	>	greater than
NKA	no known allergies	↑	increase
NWB	non-weight bearing	↓	decrease
ORIF	open reduction/internal fixation	⁻c	with
		⁻s	without
OT	occupation therapy	⁻p	after
PNF	proprioceptive neuromuscular facilitation	1°	primary
		2°	secondary
p.o.	postoperatively	x	times
pre-op	preoperatively	R	right
PRE	progressive resistance exercise	L	left

Objective information is obtained from evaluations or tests that are reproducible by others. This section guides the athletic trainer in confirming impressions drawn from the subjective section. Included in this area are vital signs, range of motion testing, strength, reflexes, measures of edema, ligamentous tests, pain on palpation, gait and posture evaluation, and functional testing. This will be the largest section of the SOAP note evaluation.

During *assessment* the athletic trainer gives his or her professional opinion based on the information acquired in the first two steps and constructs a list of problems to be dealt with, as well as both short- and long-term goals for treatment. In follow-up evaluations this section is also used by the athletic trainer in noting how the patient is progressing and reacting to treatment. Justification of any unusual goals or treatments is also done here.

Finally, the *plan* is based on goals and describes what the athletic trainer will do to achieve them. This is where the number of treatments is proposed, along with the various modalities and exercise protocols that will be used to return the athlete to competition.

Among the advantages of the SOAP note format are that the information is logically organized, the presentation does not rely on grammatical correctness, and the notes can be completed quickly.[1] Among the disadvantages are that the reader has to understand the profession and that treatments normally used for a particular injury before the record can be understood.[1]

Documentation Standards

In the clinical athletic training setting, the types of information that must be covered in the ongoing record of a patient are subject to standards from various organizations. Perhaps most important is Medicare. Since Medicare is the largest third-party payer, it makes most other insurance companies adopt similar documentation standards.[1] Medicare standards require that a record must be complete before any part of the record can be reimbursed. Clinical documentation must include four essentials: medical necessity, skilled care, significant progress, and reasonable intensity.

To be considered medically necessary, the services provided must be recognized as effective medical practice for the injury. Skilled care implies that not just anyone can administer the treatments—the services given must be sophisticated and complex, such that the caregiver must meet education, experience, and licensing requirements before being allowed to give care. Significant progress implies that the physician and athletic trainer believe the treatments will cause improvement in the condition within a relatively normal period of time. Reasonable intensity defines the quantity and quality of treatment given to a patient over the course of rehabilitation.

Medicare also requires that at some place in the documentation, specific information must be included from the referring physician, initial evaluation, plan of care, daily documentation (including change of status), progress note (including change of status), and discharge summary. The initial evaluation establishes baseline data from which to gauge necessity for treatment and change in status entered in the daily documentation.

Many professions have standards of practice, some of which codify the parts of a medical record into the standards. Herbert[7] lists thirty-seven organizations that have such standards and notes that there are many others. The American Physical Therapy Association's APTA Standards of Practice specifies the type of information required in the initial evaluation, plan of care, progress note, and discharge planning for patients treated by physical therapists.

Computers

In most clinics and many athletic training rooms, storage of medical records on the computer has become the norm. Commercially prepared **medical record software** packages for athletic trainers are available. Care must be exercised when choosing a medical records software package, because some of them are available for a short time and then are withdrawn from the market (e.g., IITS and Alfie, among others). Once they are off the market, the user support system usually shuts down as well.

Having an entire medical record at one's immediate disposal enables the athletic trainer to append information to specific items in the record as updates occur and to quickly make hard copies of portions of the record for communication with physicians, patients, and families, while ignoring the rest of the record. It requires much less space than files of papers stored in cabinets, and it provides instant access to multiple records and patients at one time without going through various locations to access the information. Athletic trainers must understand, however, that there is a significant time investment in entering the data into a record. The computer is most valuable when accessing the material already in the record (or multiple records) quickly.

Great care must be taken to be sure the daily records are backed up daily, either on tape or disk, so that vital records are not lost. If the only records of a particular injury are on a disk that was destroyed by fire, the information is permanently lost. If the athlete should become the plaintiff in a liability action, the defendants would have no way to prove what was done and when it was done during the treatment and rehabilitation of a particular injury. Most medical facilities perform backups of daily records overnight and only destroy the paper records after the backup has proven successful.

Confidentiality

An athlete's or patient's medical records are personal and private information and are subject to federal and state laws regarding confidentiality and content.[3] It is extremely important that procedures are followed to protect the athlete's right to privacy of personal information. The NATABOC Standard 4 is applicable. It states that athletic trainers shall maintain confidentiality as determined by law and communicate necessary information with the other members of the sports medicine team working with a particular patient.[12]

All medical records should be kept in a separate room or office, within a filing system that can be locked. This can be in the form of a locking file cabinet, a computer with a password, or both. In addition, the office in which they are kept should be locked after working hours.

In most clinic situations, the patient's files are controlled by one or two people who work in the records room or in the office area and who are responsible for pulling and returning files as patients are seen. Files of patients are only seen by those who will be treating them that day on a need-to-know basis. It is often the case that patients will be scheduled with the same therapist during the same time of the day for consistency in treatment and patient comfort. However, in the traditional athletic training room setting, it is possible that many different people will need access to the patient's medical records throughout the course of the year. Depending on the athlete's availability to get to the athletic training room for treatment and rehabilitation, he or she may be seen by any of the staff athletic trainers or the student athletic trainers. Some colleges and universities have various doctors and physical therapists involved in the program who may also need to see the athlete's records.

At the university or college level, an athlete's condition and progress are often shared between students and staff for the sake of education. This leads to a large number and variety of people who may view the medical record. In all cases, the athletic trainer must make sure that medical records are only seen by the healthcare professionals of the institution and those specified on the athlete's medical release form.

Patients must realize that regardless of the setting, once their medical records have been released to an insurance company for payment, all control of the record has passed out of the control of the sports medicine team. In recent hearings before Congress, insurance companies have been shown to have sold parts of the information in medical records to drug companies and others to assist in the development of marketing plans.

WHAT RECORDS SHOULD BE KEPT?

A number of different athletic training operations require record keeping. Some of these are outside the scope of a normal medical record. Four common athletic training room activities are listed here, along with descriptions of the forms that may be used for recording the information. Some of these forms are used in sports medicine clinical settings; others are modified to the needs of the clinic setting.

Blank forms must be readily available for entering new information.

Copies of sample forms for both athletic training rooms and sports medicine clinics are included at the end of the chapter.

Medical Information

Medical History Form. In an athletics program, this form must be filled out by every student athlete who wishes to participate as a part of the preparticipation physical examination. In clinical settings, patients fill out this form before they are initially seen by the healthcare provider. The form needs to cover at least three areas: a personal medical history, a family medical history, and an orthopedic history.[9] A complete history has been shown to identify between 63 percent and 74 percent of the problems that affect athletes.[11] One caution, however; in one study, only 39 percent of the histories given by athletes agreed with histories given by the athletes' parents.[11] The personal medical history focuses on what an athlete has or has not experienced in his or her lifetime. The family medical history covers possible inherited conditions and other things that may run in families with no known link or heredity. The orthopedic history covers the musculoskeletal system of the athlete and includes any surgeries, hospital stays, and so forth. Some physicians also include exercise-induced asthma on this type of preparticipation history. Each of these sections may be on a separate piece of paper, or any combination may be combined on one or more sheets of paper. The athlete should fill in all sections of this form. Everything must be completed, and any conditions that may rule out participation should be identified. If any such conditions are suspected, a certified athletic trainer and the team physician should be notified. In referral clinic settings, the detailed medical history will be with the primary care physician. Each clinic will complete an abbreviated history form to discover information that may affect the course of treatment to be followed at the clinic.

One additional type of history form is in use in college or university settings. This is a combination history and waiver of liability form used for the purpose of allowing persons to try out as a "walk-on" for varsity athletic teams. There are usually far too many "walk-ons" to give each athlete a comprehensive preparticipation physical examination. If anyone from the try-outs becomes part of the varsity team, he or she can then be given the full examination.

Physical Examination. In many collegiate jurisdictions, a physical examination is only used one time during an athlete's career. Student athletic trainers may fill in the name, age, height, weight, blood pressure, and heart rate. The head athletic trainer or assignee may do skinfold measurements to assess body fat percentages. All other information will be added by the team physician, who will rule on the athlete's fitness to participate. The NCAA policy is that such a complete preparticipation physical examination *should* be given at least once at the athlete's entry into the intercollegiate program (whether the exam is given is institutional policy)[3] (figure 8-1). A consortium of the American

Preparticipation Physical Evaluation

History

Date _____

Name _____ Sex ____ Age _____ Date of birth _____

Grade _____ Sport _____ _____

Personal physician _____ _____

Address   Physician's phone

Explain "Yes" answers below:

		Yes	No
1.	Have you ever been hospitalized?	[ ]	[ ]
	Have you ever had surgery?	[ ]	[ ]
2.	Are you presently taking any medications or pills?	[ ]	[ ]
3.	Do you have any allergies (medicine, bees or other stinging insects)?	[ ]	[ ]
4.	Have you ever passed out during or after exercise?	[ ]	[ ]
	Have you ever been dizzy during or after exercise?	[ ]	[ ]
	Have you ever had chest pain during or after exercise?	[ ]	[ ]
	Do you tire more quickly than your friends during exercise?	[ ]	[ ]
	Have you ever had high blood pressure?	[ ]	[ ]
	Have you ever been told that you have a heart murmur?	[ ]	[ ]
	Have you ever had racing of your heart or skipped heartbeats?	[ ]	[ ]
	Has anyone in your family died of heart problems or a sudden death before age 50?	[ ]	[ ]
5.	Do you have any skin problems (itching, rashes, acne)?	[ ]	[ ]
6.	Have you ever had a head injury?	[ ]	[ ]
	Have you ever been knocked out or unconscious?	[ ]	[ ]
	Have you ever had a seizure?	[ ]	[ ]
	Have you ever had a stinger, burner or pinched nerve?	[ ]	[ ]
7.	Have you ever had heat or muscle cramps?	[ ]	[ ]
	Have you ever been dizzy or passed out in the heat?	[ ]	[ ]
8.	Do you have trouble breathing or do you cough during or after activity?	[ ]	[ ]
9.	Do you use any special equipment (pads, braces, neck rolls, mouth guard, eye guards, etc.)?	[ ]	[ ]
10.	Have you had any problems with your eyes or vision?	[ ]	[ ]
	Do you wear glasses or contacts or protective eye wear?	[ ]	[ ]
11.	Have you ever sprained/strained, dislocated, fractured, broken or had repeated swelling or other injuries of any bones or joints?	[ ]	[ ]

[ ] Head   [ ] Shoulder   [ ] Thigh   [ ] Neck   [ ] Elbow   [ ] Knee   [ ] Chest
[ ] Forearm   [ ] Shin/calf   [ ] Back   [ ] Wrist   [ ] Ankle   [ ] Hip   [ ] Hand   [ ] Foot

		Yes	No
12.	Have you had any other medical problems (infectious mononucleosis, diabetes, etc.)?	[ ]	[ ]
13.	**Have you had a medical problem or injury since your last evaluation?**	[ ]	[ ]

14. When was your last tetanus shot? _____

    When was your last measles immunization? _____

15. When was your first menstrual period? _____

    When was your last menstrual period? _____

    What was the longest time between your periods last year? _____

Explain "Yes" answers:

_____
_____
_____
_____

I hereby state that, to the best of my knowledge, my answers to the above questions are correct.

Date _____

Signature of athlete _____

Signature of parent/guardian _____

Figure 8-1   Preparticipation physical evaluation form

(*Preparticipation physical evaluation [monograph]. Kansas City, MO: American Academy of Family Physicians, American Academy of Pediatrics, American Medical Society for Sports Medicine, American Orthopaedic Society for Sports Medicine, and American Osteopathic Academy of Sports Medicine. Copyright © 1992.*)

Physical Examination

Date _____

Name _____ Age _____ Date of birth _____

Height _____ Weight _____ BP _____ / _____ Pulse _____

Vision R 20/___ L 20/___ Corrected: Y N   Pupils _____

		Normal	Abnormal findings					Initials
	Cardiopulmonary							
	Pulses							
	Heart							
	Lungs							
	Tanner stage	1	2	3	4	5		
	Skin							
	Abdominal							
	Genitalia							
	Musculoskeletal							
	Neck							
	Shoulder							
	Elbow							
	Wrist							
	Hand							
	Back							
	Knee							
	Ankle							
	Foot							
	Other							

(LIMITED applies to the upper section; COMPLETE applies to the whole table)

Clearance:

A. Cleared

B. Cleared after completing evaluation/rehabilitation for: _____

C. Not cleared for: ☐ Collision

☐ Contact

☐ Noncontact ___Strenuous ___Moderately strenuous ___Nonstrenuous _

Due to: _____

Recommendation: _____

_____

_____

Name of physician _____ Date _____

Address _____ Phone _____

Signature of physician _____

Figure 8-1   Preparticipation physical evaluation form (*Continued*)

Academy of Family Physicians, the American Academy of Pediatrics, the American Medical Society for Sports Medicine, the American Orthopedic Society for Sports Medicine, and the American Osteopathic Academy of Sports Medicine[11] recommends a full and comprehensive preparticipation physical examination at the entry to athletic competition and a shorter physician-administered preparticipation physical examination in succeeding years.

In the high school setting, preparticipation physical examinations are given each year, as they are in professional sports (see chapter 13). Unfortunately, the National Federation of State High School Athletic Associations standard preparticipation physical examination form is considered too brief by most physicians.

Many of the athletes who will be seen in the sports medicine clinic will have preparticipation physical examination information on file with their primary care physician. In agency-sponsored activities, such as Little League baseball and Pop Warner football, there may be no formal requirement for a physical examination before participation in the sports activity.

Annual Health Appraisal Update. This form is used for all returning athletes in those jurisdictions that only give a complete physical examination on the athlete's initial entry into the sports program (usually college or university settings). The athlete should fill in all of the identifying information. A resting heart rate and blood pressure should be taken and recorded by student athletic trainers or staff athletic trainers. A certified athletic trainer will complete the rest of the form. Information gained with the annual health appraisal update will cover any new health conditions the athlete may have experienced within the past year, but they usually involve the summer months during the off-season. Athletes may have been placed on new medications, been involved in a motor vehicle accident, or been diagnosed with a new allergy or illness. All of these can affect athletic participation. The athlete and the person recording the information must sign the form following the appraisal. All of these forms are to be seen by the team physician, who will decide from the information obtained if any athletes need to be seen for further evaluation.

Patient Information Sheet. The patient information sheet is used extensively in clinics and physicians' offices. It contains personal identifying information about the patient, medical insurance or other method of payment, and the nature of the complaint. Additional information may be requested to determine if this is a worker's compensation or accident claim, attorneys of record, and referring physician.

Informed Consent Statement or Authorization to Treat. An informed consent statement is a standard form in most clinical rehabilitation settings that states that rehabilitation programs involve some risk of pain, fatigue, or cardiovascular incident. In addition, outcomes from this type of program cannot be guaranteed. The program or the treatment must be explained in detail. This type of form is generally not used in college or university or high school athletic training rooms, where consent to treat is often obtained as a standing order signed by the athlete and his or her parents prior to the initial physical examination.

Insurance Information Sheet. The insurance information sheet contains information on the type of insurance that an athlete carries. It should be completed by all incoming athletes and anyone who has had a recent change in his or her insurance carrier. Many athletic programs require the athlete or parents to fill out a new form each year to be certain that all information is up to date. The athlete and the carrier of the insurance covering the athlete should complete all sections and sign the bottom of the form. A modified version of this form should be used in those athletic programs that do not use any insurance, with all medical expenses being the responsibility of the athlete (as is often seen in the high school setting). Copies of this form should be kept with the team's athletic trainer whenever the team or athlete is away from the home athletic training room area for practice or competition.

Authorization for Release of Medical Information. In college or university and high school settings, the authorization for release of medical information form authorizes the head athletic trainer (not student athletic trainers) to release medical information to individuals specified by the athlete. This usually means to professional sports team medical personnel or to college sports medicine personnel. All athletic training room records are considered to be a part of the athlete's medical records, and, as such, are covered by state and federal laws regarding the right to privacy. Each time the record is to be released, the athlete should sign a specific waiver that names the party to whom the record may be released and under what conditions, including whether all or only a part of the records are to be released.[6] The athlete needs to be aware that when he or she signs this release, the designated receiver of the record will have access to a complete medical record, not simply the portions of the record that favor the athlete. In the clinic setting, this type of form applies to the release of information back to or from the patient's primary care physician and to the insurance company that will be paying the bills.

Release and Waiver of Liability and Indemnity Agreement.   This release form is to be used by team physicians (and kept in an athlete's file) when, in the physician's judgment, the athlete should not compete due to an impaired physical condition from an injury sustained before or during the time the athlete is a team member, but the athlete demands to be allowed to continue to compete. On this form the physician informs the athlete of all foreseeable potential outcomes of continued participation, both short term and long term. The forms are legal contracts in most jurisdictions,[5] but they do not protect against willful or wanton misconduct. In addition, these waivers do not cover loss of consortium by a spouse (interference with and injury to the marital relationship including companionship, conversation, comfort, sexual relations, and other aspects of life attributable to marriage[7]); therefore, separate waivers signed by the spouse may be necessary.[5]

Helmet Liability Release.   The helmet liability release form should be used at all levels of football: professional, college or university, high school, and agency sponsored. The purpose of this document is to inform football players of the risks involved in collision or contact sports and to release the sponsoring institution from legal liability due to accident. Whenever the courts have indicated that athletic trainers have a duty to warn, then that duty is fulfilled only if the information is complete regard-

ing the risk to the athlete.[14] All signatures must be present, including an independent witness and the athlete's parents in the event the athlete is a minor.

Heat Acclimatization Questionnaire.   A questionnaire such as this one is designed to identify potential heat illness risks, especially in sports that will practice during the late summer in high heat and humidity and outside. A major purpose in completing this form is to identify athletes who have a history of heat illness. Athletes with a history of heat illness are more prone to have a reoccurrence.[3,4] The athlete must understand all of the questions. It is important to stress the importance of truthfully answering all of the questions so that future heat illness can be avoided.

Evaluation of Injuries

Injury Evaluation.   All injuries must be recorded on the injury evaluation form. Figure 8-2 provides a sample form. The athlete's name, sport, chief complaint, and date and time of injury should be recorded on the top two to four lines of this form. The format should be based on the SOAP note format. The chief complaint should be described by symptoms (subjective) and signs (objective). There should be a description of the mechanism of injury and the results of any testing, palpation, and so forth. Next is an evaluation of what was found (assessment) and what will be done (e.g., refer to the doctor for diagnosis and prescription or plan). The initial treatment performed is recorded and a plan of action for treating and rehabilitating the injury is recorded. If a physician prescribes X rays, lab work, or medication, that information must be recorded. If a physician prescribes medication, it must be noted on the injury evaluation form. The athletic trainer must sign the evaluation so that any athletic trainer who works with that athlete will know who to consult should questions arise. The physician's signature for any medical coverage the physician decides on must also be obtained. Finally, the form should be filed under the athlete's name.

Reevaluation of Progress.   A reevaluation of progress form is used in clinics to establish a written record of progress during rehabilitation. It establishes the readiness of the patient to progress and to

SPORTS MEDICINE DEPARTMENT
INJURY EVALUATION

NAME: _____ Sport: _____

Report Date: _____ Injury Date: _____

EVALUATOR: _____ SIGNATURE: _____

SUBJECTIVE: _____

  Relevant Past History: _____

  Current History/Mechanism: _____

_____

OBJECTIVE: _____

  Palpation: _____

  ROM: _____

  Evaluation Testing: _____

_____

ASSESSMENT: _____

_____

_____

PLAN: _____

_____

_____

X-ray	[ ]	BAPS	[ ]	Biodex	[ ]
Ice Bag	[ ]	Crutches NWB	[ ]	Test	[ ]
Ice Massage	[ ]	Crutches PWB	[ ]	Rehab	[ ]
Slush Bucket	[ ]	Ultrasound	[ ]	Stretch	[ ]
Cold Whpl.	[ ]	NMES	[ ]	MCL Prog.	[ ]
Warm Whpl.	[ ]	Massage	[ ]	ACL Prog.	[ ]
Contrast	[ ]	Hydrocollator	[ ]	R. Cuff Prog.	[ ]
Splint	[ ]	Cryostretch	[ ]	Shoul. Flex.	[ ]
Aircast	[ ]	Traction	[ ]	SAQ	[ ]

Other: _____ Physician Referral: _____

PHYSICIAN'S COMMENTS: _____

_____

_____

_____

Physician's Signature: _____ Date: _____

Treatment Record on Next Page

Figure 8-2 Injury evaluation form

TREATMENT RECORD

DATE	TIME	TREATMENT	DISPOSITION	ATHLETIC TRAINER

Figure 8-2   Injury evaluation form (*Continued*)

return to competition or play, and it helps to protect the athletic trainer from liability actions from inappropriate progressions. This is an area that is not done in writing as often in athletic training rooms as in college or university and high school settings. It is clearly in an athletic trainer's best interest, regardless of the setting, to establish, in writing, the reasons that he or she progressed a person to the next step of a rehabilitation protocol.

Recording Treatments

Therapy Record.   The therapy record should be filled out every time an athlete is treated in the athletic training room following the initial evaluation. This information is sometimes recorded on the evaluation form for that injury and sometimes on a separate form. The athletic trainer should fill out the date, type of therapy, remarks, and initial the treatment. The remarks should be a concise, objective statement of the patient's progress since the last treatment. "AROM ↑ 10% since Friday" is an objective statement that is concise and to the point in reevaluation of an athlete. Words such as "appears to be better" are inappropriate.

Therapy Sign-Up Schedule.   A therapy sign-up schedule is kept in a location near where the athletes check in; it serves as an appointment log. The athlete must legibly print his or her name in an available time slot, and athletic trainers should explain to the athlete that he or she is expected to show up at that time. The athlete can cancel if he or she is unable to attend. It can be indicated on the sign-up schedule if the athlete was a "show" or "no-show," and this information is then recorded in the athlete's record. In college or university and high school settings, no-shows are less of a problem because the athletic trainer and coach can work together to ensure athlete compliance. It is a simple matter for the athletic trainer to inform the coach of an athlete who does not keep scheduled therapy appointments.

Injury Log Sheet.   An injury log sheet is a common form in college or university and high school athletic training rooms. The purpose of this sheet is to record initial injuries for each day. Because some state practice acts require physicians to sign off on all injury evaluation forms, but require

that this be done only one to two times a week, this form is a handy reference to quickly check initial injury dates and times. It provides information about the date of injury, the type and extent of injury, and the therapy initiated. This form also allows athletic trainers who do not work every day to catch up on recent injuries. It is important that all of this information is accurately recorded to avoid a communication breakdown. In some athletic training rooms this form is the list for entering information into the computer at the end of the day. It may be a general log-in sheet for all athletes, or there may be individual log-in sheets for each athlete.

Rehabilitation Sheet.   A rehabilitation sheet is used in some athletic training rooms to monitor rehabilitation programs that extend over several weeks. The athlete's name and the exercises and reps should be recorded, either on a card or on a sheet very much like the workout sheet the athletes use in the weight room, which may then be kept on file in the rehabilitation area. In addition, each day's workout information should be recorded completely on the form and then added to the computer record with a hard copy stored in the athlete's file. A similar form can be used with isokinetic machines.

Home Exercise Program Sheet.   Many athletic training rooms and clinics have forms for the athletes to take home with them, describing the types and frequencies of exercises they should be performing. In many clinic situations, the client will only be seen two to three times per week, and their adherence to home exercise programs has a major impact on their progress. When a patient or athlete is sent home with sheets of exercises that they are expected to perform, a copy is made and placed in his or her file. This allows the therapist to refer back to what their current rehabilitation home exercise program status should be.

Coach's Injury Report.   The coach's injury report is often used in sports with high rates of injury to inform the head coach and position coaches of the status of injured athletes from their team. It usually has areas for new injuries and recurring injuries, and it makes note of an estimated return to practice or competition. It may also act as a guideline for what level of participation an athlete may be allowed to do. For example, a football player may be healthy enough to run in that day's practice but should not participate in any contact drills. The form could be used by athletic trainers to keep all coaches informed on a regular basis.

Referrals To and From Others

Medical Service Request.   A medical service request is used to obtain services (e.g., X rays, laboratory work, health service treatment) from an outside organization when requested by a team physician or certified athletic trainer. Name of the athlete, date, appointment time, place and address of the provider, services requested, and insurance information should be recorded. Many of these services must be requested by a physician, and the service reports will be returned to the physician only. The referring physician or certified athletic trainer should fill out the "referring official" and "title" lines. The athlete should be told how to get to the place where services are to be received if he or she is not transported by a member of the sports medicine staff or by parents. Some forms of this type will seek a written diagnosis and prognosis from the physician before an athlete will be allowed to return to play.

Summary

1. Medical record content is prescribed by law in each of the states.
2. The statute of limitations defines the amount of time an injured person has to file a claim.
3. The main reasons for having medical records include communication and legal defense.
4. Secondary reasons for having medical records include research, reimbursement, and establishing athletic training room usage patterns.
5. Records in athletic training rooms should use a standard format such as SOAP .
6. Confidentiality of medical records is required by tort law.
7. In the clinical setting, documentation standards based on standards of practice or on Medicare will apply to required information in a record.
8. Forms are reviewed for various practice settings.

For Critical Thought

What possible responses would Sonya have for Darren's lawyer if she did not have such a complete record? What effect would recalling Darren's record from memory have, rather than reading from the written record?

In college athletic training education programs, current injuries are often used as teaching tools for didactic course work. The mechanism, timing, and outcome of Darren's case were used in a lower extremity evaluation class about a week after the initial injury.

The students discussed how Darren was injured and they evaluated the performance of Sonya and the entire sports medicine team from their limited base of knowledge, as to how the injury was handled. Unfortunately, the student athletic trainers were overheard discussing class by Darren's friend, specifically the injury to Darren's knee and his progress after the injury, in the athletic training room. What further consequences could happen to this case? Was confidentiality breached and/or privacy invaded?

Websites

NCAA Sports Medicine Handbook:
http://www.ncaa.org/sports_sciences/sports_med_handbook/

The NCAA Sports Medicine Handbook contains a variety of information on medical care and college athletics.

University of Missouri-Kansas City Law School:
http://plague.law.umkc.edu/

This site has superior outlines for medicolegal issues, including information on medical record keeping.

Applications for Consideration

1. The first-year student athletic trainers at Poly-inc College in Adams, California have been given an assignment in which they have to write a case study using an example they observe while in the athletic training room during the semester. As the students began working on their projects, they often had to refer back to the athlete's medical records in order to refresh their memories regarding the situation. Many students tried to save time by removing the records from the athletic training room and making copies to take home with them. Should the course instructor have emphasized any important aspects of athletes' rights to privacy before giving the assignment? What possible repercussions could arise from this situation?

2. Peter Boleski supervised Cheryl Banks for three months of postsurgical rehabilitation of her injured right shoulder during her senior year as the captain for the women's basketball team. Cheryl was not drafted by the WNBA and is now suing the university, the athletic trainers, the team physician, the clinic where Peter works, and Peter. She alleges that she was not adequately advised to adhere to the rehabilitation schedule. In addition, she claims that her records (including her rehabilitation progress and adherence) were improperly given out to the teams on her waiver list, and that she should have made more progress in rehabilitation because she was present for what she considered an adequate number of times. What information does Peter need to provide to the attorneys to litigate this case?

References

1 Arrigo, C. Clinical documentation. In Konin, JG. *Clinical athletic training.* Thorofare, NJ: SLACK, Incorporated, 1997.

2 Ball, RT. Legal responsibilities and problems. In Ryan, AJ, Allman, FL, eds. *Sports medicine,* 2nd ed. San Diego: Academic Press, 1989.

3 Bensen, MT, ed. *1999–2000 NCAA Sports Medicine Handbook.* 5th ed. Overland Park, KS: National Collegiate Athletic Association, 1999.

4 Brooks, GA, Fahey, TD, White, TP. *Exercise physiology: Human bioenergetics and its applications.* 2nd ed. Mountain View, CA: Mayfield Publishing, 1996.

5 Comodeca, JA. Release and waiver of liability forms: The most powerful player on the field. *The Sports, Parks & Recreation Law Reporter,* 6(2):17–23, 1992.

6 Hawkins, JD. Sports medicine record keeping: The key to effective communication and documentation. *The Sports, Parks & Recreation Law Reporter,* 3(1):1–7, 1989.

7 Herbert, DL. *Legal aspects of sports medicine.* 2nd ed. Canton, OH: PRC Publishing, Inc., 1995.

8 Kettenbach, G. *Writing SOAP notes.* 2nd ed. Philadelphia: F.A. Davis, Co., 1995.

9 Kibler, WB. *The sport preparticipation fitness examination.* Champaign, IL: Human Kinetics Books, 1990.

10 Marelli, TM. *Nursing documentation handbook.* 2nd ed. St. Louis: Mosby, 1996.

11 McGuire, R. One for the records. *College Athletic Management,* 2(6):22–23, 1990.

12 NATA Board of Certification. Standards for the Practice of Athletic Training. In *Credentialing information and professional practice and discipline standards for the practice of athletic training.* Omaha, NE: National Athletic Trainers' Association, Board of Certification, Inc., 1998.

13 *Preparticipation physical evaluation (PPE).* A joint publication: American Academy of Family Physicians, American Academy of Pediatrics, American Medical Society for Sports Medicine, American Orthopedic Society for Sports Medicine, and American Osteopathic Academy of Sports Medicine, 1992.

14 Roach, WH, Jr., Chernoff, SN, Esley, CL. *Medical records and the law.* Rockville, MD: Aspen Systems Corporation, 1985.

Sample Forms for Use in Colleges, Universities, and High Schools

ANNUAL HEALTH APPRAISAL UPDATE
DEPARTMENT OF SPORTS MEDICINE

Date _____

Sport _____

Name_____ Height_____ Weight_____ Date of Birth_____

School Address_____
              (Street)   (City)   (State)   (Zip Code)

Home Address_____
              (Street)   (City)   (State)   (Zip Code)

Social Security No._____ Local Phone_____

Parent or Guardian_____
            (Name)   (Address)

(City)   (State)   (Zip Code)   (Phone)

Do you have a health or injury problem about which you want to talk to a doctor?
_____ Yes _____ No

Do you have any continuing problems from injuries suffered while in athletics at (institution)?
_____ Yes _____ No

Have you seen a doctor for a medical problem in the last year? _____ Yes _____ No

GENERAL HEALTH AREAS   H.R._____ B.P._____/_____

Dental_____

_____

E.E.N.T._____

Respiratory_____

_____

Gastrointestinal_____

_____

Skin Allergies_____

_____

Head and Neck_____

_____

Genito-Urinary_____

_____

Musculotendinous_____

_____

Feet and Ankles_____

_____

Knee_____

_____

Hip_____

_____

Back_____

_____

Shoulder_____

_____

Elbow and Forearm_____

_____

Hand and Wrist_____

_____

Accidents (Industrial, Recreational, etc.)_____

_____

Comments_____

_____

_____

_____

Have you recently been placed on any medication by a physician?_____

MEDICAL INFORMATION WITHHELD, INCOMPLETE, OR INCORRECT RELIEVES THE (INSTITUTION) FROM ALL MEDICO-LEGAL LIABILITY AND MAY DISQUALIFY YOU FROM PARTICIPATION ON ANY (INSTITUTION) ATHLETIC TEAM.

THE ABOVE INFORMATION IS AN ACCURATE UPDATE OF MY HEALTH STATUS SINCE MY LAST HEALTH APPRAISAL UPDATE.

_____   _____
Athlete's Signature   Examiner

_____
Date

CONSENT FOR EMERGENCY TREATMENT

Name _____   S.S. Number _____

Address _____ City _____   State _____ Zip _____

Phone _____

Father _____   Mother _____

Address, if different from above   Address, if different from above

Employer _____   Employer _____

Employer Address _____   Employer Address _____

Employer Phone Number _____   Employer Phone Number _____

Emergency Contact Person

1. _____

2. _____

3. _____
   Name   Address   City   State   Zip   Phone

(Institution), and its athletic trainers, has my permission to seek necessary emergency treatment for

my (daughter) (son), _____, during his or her participation in

athletics, practices, games, and conditioning workouts. This permission remains in effect during the
1995–1996 academic year.

_____   _____
Father's Signature   Mother's Signature

_____
Date

_____
Witness   Date

WALK-ON TRYOUT PARTICIPANTS

RELEASE FOR PERSONAL INJURY AND DAMAGE

All physical activity has risks that may range from a fall, to muscle and ligament damage, to circulatory or heart disorders. Consequently you must make sure that your health is adequate to participate in the strenuous, vigorous physical activity involved in the (sport) tryout. It is your responsibility to check with the physician of your choice about your health status if there is any question regarding your fitness for participation. If you, at any time during your participation, experience any distress or have any questions regarding your participation, notify your coach or athletic trainer. The (name of institution) does not carry insurance to cover medical expenses of students; you must provide your own coverage and a student group plan is available through the university health service office.

WHEREAS the undersigned voluntarily desires to participate in the (name of the institution) (sport) walk-on tryout; and

WHEREAS the undersigned is duly aware of the risks and hazards that may arise through participation in said activity and that participation in said activity may result in loss of life or limb, property, or both, of the undersigned.

THEREFORE, it is agreed as follows:

THAT in consideration of being allowed to participate in said activity, the undersigned hereby voluntarily assumes all risks of accident or damage to his person or property and all risks of liability or demands of any kind sustained, whether caused by the negligence of the said (name of institution) its agents or employees, or otherwise; and

THE undersigned further voluntarily agrees that the above release shall be binding upon any heirs, administrators, executors, and assigns, of the undersigned; and,

THE undersigned hereby affirms having accident insurance coverage and having adequate health status to participate in strenuous physical activity. The undersigned further acknowledges that the undersigned has the right to refuse to attempt, or to withdraw from, the physical activity for any reason. The undersigned accepts the responsibility to report any injury, distress, preexisting condition that may impair performance, or other problems to the coach or athletic trainer.

THE undersigned, by signing this release, hereby certifies that the undersigned has read and fully understands the conditions herein provided.

Signed:_____

Date:_____

Witness:_____

AUTHORIZATION FOR RELEASE OF MEDICAL INFORMATION TO PROFESSIONAL TEAM AND REPRESENTATIVES

TO: _____

You are hereby authorized to release to the _____
_____ and to their medical examiners any and all medical information and records including x-ray reports relating to any physical, medical, or hospital examination or confinement you may have relating to my physical condition.

I understand that I have the right for this information about me to remain confidential but that upon signing this release the (institution) head athletic trainer will provide my medical information to those persons whom I have requested receive this information. After this information is released the (institution) head athletic trainer has no control over its use or confidentiality as relates to the person or persons receiving it. I realize that this information may be used in a manner beneficial or detrimental to my best interest in professional athletics by those receiving it. I further acknowledge that all questions relating to the procedures for release of and potential use of my medical information have been answered to my satisfaction.

_____

Date

_____

Athlete Signature

_____

Witness

(NAME OF INSTITUTION)
RELEASE AND WAIVER OF LIABILITY AND INDEMNITY AGREEMENT

I have been advised of the nature and extent of my injuries sustained on _____, 20__, while participating in _____

at _____, located in _____,

_____. This injury was treated by Dr. _____

in _____, _____. The team physicians have discussed

the following treatment options along with the possible outcomes, including any adverse effects if present, of such treatment that I chose to receive.

The physicians have discussed any possible risks of my continued participation in _____ following the injury described above including:

I understand the information that has been presented to me regarding possible treatments and continued participation. All of my questions have been answered to my satisfaction.

_____

Signature   Date

_____

Witness

HELMET LIABILITY RELEASE

I, the undersigned, fully understand, that there are risks involved in my participation on the (institution) football team. Furthermore, I verify that I have been warned concerning the risks of head and/or neck and spinal cord injury that may occur as a result of physical contact while wearing a football helmet during football practice or games. I have received proper instruction in the care and fitting of my football helmet and other protective equipment and understand my responsibility in the proper fitting, maintenance, and safety concerns of football equipment. I also understand that my disregard of proper technique and/or failure to comply with the rules can increase my risk of injury. If at any time I have any questions or concerns regarding the fit or safety of my football equipment, especially the helmet, I understand that it is my responsibility to bring those concerns and questions to my coach and/or equipment manager.

The undersigned does further agree to indemnify and hold harmless the (institution) and its employees or agents from any and all claims or demands for loss, cost, injury, or damage whatsoever arising from his negligence, especially for injury resulting from improper use of the helmet such as butting, ramming, or spearing another player and failure to follow safety instructions that he has received.

_____

Name

_____

Date

_____

Witness

HEAT ACCLIMATIZATION QUESTIONNAIRE

Please answer all questions at least with yes or no answers.

1. Have you ever had any form of heat stress problem (heat exhaustion, heat stroke, dizziness, fainting) before? If yes, circle the one it was.

2. If you answered yes to the above question, how many times did that particular problem occur and when did it happen?

3. Were you on any form of conditioning program during the summer? If the answer is yes, briefly explain your program.

4. Did you work in an air-conditioned building during the summer?

5. Are you presently on a diet? If yes, what kind of diet? Who designed it?

6. Have you been restricting your water intake for any reason? If yes, explain why.

7. Have you recently (last 2 weeks) had a cold, problem with vomiting, or diarrhea? If yes, please explain.

8. Are you currently on any medication? If yes, list the name and/or purpose of the medication.

_____

Name

_____

Date

INJURY REPORT

Sport:_____ Practice Date:_____ Report Date:_____

New Injuries

Name	Injury	Severity	Est. Return	Comments

Old Injuries

Name	Injury	Severity	Est. Return	Comments

Next Practice Returnees

INJURY LOG

Date	Name	Sport	Injury	Therapy	Exam By

THERAPY SCHEDULE FOR _____

		Show	NS		Show	NS		Show	NS
7:00	____	∟ ∟ ∟ ∟	____	∟ ∟ ∟ ∟	____	∟ ∟ ∟ ∟
7:15	____	∟ ∟ ∟ ∟	____	∟ ∟ ∟ ∟	____	∟ ∟ ∟ ∟
7:30	____	∟ ∟ ∟ ∟	____	∟ ∟ ∟ ∟	____	∟ ∟ ∟ ∟
7:45	____	∟ ∟ ∟ ∟	____	∟ ∟ ∟ ∟	____	∟ ∟ ∟ ∟
8:00	____	∟ ∟ ∟ ∟	____	∟ ∟ ∟ ∟	____	∟ ∟ ∟ ∟
8:15	____	∟ ∟ ∟ ∟	____	∟ ∟ ∟ ∟	____	∟ ∟ ∟ ∟
8:30	____	∟ ∟ ∟ ∟	____	∟ ∟ ∟ ∟	____	∟ ∟ ∟ ∟
8:45	____	∟ ∟ ∟ ∟	____	∟ ∟ ∟ ∟	____	∟ ∟ ∟ ∟
9:00	____	∟ ∟ ∟ ∟	____	∟ ∟ ∟ ∟	____	∟ ∟ ∟ ∟
9:15	____	∟ ∟ ∟ ∟	____	∟ ∟ ∟ ∟	____	∟ ∟ ∟ ∟
9:30	____	∟ ∟ ∟ ∟	____	∟ ∟ ∟ ∟	____	∟ ∟ ∟ ∟
9:45	____	∟ ∟ ∟ ∟	____	∟ ∟ ∟ ∟	____	∟ ∟ ∟ ∟
10:00	____	∟ ∟ ∟ ∟	____	∟ ∟ ∟ ∟	____	∟ ∟ ∟ ∟
10:15	____	∟ ∟ ∟ ∟	____	∟ ∟ ∟ ∟	____	∟ ∟ ∟ ∟
10:30	____	∟ ∟ ∟ ∟	____	∟ ∟ ∟ ∟	____	∟ ∟ ∟ ∟
10:45	____	∟ ∟ ∟ ∟	____	∟ ∟ ∟ ∟	____	∟ ∟ ∟ ∟
11:00	____	∟ ∟ ∟ ∟	____	∟ ∟ ∟ ∟	____	∟ ∟ ∟ ∟
11:15	____	∟ ∟ ∟ ∟	____	∟ ∟ ∟ ∟	____	∟ ∟ ∟ ∟
11:30	____	∟ ∟ ∟ ∟	____	∟ ∟ ∟ ∟	____	∟ ∟ ∟ ∟
11:45	____	∟ ∟ ∟ ∟	____	∟ ∟ ∟ ∟	____	∟ ∟ ∟ ∟
12:00	____	∟ ∟ ∟ ∟	____	∟ ∟ ∟ ∟	____	∟ ∟ ∟ ∟
12:15	____	∟ ∟ ∟ ∟	____	∟ ∟ / ∟	____	∟ ∟ ∟ ∟
12:30	____	∟ ∟ ∟ ∟	____	∟ ∟ ∟ ∟	____	∟ ∟ ∟ ∟
12:45	____	∟ ∟ ∟ ∟	____	∟ ∟ ∟ ∟	____	∟ ∟ ∟ ∟

REFERRAL OF VARSITY ATHLETE
to
UNIVERSITY MEDICAL CENTER

Complete and return to the athletic trainer:

_____ has symptoms related to
(athlete's name)

_____

_____

Sport: _____ Athletic trainer: _____

Phone extension: _____

Physician's diagnosis: _____

_____

_____

_____

Recommendation for practice: _____ Full

                                       _____ Limited   _____ Days

                                       _____ None for   _____ Days

_____   _____
Physician signature   Date

The NCAA does not permit the athletic department to pay for the care of illness.

ATHLETE MEDICAL REFERRAL

Athlete _____ Class _____ Date _____

Sport _____ Coach _____

Dear Physician: The athlete named above must present to the school athletic trainer written permission from a physician to resume participation in athletics. Thank you.

SIGNS, SYMPTOMS, AND IMMEDIATE CARE GIVEN:

Suspected Injury/Illness   Athletic Trainer Signature

Occasion: _____ Game _____ Practice _____ Other _____   Parent Contacted: Yes ___ No ___
                                                               Person Contacted: _____

Physician:

_____
Specific Diagnosis and/or Surgical Procedure

_____ to _____
          Period of Restriction

Prescribed Treatment/Rehabilitation/Rehabilitation Programs:

Additional Instructions/Precautions: _____

_____

Frequency: _____ Daily or _____ days per week for _____ weeks or _____ until
                                                          program is completed.

Physician Signature   Date   Phone

MEDICAL SERVICE REQUEST
NORTHERN STATE UNIVERSITY

Name _____

Date _____

Appointment Time _____

Place and Address _____

_____

Service Requested _____

_____

_____

Insurance Information Form Attached

Referring Official_____

Title _____

Sample Forms for Use in Sports Medicine Clinics

SPORTS MEDICINE CLINIC, INC.

City Office	North Suburbs	Today's Date
12 N. Michigan Ave.	98765 N. Colorado Rd.	
St. Louis, PA 75512	Dorian, PA 75115	____ / ____ / ____

THANK YOU FOR CHOOSING S.M.C.
In order to serve you more efficiently, we need the following information.
(Please Print)

Patient's Name   Birthdate   Marital Status
                                                               __Single __Married
                                                               __Widowed __
                                                               Divorced

Patient's Address   City   State   Zip   Home Phone

If minor, name and address of parent or legal guardian

Employer   Address   Phone   Ok to Call?
                                                             __yes __no

Social Security Number   Occupation

Do you have medical   If not, how do you intend to   Insurance Company and
insurance? __yes __no   pay? __check   Address
                           __ cash

Subscriber Name   Policy Number   Group Number   Through your employer?
                                                               __ yes __ no

Spouse's Name   Birthdate   Social Security No.

Is there secondary   Name and Address of   Phone
insurance? __ yes __ no   Spouse's Employer

Secondary Insurance Name and Address   Policy Number   Group Number

Medicare Number   Medicaid Number

Worker's Compensation Claim Number   Name of Company

Address of Company   Company Phone   Treatment Authorized by

In Case of Accident, Name and Address of Attorney

In Case of Emergency, Contact   Relationship to Patient   Phone

Referring Physician   Address

State Nature of Problem   Date of Onset

If Student, Grade and GPA (Optional)

PATIENT MEDICAL HISTORY
AND PERSONAL FITNESS QUESTIONNAIRE

The following questionnaire is used to gather information regarding your current and past medical status. Responses to these questions will provide you and our staff with the most appropriate guidelines for safe and effective treatment.

PERSONAL HISTORY

Check each as it applies to you. Have you ever had:

T.B.	yes __ no __ unsure __	Allergy	yes __ no __ unsure __
Heart attack	yes __ no __ unsure __	Convulsions	yes __ no __ unsure __
Angina	yes __ no __ unsure __	Paralysis	yes __ no __ unsure __
EKG abnormalities	yes __ no __ unsure __	Leg cramps	yes __ no __ unsure __
Emphysema	yes __ no __ unsure __	Headache	yes __ no __ unsure __
High blood pressure	yes __ no __ unsure __	Depression	yes __ no __ unsure __
Surgery	yes __ no __ unsure __	Shortness of breath	yes __ no __ unsure __
Diabetes	yes __ no __ unsure __	Arm pain	yes __ no __ unsure __
Stroke	yes __ no __ unsure __	Low blood pressure	yes __ no __ unsure __
Severe illness	yes __ no __ unsure __	Indigestion	yes __ no __ unsure __
Hospitalized	yes __ no __ unsure __	Ulcers	yes __ no __ unsure __
Blackouts	yes __ no __ unsure __	Asthma	yes __ no __ unsure __
Gout	yes __ no __ unsure __	Hernia	yes __ no __ unsure __
Nervousness	yes __ no __ unsure __	Back pain	yes __ no __ unsure __
Joint problems	yes __ no __ unsure __	Chest pain	yes __ no __ unsure __
Sleep interference	yes __ no __ unsure __	Cancer	yes __ no __ unsure __

Any other medical problems? If so, please describe: _____

_____

COMMENTS: _____

_____

_____

FAMILY HISTORY

Check each as it applies to a blood relative:

Heart attack	yes __ no __ unsure __	Tuberculosis	yes __ no __ unsure __
High blood pressure	yes __ no __ unsure __	Diabetes	yes __ no __ unsure __
Circulatory disorder	yes __ no __ unsure __	Stroke	yes __ no __ unsure __
Heart disease	yes __ no __ unsure __	Asthma	yes __ no __ unsure __

Any other history of family medical conditions? If so, please describe: _____

_____

Father's Age _____ Deceased _____
Mother's Age _____ Deceased _____

Comments: _____

_____

MEDICAL HISTORY

Name of your family physician _____ Date of last physical _____
What did it include? _____
Do you wear a pacemaker? _____ yes _____ no
Do you know your resting blood pressure? yes ___ no ___ _____ mmHg
Do you know your resting heart rate?   yes ___ no ___ _____ BPM
Do you know your cholesterol level?   yes ___ no ___ _____
Do you know your ratios?   yes ___ no ___ _____
Have you ever had an exercise ECG?   yes ___ no ___
Are you pregnant?   yes ___ no ___
Indicate any medications you are taking: _____
_____

EXERCISE HISTORY

Do you exercise? yes ___ no ___ What activities? _____
How long have you been exercising? _____
How many days do you exercise? _____ How many minutes per day? _____
In what kind of shoes do you work out? _____
Where do you usually exercise? _____

HEALTH HISTORY

Present Height	Present Weight	Weight:	At Age 20	At Age 30	At Age 40	One Year Ago	Most Weight	Least Weight
_____	_____		_____	_____	_____	_____	_____	_____

Approximately, your daily intake of: Coffee _____   Tea _____   Pop _____   Alcohol _____
Did you ever smoke? yes _____ no _____ If yes, how many years? _____
Approximate your daily usage of: Cigarettes _____ Cigars _____ Pipes _____
Chewing Tobacco _____
Would you consider quitting? yes _____ no _____

I certify that to the best of my knowledge the above answers are true and correct.

_____   _____

Signature   Name

SPORTS MEDICINE CLINIC

PATIENT INFORMATION:

1. Patient's Name_____ Age _____ Sex _____
2. Phone (H) _____ (W) _____
3. Referred by _____
4. Complaint: Injury _____ Pathology _____
              Sport _____
5. Family Physician _____ Phone _____

History of same injury? _____ When? _____

Physician Report

1. Chief Complaint _____
2. Pertinent History _____
3. Past Medical History _____
4. Physical Examination _____
Assessment: _____
Plan: _____
Restrictions: _____ Duration _____

_____
Physician's Signature   **Date**

Athletic Trainer's Summary

1. Evaluation _____
2. Treatment Plan _____
Restrictions: No Restrictions _____   Duration _____
                     Practice with
                        NO contact   _____
                     No Running   _____
                     No Practice   _____
Date of Next Visit _____ Location _____
Additional Comments _____

_____

_____
ATC or PT Signature   **Date**

PATIENT INFORMATION FORM

Date: _____

Name: _____ Physician: _____

Date of Injury: _____ Claim Number: _____

Type of Injury: _____

History of Injury: _____

_____

_____

Age: _____ Weight: _____ Height: _____

_____

Functional Status: Are you independent in daily living skills (i.e., eating, bathing, dressing, homemaking): YES _____ NO _____

    If NO, what areas are you limited in? _____

Do you have problems with going to sleep? YES _____ NO _____

    If YES, how long does it take you to fall asleep? _____

How many times do you wake up during the night? _____

Relevant Past Medical History: _____

_____

Educational History: _____

_____

Hobbies/Interests: _____

_____

Work History:

    Place of Employment: _____ Number of Years _____

    Job Title: _____

    Job Description (Describe your job responsibilities, number of hours per day, number of days per week, number of breaks per day): _____

_____

_____

INFORMED CONSENT STATEMENT

In the event I am required to perform therapeutic exercise, it is understood that the program is designed to develop muscular strength, muscular endurance, cardiovascular-respiratory endurance, and flexibility. I recognize that individuals vary in their response to exercise and specific results cannot always be guaranteed. Also I may experience muscle pain and physical fatigue during and after participation in exercise. A cardiovascular incident is also a remote possibility. I further understand and agree that the Sports Medicine Clinic's program is not a substitute in any way for a diagnostic evaluation by my physician and I agree to consult with my physician regarding any risk of which I now am unaware or become aware of while participating in the program. Furthermore, I understand that consultation with my physician is recommended prior to exercise.

Routines will be progressive in nature emphasizing movements to improve flexibility and cardiovascular fitness.

I will report to the exercise coordinator any change in physical condition (pain, soreness, injury), new medication, changes of medication, or changes of exercise prescription.

I recognize that development of an exercise program is not an exact science, and despite the best efforts possible, it is possible to suffer accidents and medical emergencies, such as heart attacks, stroke, or other cardiopulmonary incidents.

I have read and understand this form and the program it describes, and I do voluntarily request the right to participate in Sports Medicine Clinic's rehabilitation program. I do hereby discharge, release, and hold harmless the Sports Medicine Clinic and any of its personnel participating in this rehabilitation program, from any and all liability for damage of any kind or character resulting from any injury or condition that I may suffer, or may result from such a rehabilitation program.

THESE FORMS HAVE BEEN EXPLAINED TO ME AND I SIGN THEM VOLUNTARILY.

_____   _____
PARTICIPANT SIGNATURE   DATE

_____   _____
WITNESS SIGNATURE   DATE

_____   _____
PARENT OR GUARDIAN SIGNATURE   DATE

CONSENT FOR TREATMENT

I recognize that I am suffering from a condition requiring athletic training services and treatment. A representative of Sports Medicine Clinic, Inc., (whose name is _____) has explained the nature of my condition and the treatments I will be receiving as well as other ways that this condition can be treated. I hereby consent to the rendering of athletic training services by Sports Medicine Clinic, Inc., as described to me or as my physician or Sports Medicine Clinic, Inc., determines are necessary. I understand that the practice of athletic training is not an exact science and that athletic training treatment involves the risk of injury, or even death. I acknowledge that no guarantees have been made to me about the outcome of treatment.

CONSENT TO DISCLOSURE OF PATIENT INFORMATION

I hereby authorize Sports Medicine Clinic, Inc., and its employees to disclose information about me and the treatment being provided to me, including copies of my medical records, to my physician, to my insurance carrier, and to any utilization review organization or agency providing such benefits or reviewing or processing my claim. This information will be used by these parties to (1) determine the necessity of athletic training and related services, (2) promote the most efficient use of available health facilities and services, and (3) consider payment of all or a portion of my athletic training bills.

ASSIGNMENT OF INSURANCE BENEFITS

I hereby assign Sports Medicine Clinic, Inc., (1) all insurance, Medicare, Medicaid, and other private or governmental benefits payable for my treatments and care; and (2) all rights to payment and all money paid for any claim related to the reasons for which I am being given athletic training service and treatment. Anyone paying or receiving money for my benefits or claims shall pay the money directly to Sports Medicine Clinic, Inc., for payment of my bills. I understand that I am financially responsible for all charges not covered by my insurance or other third party payers and that any balance after insurance or third party payment has been made is due within thirty (30) days.

_____   _____
SIGNATURE OF PATIENT OR GUARDIAN   DATE

SPORTS MEDICINE CLINIC, INC.
RECORDS RELEASE

TO: _____

_____

_____

I HEREBY AUTHORIZE AND REQUEST YOU TO RELEASE TO:

Sports Medicine Clinic, Inc.
12 N. Michigan Ave.
St. Louis, PA 75512

THE FOLLOWING: _____

_____

_____

REASON FOR REQUEST: _____

_____

_____

PATIENT INFORMATION

NAME: _____

ADDRESS: _____

DATE OF BIRTH: _____

SIGNATURE: _____

RELATIONSHIP: _____

DATE: _____

WITNESS: _____

THIS AUTHORIZATION TO BE EFFECTIVE FOR ONE YEAR FROM THE DATE OF SIGNATURE.

PROGRESS NOTES

DATE

RECONDITIONING EVALUATION

NAME: _____ DATE: _____

PHYSICIAN: _____ REHAB. COUNSELOR _____

DIAGNOSIS: _____

AGE: _____ BLOOD PRESSURE: _____ REST H.R.: _____

ADL: _____

_____

_____

BEHAVIOR: _____ WEIGHT _____ INITIAL PAIN LEVEL _____

ASSESSMENT:

GAIT: _____

_____

POSTURE: _____

_____

	ROM	STRENGTH	COMMENTS
Neck:			
Flexion	_____	_____	_____
Extension	_____	_____	_____
Lateral Flex.-R	_____	_____	_____
Lateral Flex.-L	_____	_____	_____
Rotation - R	_____	_____	_____
Rotation - L	_____	_____	_____
Back/Trunk:			
Flexion	_____	_____	_____
Extension	_____	_____	_____
Lateral Flex.-R	_____	_____	_____
Lateral Flex.-L	_____	_____	_____
Rotation - R	_____	_____	_____
Rotation - L	_____	_____	_____
Finger tip to floor:	_____	_____	_____

Lower Extremities:

	Right			Left	
ROM	Strength			ROM	Strength

Hip

ROM	Strength		ROM	Strength
_____	_____	flexion	_____	_____
_____	_____	extension	_____	_____
_____	_____	abduction	_____	_____
_____	_____	adduction	_____	_____
_____	_____	internal rotation	_____	_____
_____	_____	external rotation	_____	_____

Knee

		flexion	_____	_____
_____	_____	extension	_____	_____

Ankle

_____	_____	dorsiflexion	_____	_____
_____	_____	plantar flexion	_____	_____
_____	_____	inversion	_____	_____
_____	_____	eversion	_____	_____

COMMENTS: _____

_____

_____

Fabere Test: _____

_____

Upper Extremities:

	Right			Left	
ROM	Strength			ROM	Strength

Shoulder

ROM	Strength		ROM	Strength
_____	_____	flexion 0–180	_____	_____
_____	_____	extension 0–60	_____	_____
_____	_____	abduction 0–180	_____	_____
_____	_____	horiz. flex. 0–45	_____	_____
_____	_____	horiz. ext. 0–90	_____	_____
_____	_____	internal rot. 0–70	_____	_____
_____	_____	external rot. 0–90	_____	_____

Elbow and Forearm

_____	_____	flexion 0–150	_____	_____
_____	_____	extension 0–150	_____	_____
_____	_____	supination 0–90	_____	_____
_____	_____	pronation 0–90	_____	_____

(continued)

	Right			Left	
ROM	Strength		ROM	Strength	

Wrist

ROM	Strength		ROM	Strength
_____	_____	flexion 0–80	_____	_____
_____	_____	extension 0–70	_____	_____
_____	_____	ulnar flex. 0–30	_____	_____
_____	_____	radial flex. 0–20	_____	_____

Thumb

_____	_____	MP flex.-ext. 0–50	_____	_____
_____	_____	IP flex.-ext. 0–80	_____	_____
_____	_____	palmar abduction	_____	_____
_____	_____	radial abduction	_____	_____
_____	_____	opposition cm/in	_____	_____

Index Finger

_____	_____	MP flex.-ext. 0–90	_____	_____
_____	_____	PIP flex.-ext. 0–100	_____	_____
_____	_____	DIP flex.-ext. 0–90	_____	_____

Middle Finger

_____	_____	MP flex.-ext. 0–90	_____	_____
_____	_____	PIP flex.-ext. 0–100	_____	_____
_____	_____	DIP flex.-ext. 0–90	_____	_____

Ring Finger

_____	_____	MP flex.-ext. 0–90	_____	_____
_____	_____	PIP flex.-ext. 0–100	_____	_____
_____	_____	DIP flex.-ext. 0–90	_____	_____

Little Finger

_____	_____	MP flex.-ext. 0–90	_____	_____
_____	_____	PIP flex.-ext. 0–100	_____	_____
_____	_____	DIP flex.-ext. 0–90	_____	_____

Grip Strength:	Level 1	Level 2	Level 3	Level 4	Level 5	Percentile
Right	_____	_____	_____	_____	_____	_____
Left	_____	_____	_____	_____	_____	_____

Pinch Strength:	Tip	%	Palmar	%	Lateral	%
Right	_____	_____	_____	_____	_____	_____
Left	_____	_____	_____	_____	_____	_____

Coordination:

MRMT	PLACING	Right _____ _____%	Turning
		Left _____ _____%	_____
			Total _____%

Other Tests: _____

_____

_____

_____

SENSORY TESTING: (See Semmes-Weinstein Sheet)

_____

_____

_____

_____

_____

_____

                                                    Strength Category

Bench Press Maximum Effort: _____#   _____

Leg Press Maximum Effort: _____#   _____

Pain Scale: (see sheet)

Initially: _____

Post PCE: _____

Step Test: _____ Fitness Category _____

Other Cardiovascular Screenings: _____

_____

_____

_____

_____

Maximum Heart Rate: _____

Age-Adjusted Maximum Predicted HR: _____ 60% _____ 70% _____ 80% _____

Recommendations/Summary:

    Back Education   Cumulative Trauma Prevention
    Body Mechanics Station   Aerobic Conditioning
    Stress Management   Nutritional Lecture
    Return to Work Sessions   Job Site Assessment
    Reconditioning   Work Hardening
    Physical Capacity Evaluation

_____

_____

_____

_____

_____

REHABILITATION SERVICES PLAN OF CARE

Patient's Name: _____

Address: _____

City, State, Zip: _____ Phone: _____

Diagnosis: _____ Date of Onset: _____

Patient Aware of Diagnosis: Yes _____   No _____

Rehabilitation Goals and Potential: _____

_____

PROFESSIONAL SERVICES OR CONSULTATION DESIRED

_____ Athletic Training   _____ Rehab. Counseling   _____ Speech Path.
_____ Physical Therapy   _____ Occupational   _____ Other
                                            Therapy

_____ Work Hardening/Reconditioning

Rx: __ Hot pack   __ Ultrasound   __ Massage   __ Cold pack
         __ Whirlpool   __ Ice massage   __ Therapeutic exercise
         __ Paraffin   __ Gait training   __ Traction—cervical or pelvic
         __ NMES   __ Biodex   __ Home instruction
         __ Other: _____

Area to be Treated: _____

Frequency: _____ Duration: _____ Recheck: _____

Special Instructions or Precautions: _____

MEDICAL SUMMARY

Related Medical Findings: _____

Past Medical History: _____

PROGNOSIS: _____ Excellent   _____ Good   _____ Fair   _____ Poor

I certify that the above services are required by this patient on an outpatient basis.

_____   _____
            Date   Physician's Signature

Rehabilitation Institute
2000 Health Care Drive
Lake City, Midwest 48602

Date:

Dear Doctor _____:

Please sign the attached "Evaluation/Plan of Care" and return it to our office in the enclosed, stamped envelope.

Medicare guidelines require a physician's approval for a particular plan on all Medicare patients. The prescription for Physical Therapy does not suffice. The requirements ask for problems, goals, frequency, and duration upon completion of the initial evaluation and every subsequent thirty days of treatment. We will send your office a "Plan of Care" on all Medicare patients we are treating for your signature.

If you should have any further questions, please feel free to contact our office.

Thank you.

Sincerely,

Daily Progress Note Sports Medicine and Rehabilitation

Name		Date	Visit	of
Subjective				
Objective				

CPT Time Description

CPT	Time	Description

Response to treatment
Ability to perform home program
Indication for continued treatment
Plan
Signature

Ankle Home Exercise Program

Patient name:_____

	Date instructed	Rechecked	Performed correctly	Comments
Ankle ROM—PF; DF; Inv; Erv	_____	_____	_____	_____
Alphabet exercise	_____	_____	_____	_____
Resisted dorsiflexion	_____	_____	_____	_____
Resisted plantar flexion	_____	_____	_____	_____
Resisted inversion	_____	_____	_____	_____
Resisted eversion	_____	_____	_____	_____
Gastroc stretch	_____	_____	_____	_____
Soleus stretch	_____	_____	_____	_____
Toe curls (towel)	_____	_____	_____	_____
Heel rises (Standing plantar flexion)	_____	_____	_____	_____
Single leg balance	_____	_____	_____	_____
1/2 roll plantar flexion/dorsiflexion	_____	_____	_____	_____
1/2 roll inversion/eversion	_____	_____	_____	_____
C. C. Dorsiflexion	_____	_____	_____	_____
C. C. Plantar flexion	_____	_____	_____	_____
_____	_____	_____	_____	_____
_____	_____	_____	_____	_____
_____	_____	_____	_____	_____

____ = _____
initial   Signature

Lower Extremity Evaluation

Patient:	Medical record:
Physician:	Date of eval:
Diagnosis:	Onset:
Surgery:	Date of surgery:
Precautions:	

Age:	Sex: ☐ Male ☐ Female	Injury code:

Duration of symptoms: ☐ Post Surgical ☐ < 30 days ☐ 30–90 days ☐ > 90 days

Primary complaint	
Cause	
Location of pain & Current pain level	
Description of symptoms	
What aggravates symptoms	
What improves symptoms	
Prior functional status	☐ Independent ☐ Limitations:
Current functional limitations	Disability score: ☐ Working ☐ Not working Return to work:
Mental status	☐ Alert, oriented, cooperative, able to follow instructions ☐ Limited:
Barriers to education	☐ None ☐ Barriers:
Prior treatment	☐ None ☐ Type:
Results of prior treatment	☐ NA ☐ Results:
Medical complications	☐ None ☐ Complications:

Patient Name:

Movement	Active	Passive	Active	Passive	Comments
	Right	Right	Left	Left	

Strength	Right	Left	Comments

Girth	Right	Left

Gait	Description
Assist	☐ indep ☐ min ☐ mod ☐ max
Device	☐ none ☐ cane ☐ quad cane ☐ crutches ☐ walker
Supports	☐ none ☐ brace:
Distance	☐ > 100 feet ☐ other:
Step length	☐ equal ☐ > on left ☐ > on right
Stance time	☐ equal ☐ > on left ☐ > on right
Pattern	☐ normal ☐ other:
Ascend stairs	☐ indep ☐ single step ☐ uses rail ☐ unable
Descend stairs	☐ indep ☐ single step ☐ uses rail ☐ unable
Tinetti Gait Score	☐ NA ☐ Score:

Balance	Description
Sitting	☐ normal or loses balance: ☐ left ☐ right ☐ front ☐ back
Initial standing	☐ normal or loses balance: ☐ left ☐ right ☐ front ☐ back
Standing	☐ normal or loses balance: ☐ left ☐ right ☐ front ☐ back
Standing (eyes closed)	☐ normal or loses balance: ☐ left ☐ right ☐ front ☐ back
Initial gait	☐ normal or loses balance: ☐ left ☐ right ☐ front ☐ back
Walking	☐ normal or loses balance: ☐ left ☐ right ☐ front ☐ back
Tinetti Balance Score	☐ NA ☐ Score:

Observation	Description
Tenderness	
Spasm-location	
Swelling	
Neurological findings	☐ None ☐ deficits:
Skin condition	
Additional findings	

Worksheet

Ankle

❏ **Discharge Report**   ❏ **Progress Report**

Patient: **Medical record number:**
Physician: **Age:**
Diagnosis: **Date of onset:**
Surgical procedure: **Date of surgery:**
Date of initial evaluation: **Date of report:**
Last treatment date: **Total visits:**
Injury code: **Acuity:**

GOALS	Met	Not met
1. Patient demonstrates the ability to control pain (2 or less on pain scale).	❏	❏
2. Patient will have AROM ≥ 75% of uninvolved for plantar flexion, dorsiflexion.	❏	❏
3. Strength in involved ankle musculature will be at least 75% of uninvolved for dorsiflexion, inversion, and eversion.	❏	❏
4. No gait deviations at normal walking speeds.	❏	❏
5. Ankle Rating Scale will be at least 75%.	❏	❏
6. Patient will demonstrate the ability to complete a home exercise program correctly.	❏	❏
7. _____	❏	❏
8. _____	❏	❏

Summary of current status: (address each): _____
Currently patient rates _____ ankle pain at " ____ " on pain scale. _____ ankle AROM : DF _____
Inv _____ EV _____ PF _____ . _____ / _____ ankle strength: dorsiflexion___#/___#(%); eversion
_____#/_____# (%), inversion___#/___# (%). Patient does/does not exhibit gait
deviations _____. Patient's Ankle Rating score is_____%. Patient demonstrates
the ability to perform home exercise program correctly.

_____
_____

Summary of functional progress: (ADL, walking, stairs, lifting, pushing, etc.)
_____
_____
_____

Recommendations: _____
_____

Expected duration of treatment: _____
Prognosis for meeting remaining goals:_____

Thank you for the opportunity to work with this patient.

ANKLE RATING SCALE

Patient name:_____   **Date:** _____

By completing this questionnaire, your therapist will gain information as to how your ankle functions during normal activities. Mark the box that best describes your ankle function today.

1. **LIMP**
    ( ) None   5
    ( ) Slight or periodic   3
    ( ) Severe and constant   0
2. **SUPPORT**
    ( ) None   5
    ( ) Cane or crutch needed   2
    ( ) Weight bearing impossible
3. **LOCKING**
    ( ) None   15
    ( ) Catching sensation, but no locking   10
    ( ) Locking occasionally   6
    ( ) Locking frequently   2
    ( ) Locked joint at examination   0
4. **INSTABILITY**
    ( ) Never turns or rolls over   25
    ( ) Rarely during athletic activities/physical exam   20
    ( ) Frequently during athletic activities/physical exam   15
    ( ) Occasionally during daily activities   10
    ( ) Often during daily activities   5
    ( ) Every step   0
5. **PAIN**
    ( ) None   25
    ( ) Intermittent and light during strenuous activities   20
    ( ) Marked during strenuous activities   15
    ( ) Marked during or after walking more than 2 km (1.2 mi.)   10
    ( ) Marked during or after walking less than 2 km (1.2 mi.)   5
    ( ) Constant   0
6. **SWELLING**
    ( ) None   10
    ( ) After strenuous activities   6
    ( ) After ordinary activities   2
    ( ) Constant   0
7. **STAIRS**
    ( ) No problem   10
    ( ) Slight problem   6
    ( ) One step at a time   2
    ( ) Impossible   0
8. **SQUATTING**
    ( ) No problem   5
    ( ) Slight problem   4
    ( ) Not beyond 90 degrees of flexion of the knee halfway   2
    ( ) Impossible   2

                                                    SCORE_____

Treatment Plan: Ankle

☐ Initial   ☐ Recertification

Name:	Date:
Diagnosis:	Date of onset:
Surgery:	Date of surgery:
Physician:	

PROBLEMS

☐ 1. Pain and swelling in the _____ ankle

☐ 2. Painful/limited ROM of the _____ ankle

☐ 3. Decreased strength in the _____ ankle musculature

☐ 4. Abnormal gait

☐ 5. Decreased function of the involved ankle as noted per functional rating scale

☐ 6. Decreased knowledge of a home exercise program

☐ 7. _____

☐ 8. _____

GOALS

☐ 1. Patient will verbalize rest pain at 2 or less on a pain scale.

☐ 2. Patient will have AROM ≥75% of uninvolved for plantar flexion and dorsiflexion.

☐ 3. Strength in involved ankle musculature will be at least 75% of uninvolved for dorsiflexion, inversion, and eversion.

☐ 4. No gait deviations will be noted with ambulation at normal walking speeds.

☐ 5. Ankle rating scale score will be at least 75%.

☐ 6. Patient will demonstrate the ability to complete a home exercise program correctly.

☐ 7. _____

☐ 8. _____

Above goals are expected to be met within _____ to _____ weeks.

The prognosis for meeting the above goals and potential for rehabilitation is_____.

The patient is aware of the diagnosis and the prognosis.

The _____ participated in the formation of the goals of treatment.

PLAN: Patient will be seen _____ per week for _____ weeks or _____ visits. Treatment wil consist of _____

_____.

CHAPTER 9

Insurance

After reading this chapter, you should be able to:

- Distinguish between different types of insurance (medical, health, and accident) used in the healthcare system.

- Explain the problems and benefits of self-insurance, primary coverage, secondary coverage, and managed care policies.

- Identify the scope of catastrophic insurance policies and their use.

- Describe the relationship between premiums paid in and dollars paid out by insurance companies.

- Describe who is covered by your insurance plan.

- Explain the rules of the NCAA and other athletic associations as they relate to the availability of different types of care for athletes.

- Describe the process of filing claims in the athletic department of your school.

- Explain the need for liability insurance by athletic trainers.

Key Terms

medical insurance
health insurance
accident
premium
primary coverage
secondary coverage
deductible
self-insurance
exclusion
basic medical insurance
rider
expanded coverage
managed care
fee-for-service
health maintenance organization
gatekeeper
preferred provider organization
point-of-service plan
exclusive provider organization
catastrophic insurance
liability insurance

FOR CRITICAL THOUGHT:
Types of Insurance

Sarah Jackson is in her senior year of college and is a member of the school's fencing team. During the preseason practices, Sarah injured her right foot during a lunge. She immediately went to see the head athletic trainer, Bob White. Bob evaluated Sarah's foot and thought she might have an avulsion fracture at the base of her fifth metatarsal. Bob informed Sarah that she should stop practicing immediately and begin treatments for the injury. He then told her that she should come to the athletic training room the next morning to be seen by Janice Montoya, the team physician.

The next day, Sarah came to the athletic training room and was evaluated by Dr. Montoya, who agreed with Bob's impressions. Dr. Montoya felt that Sarah should obtain an X ray, in order to determine if there was actually an avulsion fracture. Bob then called down to Southeast General Hospital, department of radiation, and informed them that one of his athletes was coming for an X ray; she would have a prescription from Dr. Montoya to have the X ray taken. Bob then had one of his graduate assistants, Li, find Sarah's insurance information from the athletic files, and made a copy. He sent Sarah to the hospital with his graduate. Upon arriving at the hospital, the two went straight to radiology for the X ray. Li gave the insurance information to the receptionist and Sarah was taken right in to have the X ray taken. After the X ray, the two returned to school.

Late that day, Bob received a phone call from Dr. Montoya's office. Dr. Montoya informed Bob that Sarah did indeed have an avulsion fracture and should be casted. Bob had Sarah taken down to Dr. Montoya's office for the application of a short leg cast.

Several weeks later, Sarah received a bill in the mail from the hospital for $20. Her parents' insurance paid 80 percent of the original $100 bill, but 20 percent was not covered. Sarah knew that she was supposed to bring all bills to Bob, so she did. He took the bill, filed the appropriate claim, and submitted it to the university's secondary carrier. Within several months, the claim to the hospital was paid.

What type of insurance did the college have to cover Sarah's injury? If her parents' coverage had been an HMO or PPO, how would the situation have changed?

As the medical cost of participation in athletics has risen, the threat of litigation has increased, and the need to purchase and use accident insurance by athletic departments has increased. The types of coverage are much more variable than those found in a homeowner's or automobile policy,[11] and athletic policies are, therefore, much more individualized. The variables to be considered include: (1) who is covered, (2) what type of plan is used, (3) what are the minimum and maximum limits, (4) what are the deductibles, and (5) what are the claims procedures.

WHO IS COVERED?

Insurance coverage is specific to each athletic program. The more people that are covered, the greater the exposure of the plan and the greater the cost to the purchaser. A study by Lehr[11] found that essentially all athletes were covered by 100 percent of the athletic policies, whereas cheerleaders were covered 69 percent, student managers were covered 61 percent, and student athletic trainers were covered 59 percent of the time, respectively. Lehr also determined that dropping from NCAA Division I to Division II and III produced proportionate decreases in the latter three groups being covered.

TYPES OF INSURANCE PLANS

When determining the type of plan to be used, some definitions must be understood. **Medical insurance** is a policy that will reimburse the policyholder a fixed percentage of the cost of medical services related to illness or injury. **Health insurance** generally covers all that medical insurance covers and also includes preventive care, which medical insurance does not. In the insurance industry, the word **accident** means an injury that results directly from trauma at a specific time and place, independently of all other causes.[11] Illness would be covered by this policy only if it can be proven that the direct cause of the illness was a specific exposure occurring as a result of athletic participation, which is extremely difficult to prove. For all practical purposes, athletic accident policies do not cover illness. **Premium** is the amount of money that the policyholder pays to the insurance company to execute the insurance policy. Premiums for basic and expanded medical coverage are in direct proportion to the number of people covered, the number of total sports offered, the number of high-risk sports offered, deductibles, and primary/secondary designation. **Primary coverage** is also called first dollar coverage. With this type of coverage, all expenses related to an injury are paid by the policy. **Secondary coverage** is a policy that pays all remaining expenses after the use of primary coverage plan.

Primary Coverage Insurance

Primary coverage insurance is coverage in which all expenses related to an injury are paid for by the athletic department's insurance policy. This type of insurance was found in Lehr's study in only 9 percent of intercollegiate athletic programs. There can be high payouts by the insurance carrier because all of the bills are covered, without exception. Because payout and premium are directly related, the most obvious problem with this type of policy is the premium cost. Other insurance plans (parents' plan, student health insurance, etc.) could have paid at least part of a claim, therefore the payout from this type of plan could have been reduced with a secondary coverage plan. The primary advantage of this plan is that usually no **deductible**, or set amount of money that will not be covered by the plan, is involved. Since there is no deductible to meet, as soon as bills are received they can be paid in a timely manner, without waiting for parents (or others) to file with their carrier, and then report the amounts paid and refile with a secondary carrier. Another disadvantage of this type of coverage is that there is often a large amount of paperwork for the local plan administrator, usually a member of the athletic training staff.[16]

Many of those who report being primary carriers are actually self-insured. **Self-insurance** is a type of primary coverage plan in which the institution places the amount of money normally paid as a premium into an escrow account and pays medical expenses directly from that account. Rather than pay a premium to an insurance company, which uses some of the money it receives for administrative expenses, the athletic department pays out from the account as needed. A major disadvantage to this plan is that during a fiscal year of heavy usage, the plan may become exhausted before the year is complete. With an outside insurance company, because the pool of monies is larger, the bills would all be paid one year and the premiums would increase the next year.

Secondary Coverage Insurance

Secondary coverage insurance pays the remaining portions of medical bills after the athlete's primary insurance carrier has made its payment. In Lehr's study,[11] 85 percent of athletic departments in intercollegiate athletics provided this type of plan. A major advantage of the secondary coverage plans is the cost can be as much as 60 percent lower than primary coverage plans. Usually the parents' insurance (or the athlete's) is the primary carrier. In some cases, the university's required student health insurance (if the student is otherwise uninsured) functions as the primary policy. However, some of these plans specifically exclude athletic participation. Many traditional medical plans covering families cover 80 percent of major medical expenses; secondary coverage insurance is a good match for this type of plan. Because most of the medical bills are paid before the athletic department's insurance becomes involved, the payouts are much lower with this type of plan. This leads to decreased cost to the institution. There is more paperwork with secondary coverage insurance because the plan administrator must deal with two (or more) insurance companies. (See figure 9-1.)

Deductibles.   Invariably, secondary coverage insurance involves deductibles. There are three types of deductible: straight, disappearing, and corridor. A straight deductible is a fixed dollar amount that

ATHLETIC DEPARTMENT INSURANCE INFORMATION

<u>PLEASE PRINT</u>

Athlete's Name: _____   SSN: _____ Date of Birth: _____
            Last   First   Middle

School Address: _____   School Phone: _____ Sport: _____

Father/Guardian to complete   ## Mother/Guardian to complete

Name: _____   Name: _____

Address: _____   Address: _____

City: _____ State: _____   City: _____ State: _____

Home Phone: _____ Zip: _____   Home Phone: _____ Zip: _____
        area code   area code

Birthdate: _____ SSN: _____   Birthdate: _____ SSN: _____

Employer: _____   Employer: _____

Address: _____   Address: _____

City: _____ State: _____   City: _____ State: _____

Work Phone: _____ Zip: _____   Work Phone: _____ Zip: _____

Name of Medical Insurance: _____   Name of Medical Insurance: _____

Address: _____   Address: _____

City: _____ State: _____   City: _____ State: _____

Phone #: _____ Zip: _____   Phone #: _____ Zip: _____
      area code   area code

Group Policy Number: _____   Group Policy Number: _____

Group Certificate Number: _____   Group Certificate Number: _____

Is your medical coverage through a Health Maintenance Organization (HMO) or a Preferred Provider Organization (PPO)?

YES: NO: Other: _____ Does it require a second opinion? _____

By signing below, the athlete, and parents/guardians do hereby affirm that they have read and understand the Midwestern State University medical policy and insurance procedures and do acknowledge that the above information is true and accurate. The signatures also authorize Midwestern State University and their insurance agency to inspect or secure copies of case history reports, laboratory reports, diagnoses, X-rays and other data. A photostatic copy of this authorization will be deemed as effective and valid as the original.

Athlete's Signature   Parent/Guardian's Signature   List any policy restrictions:

_____   _____   _____

_____   _____   _____

Figure 9-1   Sample insurance information required from athletes and parents for a university secondary coverage policy

must be paid out of pocket for each contact or procedure. With disappearing deductibles, the deductible must be paid when the primary insurance carrier does not reimburse enough money to cover the cost of the deductible, whereas if the primary reimbursement is greater than the deductible amount, the deductible is waived. This could happen if an athlete went to the emergency room for an X ray that cost $125 and the insurance plan had a $400 disappearing deductible. The $125 would have to be paid out of pocket. Another athlete needed surgery and contracted a $2700 bill under the same policy at the same hospital, but the deductible was waived after the minimum was reached. Corridor deductibles occur when the secondary coverage has a deductible that is not affected by the primary coverage payments. For an athlete with a $31,000 knee surgery covered by both his or her parents' primary coverage and the athletic department's secondary coverage, a corridor deductible would function as follows: The parents' primary coverage insurance would pay its share of the bill, then an amount would not be covered (the secondary insurance plan corridor deductible), followed by the insurance covering the remainder of the claim. Deductibles of these types are negotiable with the insurer; the lower the deductible, the higher the premium cost. Deductibles are routinely seen in athletic insurance from $250 to $2500. Many athletic departments prefer a higher deductible to prevent minor claims being rejected.

Exclusions in Coverage.   An **exclusion** is a situation that is specifically not covered by the insurance policy. A classic exclusion in athletic accident policies is for overuse injuries. In athletic accident terminology, **basic medical insurance** covers injuries sustained during competition, supervised practice, and/or team travel. It does not include nonaccident injuries from that result from sports participation, such as hernia, stress fractures, and various other situations.

Another area of concern is illness. Illnesses are extremely difficult to trace to a single event of practice or competition. Athletes are exposed to many types of illness-causing agents daily. Measles outbreaks have been occurring on college campuses all too often in the past few years. Herpes I is passed readily in wrestling when in a contagious state. The fact that others (wrestling class, karate class, etc.) had access to the wrestling mats and may have introduced the virus could be enough to deny the claim. Hepatitis-B is a dangerous illness that most colleges and universities recommend all students be immunized against before entering school. For this reason alone, hepatitis-B would probably not be covered by an accident policy.

Athletic departments must determine how much they will participate in the risk of payments with athletic accident insurance. They must decide whether they will use basic medical coverage or expanded medical coverage (which is also more expensive). Some basic coverage policies contain a provision that says that without a second opinion, the insurer will only reimburse 50 percent of the benefits they would otherwise pay. In addition, nonaccident injuries from participation in sports are routinely not covered by basic medical coverage. These include problems such as hernia (which many insurance plans define as a preexisting condition present since birth), heat illness, and overuse injuries (tendinitis, bursitis, arthritis, stress fractures, etc.).

One insurance agency refers to illness and nonathletic injury as a gray-area claim that they will pay, but only in the form of a loan to the insured institution. The money is then repaid to the carrier over a set period of time as an increase in the premium. There are problems as well as advantages to this arrangement. If this type of procedure is used and the insured decides to change to another carrier, the entire amount of the loan must be paid off at once. Also, once gray-area claims payments are started, the insured sets a legal precedent that he or she must pay. Should the insured then elect not to pay a claim, the plaintiff may well take the insured to court.

A major point of emphasis with many insurance plans is not covering preexisting conditions. This means an athlete with a documented ACL injury from high school soccer (diagnosed through an MRI and/or arthroscopic surgery) would not be covered for an ACL injury that happened during his or her first soccer practice in college. Rehabilitative braces are covered by some plans and not others, whereas prophylactic bracing is excluded by almost all plans. Finally, injuries away from the athletic arena are not covered. An in-season athlete who is involved in an automobile accident while grocery shopping is not covered for injuries by the athletic accident policy, even though the injuries may keep him or her out of play.

Managing Exclusions. One way to accommodate some exclusions in an insurance policy is to purchase a **rider**. A rider is a clause in which the insurance carrier agrees to add previously excluded situations to the coverage, but for an additional premium. Athletic accident insurance carriers have set up package deals called **expanded coverage**, which include riders for common and significant athletic medical problems that fall outside basic medical insurance. These may include death and dismemberment, and may also address subjects such as reinjury, overuse injuries, stress fractures, and other areas that cannot be identified as having a specific onset.

MANAGED CARE

Managed care has emerged as a result of rising healthcare costs and healthcare reform. This type of health care is a preplanned system that combines the financing and delivery of healthcare services to participating individuals. Under a managed care system, arrangements are made with selected providers to deliver comprehensive healthcare services. The goal of managed care is to contain costs while delivering quality health care.[1,2,3,4,9]

Types of Managed Care Organizations

There are four types of managed care organizations: health maintenance organizations (HMOs), preferred provider organizations (PPOs), point-of-service plans (POS), and exclusive provider organizations (EPOs). Each of these organizations has an established group of providers that members can use. Each also has negotiated a payment to the provider per member, rather than the traditional **fee-for-service** arrangement.[4] The differences between the different types of managed care organizations relate to which providers are included in the network, which providers members may consult,

and provider accountability to the managed care organization for the services provided.[2] Many athletes' primary insurance carrier is now some type of managed care program.

A **health maintenance organization (HMO)** is an organized group of healthcare providers that delivers a defined set of healthcare services to an enrolled population, for a fixed sum of money that is paid in advance, for a specified period of time.[2,5] HMOs offer preventive services and limit where a person can receive care. With the exception of emergencies, permission must be granted before the person can go to another provider. In general, HMOs will pay 100 percent of medical costs, as long as care is rendered at an approved facility.[5] No benefits will be paid if the athlete seeks medical attention from a provider that is not a member of the HMO. HMOs establish a set premium based on an estimate of what it will cost to provide services to the beneficiaries of the plan. The HMO tries to control the utilization of services and costs in a number of ways. The primary way to control costs is by controlling access to care by using what is called a **gatekeeper**, usually a primary care physician. The gatekeeper is assigned by the HMO to oversee the medical care rendered to a patient and initiate all specialty and/or ancillary services, such as lab tests or X rays.[9,15]

HMOs are contracts between an insurance carrier and a group of medical specialists to provide all medical care at a set fee per patient per year. When the patients do not use the services of the medical group often, the HMO makes money. When the patients use a large number of services, the HMO may lose money; therefore there may be pressure on physicians to keep expenses to the plan within set limits. In addition, when a physician refers a patient to another physician, the referral physician then receives the fee for the time the first physician was responsible for the patient's medical care. The advantage to the insured is that all expenses are covered in full when the contracted medical group renders the medical services.

A major disadvantage to athletic trainers in college or university programs is that HMOs generally require that a plan physician deliver medical services. Therefore, an athlete in Toledo, Ohio whose parents participate in an HMO in Houston, Texas, must return to Texas for surgery to repair an unstable shoulder. If the team physician in Toledo performs the surgery, the athlete's insurance carrier, an HMO, will either reject the entire claim or pay only a portion (e.g., 50 percent) of the bill. Because 100 percent of the bill would have been paid if a plan physician in Houston had done the procedure, the secondary coverage plan may also reject all remaining charges on the bill. When the athlete returns home, however, the athletic training staff and team physicians have lost all input and control of the procedures performed, length of rehabilitation prescribed, location of the rehabilitation program, and other variables that will affect the athlete's return to play. Finally, in emergency situations, many HMOs have time limits for informing the HMO of emergency room care, which may be quite short, such as forty-eight hours to one week. If the time limit is missed, then the HMO will reject the claim.

A **preferred provider organization (PPO)** is an organization of healthcare providers contracted to deliver healthcare services to a defined population. Payment to the providers in the PPO is usually discounted fee-for-service. Despite the discounted health care, members are still restricted on whom they can see and what facilities they can use. Members of the PPO will have a list of approved providers they must see if 100 percent of costs are to be covered. If the athlete would like to go to an unapproved provider, he or she will receive less in benefits.[4]

Preferred provider organizations include groups of medical providers who are marketed on a fee-for-services basis (traditional payment to the provider by the insurance company for each service performed); the PPO acts as the middleman between hospitals, physicians, and so forth, and the consumers.[6] By bringing large numbers of consumers together, PPOs may negotiate reduced rates for guaranteed use of the services available. There are definite financial incentives to the consumers to use only those providers who are within the group.

Many HMO and PPO groups will pay only partial amounts for services done outside the approved group. This makes some secondary policies difficult, because the athletic department may want the team physicians to handle a particular medical problem, but the HMO will only pay 100 percent when the services are provided by an approved physician. Some secondary plans will not pay anything when the primary coverage is an HMO (some are excluded by law from doing so). When an expanded benefits plan is in place, the plan may pay for the differences with the HMO when team physicians perform the procedures or when the HMO will only perform certain procedures and the team physician requests other procedures.

A **point-of-service plan (POS)** is a blending of the HMO and PPO. Members receive care provided by network-participating providers, but they have the option of obtaining care outside the network. This type of plan has a core HMO structure, with components of the PPO structure for added flexibility. The POS allows members, under certain circumstances and conditions, to seek care outside the network of providers.[3,4]

In an **exclusive provider organization (EPO)**, a group of providers has a contract with an insurer, employer, third-party administrator, or other sponsor. The provider agrees to a certain level of reimbursement. It also agrees to follow utilization review procedures and have patients admitted only to enrolled hospitals. Unlike PPOs, the EPO provider may be prohibited from treating any patient not enrolled in the organization. Members must seek services from participating providers in order to obtain reimbursement.[2]

Catastrophic Insurance Coverage

Catastrophic insurance refers to coverage of an injury that is so severe that activities of daily living for the patient's age group are permanently compromised. Extended care in a long-term care facility may cost more than $30,000 a year. Comatose and brain-injured individuals may need twenty-four-hour care. Costs for extended care (either in a facility or at home, and covering rehabilitation, medical, and dental expenses), home remodeling, loss of earnings potential, psychological and physical counseling, transportation and counseling for the family, and rehabilitation training of family members would be covered by this plan. The costs incurred include accidental death benefit, extended care (either in a facility or at home), home remodeling costs, loss of future earnings, counseling, and other medical costs that are accrued over and above the maximum of the primary and any secondary policies that may be in force.

All NCAA member institutions participate in the NCAA catastrophic injury plan. The Catastrophic Injury Insurance Program covers student-athletes who are catastrophically injured while participating in a covered intercollegiate athletic activity.[13] Premiums are paid out of the monies the NCAA receives from the Division I men's basketball tournament. The plan has no maximum payout. Premiums are determined by the number of sports offered, number of hazardous sports (defined by the carrier as football (fall), football (spring), gymnastics, wrestling, ice hockey, diving, lacrosse) offered, and the total number of persons covered by the plan. High schools and others participate in other private or public plans, some of which have maximum payout in the $1 million to $10 million range. Most legal professionals will explain that these amounts are inadequate.[11]

Some institutions do not carry catastrophic coverage. When athletic departments inform parents that all of their son or daughter's injury expenses will be covered, this is a potentially costly decision. For example, a shot-put specialist who was struck in the forehead by a sixteen-pound shot during practice survived the injury only to lie in a persistent vegetative state. The institution was not covered by a catastrophic policy. The expenses for this athlete's long-term care are a permanent line item in the athletic department budget as long as the athlete is living.

ATHLETIC ASSOCIATION RULES GOVERNING MEDICAL CLAIMS

The NCAA has a section in its association rules (16.4) that governs permissible medical expenses.[12] This section and subsections allow expenses related to the athletic department's purchase of medical insurance and expenses related to the treatment of athletically related injury. This includes out-of-season voluntary activity that prepares the athlete for competition as of 1992. The section also disallows expenses for illness or injury that was not a result of practice, competition, or voluntary activity preparing the athlete for

competition. The NCAA has no rules that require athletic accident or medical insurance to be purchased, but it does recommend that each student-athlete be covered by individual, parental, or institutional medical insurance, in order to defray the costs of significant injury or illness.[7] The NCAA does offer medical insurance administered through National Sports Underwriters (NSU) in Overland Park, Kansas, which is insured through Lincoln National Health and Casualty Insurance Company in Fort Wayne, Indiana. In addition, the National Association of Collegiate Directors of Athletics, the National Junior College Athletic Association, and the National Association of Intercollegiate Athletics offer plans to their members through NSU and Lincoln National. There are also private plans not affiliated with a sports governing body (First Agency and Baker Agency, both of Kalamazoo, Michigan; Health Special Risk Athletic Underwriters, and Special Insurance Services, Inc., both of Dallas, Texas, among others) that participate in the athletic accident insurance arena. These agencies all advertise, and many are exhibitors at the NATA annual meeting.

The National Federation of State High School Athletic Associations also has no requirement that accident insurance is obtained by high schools. They do not discourage the practice, either. Many school districts will require athletes to have medical insurance as a condition of being allowed to play. Some state high school athletic associations allow the schools to obtain the insurance, others do not. It should be noted, however, that many states also have laws on how public funds may be spent by school districts. Some of these jurisdictions forbid the purchase of athletic medical insurance. The national federation does make available a catastrophic insurance plan to its members; the agent has been National Sports Underwriters, underwritten by Lincoln National in Fort Wayne, Indiana.

CLAIMS PROCEDURE

In athletic departments, athletic accident insurance claims are best done as a joint venture with the claims agency and the college or university (see figure 9-2). It is most helpful if only one person at the athletic department handles claims paperwork and

Underwritten by: GUARANTEE TRUST LIFE INSURANCE COMPANY, Glenview, Illinois

Administered by:

B THE
AKER AGENCY, INC.
338 W. Allegan St.
Otsego, MI 49078

**STATEMENT OF CLAIM FOR
ACCIDENT INSURANCE**

MAIL COMPLETED CLAIM FORMS, BILLS,
EXPLANATION OF BENEFITS STATEMENTS
AND ALL OTHER CLAIM CORRESPONDENCE
TO THE BAKER AGENCY, INC.

SCHOOL OFFICIAL TO COMPLETE

SCHOOL DISTRICT: _____

INDIVIDUAL SCHOOL NAME: _____

1. Name of Student: (last) _____ (first) _____ (int.) _____
2. SOCIAL SECURITY NUMBER _____ 3. BIRTH DATE _____ 4. SEX   M   F
5. HOME ADDRESS (street) _____
   (city) _____ (state) _____ (zip code) _____
6. ACCIDENT DATE Month _____ Day _____ Year _____ HOUR _____ AM ___ PM ___
7. NAME OF SPORT _____ NAME OF ACTIVITY _____
8. TYPE OF ATHLETIC ACTIVITY _____ Intercollegiate _____ Interscholastic ___Grade _____
9. INJURED BODY PART _____ Right _____ Left _____
10. DESCRIBE IN **COMPLETE** DETAIL HOW AND WHERE ACCIDENT OCCURRED _____

    _____

11. SIGNATURE OF AUTHORIZED OFFICIAL _____ DATE _____
    TITLE _____

ATTENDING PHYSICIAN'S AND/OR DENTIST'S STATEMENT

1. PATIENT'S NAME _____ AGE _____ SEX   M   F
2. NATURE AND EXTENT OF INJURIES - DESCRIBE COMPLICATIONS, IF ANY, AND GIVE FINAL DIAGNOSIS:

   _____

   _____

3. DATE OF ACCIDENT _____
4. WHEN, WHERE AND HOW DO YOU UNDERSTAND THE INJURY OCCURRED? _____

   _____

5. DATE YOU FIRST TREATED PATIENT FOR THIS INJURY _____
6. HAS PATIENT PREVIOUSLY BEEN TROUBLED WITH THIS CONDITION? (when)_____

   _____

7. IF PATIENT REFERRED BY OTHER DOCTOR, GIVE NAME AND COMPLETE ADDRESS OF SUCH DOCTOR _____

   _____

8. IS PATIENT STILL UNDER YOUR CARE FOR THIS INJURY? WHAT FURTHER TREATMENT, IF ANY, WILL BE NECESSARY?

   _____

· If you feel that copies of your office notes will assist our office in processing this claim, please feel free to forward them to our office. Please note no payments for these copies will be issued.

An itemized statement cannot be used in place of completing this portion of the claim form.

DOCTOR - DENTIST _____

NAME (Type or Print): _____ SIGNATURE: _____

ADDRESS: _____ DATE: _____

CITY: _____ STATE: _____ ZIP CODE: _____

TELEPHONE #: (   ) _____ FEDERAL TAXPAYERS ID OR SS# _____

Figure 9-2   Sample physician's and dentist's forms to complete when validating an insurance claim (*Continued*)
(*Reprinted with permission of The Baker Agency, Inc.*)

This coverage is **EXCESS** designed to consider balances only after all other valid and collectible insurance pay their maximum benefits first and if no other coverage to consider any medical expenses **incurred within one year from the date of accident,** according to the policy provisions held by the school. Treatment must begin within 60 days from the date of the injury by a legally qualified, licensed physician, surgeon or dentist, (not a member of the insured's immediate family).

This is an accident insurance policy. This policy does not pay for treatment rendered due to an illness, diseases, degenerative injuries, conditions caused by continued stress to a particular area of the body and existing condition aggravated or exacerbated by an accident.

PLEASE BE SURE TO COMPLETE THE FOLLOWING INSTRUCTIONS TO HELP ELIMINATE DELAYS IN CLAIM PROCESSING:

I. Be sure claim form is completed in **full.**

II. Submit medical expenses to your insurance company or plan administrator FIRST. A copy of your insurance company's determination of benefits paid or denied is required.
IF YOU ARE A MEMBER OF AN HMO OR PPO, YOU MUST FOLLOW THE PROPER PROCEDURES REQUIRED BY YOUR PLAN.

III. If you are employed and no coverage is provided by your employer or the dependent is not covered by the employer plan, a letter of verification must be obtained from your employer stating this.

IV. If no insurance is provided through either employer or if you are self employed, you must submit a notarized letter verifying that you do not carry any private nor individual insurance coverage on your child.

V. Return the **completed** claim form, copies of all **itemized bills** and any insurance information to The Baker Agency, Inc., unless advised otherwise.

PARENT TO COMPLETE

1. CLAIMANT'S NAME (last) _____ (first) _____ (int.) _____
2. CLAIMANT'S FATHER _____ Phone No. ( ) _____
   (street) _____ Social Security No. _____
   (city) _____ (state) _____ (zip code) _____
3. **FATHER'S EMPLOYER** _____ Phone No. ( ) _____
4. DO YOU HAVE GROUP MEDICAL COVERAGE THROUGH YOUR EMPLOYER?___ yes ___ no
   If no or your dependent is not covered, you must submit a letter from your employer to this effect.
5. NAME OF INSURANCE COMPANY _____ Phone No. ( ) _____
6. ADDRESS OF INSURANCE COMPANY _____
7. POLICY NO. _____ GROUP NO. _____
8. CLAIMANT'S MOTHER _____ Phone No. ( ) _____
9. (street) _____ Social Security No. _____
10. (city) _____ (state) _____ (zip code) _____
11. **MOTHER'S EMPLOYER** _____ Phone No. ( ) _____
12. DO YOU HAVE GROUP MEDICAL COVERAGE THROUGH YOUR EMPLOYER? ____ yes ____ no
    If no or your dependent is not covered, you must submit a letter from your employer to this effect.
13. NAME OF INSURANCE COMPANY _____ Phone No. ( ) _____
14. ADDRESS OF INSURANCE COMPANY _____
15. POLICY NO. _____ GROUP NO. _____
16. DO YOU AS **INDIVIDUALS** CARRY ACCIDENT OR HOSPITAL INSURANCE TO COVER THIS CLAIMANT?
    _____ yes ___ no
    If no and your employer(s) does not provide insurance coverage, you must submit a notarized letter to this effect.
17. NAME AND COMPLETE ADDRESS OF PHYSICIAN WHO FIRST TREATED CLAIMANT FOR THIS CONDITION
    _____
18. HAS CLAIMANT PREVIOUSLY BEEN TROUBLED WITH THIS CONDITION? (when) _____

AUTHORIZATION TO OBTAIN INFORMATION
I hereby authorize The Baker Agency, Inc. or its representatives to inspect or secure copies of case-history records, laboratory reports, diagnosis, prognosis, x-ray and any other data covering this/previous confinements/disabilities. A photostatic copy of this authorization shall be deemed as effective and valid as the original. Drafts for benefits will automatically be sent to the hospital, doctor, or other supplier of medical services.

SIGNATURE OF CLAIMANT: _____ DATE: _____

SIGNATURE OF PARENT/GUARDIAN: _____ DATE: _____
FAILURE TO COMPLETE THIS FORM IN FULL MAY RESULT IN AN UNNECESSARY DELAY IN THE PROCESSING OF THIS CLAIM.

(continued)

Figure 9-2 Sample physician's and dentist's forms to complete when validating an insurance claim

Student's Name _____

School/College _____

ATTENDING PHYSICIAN'S AND/OR DENTIST'S STATEMENT-

This Statement MUST be Completed
With an Itemized Statement Attached

EACH DOCTOR'S BILL ATTACHED MUST BEAR DOCTOR'S I.D. OR SOCIAL SECURITY NUMBER.

1. Patient's Name	
	Age _____ Sex _____
2. Nature and Extent of Injuries (Describe complications, if any) Final Diagnosis	
3. Date of Accident	Date _____ ,20 __
4. When, Where and How do You Understand the Injury Occurred?	
5. Date you First Treated Patient for this Injury	Date _____ ,20 __
6. Describe any other disease or infirmity affecting present condition	
7. If fracture or dislocation, state whether reduced or immobilized. If fracture of long bones, state whether fracture is through shaft or extremity. Was confirmed by x-ray?	Reduction (__) Immobilization Without Reduction (__) (Check one) Yes _____ No _____ (Check one)
8. Nature of Surgical Procedure, if any (Describe fully) Where and When Performed?	Date _____ If at hospital, as inpatient _____ or outpatient _____
9. If patient hospitalized, give name and address of hospital	Admitted _____ ,20 ____ Discharged _____ ,20 ____
10. If patient referred by other doctor, give name and address of such doctor.	
11. Is patient still under your care for this injury? If discharged, give date. If not, What Further Treatment, if any, will be Necessary?	Yes _____ No _____ (Check one) Date _____ ,20 ____
12. Did you file this claim with other Insurance Company or plan. If yes, indicate name and address of Company or administrator. What payments have been received or are anticipated from any other Company or Administrator?	Yes _____ No _____ (Check one) INSURANCE CO./PLAN NAME/ADDRESS: _____ _____ _____ $ _____

IF DENTISTRY, ANSWER ALL QUESTIONS ABOVE, IN ADDITION TO THOSE BELOW

State Exactly Which Teeth Were Involved in the
Accident and Indicate Them on Chart _____

Describe Condition of Injured Teeth Prior to Accident
☐ Whole, Sound and Natural   ☐ Filled   ☐ Capped   ☐ Artificial

DOCTOR - DENTIST
NAME (TYPE OR PRINT): _____ SIGNATURE: _____
ADDRESS: _____ DATE: _____ ,20 _____
CITY: _____ STATE: _____ ZIP CODE: _____ PHONE#: ( ) _____

I.D. or S.S. No. _____ Must be filled in.

Figure 9-2   Sample physician's and dentist's forms to complete when validating an insurance claim (*Concluded*)

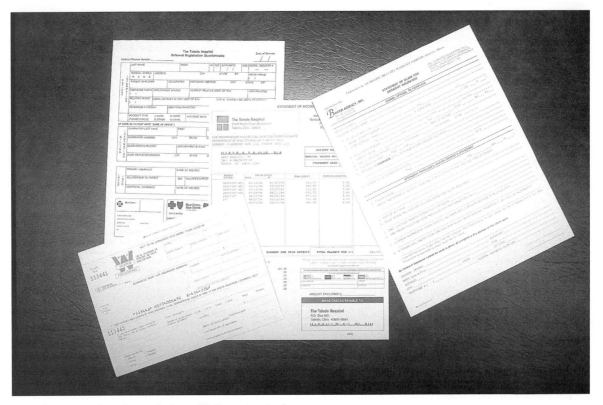

Claim forms must be submitted when all bills are received.

that person develops a good relationship with the adjuster handling that institution for the insurance company. The athletic department administrator needs to send a letter to all parents and athletes explaining the coverage and claims procedures and requesting pertinent information, including authorization to transmit medical records to the insurance carrier for purposes of evaluation of claims and payment of bills that are due. If the claims information sheet and the information form are sent to the parents together, the receipt of a signed information form by the athletic trainer is probably considered legal notification of the parents of the claims procedure. It is helpful if bills are in both the parents' and athlete's names. Special note must be taken of everyone covered by managed-care–type insurance.

It is helpful to arrange for particular providers to participate in cost savings with a program. One way may be for the team orthopedic surgeon to agree to accept payment from the athlete's insurance as payment in full and to not bill the athletic department insurance, even if the athlete may be uninsured. Another way is for the athletic department to contract directly with a provider to receive a per-patient charge in advance rather than a fee for services as rendered (HMO-type arrangement).[10]

Care must be taken that claims are submitted on time. Many athletic insurance secondary coverage plans have from one to three years to complete the claim. The athletic department administrator must work closely with parents to see that bills are submitted on time and are complete. In addition, changes in insurance status (due to unemployment, employment changes, company changes, insurance company finances, etc.) will affect the paying of bills in a timely manner. If a person stops his or her insurance, the insurance will not cover anything that happens after the date of termination, although most will pay off previous claims provided they are submitted in a timely manner. Most companies have a one-to three-year limit on claims. If it is not possible to submit all of the bills within the time allowed, many companies will extend if an initial claim is prepared and submitted within that time frame with an estimate of cost. The problem for the insurance companies is being able to get accurate factual data to set the next year's premiums.

When a claim needs to be filed with the secondary coverage carrier, the athletic department must acquire copies of all bills from the physicians, hospital, clinic, and allied health professionals that were involved. In addition, the athletic department must obtain from the athlete or the athlete's parents a copy of the insurance payout form from their primary coverage carrier stating how much was paid on the claim and to whom it was paid. All of this information is then transmitted to the claims agent, along with a claim request form for processing.

A unique way in which to facilitate claims procedures is to create your own HMO. Richard Ray[15] presents a three-step approach to devising a simple method that athletic trainers can use in their own situations. The first step is to develop a contract between the school and the athlete. This contract should inform the athlete and his or her parents what medical services will be provided by the school, the conditions under which those services will be rendered, and the limits to which those services will be paid for by the school. This is usually done at the start of each school year with a letter home describing athletic training services. The second step is to adopt the school's secondary insurance carrier's policies as your own. This will help you and your institution control costs if you only accept financial responsibility for those injuries and conditions normally paid for by your secondary insurance provider. The last step is to act as your own gatekeeper. The gatekeeper for your program may be the head athletic trainer or the team physician. This person makes decisions about referral for specialized services and procedures. The more services that can be provided in-house the better to help defer yearly medical costs and insurance payouts.[15]

CONSIDERATIONS WHEN PURCHASING INSURANCE

When selecting an insurance agency, there are some points to consider. It is important to have a face-to-face meeting with the agent at least once a year. This makes the athletic department aware of changes that happen each year. The athletic department should also receive a written report each year with claims data for its institution compared with other institutions. It is helpful if a local agency or agent handles claims rather than the home office of the insurance carrier. Having a checkbook at the institution for small claims (e.g., up to $250) that do not require claim forms is helpful when dealing with vendors. Finally, the agency should have experience dealing with intercollegiate or interscholastic sports. The best agency is one that deals in this area exclusively.[8]

Premium rates for insurance policies can vary widely with similar coverages, partly because of the amount of use the policy receives and partly because of the usual, customary, and reasonable (UCR) charges for services rendered. The basis for the UCR is a combination of the usual fee charged for a service, the customary fee charged in a particular geographic area, and the reasonable fee (usually the lower of the other two). One insurance company adjustor suggested that a geographic area could be anywhere from one to ten zip codes.

In general, premium rates are set on the concept that 60 to 75 percent of the premium will be paid to healthcare providers, with the remainder (25 to 40 percent) paying for administrative costs, agent's commission, claims agent's salary, and so forth. Premium rates will change year by year. In a study conducted by Street et al,[16] it was found that 20 percent of NCAA schools had insurance premiums falling between $10,000 and $20,000 a year. Additionally, 15 percent of schools had premiums between $30,000 and $40,000 a year, and 14 percent had premiums either between $0 and $10,000, $20,000 and $30,000, or over $70,000 a year. Some NCAA Division I programs have insurance premiums ranging from $25,000 to well over $150,000 per year.[14]

It is interesting to note that the highest month of payouts by the insurance industry is February due to the postseason football surgeries and time required to collect and submit the bills from these procedures. The second most active month is June (spring football). It is also interesting to note that in 1990 the average dollar payout for an open-cut knee surgery was approximately $13,700, whereas in 1993 that figure had increased to $17,500 (slightly more than 10 percent per year).[8]

There are two things that must be remembered about athletic medical insurance. First, it is not possible to predict who is going to get hurt. Second, even with all of the data available, it is not possible to predict the coverage in force by the primary insurance carrier on the day of the injury.

LIABILITY INSURANCE

In today's climate of litigation, protecting the personal assets of an athletic trainer takes on a very real meaning. In almost all jurisdictions, athletic trainers may not be sued for malpractice, but they may be sued for tort liability actions, usually negligence. (See chapter 15, "Risk Management," for a discussion of medical malpractice.) Many sports medicine clinics will require **liability insurance** as a precursor to employment. Some will pay the premium costs for employees after they have been hired. Most colleges or universities and high schools do not pay the premiums, but they strongly recommend the athletic trainer obtain coverage. Many athletic trainers who work for public institutions are covered by the institution's liability insurance or by governmental immunity. In many jurisdictions, governmental immunity is being defined by the courts to protect the institution rather than the individual. In addition, most institution liability policies do not deal with medical liability awards, which can cost millions of dollars. Most institution liability coverage is in the $100,000 to $200,000 range.

The National Athletic Trainers' Association offers a group liability policy that provides $2 million per incident/$4 million per year for all incidents. It includes legal fees and court costs in addition to the policy limits. Restrictions of the policy include driving a motor vehicle, functioning as another medical specialist, engaging in a business outside professional duties, or taking unlawful actions. The last point, unlawful action, is important. If an athletic trainer is sued for negligence in a civil case brought by a plaintiff, he or she is covered by his or her liability insurance. If, however, the case is a civil case brought in conjunction with a criminal complaint against the athletic trainer for practicing medicine without a license, or for violation of state or federal pharmacy laws, and the athletic trainer is found guilty on the criminal charge, then his or her liability insurance will *not* cover the actions.

For an overview of insurance types and terms, see box 9-1.

■ **Glossary of Insurance Terms**   *Box 9-1*

Types of Insurance

Accident insurance—a type of insurance that covers accidents on school grounds, while the student is in attendance; protects the institution against financial loss from medical and hospital bills.

Basic medical insurance—covers injuries sustained during competition, supervised practice, and/or team travel; does not include nonaccident injuries from participation in sports such as hernia, stress fractures, and various other situations.

Catastrophic insurance—a type of policy provided by organizations such as the NCAA; assists in the cost of long-term health care after catastrophic injury.

Glossary of Insurance Terms   *Box 9-1 (continued)*

Errors and omissions liability insurance—a type of insurance designed to protect school employees, officers, and the district against suits claiming malpractice, wrongful actions, errors and omissions, and acts of negligence; helps to cover what is not covered by a general liability policy.

General health insurance—a policy that covers preventive care, illness, hospitalization, and emergency care.

Indemnity policy—traditional health insurance that is paid by an individual's employer; also known as *fee-for-service*.

Medical insurance—a policy that will reimburse the policyholder a fixed percentage of the cost of medical services related to illness or injury.

Professional liability insurance—a type of insurance that covers claims of negligence on the part of individuals.

Types of Coverage

Primary coverage—also referred to as first dollar coverage; all expenses related to an injury are paid by the policy.

Self-insurance—a type of primary coverage plan in which the institution places the amount of money normally paid as a premium into an escrow account and pays medical expenses directly from that account.

Secondary coverage—a policy used after a primary coverage plan has made payment, in which all remaining expenses are paid.

Managed Care Terms

Capitation—a form of reimbursement used by managed care organizations in which the provider is paid a set fee per member in a predetermined period of time; not based on types or number of services provided.

Gatekeeper—the primary care physician assigned by the insurer who oversees the medical care rendered to a patient and initiates all specialty and ancillary services.

Managed care—preplanned delivery system of health care; integrates the financing and delivery of healthcare services to participating individuals.

Participating provider—a health care provider who has entered into a contract with an insurance company to provide medical services to the beneficiaries of a plan. The provider agrees to accept the insurance company's approved fee and will only bill the patient for the deductible, copayment, and uncovered services.

Third-party administrator—an independent organization that collects premiums, pays claims, and provides administrative services within a healthcare plan.

Types of Managed Care Organizations

Health maintenance organization (HMO)—an organized group of healthcare providers who deliver a predefined set of services to an enrolled population; traditionally limits the choice of providers to a specific network.

■ **Glossary of Insurance Terms**   *Box 9-1 (concluded)*

Preferred provider organization (PPO)—an organized group of healthcare providers contracted to deliver services to a defined population; members may utilize other providers for an increased fee or copayment.

Exclusive provider organization (EPO)—a group of providers who contract with an insurer or employer to provide services at a prenegotiated cost; provider may be prohibited from treating anyone not enrolled in the organization.

Point-of-service plan (POS)—a combination between HMO and PPO; members receive care provided by participating members, but, under certain conditions, have the option to seek care outside the network.

Other Important Terms

Accident—an injury that results directly from trauma at a specific time and place and independently of all other causes.

Copayment—a provision in an insurance policy requiring the policyholder to pay a specified percentage of each medical claim.

Deductible—the amount owed by the insured on a yearly basis before the insurance company will begin to pay for services rendered.

Dependent—a person legally eligible for benefits based on his or her relationship with the policyholder.

Exclusion—specified medical services, disorders, treatments, diseases, and durable medical equipment that is specifically not covered by the insurance policy.

Expanded coverage—additional coverages, including riders for common and significant athletic medical problems that fall outside basic medical insurance.

Fee-for-service—(see *indemnity plan*); the traditional form of healthcare provider billing whereby the provider charges the patient and/or payer based on a fee schedule.

Policyholder—the person who takes out the medical insurance policy.

Premium—the amount of money the policyholder pays to the insurance company to execute the insurance policy.

Rider—a clause in which the insurance carrier agrees to add previously excluded situations to the coverage, but for an additional premium.

Summary

1. Several types of insurance coverage exist, including primary and secondary plans.
2. Primary coverage insurance is coverage in which all expenses related to an injury are paid for by the athletic department's insurance policy.
3. Secondary coverage pays the remaining portions of medical bills after the primary insurance has made its payment.
4. Some insurance policies exclude coverage for certain illnesses, injuries, or conditions.
5. Riders or expanded coverage policies are two ways to manage exclusions.
6. Managed care is a system of health care designed to contain costs while delivering quality health care.
7. There are four types of managed care organizations: health maintenance organizations (HMOs), preferred provider organizations (PPOs), point-of-service (POS) plans, and exclusive provider organizations (EPOs).

8. Catastrophic insurance refers to coverage of an injury that is so severe that activities of daily living are permanently compromised.
9. The NCAA and NFSHAA do not require that athletic accident or medical insurance be purchased, but strongly recommend it.
10. Insurance claims are a joint venture between the athletic department and the insurance provider. The person on the athletic training staff responsible for this must have diligent records, good communication skills, and a comprehensive knowledge of the insurance policy.
11. Premium rates for insurance plans vary widely and will change year by year.
12. Athletic trainers should protect themselves from negligence lawsuits by purchasing liability insurance.

For Critical Thought

The college insurance plan was a secondary coverage policy. That means the college's insurance will pay for coverage that is in excess of the primary carrier, Sarah's parents' insurance. If Sarah had been covered by an HMO or PPO, she would have been obligated to return to her plan physician for evaluation and treatment. This could add substantial time to the prognosis for this injury. In addition, the treatments may not have been what Sarah's team physician had in mind. All rehabilitation may have to be done in plan facilities.

Websites

Maginnis and Associates Professional Liability Insurance:
http://www.maginnis-ins.com

This site describes the services by Maginnis and Associates. Maginnis is the administrator of the NATA's group professional liability policy.

Healthcare Providers Service Organization:
http://www.hpso.com

This website describes the insurance coverage provided by HPSO. This organization provides malpractice and liability insurance to over seventy healthcare professions.

National Collegiate Athletic Association:
http://www.ncaa.org

This is the home page of the NCAA. From the home page, the sports medicine handbook can be accessed, as well as information about the catastrophic insurance policy.

Applications for Consideration

1. Sonya Thompson is the head athletic trainer at Northwest College. Sonya just got hired in this position and would like to set up her own school-based HMO. What things must she consider? Who does she need to contact and develop relationships with? How can she convince the administration that this will be a cost-effective way of dealing with medical bills?
2. Davon Jackson is the head athletic trainer and insurance administrator at an NAIA Division II institution in Buttsville, MI. One of his gymnasts, Tony Peppitti, has been having lower leg pain for the past three weeks, despite conservative treatments. Tony's parents have an HMO, but live in New York. What does Davon need to do to help Tony get seen by a physician? What other concerns might you have knowing that this might be an overuse injury?

References

1 Albohm, M. Health care delivery and the athletic trainer. *NATA News.* (May): 28, 1996.

2 Albohm, MJ. The health care delivery system. In Konin, JG, ed. *Clinical athletic training.* Thorofare, NJ; Slack, Inc., 35–41, 1997.

3 Albohm, MJ. The health care delivery system and the ever-changing marketplace. *Proceedings from the National Athletic Trainers' Association 49th Annual Meeting and Clinical Symposia.* Champaign, IL: Human Kinetics, 22–24, 1998.

4 Anderson, E. Managed care terminology. *NATA News.* (September): 12–13, 1995.

5 Arnheim, DD, Prentice, WE. *Principles of athletic training.* Dubuque, IA: McGraw-Hill, 66–73, 2000.

6 Barger, SB, Hillman, DG, Garland, HR. *The PPO handbook.* Rockville, MD: Aspen Systems Corporation, 1985.

7 Benson, MT. ed. *1999–2000 NCAA sports medicine handbook.* Overland Park, KS: NCAA, 1999.

8 Cronen, L. Creation of athletic insurance programs and policies. Presented at the 41st Annual NATA Clinical Symposium and Workshop, Indianapolis, IN, June 12, 1990.

9 DeCarlo, MS. Reimbursement for health care services. In Konin, JG. *Clinical athletic training.* Thorofare, NJ: Slack, Inc., 89–104, 1997.

10 Entriken, J, Sacco, RM. Managing your collegiate managed care student athlete. *Proceedings from the National Athletic Trainers' Association 50th Annual Meeting and Clinical Symposia.* Champaign, IL: Human Kinetics, 292–294, 1999.

11 Lehr, C. Status of medical insurance provided to student athletes at NCAA schools. *Journal of Legal Aspects of Sports.* 2:12–22, 1992.

12 NCAA Manual, 1994–1995. Overland Park, KS: NCAA.

13 NCAA Catastrophic Injury Insurance Program. URL: www.ncaa.org/insurance/catastrophic.html

14 Rankin, JM. Financial resources for conducting athletic training programs in the collegiate and high school settings. *Journal of Athletic Training,* 27:344–349, 1992.

15 Ray, R. Create your own HMO. *Athletic Therapy Today,* 1(4):11–12, 1996.

16 Street, SS, Yates, CS, Lavery, ES, Lavery, KM. Athletic medical insurance practices at NCAA Division I institutions. *Journal of Athletic Training,* 29:9–13, 1994.

CHAPTER 10

Third-Party Reimbursement

After reading this chapter, you should be able to:

- Describe the types of managed care organizations.

- Describe reimbursement codes.

- Explain the process of filing a claim for third-party reimbursement.

- Explain the importance of third-party reimbursement for athletic trainers.

Key Terms

managed care organization
Current Procedural Terminology (CPT) codes
Universal Billing (UB) codes
International Classification of Disease (ICD) codes

FOR CRITICAL THOUGHT:
No Pay, No Stay!

Patricia Anthony was hired by a sports medicine clinic to provide outreach services to a high school and to work in the clinic in the morning. The clinic assumed that referrals from Patricia's high school would cover her salary. After one year, it was clear that this was not going to work. The clinic administrators quickly found out that referrals from the athletic trainer placed at high school would never be enough to cover her salary and benefits.

The clinic administrators decided that Patricia must be allowed to bill for third-party reimbursement in order to remain employed. They approached Patricia and said, "you must either earn your salary and benefits by billing for your services or we will have to let you go." Patricia really liked her job at the clinic and the community she lived in. She wanted to keep this job if at all possible. In order to do so, she had to find a way to make money for the clinic.

She decided to investigate whether or not she could bill for her services. She approached the HMO with which the group was contracted and asked about billing for her services. They asked her if she was licensed by the state to provide the services that she intended to bill for. She said she was. They said they did not see a problem. Next, she scheduled an appointment with the billing department at the clinic. She shared her conversation with the HMO officials and asked how she could become involved with billing for third-party reimbursement. She learned about how they processed the bills, the documentation that they used, and thought about how she could work herself into the system. She thought about what services she could bill for. She decided that general tasks performed at the high school, such as taping and bandaging, would not be billable items. She determined that injury evaluations and rehabilitation services could be billed.

She and the clinic administrators met with high school officials to explain that they could not continue to provide Patricia's services unless they were able to bill for her services. They explained that they would not bill the high school, but rather they would bill parents' insurance. They would only require the dollars recovered from the insurance companies and agreed not to pursue balances owed by the parents. In other words, they agreed they would not require out-of-pocket expenses from the parents. High school officials were willing to pursue this as an experiment. Patricia had to have some further discussions with the HMO to determine if the facilities at the high school were an appropriate place to provide service.

In today's health care environment, it is imperative that healthcare providers be able to bill for their services. It is difficult to retain personnel in times of financial strain when they cannot document their value, in dollars and cents, to their employers. The ability to bill for services also generates respect among other healthcare professions. The ability to bill for services is important in all athletic training settings. Its importance is apparent in clinical and hospital settings, but it may also be useful in college/university and high school settings, where maintaining the appropriate level of athletic

training services may only be possible if athletic trainers can generate income. This income may be necessary to pay salaries, purchase equipment or supplies, or cover other expenses incurred. Consequently, athletic trainers must understand the process of third-party reimbursement.

ATHLETIC TRAINERS AND THIRD-PARTY REIMBURSEMENT

Athletic trainers can bill for their services. It may be more difficult for athletic trainers than for other healthcare providers because there are no specific codes for athletic training services. The absence of athletic training codes does not mean that athletic trainers cannot bill, but it does present some challenges. Many third-party payers are not familiar with athletic trainers. This, coupled with the fact that athletic training practice is not protected by licensure in all states, makes it necessary for the athletic trainer to demonstrate his or her worthiness for reimbursement. It is certain that athletic trainers will not receive compensation for their services if they do not submit a bill for reimbursement. The worst thing that can happen when submitting a claim is that it will be rejected. Claims may be rejected for many reasons (table 10-1). Most of these reasons apply to all healthcare professionals. Athletic trainers may initially have claims rejected because the providers are unfamiliar with the profession of athletic training. This typically does not happen for professionals in older, more established allied healthcare professions. Once the payer becomes familiar with athletic training, then this problem ceases to exist.

Payers may ask for any of the following when determining whether athletic training services should be reimbursed: (1) Is athletic training practice regulated by the state? (2) Is this service you provided within your scope of practice? (3) If athletic training is not regulated by the state, is there a national credential, such as certification, that would describe your training? (4) Are you providing a service within the scope of your certification? Providing additional information about your educational preparation may be helpful. Documenting the

■ **TABLE 10-1** Most Common Reasons for Claim Denial

Category	Description
Appropriateness	Inappropriate service rendered
	Unnecessary service rendered
	Treatment not matching physician's orders
	No precertification
	Lack of progress of patient
Completeness	Improper forms
	Lack of clear description of progress
	Lack of client information
	Poor note quality
	Illegible documentation
	Improper coding
	Incomplete forms and documentation
	No physician referral
Timeliness	Treatment administered too soon
	Tardy documentation
	Late filing of claim
	Outdated prescriptions
	Excessively long duration of care
Compliance	No home program established or followed
	Unrealistic goals
	Nonfunctional goals
	Unsafe delivery of services
	Not following third-party guidelines
	Patient noncompliance
	Lack of progress
	Lack of reevaluations
	Patient absence of treatment sessions

Adapted from Konin[2]

success and value of athletic training services, as with published outcomes data,[1] may also help to persuade payers.

WHAT IS A THIRD-PARTY PAYER?

Third-party payers pay for some or all of the healthcare services rendered by a healthcare provider in the event of an insured's illness or accident. The first party is the patient, the second party is the healthcare provider, and the insurer is the third party. The insurer is often a managed care organization (MCO).

MANAGED CARE ORGANIZATIONS

Managed care organizations (MCOs) are designed to provide consumers with access to appropriate healthcare at a reasonable cost while controlling healthcare spending. MCOs study healthcare services and eliminate those that are unnecessary, unproven, or not cost effective. They also focus on preventative healthcare services.

As was discussed in chapter 9, there are four basic types of managed care organizations: health maintenance organizations (HMOs), preferred provider organizations (PPOs), exclusive provider organizations (EPOs), and point-of-service plans (POSs).[3]

HMOs

There are five basic models for HMOs: the staff or closed-panel model, the group model, the network model, the independent practice association or open-panel model, and the individual provider model.

In a staff model or a closed-panel HMO, the HMO directly employs the healthcare providers. This means that these healthcare providers treat only patients enrolled in the HMO. A group model is one in which the HMO contracts with a multispecialty group to provide services. This group may treat patients enrolled in the HMO as well as other patients.

The network model is just like the group model except several provider groups render care rather than just one. An independent practice association model or open-panel model is one in which providers belong to an independent association that negotiates a contract with the HMO.

The individual provider model is similar to the independent practice association model except that contracts are made with individual healthcare providers. HMOs are unique in that providers are guaranteed a predetermined dollar amount for each member in the plan regardless of whether they actually treat them. This concept is called prepaid healthcare or capitation.

PPOs

In PPOs, purchasers of healthcare services choose organizations of providers to provide healthcare services for their covered individuals. PPOs are like closed-panel HMOs in that providers treat only patients enrolled in the plan. PPOs also actively negotiate discounted rates for individuals in their plan. PPOs also allow choice of provider, but if a non-PPO provider is selected, the amount of services covered is reduced.

EPOs

EPOs are structured the same as PPOs, except if an outside provider is used, the patient must cover the entire cost of the care.

POS Plans

A POS plan is similar to a PPO except in the way the provider is reimbursed. When a person steps outside the closed panel of providers in the POS plan, the payment reverts to a fee-for-service method, and a larger percentage of the total cost is left to the covered individual. Despite the fact that POS plans require greater out-of-pocket expenses from covered individuals, they are gaining in popularity.

Some larger corporations have explored direct contracting of healthcare providers because of their dissatisfaction with MCOs. Their dissatisfaction stems from the perception that MCOs, not healthcare providers, are making medical decisions about patient care. Some MCOs have begun exploring methods of returning care decisions to healthcare providers.

REIMBURSEMENT CODES

In order to receive reimbursement for services, two basic types of information must be conveyed. First, the treatment rendered must be provided. This denotes the actual service provided. Second, codes representing the diagnosis of the problem must be presented. Coding systems for treatments rendered include Current Procedural Terminology (CPT) codes and Universal Billing (UB) codes. The International Classification of Disease (ICD) codes are used to denote the patient's diagnosis.

CPT Codes

Current Procedural Terminology (CPT) codes are developed by the American Medical Association Department of Coding and Nomenclature. A "provider," as defined in CPT codes, is anyone who is licensed to provide services. Further, the term "therapist" is meant to be a generic term and refers to no specific profession. CPT codes are for all healthcare providers to use to obtain third-party reimbursement. CPT codes are five-digit codes that represent the treatment provided (see chapter 9).

UB Codes

Universal Billing (UB) codes are similar to CPT codes in that they are used to describe the services provided. UB codes are used in hospitals to bill for healthcare services provided. A national UB Coding Committee establishes UB codes.

ICD Codes

International Classification of Disease (ICD) codes tell insurance companies what was wrong with the patient. Any services provided for that condition would use the same ICD code, even though CPT or UB codes would differ from different healthcare providers. Third-party payers may also use the ICD code to determine the appropriateness of treatments rendered.

Understanding Coding Systems

It is imperative that standard codes be understood and used properly. Different codes may be used for different payers. Typically, CPT and UB codes are used to describe the service provided and ICD codes are used to describe the condition. Improper use of these codes will delay reimbursement or possibly result in nonreimbursement.

Preparing Documentation

Properly prepared documentation may be the most important factor in successful reimbursement. Documents should be developed that provide accurate and comprehensive information about the patient's condition and treatment according to the policies and procedures set forth by the third-party payer. Many healthcare facilities develop their own forms to collect this information. Ideally, institutional forms should collect all of the information needed by the third-party payers usually encountered. Essential forms that should be used include a patient registration form, a patient encounter form, a daily journal, an individual patient accounts form, a treatment note, and insurance claims forms.

Filing the Claim

First, you must determine whether the patient or the provider (clinician) will file the claim. Call the provider relations department of the health plan to determine if you must first be assigned a provider number. They will be able to tell you what you need to do to file a claim. Review the patient's policy to see if the services provided are covered. Ask the patient to contact the health plan for coverage information. Inform patients that they are ultimately responsible for payment. Physician referral is often required to be reimbursed.

Obtain any necessary claim forms. You will need to indicate the diagnosis and treatment provided. This is usually done through billing codes, usually ICD-9-CM and CPT codes. Correct coding is essential, and you should be very familiar with billing codes that describe your services.

Filing claims for non–managed care organization insurance is similar to the process used for managed care organizations. Communication with the insurance company and using the required forms is essential.

Handling Denied Claims

If you do not agree with the health plan's decision, go back and review the patient's coverage language. If the coverage language supports payment, write an appeal letter describing the disorder and its medical nature. Include any new data that you believe further supports the claim. If the health plan continues to deny a claim that you believe is a covered benefit, consider referring the patient to small claims court. Filing a formal complaint with the state insurance commissioner should be done as well.

Your appeal letter should include the following information: facility information (name, address, phone number), date of appeal, reminder of original date of claims submission, recipient's name and address, provider information (name, address, provider number, tax number), patient information (name, address, phone number, insurer identification number), date of service and total charges, claim number, reiteration of the reason for denial, and an explanation of why the charges should be paid.

Communicating with Payers

Most third-party payer agents will not have any experience dealing with athletic trainers. They will typically not know what athletic training is or how athletic trainers are educated, certified, and licensed. Therefore, you may need to provide the necessary information to demonstrate that you are a bona fide healthcare provider before you can even discuss the claim. If you are communicating about a denied claim for reasons other than whether you are an eligible healthcare provider, the method of communication is still important. Communications should be direct, should be expressed in practical and functional terms, and should use universally understood medical terminology.

IMPORTANCE OF THIRD-PARTY REIMBURSEMENT FOR ATHLETIC TRAINERS

Third-party reimbursement for services represents acceptance as a healthcare provider. It is also required in some cases so that athletic trainers can keep their jobs. The value of third-party reimbursement for athletic trainers in clinical settings is clear. The income generated from services provided is used to pay the salary and benefits of the athletic trainer. Third-party reimbursement will also be important in other settings. In college/university and high school settings, the ability to bill third-party payers may be necessary to generate income to continue to provide the appropriate level of care. Certainly, not every service provided can be billed, but it may become necessary for certain services. The ability to recover third-party payments will also allow athletic trainers to explore more innovative methods of delivering services, perhaps in a form similar to home health care.

FUTURE STRATEGIES

The NATA Reimbursement Advisory Group has identified the following initiatives as being the most important next steps in obtaining universal billing capabilities for athletic trainers:

1. **Universal Billing Committee**: Request that the Committee create a billing code for athletic training. This will give hospitals and insurance companies an official provider code to use for athletic training services. It should alleviate some confusion and concerns relating to possible insurance fraud.

2. **CPT Coding Committee of the American Medical Association**: Work with American Medical Association (AMA) staff regarding the need for an evaluation code specific to athletic training. Continuing dialogue with the AMA regarding CPT-5 and the need for this evaluation code. Obtain official representation of the athletic training profession on the CPT Coding Committee.

3. **Health Care Practitioners Advisory Council (HCPAC)**: HCPAC is a subgroup of the National Committee for Quality Assurance. Seek inclusion in HCPAC so that the needs of athletic trainers may be expressed and included in discussions of healthcare plans.

4. **Health Care Finance Administration**: Develop a plan for athletic trainers to become officially recognized Medicare providers. A top ten law firm in Washington, D.C. that specializes in Medicare and Medicaid issues has been retained to assist with this project. There is a possibility of an ongoing relationship relating to these issues.

5. **Legal Opinion**: Retain a law firm with a specialty in Medicare and Medicaid issues to examine the Balanced Budget Act of 1997 and its impact on athletic trainers in the clinical setting. Also examine other related areas that affect the profession.

Summary

1. Athletic trainers may bill for their services.
2. Third-party payers pay for some or all of the healthcare services rendered by healthcare providers in the event of an insured's illness or accident.
3. There are four basic types of managed care organizations: health maintenance organizations (HMOs), preferred provider organizations (PPOs), exclusive provider organizations (EPOs), and point-of-service plans (POSs).
4. Coding systems for treatments rendered include Current Procedural Terminology (CPT) codes and Universal Billing (UB) codes.
5. The International Classification of Disease (ICD) codes are used to denote the patient's diagnosis.
6. Properly prepared documentation may be the most important factor in successful reimbursement.

For Critical Thought

Once Patricia and the clinic had worked out all of the details, they submitted their first claim. The HMO requested additional information about Patricia's qualifications. Once they learned that Patricia was licensed in the state and was providing services within the context of her license, they paid the claim. Patricia was now earning income for the clinic and retained her job. Although much work was involved, Patricia felt as though she was now a bona fide member of the healthcare team at the clinic. She felt better about herself because she was doing her part to keep the clinic going. The student athletes at the high school continue to get quality care thanks to Patricia's efforts.

Websites

**http://www.nata.org/Committees/
REIMBURS.HTM**

NATA Reimbursement Advisory Group web
page.

**http://otpt.ups.edu/Health_Policy/
icd-9andcpt.html**

ICD-9 and CPT codes listed by University of
Puget Sound.

http://www.hmopage.org/

The HMO page sponsored by Physicians Who
Care.

http://www.ncqa.org/Pages/Main/index.htm

National Committee for Quality Assurance
page on managed care.

Applications for Consideration

1. Your athletic director tells you that the projected athletic department budget for the next
few years looks bleak. Cuts need to be made to
all budgets within the department. You are already operating on a shoestring budget and
could not take a cut and continue to deliver
even adequate service. You decide that the only
way you can recover some income to deliver
your athletic training program is to bill for
third-party reimbursement. Explain how you
would do this. How would you present the idea
to the athletic director, the institution, and the
athletes and their parents? How would you go
about implementing the program if approved?
Identify all of the issues that you would expect
to arise as a result of this decision.

2. You are asked to develop the appropriate documents for third-party billing by athletic trainers
at your sports medicine clinic. What types of
forms would you develop? How would they be
the same as or different from the forms used by
others employed by the clinic? Develop these
forms.

References

1 Albohm, MJ, Wilkerson, GB. An outcomes assessment of care provided by certified athletic trainers. *J. Rehabil. Outcomes Meas.* 3(3):51–56, 1999.
2 Konin, J. The basics of claims filing. In Albohm, M, Campbell, D, Konin, J (eds). *Reimbursement for athletic trainers,* Thorofare, NJ: Slack, Inc., 2000.
3 Wagner, ER. Types of managed care organizations. In Kongstvedt, PR (ed). *Essentials of managed health care,* Gaithersburg, MD: Aspen Publishers, Inc., 1995.

CHAPTER 11

Financial Management

After reading this chapter, you should be able to:

- Explain the different types of budgeting systems.
- Understand the bid process.
- Identify the major elements in an athletic training facility budget.
- Prepare a budget.
- Create and maintain an inventory.

Key Terms

budget
line-item budget
program budgets
zero-based budgets
inventory
purchase plans
open accounts
bid

FOR CRITICAL THOUGHT:
A Crash Course in Budgeting

Harold Monard was hired as the first athletic trainer at the College of the Appalachians. Prior to being hired for this position, Harry had worked for three years at a rehabilitation clinic in New Jersey immediately following graduation from a master's program in athletic training at a major state university. Harry's position at the clinic included shared responsibilities as an outreach athletic trainer for visitations at numerous high schools in the area during the afternoons and working as a rehabilitation specialist at the clinic during the day. He had never been in a position where he was required to develop a new athletic training facility, let alone be responsible for acquiring equipment and supplies. Harry had accepted a new challenge.

When he arrived on campus for the first time, he met with Dr. Rashaad Walker, the current athletic director. A main item of concern Dr. Walker presented to Harry was the need to develop an equipment and supplies budget for the upcoming fiscal year. The college had never had to provide an athletic training budget before, and it needed an accurate estimate of the amount of funding needed to effectively support the facility. It was to be submitted in two weeks. After the meeting, Harry went down into what was to be the new athletic training facility to determine whether there was any existing inventory.

He found a few boxes of Band-Aids, a jar filled with Q-tips, and a few gauze bandages. He essentially had to prepare a supplies budget from scratch. Now he had to decide what to buy.

Harry was able to obtain a complete list of the number of athletes participating in each of the current active sports, which included football, ice hockey, lacrosse, and field hockey, among others. He spent some time considering both the kinds of supplies that he likes to use and the injuries that are most common in the sports that he was to cover. He also needed to outfit the facility with the appropriate permanent supplies and equipment, such as desks, tables, chairs, computers, modalities, and rehabilitation equipment. Harry had no existing data to estimate the amount of supplies he would go through during the year, so he felt it was very important to build a reserve amount of cash into the budget that could be used to cover unexpected expenses that came up during the year. He put together a complete budget request form, supplying rationales for and explanation of each of the capital and permanent supplies and equipment requests. As the fall season started, Harry decided to track inventory very carefully throughout the year. He intended to use this information to help prepare his budget for the next year.

Does it appear that Harold was thorough in his preparation for the expected needs for his athletic training facility? Are there any other routes Harry could follow in order to acquire additional funding? Is there anything that could be done differently? What else needs to be considered in this situation?

Athletic training facilities cannot effectively operate without capital. The ability to appropriately manage finances is essential to optimal facility operation. Budgets may establish parameters within which a sports medicine team may operate, but they should not inhibit the delivery of optimal health care.

In the healthcare business environment, there are six components that express the objectives of business operations.[1] While athletic trainers do not have control over all of these, they need to be aware that each can have an effect on overall operations. The first is sales. This represents gross money coming in—patient fees in the clinic setting or possibly gate receipts in college/university and professional settings. Second is cost. Costs include all expenses of doing business, from salaries to facility costs to promotional expenses. Third is profit, the amount of money remaining after the expenses have been paid. Fourth is revenue, which includes all incoming receipts and investments. Fifth is return on investment, the ratio between capital outlay and revenue generated. When the ratio is positive, the clinic generated a profit; when the ratio is negative, there was a loss. Finally, the sixth variable is growth earnings, which relates the growth in earnings over time by comparing progress from year to year.

A basic understanding of the budgeting process is necessary to effectively manage facility finances. This chapter will discuss the various aspects of the budgeting process.

BUDGETING

Managing financial resources consists of disbursing monies to cover costs and collecting monies for services rendered in an organized, objective way. For management to control the outcome of a department, control of the financial structure is critical. The process of establishing a budget enables control of the working program in realistic ways that assure that financial guidelines are being followed. A **budget** is a financial plan of operation that commits resources for projects, programs, or activities and specifies the services to be provided and the resources that must be spent to achieve these service deliveries[6]. Athletic training monies incoming are usually in the form of budget appropriations from the supervising or controlling organization. Keeping records of allotted revenues and expenditures allows the evaluation of the efficiency and effectiveness of the program in question.

There is a strong relationship between operations and financial management. According to Hy,[4] good management allows data that is input from the program to aid in decision making and planning for future growth. Knowledge of the amount of output related to the workload needed to bring about a desired result is an index of efficiency. It establishes a cost/objective ratio. Included in cost is both monies and personnel hours expended to complete the objective. The danger in using only efficiency information is that simply operating efficiently (i.e., at the lowest cost possible) does not mean that the objective is being met. The activity can be efficient but not effective. A sports medicine clinic must be able to justify the hours that it operates by demonstrating income greater than the expenditures needed to remain open. A university or high school athletic training facility must deliver comprehensive health care to an injured athlete regardless of the hours that coaches require their teams to be active during the day.

Effectiveness is the extent to which objectives are realized in relation to speed of implementation and the perceived satisfaction of the target population. Decreases in injury, along with satisfaction and recognition of positive changes from coaches, administration, and athletes, are the desired result of the effective management of a facility.

Workload is the number of hours of personnel involvement in the daily running of the program. Unfortunately, this in no way relates to the achievement of the objectives of the program. In relation to the achievement of goals, workload is only useful to establish the need to change the allocation of resources to improve efficiency and effectiveness.

BUDGET TYPES

Three types of working budgets are commonly used in sports medicine settings. The first type is the operating budget. This budget allocates money for the daily conduct of the program. It includes costs of supplies and equipment, including maintenance and repair. In a sports medicine clinic setting, revenues in the form of patient fees are generated. The expenditures generated daily to run the clinic must come into balance with the revenues generated.

Clinics cannot plan to expand or spend more money than they can generate or they will soon be out of business.

The second type is the cash budget. Most athletic training facilities do not deal in this type of budget. This budget estimates the revenues received and the monies paid out each month during the fiscal year so that there is not a shortfall in monies available to cover expenses in a particular month. This enables management to keep enough cash on hand to cover needs. It has little to do directly with planning and long-term decision making.

The third type of budget is the capital budget. This is a longer-term budget that covers monies expended on land, buildings, renovations, and large pieces of equipment. For example, the purchase of an isokinetic unit at a cost of $57,000 would not usually be in the operating budget, as it is intended to be used over a number of years. On the other hand, if a new moist hot pack unit is normally purchased each year for the athletic training room, that would be in the operating budget rather than the capital budget.

Budgets may be fixed or flexible in design. A fixed budget allocates resources on a single estimate of costs, which establishes a fixed pool of resources that can be used but not exceeded. A flexible budget allows the allocation of resources to vary in proportion to changing levels in need or activity.[6] For example, some sports medicine clinics may allocate more funds for the fall when there is a greater likelihood of seeing injuries due to high school contact sports such as soccer and football.

BUDGET SYSTEMS

There are a number of different ways to prepare a budget. Many budgets are managed throughout the year and have monies left in an account at the end of the year. If this is a limited budget, these monies then revert to the organization. This happens often in education and government. Often account managers will spend all of the monies in a given account, even if they do not need to, because higher-level managers may conclude that this account can be funded at a lower level next year since it was not used completely this year. If, however, the budget is a

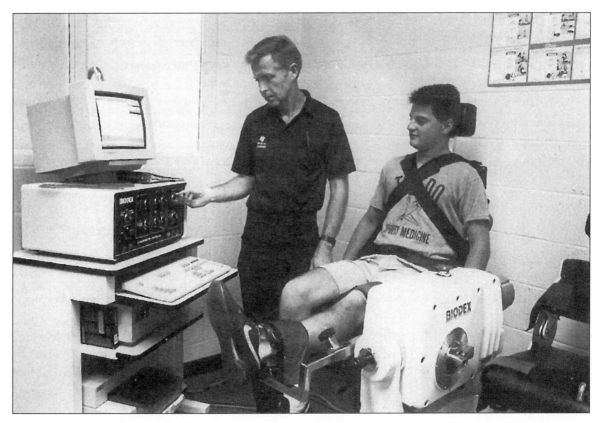

Isokinetic devices and other large equipment purchases come from the capital expenditure part of the budget. (*University of Toledo Sports Information.*)

rollover account, monies not spent in this fiscal year are carried over and may be spent during the next year. This is most useful when expenditures are not evenly spread out over a year. In an athletic training room, much of the expendable supply budget may be used in the summer getting ready for football, while in a clinic, there may be an increase in February and June, which are the biggest months for reconstructive knee surgeries.[2]

Systems to categorize budgets are varied. One in common use is the **line-item budget**. All expenditures are itemized by categories such as expendable supplies, professional expenses, operations, and capital outlays. Each main category has the potential for multiple subcategories. Expendable supplies would include tape (by size, grade, type), bandages, antiseptics, and pharmaceuticals. Managers usually have the freedom to allocate monies within a line item to various subclasses as they see fit. This system is strong on control, but weak because of overcontrol. It makes it clear where the monies for a particular area are coming from and how they will be spent. If management wants to assert control, it simply changes the amount of money allocated to a particular account. Line-item budgets do not permit the transfer of monies between accounts to cover shortfalls in other parts of the budget. This can be a weakness if the overall financial situation is not as healthy as this particular account. This type of budget also concentrates on the here and now, rather than the long-term planning and direction of an organization. Line-item budgets are often seen in athletic training rooms in college, university and high school settings.

Program budgets are functional categories within an overall budget that include all of the costs of a particular program. This type of budget is often seen in sports medicine clinics. Each area of operations (such as rehabilitation, prevention, education) is evaluated for total cost. Costs are all-inclusive. In a line item budget, the category "salary" covers the entire organization, while in a program budget, the portion of the salaries needed to run a particular program are figured in the specific program's cost. Similarly, all other costs of operating the program are included with that program, rather than the entire organization. This budget is strong in its ability to relate costs to goals and objectives and to relate programs to objectives. Long-term objectives must be considered. There may be more than one way to achieve a goal, and alternatives must be considered. A program budget details program costs. It can examine the extent to which services are actually delivered, user satisfaction, and ways to improve service delivery. It is weak in that it provides less control over some necessary accounts that may suffer when the program overspends other areas in its budget.

A performance budget is a refinement of the program budget. It is one that correlates services rendered to program objectives. The meeting of the planned objectives is the focus of achievement. The organization can see where the monies are being spent and to what extent programs are delivering, and it requires the evaluation of priorities.

Zero-based budgets are refinements of performance budgets in which the organization creates a new performance budget each year independent of performance in past years; as if it were brand new. It is based on the assumption that cost estimates are based on a fresh assessment of monies available to deliver services. All programs must justify their existence annually. Perceived inefficient programs can be eliminated or merged with more successful ones. Successful programs can see increases in funding. These budgets take a great deal of time to prepare. They may suffer from a lowering of objective standards so that those objectives will be met, thereby justifying a program's existence. These budgets are not really independent of past program performance, because the reason management would merge or eliminate a program is almost always based on previous performance. However, because this system requires a new justification each cycle, the projected need or effectiveness of an individual program in relation to

other programs will combine all efforts to assist in achieving the organization's ultimate goals.

BUDGETING PROCESS

In athletic training facilities, the monies available must enable the athletic trainers to ensure adequate care for the athletes and clients for whom they are responsible. As the scope of the program increases from high school to college and university settings to professional athletics, the dollar amounts vary a great deal, but the proportions stay remarkably the same for certain items, such as tape. Sports medicine clinics that are heavily involved in outreach programs with local high schools will most likely have a much higher allocation of funds for their sports medicine and athletic training budgets. In contrast, other clinics that are not involved externally for athletic training services and have fewer ATCs on staff will not have as much need for expendable supplies, such as tape and bandages.

In a budget request, several factors need to be considered. The first is the materials (supplies, equipment) needed to accomplish the objectives of the program. This requires knowledge of the amount of material to be used according to the estimated number of athletes or patients to be treated. Obviously, an athletic training facility that is responsible for several collision and contact sports compared with one that cares for a population of mainly recreational-type athletes will use different amounts of various materials. Another factor in the budgeting process is gaining knowledge of the amount of materials currently on hand. Therefore, a good starting place for a budget is an inventory of supplies. For each item in the inventory, assess the total needs of the athletic training program. Then count the number of the item on hand in each athletic training room. Total these and compare to the yearly need. Lastly, assess the minimum number that need to be on hand to survive, and order as needed to be above this goal and within the limits of the yearly request.

Basically, an **inventory** is the amount of materials or products kept in storage or currently available.[6] Inventories should be taken at least yearly, preferably quarterly or semiannually. These can be stored on computer and the information retrieved as needed. One inventory system is based on the economic order quantity. This method involves ordering a fixed number of items every time an inventory level falls to a predetermined point.[6] For example, some clinics will provide elastic tubing or bands for patients' home exercise programs. As the quantity of each level of resistive tubing gets down to a certain number, the facility will automatically reorder another specific amount to replenish the supplies. Changes in levels or types of supplies or equipment are initiated by the staff. In some cases, program demands change with growth or the initiation of an athletic program.

PURCHASE PLANS

The athletic trainer must be careful to specify exactly the item desired on a bid sheet or a quotation request.[1] For example, if an athletic trainer wants "Johnson & Johnson Zonas® 2-inch tape" by the case but specifies on the bid request only "2-inch tape," he or she will get the cheapest tape available that conforms to the request. In some cases a supply company will automatically replace an order for a specific brand that is unavailable with another brand that is currently in stock. Many items ordered have generic equivalents. If the athletic trainer will not accept a generic brand for the item ordered, this must be specified ahead of time, usually by indicating "do not replace."

Purchase plans that athletic trainers operate under have a major impact on what, when, and how materials are bought. In public institutions, there are usually two purchase plans in operation. Up to specified dollar limits, **open accounts** may exist to purchase supplies in smaller quantities. The dollar amount varies from institution to institution and may be covered in state law. We are aware of open accounts at various universities that range from

Using competitive bid lists is an excellent way to check for low bids.

Northwestern State University
P.O. Box 64231
Somewhere, Washington 98603

Quotation No. _____ 890-147
Page No. _____ 4

Item No.	Quantity	Description	Unit Price	Total Price
27.	4 pkgs.	Disposable Penlights, 6/pkg., single pkg.	$ _4.91_	$ _19.64_
28.	1 bx.	Double Length Elastic Wraps, 6", 6/box	_16.14_	_16.14_
29.	3 bxs.	Elastic Wraps, 6", 10/box	_7.10_	_21.30_
30.	3 bxs.	Elastic Wraps, 4", 10/box	_6.10_	_18.30_
31.	1 bx.	Elastic Wraps, 2", 10/box	_4.21_	_4.21_
32.	15 pks.	J&J Elastikon Elastic Tape, 3", 16 rls/speed pack	_40.95_	_614.25_
33.	1 rl.	Theraband Exercise Band, Medium, 50 yds.	_50.25_	_50.25_
34.	1 rl.	Theraband Exercise Band, Heavy, 50 yds.	_55.50_	_55.50_
35.	4 jars	Flex-All 454, 16 oz. jars	_10.10_	_40.40_
36.	4 bxs.	Cramers Foot Powder, 4 oz. cans, 12 cans/box		
37.	1 ea.	#BG003 Fountain WB-4S w/Cart	_312.10_	_312.10_
38.	3 ea.	Furacin Ointment, 454 gm.		
39.	2 ea.	Halstead Mosquito Forceps, 5", Straight	_2.10_	_4.20_
40.	15 bxs.	Cramers Heel and Lace Pads, 2000/box		
41.	6 ea.	Chattanooga Hydrocollator Neck Packs, 24" Long	_12.10_	_12.60_
42.	1 doz.	Chattanooga Hydrocollator Stream Pack, 10" x 12"	_10.10_	_121.20_
43.	36 tubes	Hydrocortisone Cream 0.5%. 1oz.	_1.32_	_47.52_
44.	12 btls.	Hydrogen Peroxide, 8 oz.	_.42_	_5.04_
45.	2 ea.	Igloo Ice Chest, 30.5 qts.		
46.	5 gal.	Cramers Isoquin, 1 gal.	_14.10_	_70.50_
47.	6 tubes	Ivarest Poison Ivy Cream, 1/8 oz.		
48.	12 cans	JC-5 Tape Adherent, 8 oz/can		
49.	12 cans	JC-4 Tape Adherent, 8 oz/can		
50.	12 btls.	Kaopectate, 8 oz.		
51.	12 bxs.	Beiersdorf Knuckle Coverlet, 1.5" x 3", 100/box	_5.12_	_61.44_
52.	1 sheet	Latex Foam Rubber, Plain, ½" x 21" x 36"		
53.	1 sheet	Latex Foam Rubber, Plain, 1" x 21" x 36"		
54.	25 cs.	Beiersdorf Lightplast Stretch Tape, 2", 24 rls box	_34.91_	_872.75_

Figure 11-1   Sample bid request form

$200 up to $2,500 before the bidding procedure is required.

After a minimum dollar amount has been reached, most public institutions must deal with a competitive **bid** procedure. An athletic trainer will send out a bid request sheet (figure 11-1) to prospective bidders, who will respond with prices for specified items. Usually the athletic trainer sends bid requests to at least three and as many as eight to ten bidders. Some institutions will set the minimum number of requests that must be sent, or the maximum that may be sent.

When athletic trainers send bid requests, each vendor should receive an identical bid sheet computed on common units of measurement.[1] For example, hydrogen peroxide is commonly sold in pint or quart bottles, while $1\frac{1}{2}$ inch rolls of athletic tape are sold thirty-two rolls per case and two-inch rolls are sold twenty-four per case. Often a bidder will change the specifications to a generic source, which may or may not be acceptable to the athletic trainer. Some athletic trainers must use a "low bid" purchase plan, which requires that the low bid be accepted, or the item must rebid. Others may have the ability to select the "best bid," which if it is higher than the low bid, may be accepted with justification to the budgeting office. A common justification is that a bidder is supplying an inferior generic item and the specified item is not being bid. When the option is available, price alone should not be the sole reason to purchase from a particular vendor. Superior service by the salesperson and delivery when promised are also important to the successful management of company finances.[1]

Athletic trainers may also deal with companies that will not bid from a bid sheet but will submit a list of all materials the company sells and a bid price for each. Some types of equipment may be purchased by a direct purchase plan in which the athletic trainer deals directly with the manufacturer. This is often done when purchasing isokinetic units and other large or costly pieces of equipment.

Most private institutions and some public institutions can operate under a private purchase plan. This plan involves finding an agent to sell what is needed and directly purchasing the needed material. There is no bid required. This system is open to the greatest abuse. In programs where required materials will be purchased regardless of price, higher costs than necessary may be incurred.

Oftentimes, athletic trainers deal with materials or supplies that go unused, either because they go out of date (as with tape) or because they were over-ordered. An approach to purchasing and inventory control that can help to alleviate the wasting of supplies is referred to as just-in-time scheduling or JIT, made popular by the productivity of Japanese industry. This method tries to reduce cost and improve workflow by scheduling materials to arrive "just in time" to be used.[6] This minimizes costs, as few inventories are maintained or lost due to the threat of not being used or going bad. Purchasing and storing are done in small quantities, which can open up much-needed space. Under this model, a program could order supplies in anticipation of the beginning of each season or according to the schedules of individual teams. This approach, however, requires constant attention by athletic trainers with a high degree of management skill and the time to spend in coordinating purchasing and receiving.

LINE-ITEM BUDGET CATEGORIES

Specific categories of expenditures within a budget may vary according to the type of athletic training program being funded. Salary, for example, is a part of the budget in a clinic, but probably part of a different account in a college/university or high school athletic department. Expendable supplies are a part of all athletic training programs, yet exactly what constitutes an expendable supply is open to individual interpretation. The following categories of expenditures will be discussed: expendable supplies, permanent equipment, maintenance and repair, salaries and benefits, travel and expenses, liability insurance, professional organizations, contractual services, physician retainers, and miscellaneous expenses.

Expendable supplies are those things that are consumed during daily use. This is generally the largest single portion of an athletic training room budget, 50 percent or more of the total. Usually the largest single-item expenditure in this area is for tape, which is often 50 percent of the total expendable supplies. Also included would be bandages, dressings, antiseptics, wraps, pharmaceuticals such as alcohol, aspirin, acetaminophen, ibuprofen, analgesic balm, prescription medications for physician use in the athletic training room, braces, air casts, crutches, and the like. There are obviously many other agents that could be considered here. Other considerations would include the type of facility, whether a clinic or educational institution. In addition, the level of educational institution (high school vs. college) is important to consider for items such as pharmaceuticals.

Permanent equipment is expected to last over a number of years. This would include basic items like tables, chairs, desk, file cabinets, ice machines, refrigerator/freezers, modalities such as moist hot pack units (Hydrocollator), ultrasound, electric muscle stimulators, whirlpools, diathermies, paraffin baths, intermittent pressure units, intermittent traction units, and rehabilitation equipment such as an isokinetic dynamometer (Cybex, Biodex, Kin-Kom), bicycle ergometer (Fitron, Lifecycle, Monarch, Tunturi), upper body ergometers (Cybex UBE), free weights, Hammer or Nautilus equipment, BAPS board, stair climbers, cross country ski simulators, and weight tables and benches. These pieces of equipment range in cost from a few hundred to many thousands of dollars and are not usually purchased all at one time after the program is established. Budgets for these types of purchases are anywhere from nonexistent to unlimited, based upon justification of need and monies available.

As new facilities are created and current facilities are updated to become more modern, another consideration is computers. Many athletic training facilities include a line item in the budget for computers. They are mandatory pieces of equipment in a clinic setting and are useful tools in all athletic training settings. Medical records, insurance records, athletic training room usage patterns, inventories, budgets, communications, and many other types of data can be stored on computers. Computer expenses include the hardware (computer, monitor, hard drive and/or disk drives, printer), software (programs such as word processing, databases, spreadsheets, and record keeping and educational programs such as study guides for the NATA Certification Examination), and supplies (paper, printer ribbons or ink, blank disks, disk storage boxes). One caution to remember: always make hard copies of records entered on a computer and back up data disks, otherwise irretrievable data may be lost.

Maintenance and repair is an often-overlooked expense of major importance to the service life and well-being of permanent equipment. Electric modalities must be calibrated yearly to be accurate in their delivery. Heating units must be kept clean and temperatures monitored so they do not harm patients.

Dynamometers must be cleaned and calibrated. Failure to do these things may allow contamination to alter the internal workings of a piece of equipment, leading to expensive repairs or replacement before the usable life is obtained. Athletic training facilities are healthcare facilities, and they need to be kept clean and sanitary. Not all facilities will have designated staff responsible for cleaning the room and equipment. Items such as bleach, disinfectant, mops, brooms, towels, and brushes, are needed to ensure a sanitary environment. In some budgets this is a well-funded area, while in others it does not exist, leading to problems later on. Some athletic trainers without this category have had to switch monies from other areas or collect monies from outside fund-raising to cover these expenses.

Salaries and benefits for athletic trainers are an important budget item in sports medicine clinics and are usually not considered a part of the traditional athletic training room budget. In general, beginning salaries are highest in the high school teacher/athletic trainer position and lowest in the college/university assistant athletic trainer position. Benefits vary from one type of position to the next. Included in benefits could be health insurance, life insurance, dental insurance, vision insurance, paid vacation days, malpractice insurance, retirement program contributions, union dues, professional association dues, continuing education expenses (which could include tuition and expenses for seminars, courses, or degree programs—some college/universities offer free tuition or partial tuition waivers to employees and dependents), moving expenses, child care expenses, profit sharing, and sign-on bonuses. Additional compensation may also come in the form of playoff shares for professional athletic trainers. Benefits packages traditionally have run in the area of 15 to 20 percent of salary but, depending upon the options in the package, may be 50 percent or more.

Travel expenses usually refer to attendance at professional meetings, such as the annual National Athletic Trainers' Association Clinical Symposium and Workshop, district meetings, state association meetings, and allied professional meetings such as the American College of Sports Medicine, American Kinesiotherapy Association, and the American Physical Therapy Association. This may also cover expenses to attend conferences or seminars conducted by educational and/or medical organizations. Since continuing education is a requirement to maintain NATA certification, this is an important section to be considered in the budget. Many high schools include this category, as do college/universities, clinics, and professional teams.

Liability insurance is a must in this litigious society. The cost will vary from company to company, but both the NATA and the ACSM provide liability insurance programs at reasonable rates to cover athletic trainers. Most companies recommend athletic trainers' coverage of at least $1,000,000 per injury and $3,000,000 per policy. Many athletic trainers carry higher limits. Liability insurance is a requirement for many jobs but may be paid by the employer as a staff benefit.

Professional organization memberships are often paid for out of the athletic training budget, most often to the National Athletic Trainers' Association. Some budgets also will pay state dues and allied association dues, such as APTA or ACSM. Some institutions will even provide release time for staff members who are officers in national organizations.

Contractual services may be a part of the athletic training room budget. These services include mortgage or rent, heat, electricity, water, sewer, phone, and debt service for long-term loans. In a traditional athletic training room setting, water is not a major expense, but in a large physical therapy clinic, it is not uncommon to go through 100,000 gallons of heated water daily for whirlpool treatments.[3] The turbines to power the water, the electrical modalities, light, sometimes heat and air conditioning, all consume large amounts of electricity. Telephone expenses, especially long distance charges, may be considerable. Many college/university programs have limits of fifteen minutes per call for long distance, and anything over the limit must be explained and defended. In most traditional athletic training settings, the phone, heat, lights, water, and the like are paid out of the athletic department's operating budget rather than the athletic training room budget.

Physician involvement in athletic training programs is often on a contract-for-fees basis. Many team physicians are paid retainers or stipends to provide athletic training room visits and game coverage. In many cases at the college/university level, the team physician is associated with the campus health center or medical school. Sometimes coverage of athletics is built into this physician's contract. If the physician on stipend is an orthopedic surgeon, there may be additional fees from the surgeon for surgical procedures. This is traditionally a contract provision. In a clinic setting, the physician may own the clinic or may have a contract with the clinic to use the staff and facilities for the rehabilitation of athletic injuries treated in the physician's practice. In some cases the clinic and the physician are located in the same facility, such as in a hospital. In many high school settings and college/university settings, the physician is a volunteer who receives no payment for services to the athletic training program. An athletic trainer is at the mercy of the physician's dedication to the program in this situation. When a physician has other commitments, he or she may not cover the athletic training room needs or arrange substitute coverage, and the needs can go unmet.

Miscellaneous expenses include a variety of categories. Student athletic trainer expenses include such things as clothing, awards, and scholarships or salaries. Many NATA-approved athletic trainer education programs do not pay student athletic trainers because the clinical hours are required for NATA certification. In many institutions, the only financial aid available to student athletic trainers is that available to all students through the financial aid office of the college or university. Some institutions will pay a stipend to those student athletic trainers who return early from their summer jobs for early fall sports before classes start. Some institutions will pay their student athletic trainers a weekly stipend or a scholarship, which may range from a full scholarship to a progressive increase in monies as class standing increases.

Miscellaneous expenses also include the purchase of journal subscriptions and books for the athletic trainer's professional library. This area may also include slides, videotapes, and overhead transparencies for use in patient education and/or public speaking engagements. Athletic trainers are often asked to speak at coaches' meetings, career clubs in high schools, and education programs for athletic trainers. Some states require those faculty members in secondary schools who direct student activity programs to have continuing ongoing training in sports medicine, and athletic trainers provide much of this training.

DIFFERENCES BY SETTING

Athletic training facilities depend upon monetary support to effectively operate and provide optimal healthcare to their target populations. One of the main considerations in developing a budget for a specific program is the type and size of the facility. High schools and clinics will have different populations to care for, and their ability to buy supplies and materials will vary.

It is a well-known fact among athletic trainers in college/university settings that the monies available to an athletic training budget will depend to a great extent on the size and scope of the athletic program that generates funds to cover its costs of operation. Large NCAA Division IA football schools, such as those in the Big Twelve, Big Ten, Southeastern, and Pac 10 conferences, have much more money to deal with than smaller Division IA or Division IAA schools, such as those in the Ohio Valley, Association of Mid-Continent Universities, or Mid-American conferences. There is proportionally even less money at Division II, Division III, and high schools, and different types of financing in clinics and professional sports as compared to these college and high school settings.

A study by Rankin[5] in 1992 found that the discrepancy between big-time football NCAA Division IA schools and NCAA Division III schools showed a disparity of $745 per athlete available for athletic training services ($926 and $181, respectively). A comparison of various budget items from the study categorized against program type is shown in table 11-1. Salary is the mean for all full-time athletic trainers (both head athletic trainers and assistant athletic trainers) as reported. Care must be exercised interpreting the data from Division IAA, as there was a small number of responding schools compared to the other categories.

Expenditures in professional athletics are more performance driven than in other settings. When an

■ **TABLE** **11-1** Mean Expenditures by Selected Categories

Program Level	Expendable Supplies	Capital Equipment	Maintenance Repairs	Student ATs	Dollars Spent Per Athlete
BigDivIA	$85,903.67	$11,906.74	$4,409.46	$25,476	$926
SmDivIA	$29,914.47	$ 2,730.47	$ 621.43	$ 8,147	$462
DivIAA	$23,385.25	$ 700.00	$ 520.00	$ 4,200	$293
DivII	$15,625.56	$ 2,071.19	$ 578.64	$ 1,743	$301
DivIII	$11,716.56	$ 1,880.84	$ 380.95	$ 3,900	$181
High School	$ 4,150.57	$ 735.00	$ 234.28	$ 45	$ 96

	Salaries	Benefits	Medical Services	Medical Insurance	Education/ Travel
BigDivIA	$30,706	$1,956	$83,085	$58,620	$5,232
SmDivIA	$27,412	$2,218	$ 9,230	$36,838	$1,676
DivIAA	$32,375	$2,423	$ 8,265	$22,306	$2,400
DivII	$30,155	$3,115	$ 3,237	$29,000	$ 802
DivIII	$27,702	$3,943	$ 2,012	$10,273	$ 611
High School	$31,730	$2,518	$ 0	$ 2,008	$ 424

organization has enough money to pay the athletes, the expenses of the sports medicine program are rather minimal. When a large expense is requested for a piece of equipment, the team will either buy or rent the equipment with proper justification. A frequent justification is the specialized need for the rehabilitation of a particular athlete. In those sports with minor leagues affiliated with major league teams, various purchases may be made by the parent organization to be used throughout the organization.

In an industrial setting, cost effectiveness is the single most important reason for the existence of an on-site facility, rather than sending injured workers off-site to a rehabilitation facility. It is estimated that in the automobile industry, the cost of one off-site rehabilitation session is four hours of replacement time, while on-site the cost is 45 minutes (personal communication, Wayne Vaupel, Work-Fit, March 1999). While most medium and large manufacturing facilities have safety engineers, they are concerned with equipment safety instead of the po-

tential for worker injury through repetitive motion activity or movement at an awkward angle for a particular body part. Industrial athletic trainers can save a company money through injury prevention and ergonomic assessment, in addition to rehabilitation programming after an injury has occurred.

After considering the type of facility and the needs of their athletes or clients, athletic trainers must design their budgets according to the organization's guidelines and procedures. If a bidding process must be initiated, it needs to be done early enough to avoid exhausting the current supplies. All items of a program's budget should be updated and properly supported. Insurance, benefits, and expenses deserve as much scrutiny in estimated costs as the supplies and materials needed to run the program. Effective inventory management and control ensures that all materials are being used and are replaced before they run out. Athletic trainers also should develop relationships with other organizations that may be able to provide additional funding or equipment.

Summary

1. There are six variables in the financial life of an organization: sales, costs, profits, revenue, return, and growth.
2. A budget is a financial plan of operation that commits resources for projects, programs, or activities and specifies the services to be provided and the resources that must be spent to deliver these services.
3. Budget types include operating, cash, and capital.
4. Budget systems include line-item, program, performance, and zero-based budgets.
5. Inventory assesses supplies on hand.

6. Purchase plans include competitive bid (either low-bid or best-bid), open account, and private purchase arrangements.
7. Categories to be considered in a line-item budget include expendable supplies, permanent equipment, maintenance and repair, salaries and benefits, travel expenses, liability insurance, professional organization memberships, contracted services, physician retainers, and miscellaneous expenses.
8. There are wide differences in available monies based on practice setting.

For Critical Thought

Now that Harold has completed the first year, he realizes that he had to request additional funding from the athletic director for expendable supplies. Two of the pieces of permanent equipment were not used as often as he thought they would be based on his clinic experiences. At the end of the year he realized that he

might have been farther ahead had he consulted with the college athletic trainers he knew, starting with the head athletic trainer at the university he attended for his master's degree. Two of his fellow G.A.s are now in small college programs and would have been excellent resources had he thought to utilize them, a mistake he will not repeat. As he began to prepare the next year's budget, he spoke with his friends and obtained copies of their bid sheets. He also traded the underutilized equipment with a local sports medicine clinic for additional closed-chain rehabilitation equipment. He was well received by the coaches and administration for the invaluable service he provided to the college. Harry is happy he accepted a position where he is appreciated and had the opportunity to learn and grow on the job.

 ## Website

**http://ashley.ivey.uwo.ca/~dszpiro/
capbud_paper/capbud.html.**

An interesting study detailing the real-world mechanics of capital budgeting. The study provides an interesting discussion of how capital budgeting is performed in the real world. It is fairly nontechnical.

Applications for Consideration

1. Larissa Kullinski has been the head athletic trainer at Southcentral College, a small Divison III school, for eight years. Larissa minored in business during her undergraduate years and has always dreamed of opening up her own sports medicine clinic. She has her master's degree and has been slowly completing her doctoral work in administration. She recently accepted a position at a local clinic associated with the city hospital as the director of the sports medicine program. She starts in the summer. Under her supervision will be athletic trainers, physical therapists, exercise physiologists, support staff, and aides. One of her first duties will be to create the upcoming year's budget. The hospital operates on a zero-based budget system. What factors will Larissa have to consider? What items will most likely be included in the budget? What justifications should be made for those items?

2. You are the director of athletic training for The Central State Institute of Sports Medicine and Rehabilitation. You have ten high schools on contract and ten athletic trainers assigned to them. There is no charge to the high schools for the athletic training service; the clinic relies on referrals for rehabilitation for revenue. Each schools is expected to supply their ATC with the appropriate materials to provide adequate health care. Many of the athletic trainers have been complaining for the past few seasons that their increasing needs are not being met. It is an issue that is touchy with the clinic owners; they don't want to see the high school sites too well equipped, otherwise referrals aren't necessary. However, some of the cases being brought to you suggest that the high schools may not be supplying the athletic training program with enough funds, due to either lack of education or simple lack of resources. The clinic you work for is the only one in the area and is not hurting for money. What directions and what approaches can you adopt in order to better equip your high school's athletic training facilities? What rationales and justifications should you provide? How do you best meet the needs of the athletes who suffer from this situation?

References

1 Barnes, RP. Fiscal management. In Konin, JG. *Clinical athletic training.* Thorofare, NJ: Slack, Inc., 1997.

2 Cronen, LL. Certification of athletic insurance programs and policies. Presented to the 41st Annual National Athletic Trainers' Association, Inc., Clinical Symposium and Workshop, Indianapolis, IN, June 12, 1990.

3 Griffin, JE, Karselis, TC. *Physical agents for physical therapists.* 2nd ed. Springfield, IL: Charles C. Thomas, 1982.

4 Hy, RJ. *Financial management for health care administrators.* New York: Quorum Books, 1989.

5 Rankin, JM. Financial resources for conducting athletic training programs in the collegiate and high school settings. *Journal of Athletic Training,* 27:344–349, 1992.

6 Schermerhorn, JR. *Management.* 6th ed. NY: John Wiley & Sons, Inc., 1999.

CHAPTER 12

Emergency Care Planning

After reading this chapter, you should be able to:

- Establish emergency care standard operating procedures.

- Prepare a written emergency care plan.

- Distinguish between life-threatening and non–life-threatening emergencies.

- Determine who is covered by an emergency care plan.

- Utilize or develop the appropriate medical records for emergency situations.

Key Terms

emergency care plan
standard operating procedures
life-threatening emergency
non–life-threatening emergency

FOR CRITICAL THOUGHT:
Activating the Emergency Care Plan

Antonio Montana is the athletic trainer for the University of Eastern's football team. He and his medical staff responded to an unresponsive athlete who was hit in the head during practice last Wednesday. Following Antonio's primary assessment, it was determined the athlete did not have a heartbeat. He began the process of initiating the emergency care plan by signaling his emergency medical team with a prearranged hand signal (i.e., hands crossed in front of his chest). At this point everyone on the emergency care team knew what their role was to properly care for the injured athlete.

The assistant athletic trainer came onto the field to assist Antonio in cardiopulmonary resuscitation (CPR). He went right to his previously designated position at chest to continue chest compressions. The head athletic trainer and the assistant athletic trainer continued to perform CPR until the emergency rescue squad arrived on the scene and assumed control of the situation.

There were three student athletic trainers (Alexa, Walt, and Melissa) assigned to the emergency care plan. Alexa's responsibility was to contact the emergency medical services (EMS) by dialing 911 at the predetermined telephone. The operator answered the phone and began asking several questions about the injury. Alexa was able to answer these questions thoroughly and without panic. She remained on the phone with the operator until the ambulance arrived and the operator told her she could hang up the phone. She then went to the field where the injury was located and remained on standby until she was needed to assist with the injury.

During the phone call, Walt was responsible for unlocking the gates to the athletic practice field. He remained at the gate to guide the ambulance to the correct location on the field. He remained in contact with the assistant athletic trainer and Alexa via two-way radio. This enabled Alexa and the athletic training staff to know when the ambulance had arrived at the scene.

Melissa was in charge of getting copies of the athlete's medical history and insurance forms from the file in the athletic training room. These would follow the athlete to the hospital to let the doctors there know if there were any preexisting conditions that might have caused the emergency.

The ambulance arrived on the scene and prepared to transport the athlete. Antonio and the assistant athletic trainer had removed the face mask to initiate CPR, which they were continuing. The emergency medical technicians did not try to remove the helmet but prepared to attach a defibrillator to the athlete. The athlete was placed on a backboard with Antonio at the head, one EMT at the shoulder, one EMT at the waist, Alexa at the knees, and Melissa at the feet. The athlete was placed on an ambulance gurney and transported to the hospital in the ambulance. Antonio rode in the ambulance to escort the athlete to the hospital with his medical records.

Following the return of Antonio from the hospital, he reported that the athlete survived and was currently in an intensive care unit. He began to talk to the other staff about the situation and how it was handled in the after-action briefing. The situation was analyzed to see where things could be improved and where procedures should remain in place. All on the staff thought the situation was handled appropriately because of careful preplanning and practice of the emergency care plan throughout the year.

Fortunately, medical emergencies are rare in athletics. Former NATA President Bobby Barton once said at a state meeting that a person involved in athletic training at the college or university level for more than five years will see at least one potentially catastrophic injury. The **emergency care plan** is a written document that defines the standard of care required in every conceivable event during an emergency on the practice or playing field.[5] Standard operating procedures must be explicit, the scope of coverage must be specified, and the appropriate medical records must be identified and prepared. A well-conceived emergency care plan will minimize the time needed to enter the injured athlete into the emergency care system. This detailed document also provides the athletic trainer with the guidance and protection necessary to protect all members of the sports medicine team against legal ramifications.

STANDARD OPERATING PROCEDURES FOR DEVELOPING AN EMERGENCY CARE PLAN

There are a number of **standard operating procedures** used to develop an emergency care plan (ECP). These procedures will inevitably be specific to the needs of each institution and athletic facility. Some fundamental guidelines, however will help the athletic trainer to determine and identify key personnel and their qualifications and roles the ECP. Standard operating procedures will also ensure that all necessary emergency equipment is available for providing an appropriate standard of care during an emergency.

Key Personnel

Available resources will dictate what personnel will be involved in the ECP. For instance, a high school–certified athletic trainer may not have access to several different types of medical personnel. It would, therefore, be advantageous for the athletic trainer to choose members who have "multiple skills or credentials."[14] Where there are many resources, key personnel may involve several types of healthcare professionals such as physicians (i.e., emergency medicine, orthopedic, cardiologist, or podiatrist), emergency medical technicians, physician assistants, and/or nurse practitioners. There must also be consideration of nonmedical personnel's involvement in the ECP. Open communications with law enforcement, security, athletic administration, university administration, and custodial personnel are essential to the efficient operation of an ECP.[1] Thus, responsibility for developing an ECP should be shared by the athletic department, coaches, and essential medical and nonmedical personnel.[9]

Qualifications

The qualifications of all persons delivering emergency health care to a large extent determine the quality of the care that is delivered to the athlete. The NCAA and the American College of Sports Medicine[3] have both published guidelines for ensuring that qualified individuals are available during an emergency. Currently, the National Athletic Trainers' Association requires that all certified athletic trainers maintain certification in cardiopulmonary resuscitation (CPR).[8] Noncertified student athletic trainers should also receive certification in basic or advanced first aid in order to increase their ability to function within the emergency care plan. The consequences of inadequate preparation and the ease of obtaining this training make certification requirements both reasonable and prudent.

Roles

Following the identification of all key personnel and their qualifications, the next step in developing an emergency care plan is to define the role of each member of the sports medicine team. Team members may assume different roles depending on the site, their specific skills or certifications, or the presence of other personnel. Items such as, but not limited to, the following should be considered:

- Who will go onto the field when an athlete goes down?
- How is the emergency medical system activated?
- Where is the communication equipment (phone, two-way radio)? Who will make sure the rescue squad finds the accident scene? Who will provide emergency first aid or CPR if necessary?
- Who will provide crowd control?
- Who will complete an incident report that is thorough and accurate?

People involved with the ECP must be assigned to their roles before an emergency occurs. This will eliminate confusion during the emergency, because everyone on the ECP will know exactly what is expected of them. These roles may be rotated or they may be permanently designated among the professional staff. It is also important that backup personnel be given roles within the ECP in the event that a key member is not available at the time an emergency arises. Box 12-1 identifies the specific emergency response team roles.

Equipment

The appropriate emergency equipment must be available in order to administer sufficient advanced life support techniques whenever a practice or competitive event is in progress.[2,4,9] Types of equipment and the extent of inventory for equipment will depend on budget constraints, activity type, professionals' preference, individual athletes' needs, and team physician preference.[2,11] It is essential that everyone on the emergency care team know where all equipment is before an emergency occurs. Likewise, all emergency equipment should be easily accessible to each member of the emergency care team. Team members must be proficient in the use of equipment for which they are certified and familiar with the equipment for which they are not certified. This will avoid critical time loss when those who are qualified to use this equipment arrive at the scene. It must be emphasized, however, that this equipment must not

---

■ **Specific Emergency Response Team Roles** *Box 12-1*

....

Role 1 (Physician, highest ranking staff ATC, or designated person)

1. Take charge of the emergency until relieved by higher authority.
2. Assess patient. Begin rescue breathing or CPR as needed.

Role 2 (Next highest staff ATC, student athletic trainer or designated person)

1. Assist with rescue breathing or CPR.
2. Keep written record of all conditions and actions.

Role 3 (Next highest staff ATC, student athletic trainer or designated person)

1. Activate the emergency medical system; call 911.
2. Assist emergency personnel to the emergency site.

Role 4 (Student athletic trainer, coach, or designated person)

1. Bring crash cart to the scene.
2. Assist with rescue breathing or CPR as needed.

Role 5 (Student athletic trainer or designated person)

1. Bring biohazard disposal containers to the site.
2. Once the athlete and medical personnel have left the scene, clean the area using OSHA standards for handling blood-borne pathogens.

---

be used by untrained or unlicensed personnel (see individual state athletic training practice acts).

The location of all standard emergency equipment such as backboards, splints, stethoscopes, sphygmomanometers, and blood-borne pathogen containers should also be documented within the ECP. Additional equipment may include oral pharyngeal airways, tongue forceps, one-way-valve pocket mask, oxygen, suctioning apparatus, defibrillator, and cellular phones or other communication devices. Emergency care plans should also list those materials found within the physician's "crash" kit. These materials and equipment are to be used *only* by a physician in order to provide immediate life support and pain management.[10] Items located within the "crash" kit may include nasal airways, cricoid thyrotomy unit, prescription medications, syringes, needles, IV bags, and/or oral and metered injectable units.[10]

Implementation

All personnel involved with the emergency plan should know it well enough that they do not have to refer to the written version in the event of an emergency. It is helpful, however, to provide each member of the team with a laminated card to carry on their person. This card includes emergency information that is pertinent to the specific location of the practice or athletic contest.

The best and possibly the only way for the team to become competent in using the ECP is to rehearse it throughout the year. Herbert's[4] summarization of the ACSM's Health and Fitness Facility Standards and Guidelines (1997) indicates that rehearsals should be completed a minimum of twice per year. The biannual tests should serve as the dress rehearsal for an actual emergency. Periodic drills, however, should come in between these dates to allow for changes to be implemented within the plan, as well as for new staff members to become familiar with the plan. Rehearsals can occur both announced and unannounced throughout the year. Announced drills during in-service sessions serve as excellent educational situations for everyone to become familiar with the plan, especially in the early stages of plan development. Unannounced drills give a better indication of how members will respond during an actual emergency. Following the rehearsal, an after-action report should be written and presented to the team members. Recommendations for improving the ECP should be discussed and implemented.

Failure to carry out the emergency care plan can have catastrophic results to the victim (not to mention the liability action against the sports medicine team). For example, Hank Gathers, a prominent college basketball player with a known ventricular arrhythmia, collapsed during a game in March 1990. A defibrillator was located courtside along with qualified physicians who could use it. However, he was removed from the playing area before either aggressive CPR or defibrillation was attempted.[7] These issues were among several litigated by his family against the university and associated personnel when he later died.

Many high school, college, and university athletic teams practice in multiple facilities. In addition, teams playing on the road will be in a facility that is different from the one in which they regularly practice. Emergency care plans must be developed for *each* site in which the team will compete or practice.[1] In these cases, it may be helpful to color-code the laminated emergency care cards to ensure that no confusion exists over which ECP should be used at which playing field or court. It may also be helpful for athletic trainers to refer to the fields and courts according to their color-coded ECP cards.

It is not an acceptable defense to depend on the home team's sports medicine personnel to have developed an adequate emergency care plan in the event of a catastrophic injury. The athletic trainer should also not assume that medical team members from the host institution, other than possibly a student athletic trainer, will be present during practices. The visiting athletic trainer must contact a representative from the host institution to collect the same information available in his or her institution's emergency care plan. It is imperative that the host's ECP procedures be put in writing prior to traveling. Likewise, the host institution should send the visiting athletic training and sports medicine team the pertinent information from its emergency care plan for their preparation to travel.

Professional sports provide a good example of the cooperation that exists between host and visiting teams in the sharing of ECP information. The sports medicine personnel in various professional sports have compiled a data book that provides the athletic trainer with host athletic trainers' and assistants' telephone numbers, local hotels, athletic trainers' spouses, team physicians, neurologist, internist, access to local emergency medical service, and nearest hospital to the playing site and the team's hotel. This information allows effective contact between visiting and local personnel in the event of an emergency. It is critically useful information, especially when the athletic trainer is new to the area of competition. This plan may actually become familiar to the visiting athletic trainer when his or her team competes at that site often.

Since the team physician is the ultimate decision-maker in emergency situations, he or she reserves the right to assume or delegate any role in emergency care. It is therefore absolutely necessary to involve the team physician, as well as the institution's legal counsel, and the local emergency medical service in the development of an emergency care plan. The physician can express his or her preferences regarding his or her role in emergency situations, as well as the roles of others within the ECP.

An important point to consider when developing an emergency care plan is to determine whether the institution has an emergency care plan already adopted both at the institutional and/or the departmental level. The number of institutions that do not have a written emergency response plan in place is surprising! For example, upon requesting a copy of his institution's emergency care plan, one author was informed that there was no formal plan and that everyone went by the instructions on the back of the university phone directory. The institution then requested that a plan be created and forwarded to the safety committee for consideration.

Consistency

If a departmental emergency care plan is in place, it is a good idea to check it against the institutional emergency care plan for consistency. The sports medicine team emergency care plan must be consistent with the institutional care plan. If it is not, the program may be open to liability suits. The athletic trainer must seek guidance from institutional legal and medical representatives to instigate needed changes if the institutional emergency care plan is inadequate. Assistance from these people will yield suggestions for policy and procedural changes. However, those policies that are already established cannot be ignored until the new ECP is officially implemented.

Contacts

It is important to determine who must be contacted according to the institution's emergency care plan in the event of an emergency. At some colleges and universities, the campus police must be informed if there is an emergency on institutionally owned grounds, including those fields and courts that are considered off-campus. In addition, some institutions also mandate that campus police must approve emergency squad dispatches. Campus police telephone numbers are essential and should be placed in a conspicuous place within the athletic training facility. A page within the emergency care plan document should list these and other primary phone numbers. These numbers may also be laminated and placed in the athletic trainer's personal kit for easy access during an emergency.

An emergency may warrant contacting emergency medical services. In many legal jurisdictions, emergency medical technicians (EMTs) take control over all actions surrounding the stabilization and transportation of the injured athlete once they are called to the scene. This means that the athletic trainer no longer has any voice in such matters as removing football helmets.[13] For example, emergency medical technicians were once taught to remove all helmets regardless of type, whether motorcycle or football. This is because EMTs predominantly deal with motorcycle helmets that often have a face mask that cannot be removed, thus requiring helmet removal for adequate CPR or rescue breathing. Athletic trainers who have questioned this practice during emergencies or tried to interfere in the removal of a helmet have been threatened with arrest for interfering with the job performance of an EMT. Emergency medical technician training has changed in recent years so that football helmet removal is no longer mandatory. It is wise, nonetheless, to include EMTs in the planning and practice of an emergency care plan. An in-service to demonstrate the way to access the head for rescue breathing without removing the football helmet may educate those EMTs not trained in or skeptical of this practice. Hopefully, this type of exchange will eliminate any confusion or problems that have often occurred on the football field.

Writing the Plan

Writing an emergency care plan can be time-consuming and tedious, but it is a necessity. Certainly each institution's emergency care plan will be somewhat different from other institutions' plans, but certain issues always need to be addressed. Box 12-2 provides a skeleton outline of the contents of an emergency care plan.

Once completed, the emergency care plan should be approved by the institution's administration and legal staff, team physicians, and emergency medical service representatives who will operate in conjunction with the plan. It is important that each person covered by the emergency care plan be informed of its contents by providing each with a copy of the plan, providing an in-service on what it contains, and establishing practice opportunities at each site where the plan will be used.[4,15] It is also good practice to prepare a condensed version of the emergency care plan for the athletes' parents. Providing them with this document accomplishes three things. First, it informs parents that a structured healthcare plan is in place for their daughter or son. Second, it presents a standard of care that they can expect the sports medicine team to uphold. Finally, it provides positive public relations for the sports medicine team.

■ **Outline of an Emergency Care Plan**   *Box 12-2*

I. Materials
   A. First aid kit
   B. Appropriate medical forms
   C. Emergency care equipment
   D. Detailed maps of facilities (gates, doors, fields, phone location)
II. Procedures
   A. Identify responsibilities of emergency care team
      1. Supervisor or facilitator: coordinates emergency care
      2. Emergency care provider(s): handle(s) emergency situation
      3. Traffic controller: keeps site of injury clear of observers
      4. Emergency medical assistance contact: telephones for emergency care personnel
      5. Emergency vehicle escort: flags down and escorts emergency vehicle
   B. Assign individuals to responsibilities
   C. Assign duties to responsibility
      1. Supervisor or facilitator
         a. Take charge of situation
         b. Send team members to their assigned tasks
         c. Contact athlete's parent(s) or guardian(s)
         d. Make sure injury evaluation form is completed
      2. Emergency care provider(s)
         a. Calm and reassure athlete
         b. Evaluate injury
         c. Explain nature and severity of injury to emergency medical assistant
         d. Provide appropriate emergency care
         e. Release to emergency medical personnel, if necessary, for transport
         f. Supply emergency medical personnel with appropriate medical forms
      3. Traffic controller
         a. Keep uninjured athletes away from site of injury
         b. Keep spectators, press, and so forth away from injury site
      4. Emergency medical assistance contact
         a. Identify location and number of nearest phone to emergency operator
         b. Report nature and severity of injury
         c. Give directions to injury site
         d. Name and location of emergency vehicle escort
         e. Remain on phone until operator hangs up
         f. Inform emergency care provider of status of emergency medical assistance
      5. Emergency vehicle escort
         a. Go to designated location to flag down emergency vehicle
         b. Have keys to gate or door locks available
         c. Direct emergency vehicle to injury site

Adapted from Kimball et al.[5]

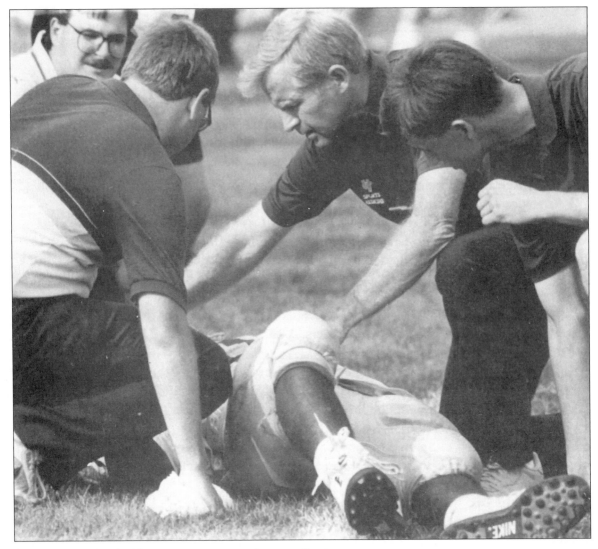

Reassuring an injured athlete is an important step in responding to an emergency. (*University of Toledo Sports Information.*)

PROCEDURES

Once policies have been established, procedures must be developed. Establishing the chain of command, classifying emergencies, and activating the emergency medical system must be detailed.

Chain of Command

The chain of command is a list of the emergency care team members and their rank in the emergency care decision-making process. Establishing a chain of command will depend on the personnel available and the different facilities where services are rendered. The chain of command for each site should be in writing, distributed to appropriate individuals, and strictly observed.

The chain of command for athletic emergencies should be in agreement with institutional policies. Failure to comply with the institutional chain of command may result in undesirable legal ramifications (see chapter 16). If the institutional chain of

■ **Chain of Command**   *Box 12-3*

Team Physician
  Makes all decisions about transport and care of athlete

Certified Head Athletic Trainer
  1. Makes all decisions about transport and care of athlete when physican is not present
  2. Never outranks the team physician

Certified Assistant Athletic Trainer
  1. Makes all decisions about transport and care of athlete when head athletic trainer is not present
  2. Assists when head athletic trainer is present

Student Athletic Trainer
  1. Assists any certified athletic trainer or physician when present
  2. Is a supervised member within the chain of command

Emergency Medical Services
  1. Depends on local/state jurisdictions
  2. May outrank everyone except the physician if called to the scene

Nurse
Security Personnel
Athletic Administrators

command hampers the team's ability to effectively handle emergencies, it should be brought to the attention of the appropriate administrators and avenues for change should be explored.

The responsibility for making decisions about the disposition of an injured athlete in any emergency generally belongs to an attending physician. Although this is usually accepted and straightforward, the placement of other allied health professionals (i.e., physician assistants or nurses) within the chain of command is not always clear. Questions often asked include: Who is in charge if the physician is not present? Does this add another phone call to the notification procedure (to the physician)? What is the response if a person comes from the stands and announces, "I am a doctor, I am taking over?" Is the response different in a high school setting than in other settings? Answers to questions such as these are important to discuss when developing an effective emergency care plan with

designated key personnel before an emergency arises.

The head athletic trainer or team athletic trainer is generally second in the chain of command to a physician. At some institutions, a physician's assistant or a nurse may be in charge. In some settings, the administrator, school nurse, security personnel, and so forth must be notified prior to taking action. This is particularly true when outside agencies, such as ambulance crews, must be called in to provide assistance. Box 12-3 provides an example chain of command for an emergency care plan.

Emergencies

The ECP is activated when the main decision-maker determines that emergency services should be summoned.[15] The procedures to be followed during an emergency will depend largely on the nature or severity of the injury. A **life-threatening emergency** must receive top priority, and all resources available to provide care must be used to assist the cardiopulmonary function of the athlete. Life-threatening emergencies are situations in which the victim's life is in immediate danger. In general, these incidents comprise cardiovascular or respiratory systems failure, shock, or severe hemorrhaging. If the injury is considered a **non–life-threatening emergency**, the resources at one's disposal may be limited to stabilization of the athlete until EMS arrives at the scene. Procedures to be followed in these situations must be clearly defined in the emergency care plan.

Certain guidelines must be followed when contacting emergency assistance. These five elements are essential:[10]

1. *Identification*: The emergency operator needs the caller's name, the patient's name, the telephone number, and the location where the call is being made.

2. *Nature of emergency*: The operator will ask about the type of emergency (heart attack, seizure, etc.), the number of people injured or ill, and the seriousness of the injury or injuries.

3. *First aid implemented*: The operator needs to know what has been done to the victim and what type of assistance and/or equipment is needed.

4. *Directions*: The operator needs directions to the site of the emergency. It is also recommended that someone be available to meet the ambulance at a gate or entrance with keys to all doors to expedite the entry of emergency personnel.

5. *Termination of phone call*: The operator will tell the caller when to hang up the phone. It is essential not to hang up before this, even if one sees the ambulance arriving at the scene.

Information from the athlete's preparticipation examination should be used when making any

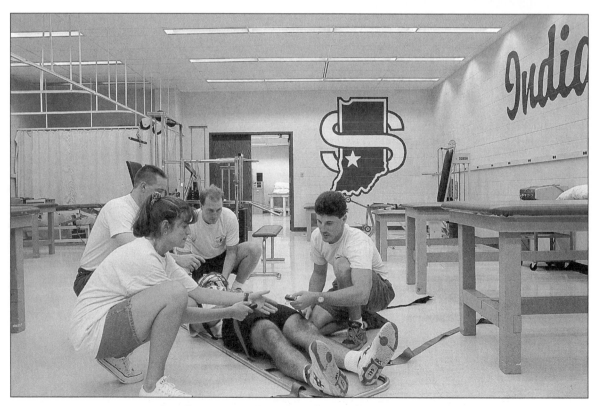

Practicing an emergency care plan allows for smooth implementation should it become necessary to use.

decisions. By keeping each athlete's medical information on-site for each practice and game, it is possible to quickly determine if the athlete has allergies, preexisting conditions, and so forth. This information may be vital for the proper care of the athlete.

Copies of consent forms and insurance information can also expedite emergency care. If a consent form is available, there is no question that the sports medicine team is authorized to provide emergency care to the athlete. Having the athlete's insurance information readily available will expedite care once he or she arrives at the hospital.

Notification of Parents

It is imperative that the athlete's parents are contacted during an emergency when the athlete is a minor. *Actual consent* is notification that permission is granted to give treatment for a particular incident. Actual consent to render care to minors can be given in writing before or during emergencies. Actual consent is a valid precept only when it is informed consent. The informed consent would consist of informing the athlete and/or parents of what the athletic trainer believes to be wrong and what he or she intends to do about the situation. Obtaining actual consent in writing about parents' preferences for hospitals and medical procedures (i.e., religious beliefs for or against medical treatment) helps to eliminate confusion and potential problems with emergency medical decisions. It is absolutely imperative that parents of minors are contacted as soon as possible, even if actual consent has been given before an emergency occurs. In the event that the athlete's parents cannot be contacted, the predetermined wishes of the parents can be enacted.

If the parents are not available and there is no consent on file, then *minor consent* may apply in which the minor gives binding consent. It is pertinent to continue to try to contact the parents even after emergency care has been administered or hospitalization has occurred. *Implied consent* takes over when parents cannot be contacted, consents are not on file, and the athlete is unconscious. Implied consent assumes that the athlete would consent to treatment to save his or her life if he or she were able to do so. This applies to both adults and minors.

SCOPE OF COVERAGE

Rieff[14] has described the scope of coverage, ". . . as a statement that will drive your functional goals which in turn formulates your entire medical operation." Several issues must be considered when discussing the extent of coverage by the emergency care team. These may include but are not limited to: budget constraints, number of spectators and participants, in and out of season activities, indoor and outdoor facilities and personnel available.[15] A scope of coverage statement may be individualized to each specific athletic site, institution, or both. Appropriate clearance from the proper administration must occur in advance of the adoption of the ECP's scope of coverage statement.

The development of the ECP should center on the care of athletes.[15] Spectators, coaches, and other staff are considered secondary to the athletes' care. The extent to which the emergency care team's responsibility lies outside the athletic realm will most likely be determined by the administrative policies for a particular institution. If the athletic emergency care staff is responsible for nonathletic personnel, then medical coverage must be made available for this population. Alternatively, it may be decided that a separate medical team will have responsibility for spectators, press members, etc., consequently relieving the athletic emergency care team of the responsibility for nonathletic populations. This is ideal, because full attention can be given to the events that are occurring on the playing field or court without interruption. It may, however, increase medical costs due to the extra medical staff and equipment being available for nonathletic injuries.

RECORDS

After an emergency has occurred, it is imperative to record the findings on the appropriate medical forms (see chapter 8 for more information on these records). It is critical that an incident report be completed and appropriately filed. Make sure that *all* of the findings are recorded, dated, and signed. There should also be informed consent forms for administering emergency care and transporting the athlete, and insurance information forms with the athlete if he or she is to be transported.

Summary

1. Standard operating procedures for developing a care plan vary with the site.
2. Key personnel should ideally include physicians, athletic trainers, and other medical specialties.
3. The role of each member of the team must be defined.
4. Implementation of the emergency care plan requires rehearsal throughout the year.
5. Contact with the local emergency medical service is critical to the plan's success.
6. Chain of command must be established within institutional, EMS, and legal guidelines.
   Should there be a conflict, this must be solved in advance.
7. Life-threatening emergencies take precedence.
8. Parental notification is only required when the athlete is a minor.
9. The central focus should be on the care of athletes.
10. Appropriate records must be completed.
11. Finally, the area must be cleaned of any biohazardous materials.

For Critical Thought

In this instance the emergency care plan worked the way it was intended to. What would the ramifications have been if there was poor communication between the athletic trainers and the emergency medical service staff? What could have happened if the EMS was already on site and athletic trainers or team physicians requested that the squad move onto the field, yet EMS personnel walked out to assess for themselves whether the unit was needed? Worse yet, what if the squad loaded the athlete and then remained in place for fifteen minutes while the EMS personnel removed all supporting splinting, backboard, and restraint that the team physician had supervised? Could this have been prevented with communication during the formulation of the ECP?

Websites

National Association of Emergency Medical Technicians Online:
http://www.naemt.org/

   This site has a lot of information on EMT.

Michigan Department of Public Health:
http://www.orcbs.msu.edu/biological/miosha1.htm

   MIOSHA Blood-borne Pathogen Standard.

Applications for Consideration

1. Roberto Vasquez is the certified athletic trainer for a local high school. An athlete has collapsed on the football field. Upon evaluation, Roberto begins CPR because he has determined that the athlete is in cardiac arrest. During this time, other staff members (student athletic trainers and coaches) are unsure what to do to assist the athlete. They are also unsure where much-needed equipment is located.
   How would an emergency care plan alleviate this problem?
2. The certified athletic trainer, Malfalda Mastacci, has assessed an athlete on the field who has sustained an axial load to the cervical spine. Malfalda determines that the emergency medical services are needed on the field to assist with the management of this injury. The EMT determines that the helmet must be removed for safe

transport to the hospital. Malfalda, however voices her opinion based on training that it is safer to keep the helmet in place to avoid excessive movement. The consequence of the difference in opinions is that the EMT and the ATC debate their points for several minutes while the athlete lies on the field. Who has jurisdiction in this situation? What should have been done in order to prevent this situation from occurring?

3.   The certified athletic trainer's name for Southern Glens Falls High School is Hiroshi Yokohoma. He has traveled to Luzerne Boys School with the ice hockey team for an overnight stay before the state championship game. During practice, an athlete is checked into the boards and is now unresponsive. In addition to caring for the athlete, Hiroshi learns that there is no other certified athletic trainer or medical personnel available to assist in activating the emergency care plan. Hence, he has no knowledge of key information such as phone locations, phone numbers for EMS or police, etc. What could Hiroshi have done before traveling to Luzerne's ice hockey facility? What legal ramifications could occur as a result of Hiroshi's situation?

References

1   Ball, RT. Legal responsibilities and problems. In Ryan, AJ, Allman, FL, eds. *Sports medicine.* 2nd ed. San Diego: Academic Press, 1989.

2   Harris, AJ. Disaster plan–A part of the game plan. *Journal of Athletic Training.* 23(1):59, 1988.

3   Herbert, DL. Do you need a written emergency response plan? *The Sports Medicine Standards and Malpractice Reporter.* 11(s):17, 20–24, 1999.

4   Herbert, DL. Deficiencies in emergency response planning and execution. *The Sports Medicine Standards and Malpractice Reporter.* 10(4):49, 52–57, 1998.

5   Herbert, DL. Developing a comprehensive sports medicine emergency care plan. *The Sports Medicine Standards and Malpractice Reporter.* 7(4):49, 52, 1995.

6   Kimball, R, Brown, EW, Lillegard, W, Nogle, S, Mackowiak, T. Care of common sports injuries. In Seteldt, V, Brown, EW, eds. *Program for athletic coaches' education.* Indianapolis. IN: Brown & Benchmark, 11–15, 1992.

7   Munnings, F. The death of Hank Gathers: A legacy of confusion. *The Physician and Sports Medicine.* 18(5):97–102, 1990.

8   NATA Board of Certification, Inc. *Certification standards.* www.nataboc.org., 1998.

9   *NCAA sports handbook.* Guideline 1A: Sports Administration. Revised August 1999.

10   Neal, T. Ready to rescue. *Athletic Management.* 9(5):42–45, 1997.

11   Nowlan, WP, Davis, GA, McDonald, B. Preparing for sudden emergencies. *Athletic Therapy Today.* 1(1): 45–47, 1996.

12   Parcel, GS, Rinear CE. *Basic emergency care of the sick and injured.* 4th ed. St. Louis: Times Mirror/Mosby College Publishing, 1990.

13   Rehberg, RS. Football helmets: To remove or not to remove . . . should there be a question? *NATA News.* 4–6, (June) 1993.

14   Rieff, R. The medical management of sporting events. NATA Annual Meeting and Clinical Symposium, Baltimore, MD, June 17–20, 1998.

15   Walsh, K. Development of an emergency action plan. NATA Annual Meeting and Clinical Symposium, Kansas City, MO, June 16–19,1999.

CHAPTER 13

Organizing and Administering Preparticipation Physical Examinations

After reading this chapter, you should be able to:

- Discuss the principles governing preparticipation examinations.

- State the goals of the preparticipation examination.

- Develop forms to evaluate an athlete's medical history.

- Identify appropriate medical and musculoskeletal examination tests.

- Develop appropriate sport-specific tests.

- Recognize specific skills of professionals involved in the preparticipation examination and use them appropriately.

- Discuss important legal ramifications of the preparticipation examination.

Key Terms

preparticipation physical examination
health appraisal update

medical history
medical examination
maturity
sport-specific
disqualification
personnel
consent
waiver

FOR CRITICAL THOUGHT:
The Station Exam

Duane Johnson is a sophomore wrestler at Gemini State College. He is returning for his second year at school and is anxious for wrestling practices to begin. Over the summer he received several mailings from Tim Best, the college's head athletic trainer, regarding insurance and physical exams. Duane's parents mailed the insurance forms and he knows that physicals will be the first Saturday afternoon here at school.

On Saturday Duane goes to the field house where the physicals will be conducted. They are set up differently than they were his freshman year, and things seem a little simpler this time around. Duane starts at the check-in room, where he sees his coach and several teammates and checks in with a student athletic trainer. The SAT makes sure that Duane's medical file is on hand, and that he has mailed in his insurance information. The student then tells Duane that he can go ahead to the next station. Duane proceeds to the next station, where he encounters another student athletic trainer, who records Duane's height and weight. Duane is then sent to the next room and asked to sit for a few minutes so that a resting heart rate and blood pressure can be taken by one of the nurses who came from the local hospital to help with physicals. After Duane has his blood pressure and heart rate assessed, he proceeds to the next station with an assistant athletic trainer, Janice. Janice oversees medical care for the wrestling team and proceeds to take an updated history from Duane. She asks him about injuries from last season and if anything occurred over the summer. Duane remembers that he sprained his ankle playing pick-up basketball sometime in July. He said that he couldn't walk on it for a few days, and was unable to work at his job as a lifeguard for a week because he couldn't run on the beach. Duane also states that even though he could go back to work, his ankle still swelled and bothered him at times. Janice notes the information, asks other questions about Duane's upper extremity and overall health, and then performs an evaluation on Duane's injured ankle. Janice notes some mild effusion, but mainly finds decreased strength in the dorsiflexors and everters. Duane also has a positive anterior drawer test. She then accompanies Duane to the next station.

At the next station, Janice introduces Duane to Dr. Billy Yoshi, an orthopedic fellow who will be working with the college this year. Janice updates Dr. Yoshi on the ankle injury Duane sustained this summer, gives him her impression, and asks if Dr. Johnson could also make an assessment. Dr. Yoshi confirms Janice's suspicions and together

they agree to implement a comprehensive ankle rehabilitation program prior to the wrestling season. Janice informs Duane of what occurred and why he is still having trouble with his ankle, and explains the importance of seeing her in the athletic training room on Monday morning. Duane agrees and is sent to the next station.

The next station is the check-out station, where Duane speaks to Tim, the head athletic trainer and Dr. Mohamed, the head team physician. Duane is told that based on the findings of his annual health appraisal, he has conditionally passed the physical examination. He will not be cleared to fully participate in wrestling until his ankle strength has returned to normal.

The **preparticipation physical examination** (PPE) is a principal tool for injury prevention. Generally, the PPE is an athlete's initial exposure to the sports medicine team. Likewise, it is the sports medicine team's initial exposure to the athlete. The ability to provide optimal health care to the athlete begins here. The PPE requires in-depth planning. This chapter is designed to assist with this planning effort. Principles and goals of the PPE are identified, potential components of the PPE and the personnel necessary are explained, and selected legal ramifications of decisions made following the PPE are discussed.

PRINCIPLES GOVERNING PREPARTICIPATION PHYSICAL EXAMINATIONS

The preparticipation physical examination (PPE) is designed to collect medical information about athletes to ensure their readiness to participate in a chosen sport. The design of the PPE should allow assessment of risk factors and detect any disease and/or injury that might create problems for the athlete during activities. At this time, there is no uniform agreement concerning the format and objectives of the PPE. However, most believe that the PPE should permit athletes to participate in the safest manner possible.[9,13,14] The reasons for collecting such information should be clear in the athletic trainer's mind before the PPE is administered. It is important to realize, prior to designing the PPE, that different age groups under different situations call for different types of screening examinations.[18] Each component of the exam, and each aspect of the athlete's past and present history, should contribute to the quality of health care provided. The components selected for the PPE must also be necessary and ethical.

Each instrument used in the PPE, whether it is a diagnostic test or a questionnaire, should be valid and reliable. Failure to measure the desired attribute may result in a threat to the well-being of the athlete. The athlete must understand each item on a questionnaire. It is also important to ensure that any instruments used to measure physical attributes or performance (i.e., scales, body fat analyzers, dynamometers, ECG, etc.) are properly calibrated and operated by trained individuals.

Elements of the PPE should be evaluated for their appropriateness based on the physical demands of athletes for that particular sport. As with rehabilitation, assurance that the athletes can safely perform their selected sport is mandatory.

GOALS OF PREPARTICIPATION PHYSICAL EXAMINATIONS

Kibler[14] identified five goals of a PPE:

1. Provide an objective, sport-specific musculoskeletal exam.
2. Obtain negative information that alters participation options.
3. Obtain positive information to decrease injury potential and increase performance.
4. Provide a reproducible record for comparison in the future.
5. Provide baseline data for sport-specific conditioning.

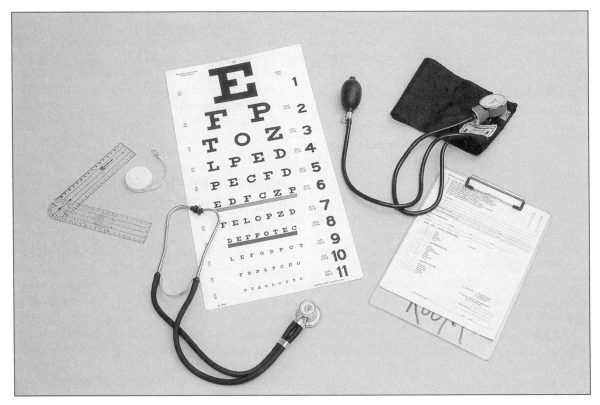

Preparticipation physical examinations require a variety of diagnostic equipment.

Because the PPE is designed to determine an athlete's readiness to participate in his or her chosen sport, sport specificity is essential. Observing an intact musculoskeletal system does not ensure that the athlete is physically prepared to participate in the sport. For example, adequate strength for the functions of daily living is by no means adequate for participation in athletics.

The PPE should be used to identify conditions or injuries that would disallow or require changes in participation for the athlete. Again, findings that may contraindicate participation must be considered in light of the expectation and demands of the athlete's particular sport. The American Academy of Pediatrics Committee on Sports Medicine[6] provides recommendations regarding contraindications for sports participation. Its recommendations are based on the demands of different types of sports: contact/collision sports, limited contact/impact sports, strenuous noncontact activities, moderately strenuous noncontact activities, and nonstrenuous non-contact activities.

The PPE is not designed to rule out participation for athletes, but more importantly to identify factors that may decrease injury potential and improve performance. For example, the athletic trainer may wish to assess flexibility or range of motion (ROM) during the PPE. Evaluation of hamstring flexibility in football players or shoulder range of motion in baseball players may assist in preventing eventual injury. Hamstring tightness may lead to low back pain and/or eventual injury, while decreased shoulder ROM in a baseball pitcher will certainly lead to compensation and overload placed on other upper extremity structures. Measurements of these attributes may allow the athletic trainer to identify athletes with certain deficits that will predispose them to injury. Once these are identified, the athlete can be placed on a daily stretching or ROM program for the affected extremity, thereby preventing future injury and perhaps increasing performance.

Accurate and reproducible records of the athletic trainer's findings during the PPE are essential. If inadequate information about a condition or injury is collected, later efforts to alleviate the problem may be thwarted. If later action is affected, much of the value of the PPE is lost.

Information recorded during the PPE can also serve as baseline data for the attributes measured for the athletes. This information allows comparisons of past and present athletes and may be helpful for making sport-specific decisions about an athlete's readiness to participate. For these reasons, never dispose of old PPEs.

Three methods of administering the PPE include the office visit, the assembly line approach, or the mass screening station approach. The office visit simply involves the athlete making an appointment with his or her family physician to have a physical examination performed. The assembly line method usually involves the athlete's lining up in a locker room where the examiner examines each athlete in turn.[9] The station approach may be set up in one of two manners. The first method is a "space-available" format and the second is a "straight-line" approach.[16] In the space-available format, the athlete goes to whatever station is available, after checking in. Once the athlete has visited all stations, he or she then checks out. In the straight-line method, after checking in, the athlete will go to each station in a predetermined order (see figure 13-1).

Where and how the PPE is administered usually depends on the type of institution involved. Almost all college and university programs use a station-based approach. In high school and junior high school settings, PPEs are performed in the physician's office, via the assembly line method, or in a station-based mass screening. There are advantages and disadvantages to each of these methods[9,10,20] (see table 13-1).

DuRant et al.[7] have compared the results of single examiner (office visit or assembly line method) against multiple examiner in the PPE. Multiple examiners detected a greater number of musculoskeletal abnormalities than single examiners. Additionally, Linder, et al.[15] suggested that the success of the station method is highly dependent on the examiners' specialties.

FREQUENCY AND TIMING OF THE PREPARTICIPATION PHYSICAL EXAMINATION

Many researchers[9,13,15,18] recommend that the PPE be conducted at least four to eight weeks before the start of the season. This allows enough time for

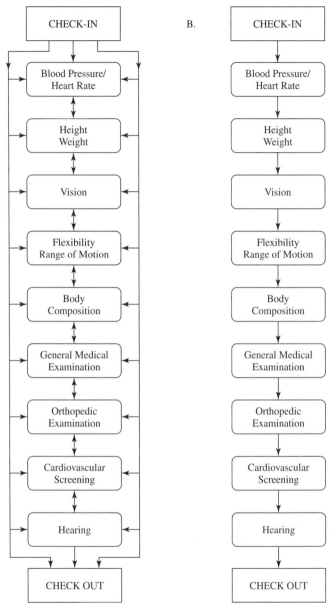

Figure 13-1 Traffic flow patterns when using the station-based method of performing physical examinations. A. Example of the space available setup. B. Example of the straight-line method.

follow-up, rehabilitation of injuries, or further evaluation if deemed necessary. Some recommend the PPE take place in May or June for fall sports. The problem with scheduling the PPE at that time is that many things can occur to the athlete over the course of the summer, and therefore a recheck should be completed when the athlete returns to school.[20]

The frequency of the PPE is another matter of controversy. Some recommend that the PPE be performed before the beginning of each sport season,

■ **TABLE 13-1**   Comparison of Various Settings for Administering the PPE

Office-Based PPE

Advantages	Disadvantages
• Established relationship between the physician and the athlete • Established relationship allows facilitated discussion of sensitive issues • Continuity of care • Conducive to counseling on health-related issues • Knowledge of past medical history • Better assessment of motivation • Easier to make arrangements for a quick follow-up if necessary	• Lack of established relationship between many adolescents and their primary care/family physicians • Potentially difficult to schedule PPE in relation to the season • Potential increased cost • Physician may lack sport interest and/or knowledge about the demands of the activity • More difficult communication with the ATC, team physician, and other members of the sports medicine team • Lack of consistency in judgments regarding qualification, disqualification, and referral standards

Assembly Line Method

Advantages	Disadvantages
• Fastest method • Allows the physician to see the most athletes in the shortest amount of time	• Does not provide the examiner access to past medical history unless the athletes have an established record on hand or complete a checklist prior to the exam • Does not allow time for personalized attention • No continuity of care

Station-Based Examination

Advantages	Disadvantages
• Use of specialized personnel with an interest in and knowledge of athletics and demands of sport • Cost effectiveness • Can utilize lay personnel (coaches, etc.) to assist with certain stations such as sign-in, traffic flow, height, or weight • Better communication between members of the sports medicine team because most are participating in the screening procedures • May be able to include performance testing • Ability to screen a large number of athletes	• Need an adequate number of personnel • Need adequate and large enough facilities • Lack of privacy • Disruptive environments • Medical personnel may feel hurried due to the large number of athletes usually involved • Difficult to communicate with the athlete's parent or legal guardian • Difficult to follow up if the physician is not the institution or athlete's regular physician • May not be familiar with the medical history or history of previous injury. This is dependent on the materials forwarded from the athlete's previous physician • Difficult to establish a doctor-patient relationship

while others recommend a PPE when moving from one level to the next.[9,18,20] The American Medical Association (AMA) recommends for adolescents that a PPE be done at the beginning of any new level of competition, such as going from junior high school to high school.[2] The AMA also recom-

mends that a review of the athlete's medical history should occur at the start of each season. The NCAA requires a PPE upon entrance into a collegiate athletic program. After the initial examination, it is recommended that an updated history be performed annually to detect any problems or conditions. Further PPEs are not deemed necessary by the NCAA,[4] unless warranted by the updated history. The NCAA instead allows a **health appraisal update** for all returning athletes. Essentially, the athletic trainer is required to identify and document all conditions or injuries that have developed since the last PPE or health appraisal update. This is in contrast to the recommendation of a consortium of medical associations that a comprehensive physical examination be done upon initial entry and thereafter.[22] The consortium suggests that the examination could be done biannually if there is well-trained support staff such as athletic trainers available to review the interim history and notify physicians of potential problems requiring physician evaluation.

COMPONENTS OF THE PREPARTICIPATION PHYSICAL EXAMINATION

The PPE is generally comprised of questionnaires to assess past medical history, specific physical examinations, and sport-specific assessments.

History Examination

Various **medical history** forms are used during the PPE. All of the information may be collected on one general form or it may be separated. If at all possible, the athletic trainer should conduct verbal interviews to determine the history. In this manner, additional and follow-up questions can be asked of the athlete, possibly uncovering important medical information. Most studies suggest that approximately 70 percent of problems are identified during the PPE through adequate history taking alone.[16] An athlete's personal medical history (immunizations, removal of spleen, hepatitis, surgeries, etc.), family medical history (asthma, diabetes, genetic disorders, alcohol abuse, cardiovascular disease prevalence, etc.), and personal orthopedic history (previous injuries, surgeries, rehabilitation, etc.) should all be ascertained. Other important components of the preparticipation history include obtaining information on the following:

General history: Hospitalizations, surgeries, chronic medical problems, or illnesses since the previous examination.

Cardiovascular risk factors: Dizziness, lightheadedness, syncope during or after exercise; chest pain and palpitations during or after exercise; shortness of breath and fatigue out of proportion; high blood pressure, high cholesterol, recent viral illnesses (mononucleosis, myocarditis); family history of hypertrophic cardiomyopathy or of sudden cardiac death prior to 50 years of age; family history of Marfan syndrome; cocaine use or anabolic steroid use; prior restrictions to athletic participation due to cardiovascular concerns.

Dermatologic: Current skin problems such as warts, rashes, acne, herpes, or blisters.

Drug use: Medication usage, including prescription and over-the-counter; allergy information should be obtained, including allergy to medications, as well as to the environment, food, and/or insects; drug or alcohol abuse in athlete or family members; steroid usage.

Female athletes: Menstrual history, including age of onset (menarche), most recent menstruation, regularity of cycle, and any missed cycles (amenorrhea); adequate nutrition and calcium intake; any irregular eating habits.

Heat-related illness: Prior incidences of problems with the heat, including heat cramps, exhaustion, stroke, or malignant hyperthermia.

Musculoskeletal: Type and severity of prior injury, such as sprains, strains, fractures; swelling or pain; past treatment and rehabilitation of any prior injuries.

Neurologic: Frequent headaches, migraines, and/or seizures.

Concussion: Incidence, type, and severity of prior head injuries; presence of concussive symptoms.

Spinal Injury: Prior burners or stingers, any numbness or tingling in arms, legs, hands, or feet.

Pulmonary: Shortness of breath, wheezing, or coughing during or after activity; seasonal allergies; any episodes of exercise-induced asthma.

Sickle cell trait: Athletes of African ancestry should be asked if they carry the sickle cell trait.

Solitary organs: Prevalence of one paired organ (eye, testes, kidney, etc.).

Weight: Questions regarding body image, perceived ideal weight, and recent weight changes.

Other: Depression, anxiety, general stress.

Medical Examination

It is not enough to simply determine an athlete's past injuries or conditions. It is also essential to examine the athlete. This is usually accomplished with a general **medical examination**, a musculoskeletal (or orthopedic) examination, and a sport-specific (performance) evaluation.[14]

The *general medical examination* starts with some vital statistics of the athlete such as age, sex, height, weight, blood pressure, and heart rate. The exam then proceeds to evaluate various body regions and systems, including head, eyes, ears, nose, throat, chest, abdomen, skin condition, genitalia, and possible hernia. The general medical examination is designed to identify the presence of common medical conditions.

Additionally, Arnheim[3] advocates Tanner staging as a guide to physical **maturity** when adolescents participate in collision or contact sports. The AMA Board of Trustees[2] also recommends that athletes have a proper assessment of physical maturity to ensure a proper match within their level of athletic participation. Tanner staging rates pubic hair and genital development in males, and pubic hair, hip, and breast development in females. The consortium PPE[22] recommends that Tanner staging be done; however, it also states that there is no data to support claims of physical or psychological harm where athletes participate against those of higher stages.[22] It is thought, however, that physical maturity staging will help to identify athletes at risk. The greatest incidence of epiphyseal injuries occurs during pubescence. Also, it is felt that during a growth spurt, the young athlete is predisposed to overuse injuries resulting from relative tendon tightness and decreased flexibility.[9] The examination itself can be a concern and source of embarrassment for the young athlete. To avoid this additional stress, self-rating by the athlete can be performed. This method has been shown to be as accurate as one performed by an examiner.

The *musculoskeletal (orthopedic) examination* is designed to assess the integrity of the athlete's joints and muscles. This component of the PPE may include an assessment of major joints; manual, isotonic, or isokinetic muscle strength assessment; and joint flexibility. Consideration of the demands of an athlete's particular sport is essential during this examination. The more extensive this examination, the more powerful the PPE can be as an injury prevention tool.

Cardiovascular Screening

In 1996, the American Heart Association (AHA)[17] published recommendations for cardiovascular preparticipation screening for athletes. The AHA states that "some form of preparticipation cardiovascular screening for high school and collegiate athletes is justifiable and compelling, based on ethical, legal, and medical grounds." The recommendations for PPE cardiovascular screening include:

- Family history of premature or sudden death or heart disease in surviving relatives
- Personal history of heart murmur, systemic hypertension, excessive fatigability, syncope, exertional dyspnea or chest pain, as well as parental verification of the history
- Physical examination for heart murmur, femoral pulses, stigmata of Marfan syndrome or blood pressure measurement, which includes the recommendation of precordial auscultation in both supine or sitting and standing position to identify heart murmurs consistent with left ventricular outflow tract obstruction[17]

The AHA also recommends that trained individuals perform the cardiovascular screening portion of the PPE.

Sport Specificity

Different sports have different demands. Consequently, it is essential that the PPE evaluate an athlete's readiness to participate in his or her particular sport. **Sport-specific** tests can be designed to evaluate the athlete's readiness to participate. As examples, the following tests may be considered:

- Flexibility, strength, power, anaerobic endurance, aerobic endurance
- Establish flexibility with a sit-and-reach test and goniometer measurements
- Establish strength with manual exercises, dynamometers
- Establish power with power activities (vertical jump, etc.)
- Establish anaerobic endurance with specific activity (40-yard dash, shuttle run, sit-ups in one minute, etc.)
- Establish aerobic endurance with specific activity (distance in a twelve-minute run, step-test, submaximal treadmill or bicycle tests, etc.)[14]

It is essential that the person responsible for setting up the sport-specific testing protocols understand the demands each sport places on the human body. A twelve-minute run is not a good test of the readiness to play softball, but may be useful in endurance sports such as soccer or road bicycling. Conversely, maximum power testing would be invalid to assess cross-country running but helpful in football. As a result, mixed anaerobic-aerobic load sports are the most difficult to get an accurate assessment of readiness.

A neurological examination may be performed during the PPE for those athletes who will be participating in collision and contact sports. Several tests or assessment tools should be completed in order to evaluate the athlete's neurological and psychomotor abilities before athletic participation. In the event that a head injury is sustained, the athletic trainer will have a baseline to compare to when assessing the extent of the injury. One example of an evaluation tool is the SAC (Standardized Assessment of Concussion), which can easily be performed during a PPE, on the sideline, or in the athletic training room.

Medical Disqualification

The physician administering the examination determines whether the athlete is fit to compete.

Disqualification from participation in a particular sport must be based on valid medical reasons that the athlete is at risk if allowed to compete. Physicians generally will clear an athlete for all possible activity, clear the athlete pending follow-up examination, or disqualify the athlete for some or all levels of activity.[22]

According to the American Academy of Orthopedic Surgeons,[1] a physician has six options for qualification versus disqualification. They are: passed, passed with conditions, passed with reservations, failed with reservations, failed with conditions, and failed. The conditions for each of the six options are:

1. Passed:
   - Unconditional
   - No reservations
   - Cleared for all activities and all levels of exertion
   - No current or preexisting medical problems
   - No contraindications for collision or contact sports
2. Passed with conditions:
   - Has a medical problem that needs follow-up
   - Able to participate in sports at present
   - Follow-up must occur before athletic participation
3. Passed with reservations:
   - No collision sports
   - No contact sports
4. Failed with reservations:
   - Not cleared for requested activity (may be considered for other sports)
   - Collision not permitted, contact limited
   - Contact not permitted, noncontact sports allowed
5. Failed with conditions:
   - Can be reconsidered after medical problem is addressed
6. Failed:
   - Unconditional
   - No reservations
   - Cannot be cleared for any sport or any level of competition

Personnel

The PPE is a large undertaking. Therefore, many professionals are needed to provide quality PPEs. Because the services of those who do not work with the athletes on a day-to-day basis may be necessary, it is important to provide all **personnel** with advanced notice. For example, if PPEs are planned for July, it is best to advise all personnel of the day, time, and requested time commitment in March. This allows advanced planning. Providing such an advanced notice may also require written follow-up notes.

An effective use of personnel enhances the quality of the PPE. Before assigning tasks, carefully evaluate the skills of each member of the PPE team. Professionals have specific skills. Take advantage of the expertise available. Table 13-2 lists potential stations of a PPE and professionals to operate them.

Who can give exams and what they must include in writing is extremely varied. The National

■ **TABLE 13-2**   Stations and Staffing for Preparticipation Physical Examinations

Station	Professional
Aerobic capacity	Team/consulting physician, resident, or intern
	Team/consulting exercise physiologist
Anaerobic capacity	Team/consulting physician, resident, or intern
	Team/consulting exercise physiologist or strength coach
Audiometry	Staff athletic trainer
	Student athletic trainer
	Team/consulting physician, resident, or intern
Blood pressure and heart rate	Staff athletic trainer
	Student athletic trainer
Body composition	Team/consulting exercise physiologist
	Staff athletic trainer
	Student athletic trainer
Check-in	Athletic department personnel
	Student athletic trainer
	Staff athletic trainer
	School nurse
Check-out	Student athletic trainer
	Staff athletic trainer
	School nurse
EKG	Team/consulting cardiologist
	Team/consulting exercise physiologist
Family medical history	Staff athletic trainer
	School nurse
Flexibility testing	Staff athletic trainer
	Staff/consulting physical therapist
	Student athletic trainer
	Team/consulting exercise physiologist
Medical exam	Team physician
	Team/consulting family physician
	Team/consulting internist
	Local medical residents or interns
Orthopedic exam	Team/consulting orthopedic surgeon
	Team/consulting family physician
	Orthopedic fellows
Personal medical history	Staff athletic trainer
	School nurse
	Staff/consulting physical therapist

(continued)

■ **TABLE 13-2** Stations and Staffing for Preparticipation Physical Examinations (*Concluded*)

Station	Professional
Personal orthopedic history	Staff athletic trainer
	Staff/consulting physical therapist
Power assessment	Staff athletic trainer
	Student athletic trainer
	Team/consulting exercise physiologist or strength coach
Strength assessment	Staff athletic trainer
	Staff/consulting physical therapist
	Team/consulting exercise physiologist or strength coach
Traffic flow	Athletic department staff/coach
	Student athletic trainer
Urinalysis	Staff athletic trainer
	School nurse
	Student athletic trainer
Vision screening	Team/consulting opthalmologist
	Team/consulting optometrist
	Staff athletic trainer
	Student athletic trainer
Weight and height	Staff athletic trainer
	School nurse
	Student athletic trainer

Federation of State High School Associations (NFHS) has no blanket policy requiring their use; instead, each state has its own guidelines for requiring and conducting PPEs.[5] On November 4, 1998 the NFHS[21] stated in a press release that PPEs for high school–age athletes "are a necessary and desirable pre-condition to interscholastic athletic practice and competition."[21] The NFHS, however, has not endorsed a nationwide standard format or form for the PPE, stating that adopting a standardized form would not be practical because state laws and local conditions vary. This has resulted in uneven administration and documentation of information.

For example, Glover and Maron,[8] in a study of all fifty states and the District of Columbia, found much diversity in the PPE forms used. Eight states (CA, GA, ME, MS, NH, NJ, OR, RI) do not have recommended history or physical questionnaires. Most forms used for the PPE were developed by state high school athletic associations, usually in collaboration with state medical associations. The same study evaluated how much the state PPE included the

1996 AHA recommendations for cardiovascular screening. It was found that 40 percent of state associations do not offer approved history and physical examination questionnaires, have no screening requirement, or have screening forms deficient according to AHA recommendations. Based on their findings, the authors suggest that there be a national standardization of the history and physical exam forms for preparticipation screening of high school athletes.

SELECTED LEGAL RAMIFICATIONS OF PREPARTICIPATION PHYSICAL EXAMINATIONS

The utilization of the PPE has brought about some legal concerns that should be weighed. Some athletes or their parents may assume that this physical is equivalent to a family physician's comprehensive physical examination. This is not the case and was never intended to be. A certain percentage of underlying problems that could affect future activities of daily living (and even life itself) will not be found by the PPE. In addition, not all problems will necessarily be identified that will have an impact on an athlete's ability to withstand participation in a sport. Some athletes assume that if they pass the exam, they will be invulnerable to injury in their sport. Because the exam should involve some exertion, there is a possibility that the exam can induce injury, and the athlete must be forewarned before any action takes place. All of these things need to be discussed in writing with athletes, parents, and coaches.

During the 1990s, the number of persons accusing physicians of sexual impropriety during physical examinations increased.[12] Such claims are usually made by members of the same or opposite sex under the battery section of malpractice laws. Often actions such as listening to heart and respiratory sounds through a stethoscope or palpation of abdominal, pelvic, or breast areas for legitimate medical reasons may be seen by the patient as having sexual overtones. To prevent this occurrence, Herbert[12] suggests that the physician have an allied healthcare professional, preferably of the same sex as the patient, present during the exam. This witness should be noted in the record. If the patient refuses to allow a witness, Herbert further suggests the physician refer the patient to another physician. If the patient persists in requesting the examination continue without a witness, this should be noted in the record and countersigned by the patient.[12]

A **consent** form granting actual consent should be obtained allowing the exam to be given, including the physical exertion assessments. In athletes eighteen years of age or older, this may be done directly. If the athletes are minors, consent must be obtained from the parents or guardians. Remember that the athlete in no way waives rights in this situation, only the parents do (see chapter 16).

With the passage of the Americans with Disabilities Act, disqualification must be based on factors that adversely affect the health of the athlete should they be allowed to participate. People with disabilities can only be excluded from intramurals or team activities if their participation is likely to result in

danger to other participants.[19] When the disability affects the skill level of an athlete, but not the athlete's potential to become injured, then the athlete may be cut from the squad by the coach for lack of skill but not prohibited from trying by the physical examination findings.

Athletic trainers must keep complete, detailed, written records of the history findings, the medical examination findings, and the orthopedic findings in each athlete's medical file (it is a good idea to use carbonless paper and make multiple copies to be kept by the athletic training room and by the physician giving the examination in case a patient record is lost).

Should an athlete wish to participate after having been disqualified, and the parents agree, then **waiver** of liability forms are the only safeguard against later legal action. The athlete must be given "full disclosure of all information" that would allow the athlete to make a reasoned and competent decision to participate.[10,11] This includes all foreseeable risks of participation. These waivers have been upheld in various courts.

In some conditions, such as cardiovascular or neurological complications, the team physicians may disqualify a person who still wishes to play. Under these conditions, the conservative approach would be for the athlete to file suit against the physician for denying the right to participate, allowing the courts to issue an order allowing the participation to occur. A copy of the order should then be entered in the athlete's medical file. This resolves somewhat the issues of informed consent and waivers that may be declared by a court not to be in the public interest at a later date. As long as there is no negligent conduct on the part of the medical staff, they would theoretically be protected from suit later if participation has adverse results (e.g., the deaths of Flo Hyman, Hank Gathers, and Reggie Lewis). It should also be noted that if the athlete is married, unless a spouse also signs a waiver, the spouse is not precluded from bringing action for "loss of consortium" against the school or team, athletic trainers, and physicians. This is more of a problem for colleges and universities and for professional teams than high schools. (For a more comprehensive discussion of waivers, see chapter 16.)

Summary

1. PPEs should be designed to allow athletes to participate in the safest manner possible, as well as assess any risk factors the athlete may possess.
2. Each component should have a specific purpose for its inclusion in the PPE.
3. The PPE may be conducted in a physician's office, in an assembly line approach, or via the station-to-station approach. There are advantages and disadvantages to each method. The athletic trainer should weigh all factors when designing the PPE.
4. PPEs should be performed before the sport season and, at the least, at the beginning of any new level of competition.
5. The components of the PPE include various questions for determining medical history. This should include sections to determine specific risk factors. A medical examination includes a general medical assessment, orthopedic screening, cardiovascular screening, and sport-specific tests.
6. The physician makes the final decision regarding participation or disqualification.
7. Qualified and educated medical personnel should perform each section of the PPE.
8. The PPE is not meant to be a comprehensive annual physical examination. This should be fully explained to athletes and parents.
9. The athletic trainer should document all PPE findings and should maintain all appropriate records and forms from the physical examinations.

For Critical Thought

When large numbers of athletes are involved, most sports medicine programs find it convenient to do group physical examinations. Station examinations are common. There are distinct advantages and disadvantages to this type of preparticipation physical examination. When an athlete is encountered who was injured, what problems may arise? What is the chain of command? Should Janice have consulted with the head athletic trainer before consulting with the team physician? Would a physical examination in the physician's office have been better? What factors were against this type of examination?

Websites

NFSHSA:
http://www.nfhs.org/home.html

Official web site of the National Federation of State High School Associations (NFSHSA). Contains several links to sites dealing with important issues in high school athletics, including a sports medicine link.

NCAA Sportsmed Site:
http://www.ncaa.org/sports_sciences/sports_med_handbook/

A link from the NCAA website. This site is the online version of the most recent NCAA Sports Medicine Handbook, which is published annually.

AAP:
http://www.aap.org/

This is the home site for the American Academy of Pediatrics. The site contains important information, including medical disqualification criteria and links related to pediatric medicine.

AMSSM Home Page:
http://www.sportsmed.upmc.edu/~amssm/

The home page for the American Medical Society for Sports Medicine.

American Heart Association:
http://amhrt.org/

Home page for the American Heart Association. Search for "preparticipation physical examination" to obtain their position paper.

Applications for Consideration

1. Darlene Mandella just took a position as the head athletic trainer at City High School. It is June and she would like to begin preparing for the fall season. City High School has 2500 students, and 1500 of these students participate in the interscholastic sport program. Darlene knows that setting up physicals for 1500 athletes will be difficult, but feels that by organizing the PPE herself, she will gain a better knowledge of any conditions that may be detected. What steps will Darlene need to perform in order to organize the physicals? Approximately how many physicians and sites does Darlene need to achieve her goal of qualifying more than 1500 athletes? How many athletic trainers and other allied medical personnel does she need to complete the task? Where could these examinations take place, and how long will it take to complete the task?

2. Johnny Monk, a blue-chip basketball recruit, is attending Southern Junior College on a scholarship. During the PPE, the physician determines that Johnny has strong risk factors for Marfan syndrome and sudden cardiac death. After a full cardiovascular workup, including echocardiogram and ECG, Dr. Young disqualifies Johnny from participation on the team. Johnny and his family are upset about this and file suit against the athletic trainer, physician, and school. What could be done before the PPE to avoid this type of suit? What can the athletic trainer do in this situation? Is there anything that could have prevented Johnny from filing suit?

References

1 American Academy of Orthopedic Surgeons. *Athletic training and sports medicine.* 2nd ed. Park Ridge, IL: AAOS, 49–64, 1991.

2 American Medical Association Board of Trustees, Group on Science and Technology. Athletic preparticipation examinations for adolescents. *Archives of Pediatric and Adolescent Medicine.* 148:93–98, 1994.

3 Arnheim, DD, Prentice, WE. *Principles of athletic training.* 10th ed. Dubuque, IA: McGraw-Hill, 46–53, 2000.

4 Benson, MT, ed. *1999–2000 NCAA sports medicine handbook.* Overland Park, KS: NCAA, 1999.

5 Bonci, C. Anatomy of a physical. *Athletic Management.* 4(4):22–30, 1992.

6 Committee on Sports Medicine. Recommendations for participation in competitive sports. *Pediatrics* 81:737–739, 1988.

7 DuRant, RH, Seymore, C, Linder, CW, Jay, S. The preparticipation examination of athletes: Comparison of single and multiple examiners. *American Journal of Diseases of Children.* 139:657–661, 1985.

8 Glover, DW, Maron, BJ. Profile of preparticipation cardiovascular screening for high school athletes. *Journal of the American Medical Association.* 279:1817–1819, 1998.

9 Grafe, MW, Paul, GR, Foster, TE. The preparticipation sports examination for high school and college athletes. *Clinics in Sports Medicine.* 16:569–591, 1997.

10 Herbert, DL. Proof of fraudulent concealment of medical information requires findings in favor of professional football player. *The Sports, Parks & Recreation Law Reporter.* 1:23–25, 1987.

11 Herbert, DL. Reexamining team physician/athletic trainer relationships with athletes in light of fraudulent concealment of medical information and similar claims. *The Sports, Parks & Recreation Law Reporter.* 1:44–47, 1987.

12 Herbert, DL. Professional considerations related to the conduct of preparticipation examinations. *The Sports Medicine Standards and Malpractice Reporter.* 6(4):49–52, 1994.

13 Johnson, MD, Kibler, WB, Smith, D. Keys to successful preparticipation exams. *Physician and Sportsmedicine.* 21(9):109–123, 1993.

14 Kibler, WB. *The sport preparticipation fitness examination.* Champaign, IL: Human Kinetics Books, 1990.

15 Linder, CW, DuRant, RH, Seklecki, RM, Strong, WB. Preparticipation health screening of young athletes: Results of 1268 examinations. *American Journal of Sports Medicine.* 9:187–193, 1981.

16 Magee, DJ. Orthopedic physical assessment. Philadelphia: W.B. Saunders Co. 758–781, 1997.

17 Maron, BJ, Thompson, PD, Puffer, JC, McGrew, CA, Strong, WB, Douglas, PS, Clark, LT, Mitten, MJ, Crawford, MH, Atkins, DL, Driscoll, DJ, Epstein, AE. Cardiovascular preparticipation screening of competitive athletes: A statement for health professionals from the sudden death committee (clinical cardiology) and congenital cardiac defects committee (cardiovascular disease in the young), American Heart Association. *Circulation.* 94:850–856, 1996.

18 McKeag, DB. Preparticipation screening of the potential athlete. *Clinics in Sports Medicine.* 8:373–397, 1989.

19 Munson, AL, Comodeca, JA. The act of inclusion. *Athletic Management.* 5(4):14–19, 1993.

20 Myers, A, Sickles, T. Preparticipation sports examination. *Primary Care,* 25:225–236, 1998.

21 National Federation of State High School Associations. NFHS Encourages Preparticipation Physical Evaluations. Press release; http://www.nfhs.org/PR-eval.htm.

22 Swander, H. ed. *Preparticipation physical evaluation.* American Academy of Family Physicians, American Academy of Pediatrics, American Medical Society for Sports Medicine, American Orthopedic Society for Sports Medicine, American Osteopathic Academy of Sports Medicine, 1992.

CHAPTER 14

Public Relations

After reading this chapter, you should be able to:

- Prepare a presentation addressing the duties and professional/educational requirements of an athletic trainer.

- Prepare a presentation addressing when an athletic trainer can provide services.

- Prepare a presentation addressing the various employment settings of athletic trainers.

- Prepare a presentation addressing the necessity of hiring an athletic trainer.

- Prepare a presentation addressing how an athletic trainer can provide a service to an organization.

- Develop a plan to promote athletic training services provided by a sports medicine clinic.

- Evaluate a public relations plan.

Key Terms

public relations
athletic training services
public relations plan

FOR CRITICAL THOUGHT:
I Am Not a Trainer!

*Thursday afternoon, football practice field, coach:
"Hey, trainer! We have someone down on the field."*

•

*Friday evening, football stadium, PA announcer:
"Ladies and gentlemen, we have a player down on the field. Here comes the trainer to check out the situation."*

•

Friday evening, in the locker room after the game, reporter: "Boy, it's a good thing the team has a trainer. Those boys are really in good shape. I bet you spend a lot of time working them out."

•

Friday evening, outside the football stadium after the game, parent: "I am sure glad you were there to help Johnny when he got injured. I didn't realize trainers had so much medical training. I knew you knew a lot about getting people in shape, but I had no idea you knew how to handle injuries in a medical way. Trainers sure are a lot more talented than I thought. Thanks again for helping Johnny."

•

Football awards banquet, head coach: "I would like to take a moment to thank our head trainer,

John Alseeing. He was instrumental in helping us handle injuries all season long. I very much enjoyed having him as an assistant. Many of you do not know how much work the trainer puts in to keep the guys healthy. He has been a real godsend. Thanks, John!"

●

John went home the evening after the awards banquet and began to think about how he was perceived by his patients, their parents, the coaches, and all the others at the high school. It was clear that they all had a misperception about what an athletic trainer was. How, he thought, could he begin to educate them about the job responsibilities and educational preparation of an athletic trainer? He had a sense that he was being confused with personal trainers, such as those on TV selling exercise equipment. He decided it was time to launch a public relations campaign with all the people he was working with. Why is it important for those that John works with to understand the importance of referring to him as an athletic trainer instead of a trainer? What types of educational materials can John put together? Where can he find literature to support his view?

Athletic training is a relatively new allied health profession. The National Athletic Trainers' Association was founded in 1950. It is not surprising that the general public is generally uninformed about athletic training and athletic trainers. Those not familiar with athletic training or athletic trainers often do not realize the full scope of services available from athletic trainers. They may be familiar with a small percentage of services (e.g., taping), or they may misunderstand what an athletic trainer does (e.g., confuse athletic trainers with personal fitness trainers). There has been little effort, historically, by media, moviemakers, and others in the entertainment business to investigate the true capabilities and qualifications of certified athletic trainers when portraying them in film. Therefore, the public's exposure to athletic trainers from media has typically been portrayed by an actor who is cast as an athletic trainer. A recently released film directed by Oliver Stone, *Any Given Sunday*, hired certified athletic trainers to treat injuries to the cast and actors, and even had them portray the roles of athletic trainers in the movie itself.

The term *athletic trainer* doesn't help matters, either. The title of athletic trainer suggests one who "trains" athletes. Consequently, persons who do not live in North America, and some who do, assume that an athletic trainer is a coach or a personal fitness trainer.

To overcome this misinformation or lack of information, we need to promote athletic training and athletic trainers. This is often difficult. Athletic trainers tend to be "givers," and they are reluctant or embarrassed to articulate their own worth. To accomplish the great undertaking of educating the masses, it will be necessary to demonstrate your value, particularly now in this era of healthcare reform. Essentially, you need to convince anyone who will listen that athletic training is a necessary allied healthcare profession.

A planned **public relations** presentation should be a mandatory part of an ATC's professional materials. If asked to talk about athletic training, whether to a booster club, a service club, a hospital administrator, or an athlete's parent, one will be prepared to positively represent the profession.[4]

Any attempt to promote athletic training should coincide with the mission of the National Athletic Trainers' Association, ". . . to enhance the quality of health care for athletes and those engaged in physical activity, and to advance the profession of athletic training through education and research in the prevention, evaluation, management and rehabilitation of injuries."[5]

When encountering something new or not fully understood, we instinctively ask the following questions: who? what? when? where? why? and how? The following section takes each of these questions into consideration.

WHO ARE WE?

The question, "Who are we?," can be answered by explaining the six domains of athletic training; outlining the educational and professional requirements for athletic trainers; explaining the certification, licensure, and/or registration processes that apply; and describing the organization and function of the National Athletic Trainers' Association.

The six domains of athletic training include (1) prevention, (2) recognition, evaluation, and assessment, (3) immediate care, (4) treatment, rehabilitation, and reconditioning, (5) organization and administration, and (6) professional development and responsibility.[6] When explaining the six domains of athletic training, be sure to include examples that are easily understood by the audience being addressed. For example, when explaining the prevention of athletic injuries, it may be appropriate to relate a story such as implementing an ankle-strengthening program one season and reducing the number of ankle injuries by 50 percent. Try to think of an example other than taping—this reinforces a negative stereotype.

Important points to mention regarding educational and professional requirements of athletic trainers include academic preparation, clinical experiences, and continuing education requirements. Certified athletic trainers must obtain a baccalaureate degree with designated course work and/or documented clinical experiences addressing anatomy and physiology, physiology of exercise, kinesiology/biomechanics, psychology, rehabilitation, injury evaluation, and emergency care, among others. At least 800 clinical hours of experience (1500 hours if not from an accredited athletic training education program) must also be acquired before one can take the certification test. Emphasize that educational requirements do not end once the athletic trainer enters the workforce. The NATA requires continuing education units (CEUs) to maintain certification status. Many athletic trainers also continue their education by obtaining master's and doctoral degrees.

Athletic trainers are involved with the development of health care. Many of the techniques developed by athletic trainers are eventually used in the health care of everyone. Athletic trainers are also involved in research. The scientific bases of injury evaluation, care, and prevention of athletic injuries are advanced by athletic training researchers. Essentially, people are getting better faster and more completely thanks to athletic trainers.

It is important to discuss the certification, licensure, or registration process. Credentialing suggests quality. Discuss the quality and difficulty of the NATA Board of Certification Examination. This test is widely acclaimed to be a model examination for allied health professionals. If the state you work in has licensure, explain that state law regulates the practice of athletic training and mention additional tests or competencies needed to obtain licensure.

Discussing the organization and function of the NATA establishes that athletic training is a strong, focused organization with a commitment to the welfare of those who can benefit from our services. Some important points to mention include the membership of the NATA, the NATA board of directors, important committees and foundations of the NATA, and professional leadership.

The membership of the NATA is growing at a tremendous rate; approximately 1100 students become certified every year. This includes approximately the same number of males and females, so athletic training is becoming an equal opportunity profession, even though sport has historically been a male-dominated enterprise.

The board of directors includes representatives from ten districts encompassing the entire United States and parts of Canada. This group is responsible for developing standards of athletic training that continually improve the quality of care for our patients.

A brief mention of key committees or foundations affiliated with the NATA will illustrate the means by which quality is promoted. The Board of Certification, the Education Council (and its relationship to the Joint Review Committee—Athletic Training), continuing education committee, journal committee, and Research and Education Foundation should be identified.

WHAT DO WE DO?

The six domains that describe athletic training explain what athletic trainers do. A recounting of the six domains, with specific references to domains important for the specific setting being promoted, will inform your listeners of the variety of tasks an athletic trainer is prepared to perform.

For school settings, injury prevention, evaluation, rehabilitation, and emergency care may be

Staying up-to-date with the current literature.

emphasized. Having qualified personnel on-site when an injury occurs is a unique service of athletic trainers. Injury prevention and rehabilitation can reduce claims on insurance policies.

High school athletic trainers may have an opportunity to make a presentation to the board of education, either as an annual report or as a proposal for the initiation of an athletic training program. Before the presentation, the athletic trainer should make the effort to find out the board's and the superintendent's position regarding such presentations. Some may ask for information about the person who will provide the service, while others may only be interested in what athletic training is as a profession and why they may wish to include it in their district. Either way, the athletic trainer should prepare a presentation booklet to hand out to the audience to act as a guide to the presentation.[2]

Emphasize the fact that athletic trainers are the only allied health professionals specifically trained to care for physically active people. Briefly discuss how physically active people respond differently to treatment and how aggressive rehabilitation not only saves time, but is better for the patient than slower-paced rehabilitation programs.

WHEN ARE OUR SERVICES NECESSARY?

Athletic training services are necessary to provide prompt, effective health care for physically active people. Combined with the care provided by the person's team or personal physician, a person can quickly and safely return to athletic competition or their exercise regime.

In some situations, the athletic trainer represents an athlete's only means of access to the medical system. Inner-city schools may have athletes who have never seen a physician until they were referred to one by their athletic trainer.

WHERE DO WE WORK?

Athletic trainers can be found working in settings where physically active people are found. This includes high schools, colleges/universities, professional sports, amateur sports, sports medicine clinics, health clubs, industry, and even show business. Identify the role of the athletic trainer for each of these sites.

Athletic trainers serve different roles depending on the site in which they work. College/university, professional sports, amateur sports, and high school athletic trainers spend a large percentage of their time in prevention, evaluation, and management of injuries. Athletic trainers in sports medicine clinics and industry may spend more time on rehabilitation (table 14-1).

■ **TABLE 14-1**   Employment Sites of NATA Members (N = 19,624)

Site	Percent Membership*
Clinical	20.7%
Clinic/industrial	0.1%
Corporate	0.7%
College student	18.9%
High school/clinic	13.2%
Hospital	5.1%
High school	14.3%
Industrial	0.8%
Junior college	1.4%
Other	4.8%
Professional basketball	0.3%
Professional football	0.6%
Professional golf	0.03%
Professional hockey	0.5%
Professional soccer	0.2%
Professional tennis	1.2%
University/college	15.5%
No data	1.7%

*Percentages total slightly more than 100% due to rounding.

WHY IS AN ATHLETIC TRAINER NEEDED?

In order to convince someone that they need an athletic trainer, start by convincing them that they need the types of services offered. Most people will agree that athletic training services are desirable if you positively represent the profession. The most common reason for not employing an athletic trainer is lack of funds. Consequently, convince listeners that their money is well spent. Again, depending on the setting being promoted, cost effectiveness must be demonstrated.

In a high school setting, it may help to provide examples of how athletic trainers can save the school money. Identify the number of treatments an athletic trainer would provide in one school year and project the cost of such services if the athlete were referred to a clinic or physical therapy setting. This number can easily approach six figures. Point out the number of emergency room visits avoided by employing athletic trainers. Remember, someone has to pay for the emergency room visit, and it may be the school's insurance policy. A low number of claims against an insurance policy helps reduce premiums in subsequent years. The flexibility of an athletic trainer's preparation is also an asset. A teacher/athletic trainer is usually paid a regular teacher's salary plus a head coach's stipend. This head coach's stipend lasts all year, rather than a single season.

The fact that a clinic or factory employs an athletic trainer demonstrates a commitment to optimal care for physically active persons. Athletic trainers' flexibility in providing services in the clinical or industrial setting, their ability to serve in outreach programs, and their rapport with the athletic community are all assets for a sports medicine clinic. This is particularly true in a very competitive sports medicine market.

Promoting athletic training in the industrial setting, particularly in terms of revenue savings, is not difficult. Large industries can save millions of dollars in insurance claims alone by employing athletic trainers. Factor in reduced absenteeism and increased general health of the employees, and you can build a very strong case for investing in athletic trainers.

College/university, professional, and amateur sports settings have already recognized the value of employing athletic trainers. There are relatively few new positions in these settings.

HOW CAN WE HELP?

At this point of the presentation, listeners have been provided with a great deal of information. To explain "How we can help you," merely restate some of the important points made earlier in the presentation. Try to make the discussion interactive; this can help reveal what the interested parties are looking for and accentuate the points that were most important to them.

PROMOTING ATHLETIC TRAINING AS A PART OF SPORTS MEDICINE CLINIC SERVICES

The promotion of athletic training services provided by a sports medicine clinic is usually included as part of an overall **public relations plan**. Public relations/advertising plans are usually relatively simple documents: state your goal(s), objectives, and strategies to realize your objectives.

Realistic objectives may include any or all of the following:

- Sponsorship of recreational/youth sports teams
- Web page/Internet advertising
- Radio advertising
- Cable television commercials
- Newspaper advertisements or sports medicine advice column
- Presentations to local physicians and managed care providers
- Yellow page listings
- Presentations to organized sports groups
- Participation in health fairs
- Sponsorship of athletic events (5K runs, triathlons, etc.)
- Banners/billboards at athletic events
- Program brochures, newsletters, and educational materials
- Relationships with other sport-related enterprises
- Sponsoring interdisciplinary study groups and sports medicine symposia

- Developing a speaker's bureau
- Establishing a tradition
- Receptions for physicians or coaches

Sponsorship of Recreational/Youth Sports Teams

Sponsoring recreational or youth teams will increase the visibility of a clinic. The uniforms of a sponsored team can bear the logo and name of a clinic. Some sports facilities may provide permission to display a billboard on the playing field/court. Athletes, parents, coaches, and fans will all be exposed to the facility.

Web Page/Internet Advertising

Web pages are used extensively to advertise businesses. Much more information can be provided on a web page than in any other advertising medium. People have come to expect companies to have web pages, and they depend on them to be accurate and up to date. It is imperative that web pages be updated frequently.

Radio Advertising

Radio advertising should be well planned in terms of air time and theme. Commercials airing during athletic events or sports news will reach athletic-minded people. Tell the listening audience about the cutting-edge, sympathetic nature of the services provided. Returning to sport participation quickly, state-of-the-art equipment, and specialized personnel are just a few of the points to emphasize. There may also be an opportunity to host a sports medicine talk show in which one could answer callers' questions about sports/exercise injuries.

Cable Television Commercials

Cable television commercials have the capacity to address a very specific audience. Cable watchers can tune to specialized channels. Advertisements on sports channels will reach people who may benefit from your services. Television also provides visual, as well as audio, impact. Featured shots of the facility, staff working with celebrity athletes, and so forth can be appealing to viewers. Interviews on the local news or hosting a sports medicine program will also increase awareness of a sports medicine facility.

Newspaper Advertising or Sports Medicine Advice Column

Newspaper advertisements, particularly those in and around the sports page, can also reach intended audiences. These ads offer the opportunity to display a clinic's logo, list available services, and provide necessary contact information for potential patients (telephone number, address). Incentives can be provided for visits to a clinic, such as including discount coupons in an ad or offering some type of free service (body fats analysis, nutrition evaluation, etc.). Sports medicine advice columns are quite common in local newspapers. If the local newspaper does not have one, contact the newspaper's editor to pursue the matter. Make sure to accurately describe the affiliation and keep in mind professional preparation when contacting the newspaper.

Presentations to Local Physicians and Managed Care Providers

A clinic often may rely solely on referrals for patients. If so, try to create a network of referring healthcare professionals. One-on-one time spent with local physicians is time well spent. Preparing a brief presentation and promotional materials and inviting physicians for a site visit helps promote a facility.

Yellow Page Listings

Yellow page listings, like newspaper ads, provide an opportunity to display a clinic's logo, list available services, and provide necessary contact information for potential patients (telephone number, address). The ad should be placed under a "Sports Medicine" heading, if available. Otherwise, place a listing under all pertinent categories.

Presentations to Organized Sports Groups

Direct communication with officials from organized sports groups will help increase visibility among the athletes who participate in the league(s) sponsored by the organization. Emphasize the importance placed on quickly returning athletes to play. This is an important inroad to the "weekend warriors."

Participation in Health Fairs

Health fairs are often sponsored by schools, universities, and community groups. Health fairs provide an opportunity to promote the services provided as well as increasing public awareness of the professions represented in a clinic. Provide simple services such as cholesterol analyses, blood pressure assessments, and/or body fat analyses. This type of service is currently quite popular. Visitors and patients to a clinic often receive items that display a clinic's logo and contact information (e.g., mini footballs, water bottles, key chains, etc.)

Sponsorship of Athletic Events (e.g., 5K Runs, Triathlons, etc.)

Sponsoring athletic events provides an opportunity to display banners/billboards, provide sports medicine care to participants, and distribute promotional materials. Such events provide an opportunity to supply participants with many items that promote a sports medicine clinic: T-shirts, water bottles, trophies/plaques, hats, and others.

Banners/Billboards at Athletic Events

Banners or billboards that are displayed at organized athletic events are a constant reminder of a facility's services. Banner/billboard space can be purchased and may be included as part of the outreach services program.

Program Brochures, Newsletters, and Educational Materials

Program brochures serve as a brief but all-encompassing announcement of the major characteristics and descriptions of a specific program. The brochures should be written and edited clearly for communication and targeted toward specific audiences.[7] For example, a sports medicine athletic training program brochure can be written specifically for high school students for recruiting and profession description purposes.

Distributing newsletters and other educational materials to current or former patients, referring healthcare professionals, and sports organization officials promotes injury prevention and serves as a reminder of services received. These materials reinforce the profession's commitment to serve physically active people. These materials can be created very efficiently with modern software programs and can be produced in various forms and designs.

Relationships with Other Sport-Related Enterprises

Developing relationships with health clubs, sporting goods stores, and other sport-related enterprises may provide for expansion of the promotional program. Posting banners, business card/brochure displays, or other promotional materials in these facilities will reach potential patients.

Sponsoring Interdisciplinary Study Groups and Sports Medicine Symposia

Sponsoring interdisciplinary study groups and sports medicine seminars demonstrates a commitment to staying on the cutting edge. Study groups can serve as a "grand rounds" experience. This encourages staff to communicate with professionals in other fields and to learn from one another. Sports medicine seminars may focus on specific sports or injuries and can feature prominent sports medicine professionals and athletes. They can be designed for sports medicine professionals, coaches, or the lay person.

Developing a Speaker's Bureau

Developing a speaker's bureau and publicizing it may make staff available for specialized needs. A booklet listing can be developed to introduce personnel, their occupation, the topics they have expertise in, and how to contact them. Allowing personnel to make presentations allows promotion of their occupation and increases their individual notoriety. Patients prefer to be treated by well-known, respected

professionals. Involvement in speaking activities allows staff to attain notoriety. Such notoriety greatly benefits a facility.

Establishing a Tradition

Become the sports medicine sponsor or cosponsor of an annually held athletic event. Endow a scholarship to a local university. Present a scholarship to a college student who is majoring in athletic training.

Receptions for Physicians or Coaches

Let these people know how important they are to the success of your facility. Thank them for their continued support. Hold a golf outing where the two groups can see each other socially away from their employment.

A multifaceted promotional plan is more effective than a sporadic, unidimensional one. Implementing only one or two of the strategies mentioned here will most likely be ineffective. The activities selected will be determined by budget, staff, and the availability of such strategies in the surrounding market. Each major promotional technique has strengths and drawbacks. These need to be evaluated in light of cost, ease of production, target audience, and flexibility.[1] The sports medicine market is very competitive. The ability to reach potential patients highly affects success.

The National Athletic Trainers' Association provides a member PR kit that contains the following resources to aid in the development of public relations activities:

Minimizing the Risk of Injury in High School Athletics is a brochure targeted toward secondary schools. It explains how athletic trainers participate in implementing guidelines to reduce injuries in high school sports. The brochure is aimed at coaches, athletic directors, administrators, and the media.

The Certified Athletic Trainer is a brochure that describes the profession and how we affect athletic programs. This brochure is for parents, school administrators, and the media.

Athletic Training Career Information presents the profession, practice settings, and the basic qualifications for certification. This one is for high school students and their parents.

The address from which to request any of these brochures is:
National Athletic Trainers' Association
NATA Brochure Request
2952 Stemmons Freeway
Dallas, TX 75247

In addition, the NATA has a large collection of documents through a Fax-on-Demand service. The service is available from the NATA office in Dallas, phone 1-888-ASK-NATA (1-888-275-6282). The document list is published periodically in the NATA News and is also available as document number 700 from the Fax-on-Demand service.

PROFESSIONALISM

An effective promotions plan and a persuasive public relations presentation must be complimented by a positive image and must exemplify professionalism. If physicians, parents, or an organization's administrators visit a facility and the athletic trainer is dressed in faded blue jeans and a torn T-shirt, while using poor interaction and communication skills, the person will not be viewed as a healthcare professional. It is vital that an athletic trainer dress and act as a professional, regardless of the employment setting or situation. Swartz[8] explains that it is also just as important to display professionalism when interacting with other NATA members and other healthcare professionals, such as at national, district, and state meetings or symposia.

It is important to wear clothing that is neat, conservative, functional, and identifiable. If working on the field, a shirt or jacket that can identify you as an athletic trainer will make it easier for athletes to find you. If you are dressed in gym shorts and a muscle shirt, people who do not personally know you will have difficulty identifying you. Many athletic trainers for indoor sports and clinical/industrial settings will wear formal attire.

Even more important, behavior must also be professional. Professional behavior includes the language used, interaction with people, the manner in which one projects himself or herself, and even everyday health habits. Using excessive foul language is not professional. In most cases, it is possible to articulate ideas without the use of vulgarities. Interaction with people should be civil. The regular use of confrontation will decrease athletes' willingness to confide in an athletic trainer. Other members of the sports medicine team will also be less inclined to communicate with an athletic trainer if they do not interact in a civil manner.

When one is serving as an athletic trainer, many eyes will be on that person throughout the working week. Physicians, athletes, student athletic trainers, parents, and others will be watching how the athletic trainer projects himself or herself. It is important to project a calm, assured presence. If an athletic trainer appears to be in control, people will be more likely to respond to that person in emergency situations. If the athletic trainer does not seem capable of controlling emotions, others will be apprehensive. Catastrophic injuries are frightening for everyone. It is OK to be frightened on the inside as long as the distress does not show on the outside.

Personal health habits also project professionalism. If one does not wash their hands after using the rest room or tends to eat bacon and eggs for breakfast every morning, this is not reinforcing a healthy lifestyle. Athletes look to the athletic trainer for counseling on health-related matters. Athletic trainers need to practice what they preach.

EVALUATING A PUBLIC RELATIONS PLAN

Evaluating the success of a public relations plan in school settings may be difficult. However, increased support for the position may occur (i.e., retention during budget crunches) or there may be new funding available for additional staff. Support from booster clubs and interaction with parents may also increase. Ideally, those interacted with will consider athletic training services as necessary as desks and chairs in the classroom.

In the clinical setting, there are a number of indices that can be used to evaluate a program's public relations plan. An increase in patient referrals is perhaps the most important. Since the plan will most likely be multifaceted, it is important to collect information from patients or referring healthcare professionals about how they learned of the facility.

A brief questionnaire on patient information forms, phone calls or personal discussions with referring healthcare professionals will provide insight into successful marketing strategies.

Summary

1. To promote athletic training, we must first identify what athletic training is.
2. Identify who athletic trainers are by emphasizing the six task domains as outlined in the NATABOC Role Delineation Study.
3. Emphasize educational and professional requirements, including academic preparation, clinical experiences, and continuing education.
4. Stress that athletic training is recognized as an allied health profession by the AMA and is credentialed in more than thirty-five states (especially if yours is one of those).
5. What athletic trainers do must be integrated into the healthcare delivery system.
6. Athletic trainers work in a variety of settings (see chapter 3).
7. Athletic trainers are specialized healthcare providers.
8. There are many ways to promote the profession as part of the services of a sports medicine clinic.
9. Developing a strong, positive public image is enhanced by the way athletic trainers dress and portray themselves in public.

For Critical Thought

Now that John has thought about his status within his community, he realizes he needs some help. On the NATA web page he finds the Public Relations Committee's web page. John obtained the NATA Member Public Relations kit with suggestions for increasing public awareness. He also found some further resources on the District IV web page and the state web page in his home state. Some of the suggestions that the page offers are easy for John, while others require some time, thought, and money to complete. What would be most appropriate for John?

Websites

http://www.nata.org/Departments/communi-cations/public.htm

NATA Public Relations Committee web page

http://www.nata.org/

Home page of the NATA, with a variety of links dealing with injury information related to high schools, outcomes assessment, public relations, committees, and placement, among other areas.

Applications for Consideration

1. The Southside Unified School District has been presented with a proposal to hire an athletic trainer by a local physician. Since you are a graduate of Southside High School, you have been asked to make a thirty-minute presentation to the school board outlining the advantages/necessity of hiring an athletic trainer. Money is tight in Southside. Prepare a presentation that includes all necessary information about the advantages of employing an athletic trainer but also includes several plans for securing an athletic trainer's services.

2. You are the head athletic trainer at Port Correlation University. The athletic department at PCU has recently experienced a budget cut. Their plan includes cutting one position. They are considering elimination of a member of the athletic training staff. Prepare a presentation that would convince the athletic director that cuts in the athletic training staff would adversely affect the health care of the athletes.

3. Part of your new responsibilities at Metro Sports Care includes recruiting high schools for their outreach program. Describe how you would (a) arrange visits with school officials to discuss the possibility of providing services, (b) present an athletic healthcare package to school officials, and (c) follow up your visit with written materials.

References

1 Clover, J. Clinical marketing. In Konin, JG. *Clinical athletic training.* Thorofare, NJ: SLACK, Incorporated, 1997.
2 Hossler, P. Promoting athletic training. *NATA News.* (June): 16–17, 1994.
3 Hunt, V. Certified athletic trainers debut in upcoming Oliver Stone flick. *NATA News.* (August):24–25, 1999.
4 Marks, L. Public relations, public image, public education. *NATA News.* (August):21, 1991.
5 National Athletic Trainers' Association. *NATA annual report* 1991–92.
6 NATA Board of Certification. *Role delineation study,* 4th ed. Omaha, NE: NATA Board of Certification, 1999.
7 Ray, R. How well do you communicate? *Athletic Therapy Today.* (March): 26–27, 1996.
8 Swartz, E. Professionalism is important. *NATA News.* (June): 36, 1999.

Recommended Reading

1 Hossler, P. Promoting sports care in the secondary school setting. *NATA News.* (September):14–15, 1993.
2 Stopka, C, Kaiser, D. Certified athletic trainers in our secondary schools: The need and the solution. *Athletic Training.* 23:322–324, 1988.
3 Smaha, M, Powell, J. Effectively communicating the importance of injury prevention and management. *NATA News.* (April):22–25, 1994.

NATIONAL ATHLETIC TRAINERS' ASSOCIATION

1999 National Public Relations Plan

The NATA Public Relations Committee has been working with a public relations firm to develop a plan to focus on the general public's awareness of athletic training. This appendix is a working document between the two groups.

1. Overview

Host Communications, Inc. proposes a public relations campaign with a primary mission of increasing National Athletic Trainers' Association membership awareness among NATA's key constituencies and the general public.

HCI will incorporate elements of television, radio, Internet, print and grass roots PR efforts to accomplish this goal. Cornerstone to the general efforts of exposing the membership, is a long-range campaign to differentiate a Certified Athletic Trainer from the general name "trainer", which alone does not do justice to the membership's individual qualifications.

NATA membership has spread from sports to include the corporate world. Our campaign will address and further expand the role of the membership, but will use access provided by the sports world as its main stage.

It is our opinion that the membership will find that it has clout in the sports world perhaps not apparent in the past. Part of our mission will be to uncover this and use it both to benefit the sports institutions and the NATA membership.

Our approach will be to point out that the existence of staff within the sports organization with the qualifications and training of an ATC is something that the public does not now know and should know. Our case will be that if the public knew what the ATCs are and do, their opinion of the sport in general will rise.

2. Call Me ATC

Rationale

A long-range campaign to differentiate a Certified Athletic Trainer from the general name "trainer", which in our view does not do justice to the membership. Getting the public to view the Certified Athletic Trainer as an ATC rather than its current broad and vague perception of "trainer" will produce a paradigm shift as significant as changing from simply "doctor" to "surgeon", from "ambulance driver" to "EMT" or from "businessman" to "CEO".

All of these professional descriptions at one time were once commonly underestimated and through repeated exposure over time have come to mean something completely different.

Strategy

We will use this theme throughout the campaign and will do some primary membership work to achieve buy-in. The perfect forum may be regional meetings in the spring and the national meeting in the summer, however the plan can be rolled out in the NATA publications and web site right away.

Other specific items will include:

- Placement of the ATC logo on key "highly visible" Certified Athletic Trainers, particularly those with potential television screen time.
- A broad campaign to the membership of incorporating the ATC logo into game-day apparel where possible. This will follow already established guidelines by NATA Public Relations staff and will use the logo adopted by membership vote.
- Correspondence to inform the media that the proper terminology is now "ATC" or "Certified Athletic Trainer", but never just "trainer".
- Organization of terminology notes for use during conference "media days" or other opportunities where ATCs have an audience with the media.

3. Press Kit

HCI will work with the NATA Public Relations committee and staff to produce press kits that will be used to distribute to national media and that will serve as material that any NATA member can use to assist in publicity in his or her local market. The below materials will complement and work in concert with other pieces being organized within NATA. Our suggested initial components would include:

Media Background Pages

- "What is an ATC?"-Printed description of what ATCs do and notes about what their value is to the organization
- "What You Don't Know about Certified Athletic Trainers"-Bullet lists of Items not commonly known about ATCs
- Biographies (where appropriate)
- Web site information
- Key contact lists

Public Speaking and Function Tools

- Video-Five to eight minute video on what ATCs do for use at school groups, classes and community functions (dubs distributed as-needed)
- Speaking points and tips-Items that have been effective for other NATA speakers and tips on both to get the engagement and what to say.

Media Exposure Tools

- National TV and radio PSAs (To save cost, we'll only send out dubs on an as-needed basis)
- TV and Radio Drop-In copy
- Internet Instruction and template files
- Instruction on how to get a link from an athletics page and boilerplate content on ATCs, graphic images and good ATC links that high school, college or professional team official pages would find useful

4. Television & Radio Media

PSAs

HCI will produce two "PSAs" (Public Service Announcements) focused on what ATCs do and the often unseen benefit they bring to sports and industry. One thirty-second and one fifteen-second PSA will be distributed. Creative will include athletes talking about how their ATC helped during rehabilitation or how conditioning improved performance.

Rationale

Television

There are few more effective ways to communicate a message than television. While its impact is eroding due to fragmentation by cable outlets and other new media like the Internet, it is still a highly effective way most companies, institutions distribute their message.

Radio

Radio provides for sports fans the most consistent way to follow their favorite teams. Television games jump from station to station with different, usually impartial announce teams. Radio offers the same announcers and a friendly bias, making the emotional tie strong to the "home team" radio broadcast. In this atmosphere, messages have a higher level of impact with listeners.

Strategy

We will attempt to get the spots aired as PSAs through access provided to leagues and institutions during network, regional and local broadcasts on both radio and television. We will use the access provided by the sports angle, but will give an overall picture of NATA membership.

By arming the membership with the PSAs and a battle plan to get the spots aired, we should be able to garner some airtime, perhaps with effort, on the national level.

HCI will organize the approach, provide talking points on the best arguments to make in our appeal (generally to an Athletics Director or club Marketing Director). HCI will make the actual pitch, where appropriate, in selected cases.

Electronic Media Stories and Features

Rationale

There are dozens of television and radio shows that deal with sports at every level. Getting an interview for an ATC will expose the profession as well as the individual.

Strategy

We will use HCI's contact base to encourage placement of ATCs into stories. While we do this, we will use the telephone time to explain what the ATC is and

then follow with background notes so that when the opportunity arises, all of the information is there.

5. Internet Exposure

Rationale

Nearly every organization has an official Internet site, often highly trafficked. Creating links on these sites will generate traffic to areas set up to inform the public about ATCs and the NATA.

Strategy

We will send boilerplate stories and information to webmasters of official sites. If we can make the workload small for the webmaster, we can very likely get an ATC link and a page of information.

6. Industry Print Exposure

Rationale

Game day programs, NCAA Championship programs, industry newsletters and media guides all provide opportunities that we should be able to exploit for the ATC and their mission.

Strategy

HCI will use its understanding of the athletics world to get access for the ATC in publications by lobbying SIDs and marketing directors.

7. Injury Survey

Rationale

The survey provides an excellent atmosphere to expose the association and places the focus of the public on NATA in a medical context.

Strategy

We will organize key points from the survey and distribute releases to key news organizations. We will use follow-up telephone calls to increase use of the information and we will attempt to expand coverage by organizing interviews of members.

(provided by the National Athletic Trainers' Association with permission of Host Communications, Inc.)

PART FOUR

Legal Issues

CHAPTER 15

Athletic Training Practice

After reading this chapter, you should be able to:

- Define the ways in which athletic trainers are credentialed.

- List the NATABOC Standards for the Practice of Athletic Training.

- Explain how practice standards define the standard of care.

- Describe the various concepts of tort law as they involve liability, negligence, and medical malpractice.

Key Terms

licensed
registration
certification
exemption
standard of care
tort
profession
negligence
malpractice
liability
duty
breach of duty
causation
damage

FOR CRITICAL THOUGHT:
A Case of Negligence

During late summer conditioning, Dave felt a twinge in his back that accompanied a burning sensation down his leg. The pain went away quickly and Dave told no one. Later, during two-a-day practices, he felt the same pain, only it lasted longer. When he went to lift after practice, the pain intensified. Dave reported to the athletic trainer, Tom, and told him he had a painful back. Knowing he could not afford to miss any practice time, Dave did not tell Tom that the pain was radiating down the leg. Tom placed an ice pack over the lumbar musculature and then wrote an injury report of this incident. The pain decreased in the back during and for a short time after the treatment. Tom spoke with the team physician and told her that Dave had a muscle spasm that he was treating with cold and electrical stimulation, to which Dr. Ryan added Advil.

The next day Dave reported to the athletic training room, where he had cold and electrical stimulation. He finally reported the pain radiating into his leg, but Tom found no signs during his observation of Dave's gait. Tom told Dave to continue with the cold and stimulation and to increase the dosage of Advil to four per dose, three times a day. He also gave Dave a TENS unit, placed the electrodes and showed Dave how to adjust the intensity.

The following three weeks had no change. Every day Dave felt a burning pain in his leg and discomfort in his back, and every day he complained that his back was getting worse. Tom switched to heat after the first week and continued the electrical stimulation. Dave requested an appointment with Dr. Ryan twice, but Tom did not think this was necessary, since he was in daily consultation with the doctor on this injury.

About halfway through the fourth week, Melissa, the football graduate assistant athletic trainer, asked Tom if he noticed that the medial head of the gastrocnemius muscle in Dave's right leg was severely atrophied. Tom inspected Dave again, and immediately sent him to Dr. Ryan for referral to a neurosurgeon.

Dave was referred to Dr. Hammoud, a specialist in disk and nerve injuries. Dr. Hammoud scheduled Dave for evaluation and an MRI. After obtaining the test results, Dave was scheduled for surgery to remove two damaged disks and to fuse three lumbar vertebrae. The surgery was performed December 4 and recovery was uneventful. One year later the gastrocnemius was still atrophied 50 percent.

Dave retained the services of an attorney and filed a negligence claim against the university, the athletic director, and the associate athletic director who supervised the athletic trainers and the team physician. All were charged with engendering a win-at-all-costs mentality, excessively pressuring players to perform, conditioning payment for medical services on an athletic trainer's determination of medical need, and employing unqualified personnel to diagnose and treat football-related injuries and evaluate his medical fitness to play football. Tom was named in the suit, alleging violation of the medical standards of care and unauthorized practice of medicine on the theory that Tom was making diagnoses and improperly prescribing treatments that are the sole province of a physician. Dr. Ryan

was charged with malpractice, as she did not completely examine this patient for six weeks, instead relying on Tom's observations relayed through phone conversations. Dave also claimed she injected his lumbar musculature with a local anaesthetic to enable him to play without performing a complete diagnosis.

What went wrong in this case? Does Dave have a cause of action? Tom and Dr. Ryan both claimed that they were not liable due to discretionary function immunity. This defense (see chapter 16) asserts that a state employee using discretionary judgment in the performance of his or her duties is immune from negligence action. It is within the law in few states such as Alabama. Can this line of defense succeed? What would a reasonable athletic trainer have done the first time that Dave came to see him or her?

Athletic training has been identified by the following content domains: (1) prevention; (2) recognition, evaluation, and assessment; (3) immediate care; (4) treatment, rehabilitation, and reconditioning; (5) organization and administration; and (6) professional development and responsibility.[20]

The practice of athletic training is regulated in some manner by more than 36 states.[4] Athletic trainers may be licensed, registered, certified, or exempted from allied medical practice acts. Any profession is credentialed to define what the profession is and what practitioners can do in their jobs, and to protect the title of the profession.

In states where athletic training is a **licensed** profession, a person must meet qualifying standards and pass an examination. Frequently, state licensing boards will purchase results of the NATABOC Certification Examination as the test of the body of knowledge making up athletic training. Some states will further test the rules and regulations set forth in the state practice act. Upon licensure, the athletic trainer is subject to either laws or administrative rules that make up a state practice act that defines the profession, scope of practice, and allowed and disallowed roles. State practice acts supersede NATABOC direct service and service program standards. Due in large part to the influence of other allied health professions, athletic training is the *only* allied health profession that in many state practice acts defines the patient group on which athletic trainers can practice.[23]

States that register athletic trainers most often will not require an examination at the state level. The athletic trainer must meet standards of eligibility and pay a fee, and he or she will be placed on the state **registration** list of those legally allowed to use the term *athletic trainer*. This is the least restrictive form of regulation. There is usually no practice act or administrative board to set rules governing what an athletic trainer is allowed to do, but there is title protection.

Certification at the state level is different from NATABOC certification. Within a state, certification usually means the person has submitted minimum credentials of eligibility and then taken some form of state-administered examination. State certification does not usually restrict the title of a profession, but it can restrict the application of specific skills and knowledge to persons who are regulated.[4]

Exemption is the process of identifying a specific profession or group of practitioners and allowing that group to use the methods of a licensed profession. Without exemption, those practicing the profession would be in violation of the practice act of the licensed profession. Usually, in regard to athletic training, exemption is granted from the physical therapy practice act.

In those jurisdictions without regulations, other medical or allied medical practice acts may have an impact on the delivery of athletic training services. In the absence of uniform qualifications among states, the most universally accepted credential is certification according to the criteria of the National Athletic Trainers' Association Board of Certification.[9] The credential is recognition of qualification by employers, rather than a government agency. In such states the use of therapeutic modalities or rehabilitative exercise may be in violation of physical therapy law. To date, athletic trainers have not been challenged on this point while practicing in college/university, high school, or professional athletic training rooms.

STANDARD OF CARE AND SCOPE OF PRACTICE

The practice of medicine is unlimited in scope when performed by allopathic (M.D.) or osteopathic (D.O.) physicians. This is defined state to state. In Michigan the practice of medicine means the "diagnosis, treatment, prevention, cure, or relieving of a human disease, ailment, defect, complaint, or other physical or mental condition, by attendance, advice, device, diagnostic test, or other means, or offering, undertaking, attempting to do, or holding oneself out as able to do, any of these acts." (MCLA §333.17001(c)) In New York the practice of medicine is defined as "diagnosing, treating, operating or prescribing for any human disease, pain, injury, deformity, or physical condition." (NYA §6521) There are no limitations placed on physicians regarding methods that conform to standard practice.

All other medical or allied medical personnel have a limited scope of practice that is subordinate to physicians. For the most part, diagnosis, as done by a physician, surgery, and prescribing, especially medications, are forbidden to all but physicians. Limited scope, therefore, means that an allied profession such as athletic training or physical therapy works under the auspices of a physician or other licensed designated medical professional. Allied professionals have the freedom to apply their knowledge, but within a narrow scope of practice. Athletic trainers may not perform surgery. Physical therapists may not reduce dislocations and prescribe pain medications.

The concept of standard of care is directly related to these limitations. **Standard of care** is the level of medical sophistication and competency that must be demonstrated by someone who has similar education and training to other members of a particular group. In the area of sports medicine the standard of care is somewhat difficult to establish due to the large number of medical and allied health professionals caring for athletes.

Due to the general lack of uniform athletic trainer practice legislation, what is accepted practice in one state may be forbidden in another. Before 1999, the licensure law in New Jersey (NJSA §45:9–37.36[d]) stated that athletic training is limited to the physical conditioning and reconditioning of athletes and the prevention of injuries unless physical modalities are prescribed by a physician. The Ohio licensure law (Ohio Rev. Code §4755.60–4755.65) specifies that athletic training is the practice of prevention, recognition, and assessment of an athletic injury and the complete management, treatment, disposition, and reconditioning of acute athletic injuries upon referral of an individual authorized under other sections of the law. There is no distinction requiring a physician prescription for modality use. In Georgia (Code Section §43-5-7), any person holding themselves out to be an athletic trainer must be licensed except when the individual is a "student-trainer, assistant-trainer, teacher-trainer, or any similar position . . . and is carried out under the supervision of a coach, physician, or licensed athletic trainer." It is important to remember that state law may well supersede the domains identified in the *Role Delineation Study*,[20] or *Competencies in Athletic Training*[18] (*Athletic Training Educational Competencies*[19]), which is a list of objectives written according to the cognitive, psychomotor, and affective domains of Bloom's taxonomy.

Within the healthcare spectrum there are approximately 30,000 statements that are considered standards.[12] There are approximately 100 standards-type statements that deal directly with sports medicine.[13] These standards are used to provide evidence of a duty to act.

Standards that affect athletic training come from a variety of sources. The most important are those found in state practice acts, which supersede agency standards. In the absence of state standards, or where the standards are unclear, then agency standards will become part of the definition of duty. Additional standards affecting the practice of athletic training include OSHA standards and guidelines, Americans with Disabilities Act, Drug Enforcement Agency, Title IX of the Federal Education Amendments of 1972, and the Civil Rights Act of 1964 as amended.[20]

Standards are produced by the NATABOC.[21] There are fifteen standards divided into two groups, seven direct service standards, and eight service program standards. Direct service standards

describe those who supervise athletic trainers, documentation, confidentiality, initial assessment, and program planning and discontinuation. The service program standards include setting objectives for activities, planning objectives, evaluation, types of service offered, personnel and facilities available, records kept and annual reporting on all aspects of the service program. These statements help to establish the minimal requirements of action for practicing athletic trainers. Other standards statements relating to athletic training have been produced by the American Athletic Trainers' Association,[14] the American Medical Association,[14] and the NCAA.[8]

In 1992, Webster, Mason, and Keating completed *Guidelines for Professional Practice in Athletic Training*,[24] which was intended to develop written procedures with which to judge a person's standard of conduct in relation to the standard of care. Courts have shown that they may be willing to differentiate between standards as mandatory policies and procedures that must be incorporated and guidelines as recommended policies and procedures.[7] Where there are nationally published standards that are violated by employees of an institution, there may also be vicarious liability for the care given by the employee.

In determining duty to act as one of the standards of negligence, expert testimony is often used. Frequently the expert will introduce written standards to determine that the defendant in the action had a duty (due to published standards) and has breached that duty.[7] Athletic trainers and other sports medicine providers need to understand the relevant standards most often found in the literature that can be used to assess the level and quality of care received by patients.[11] While some professionals decry standards-type statements as a "cookbook" approach, the reality is that these standards are in public dissemination and are being used in court to set the standard of care and define the duty owed to a patient.

The standard of care normally present for athletic trainers may be elevated to that of physicians if the athletic trainer engages in the unauthorized practice of medicine. In *Gillespie v. Southern Utah State College*, 669 P.2nd 861 (Utah 1983),[2] an athletic trainer prescribed a series of ice pack treatments to the plaintiff for a sprained ankle. The ice packs resulted in frostbite and amputation of a part of the plaintiff's foot. The trial court ordered the jury to hold the athletic trainer to the standard of care associated with a physician. The jury found in favor of the defendant because the athlete had left the ice packs on his ankle at home for much longer than the prescribed time factor.[5]

Lawyers warn that when nonmedical treatment of minor injuries becomes habitual, the athlete may then believe that the athletic trainer has medical training and trial courts may order the athletic trainer to be judged by the standards of the physician.[2] In this event, the conduct would be compared to the presumed standard of care of someone with the qualifications to perform the task the athletic trainer tried to perform.[10]

TORT

Tort law involves legal wrong other than breach of contract for which the courts provide some remedy, usually in the form of monetary damage. This action is a civil, rather than criminal, proceeding. Most of the tort actions for malpractice are brought in the area of negligence. Two definitions are important here. The first defines undertaking a **profession** and states that professionals have a duty to exercise the skills and knowledge normally employed by members of the profession to prevent unreasonable risk of harm to others.[1] The second is a definition of **negligence**, which states that negligent conduct can either be an act of commission that invades the interests of another or an act of omission where another is injured by failing to act when there was a duty to act.[1]

Malpractice

The most common legal problem faced by physicians is malpractice. Individual state laws will determine whether an athletic trainer can be sued for negligence or malpractice. **Malpractice** is a liability where there is an unfavorable outcome of patient–practitioner interaction.[22] **Liability** is the responsibility for actions that cause harm to others. Liability can be due to any number of reasons,

among them negligence, failure to inform, breach of contract, or assault and battery.[17]

Some state malpractice laws define the specific job classifications that can be sued for malpractice.[17] Other states refer to "healthcare providers" when assessing who is subject to their medical malpractice law. In six jurisdictions (Alaska, New Hampshire, West Virginia, New Jersey, District of Columbia, and Puerto Rico) there are no malpractice laws; therefore proceedings are brought under negligence laws that usually have longer statutes of limitations (discussed later in the chapter). Pennsylvania has a detailed malpractice law but uses the statute of limitations for simple negligence. In most states if a profession is not licensed, the practitioners are not covered by malpractice acts.

Negligence

To prove negligence, four points must be shown. These are duty to use reasonable care to conform to a standard, breach of duty, causation, and damage.[3] If all four points are not proven, there is no negligence.

Duty to use reasonable care to avoid unreasonable risk to another exists through employment for most athletic trainers. The standards and guidelines statements previously mentioned are often used in legal proceedings to establish the duty to act. Where the athletic trainer agrees to provide services in return for payment, a written contract is the best way to delineate the duty to act.[6] If there is no written contract, the duty to act is open to interpretation. Athletic trainers who witness unsafe playing conditions, see an athlete injured, or follow up with rehabilitation and reevaluation have the duty to perform the domains of athletic training while doing no harm. It should be noted that the courts have found that education institutions have a duty to provide emergency care to injured varsity athletes, whether on a scholarship or not.[15]

Breach of duty is a condition in which the standard of care has been violated. Breach of duty may generally fall within three areas: prevention, standard of care, and disclosure.[5] An athletic trainer who does not monitor environmental conditions in August while fall sports are beginning practice could have a potentially catastrophic heat illness problem. When an athlete is injured on the playing field, failing to properly evaluate the injury can have far-reaching consequences. After an athlete has been injured, failing to give the athlete all information that pertains to his or her case does not allow an informed decision by the athlete concerning the direction the case would take. In these cases, duty is breached.

Causation is the determination that the actions led to damage and to what extent the person was responsible for the damage caused (there may be more than one perpetrator, even including the injured party). In part, causation requires the action of the athletic trainer to have been *foreseeable* as a cause of damage. Results that are unforeseen by a reasonable and prudent athletic trainer are forgiven under this test. Athletic trainers must carefully supervise student athletic trainers, because incompetent actions of student athletic trainers have been found liable as a breach of the standard of care.[5] In *O'Brien v. Township High School District* (1980), an athlete sued the school, coach, athletic trainer, and the student athletic trainer for injuries experienced when an athletic trainer delegated to a student athletic trainer a task that was practicing medicine without a license.[5]

Finally, the athletic trainer's conduct (act of omission or act of commission) must be proven to have caused the plaintiff to suffer **damage**. Where there is no damage, there is no negligence, even if the athletic trainer acted improperly. Recently an athlete fractured and partially dislocated the fifth cervical vertebra during a college football game. The athletic trainer found an unconscious individual and summoned the team physician. The evaluation by the team physician was conducted while the athlete regained consciousness. With all neurological, structural, and functional tests normal, the athlete was allowed to sit, then stand and walk off the field. As the athlete sat down, he complained of shooting pains down both arms. He was secured to a backboard held vertically while the athlete was in a sitting position, lifted up, and then the board was laid horizontally on the bench. The athlete was repositioned, secured to the board, and sent to the emergency room. The neck was surgically repaired a week later. The athlete has no residual deficits. With no damage, there was no negligence, even though an athlete with a fractured, partially dislocated neck was allowed to get up and walk.

In assessing the duty to act without causing harm to others, the courts will assess whether the injury or circumstances leading to the injury were foreseeable. The courts have found that no person is able to prevent harm that is completely unforeseeable or for which the risk is so small that it is usually disregarded.[3] In assessing the standard of care, what a reasonable and prudent person would do in the same circumstances is considered an objective standard.

When assessing the standard of care for professionals, *Blond's Torts*[3] lists seven criteria:

- *Locality rule.* There is a duty to follow the standards of the profession as it is practiced locally.
- *Success is not guaranteed.* The only requirement is for the professional to act with a fundamental level of skill.
- *Differing schools of thought.* Where professionals may reasonably differ, a person may choose any reasonably acceptable method.
- *Specialists.* Specialists are held to a higher standard of care than those who are not specialists.
- *Novices.* Those who are newly licensed are held to the same standard as experienced professionals.
- *Unreasonable standard.* If a court declares a standard unreasonable, then those practicing that standard are negligent.
- *Doctrine of informed consent.* Unless the treatment is an emergency, professionals have a duty to inform a patient of all risks inherent in the procedure.

Negligence is proven through expert testimony or circumstantial evidence. Expert testimony involves the use of professionals with the same qualification as the defendant to establish what is the applicable standard of care and what would a reasonable person have done in the same circumstances. Circumstantial evidence is the presentation of a set of facts from which another set of facts may be inferred.

When negligence has been established, damages are awarded by the court as a remedy. For negligence to succeed, actual damages have to be shown by the plaintiff, usually including some form of physical injury. Damage awards may include medical expenses, lost earnings, future earnings, pain and suffering, mental distress, and property damage.[3]

These damage awards are tax free. In addition, punitive damages may be awarded in excess of the actual harm as punishment to the defendant for reckless behavior. The plaintiff's attorney fees and interest on the damage award are considered unrecoverable damages. The amount of damages are not affected by recovery from other sources such as social security or disability insurance.[3]

WHAT TO DO IF AN ATHLETIC TRAINER IS SUED

If an athletic trainer is sued, he or she needs to consult with an attorney at once. Do not discuss anything with the plaintiff or plaintiff's attorney. If the athletic trainer has liability insurance, the insurer will wish to assign counsel. If you have an attorney in mind, inform the insurance company, which will usually grant your request. After an attorney is assigned, he or she will review a copy of the plaintiff's file. Next, a meeting will be arranged for you to meet the attorney and discuss the case. Do not hold back any information, as it will invariably come out during discovery or testimony.

Discovery is the process of obtaining information from the other side in a case. During civil procedures, discovery takes place after the filing of the suit, unlike criminal law when discovery is often done in secrecy and before the charges are filed. During discovery, written requests are made for all pertinent documents. These requests cover the defendant's background, education, training, and experience. Witnesses are interviewed by deposition. These interviews can be videotaped. Depositions can take place two or more years after the initiation of a suit, hence complete, accurate, written records are a must. Depositions are done under oath in the presence of a court reporter. Transcripts of the deposition will be available to all of the attorneys in a case. At trial, care must be given that testimony is consistent with that given during a deposition.

When preparing for a deposition, it is a good idea to bring a copy of your comprehensive resume or vita. This will simplify the questions about your background. Careful review of the patient record is a must. Being able to recall from the written record the facts of a case is extremely important. Rather than guessing, or speculating on what an athletic trainer thinks happened, the answers should be short, to the point, and cover only the question asked. If there is no written prompt in the records, it is better to say, "I do not know," than to guess. Care should be given not to educate the plaintiff's attorney in the nuances of a profession about which he or she may have little understanding.

During the trial the athletic trainer will be expected to present the same points of fact in answering questions that he or she did during the deposition. Where there are discrepancies, the plaintiff's lawyer most likely will try to infer the defendant is lying, either during the deposition or now, during the trial.

The usatrainers.com website lists ten common mistakes that encourage litigation. These include:

- Alter the client's record.
- Fail to document what you did or did not do and why.
- Fail to follow your own policies and procedures even though your actions may fall within the standard of care.
- Treat a client like he or she is unimportant and what he or she has to say is insignificant.
- Speak in a superior manner to a client using terminology they do not understand.
- Refuse to treat a client because of his/her condition.
- Tell a client that a co-worker made an error which caused the client's problem.
- Fail to obtain informed consent from the client and a bad result, but known risk, ensues.
- Discuss individual cases with friends or family members, breaching the client's confidentiality.
- Speak of confidential client information in the hallways where unsuspecting family members or others may hear."[16]

Remember that even if the athletic trainer prevails in the action before the court, the tide of public opinion does not always stay with the winning side. Reputations may be damaged to the extent of losing referrals and patients. In addition, the work of preparation, discovery, deposition, and trial is time-consuming. This is time away from the job, disrupting an athletic trainer's daily work life.

Summary

1. Athletic training is identified by the content domains of the *Role Delineation Study*.
2. The practice of athletic training is regulated in more than 36 states.
3. Licensure requires a person to meet minimum standards and pass an examination. There is a practice act defining what can and cannot be done in the practice of athletic training.
4. Registration requires a person to meet minimum standards and pay a fee to be placed on an approved list.
5. Certification requires a person to meet minimum standards and pass a state certification examination.
6. Exemption is a method of allowing a profession to be exempted from another licensed profession's practice act.
7. Physicians have an unlimited scope of practice.
8. All other medical and allied medical professions have a limited scope of practice under the direction of a physician.
9. Standard of care is the level of medical sophistication and competency that must be demonstrated by someone with similar education and training to other members of the same group.
10. Due to a lack of uniform practice acts, standard of care is variable between states.
11. Standard of care can be defined by the use of national or agency standards or state practice acts.
12. The NATABOC has defined seven direct service standards and eight service program standards.
13. Standards are firm statements, while guidelines are much more open to interpretation.
14. Tort is the branch of civil law dealing with legal wrongs other than breach of contract.
15. Malpractice is a liability for physicians and other named professions when there is an unfavorable patient outcome.
16. Negligence is liability for actions through either an act of omission or an act of commission.
17. The four cornerstones of negligence are duty, breach of duty, causation, and damage.
18. Duty for an athletic trainer is often established by employment.
19. Breach of duty is a condition in which the standard of care has been violated.
20. Causation is the determination that the actions led to damage.
21. Damage is injury, either physical or mental, arising from another's conduct.
22. If an athletic trainer is sued, he or she must consult with an attorney.
23. Discovery is the exchange of information between the parties to a suit before the trial.
24. Deposition is taking testimony in the presence of attorneys and a court reporter.
25. During a trial, an athletic trainer will be expected to present the same points of fact as in the deposition.
26. There a number of factors that encourage litigation.

For Critical Thought

Tom is caught in an indefensible position. He has committed negligence through acts of commission (diagnosing and treating an injury without formal approval of his team physician) and acts of omission (failing to refer Dave to Dr. Ryan). Tom relied on his observation of Dave's gait pattern alone to assess his back injury. Tom also told Dave to use a prescription strength of ibuprofen, in violation of various pharmacy laws. By the time the atrophy was noted, damage had been done. Dr. Ryan erred by not examining this patient thoroughly when Tom first discussed Dave with her. She did not perform a complete diagnosis before administering a local anaesthetic. The university's insurance company, Tom's insurance company, and Dr. Ryan's insurance company should settle this claim as quickly as possible.

Websites

www.osha.gov

The site for OSHA standards and guidelines.

http://www.usdoj.gov/dea/index.htm

Department of Justice, Drug Enforcement Agency homepage.

http://www.usdoj.gov/crt/ada/adahom1.htm

U.S. Department of Justice ADA homepage.

http://www.usbr.gov/laws/civil.html

Civil Rights Act of 1991, which expanded Title VII of the Civil Rights Act of 1964 by allowing damages to be collected for violating the original act, ADA, or the Rehabilitation Act of 1973.

http://nfb.org/rehabact.htm

Rehabilitation Act of 1973.

http://usatrainers.com

A website with information on what to do if you are sued and ways to minimize the risk.

Applications for Consideration

1. Jorge and Jerome are athletic trainers at competing clinical sites and best friends since college. Jorge and Jerome were on opposite sidelines last week during a high school football game and one of Jorge's athletes was severely injured. Jerome came over to Jorge's work site to pick him up for lunch a few days later and began to ask questions about the outcome of the injury. Can Jorge disclose this information? What possible problems could arise from such a discussion? What problems could arise if the injured player's girlfriend and sister are working out in the health club section of the clinic and overhear the conversation?

2. Mark and Mitch are doing research at Enormous State University's Sports Injury Research Institute. Mark and Mitch see Jeff performing what they consider to be highly unethical treatments to an athlete. Later the athlete asks Mitch if the treatments will be successful. What should Mitch say in this situation?

References

1 The American Law Institute. *Restatement of torts, second: Torts 2d.* St. Paul, MN: American Law Institute Publishers, 1965.

2 An athletic trainer's standard of care can be elevated: A look at Gillespie v. Southern Utah State College. *The Sports, Parks, and Recreation Law Reporter.* 2:62–63, 1989.

3 Blond, NC. *Blond's torts.* 3rd ed. New York: Sulzburger and Graham Publishing, Ltd., 1993.

4 Campbell, D, Konin, JG. Regulation of athletic training. In Konin, JG, ed. *Clinical Athletic Training,* Thorofare, NJ: SLACK, Incorporated, 1997.

5 Ciccolella, M. Caught in court. *College Athletic Management.* 3(4):10–13, 1991.

6 Drowatzky, JN. Legal duties and liability in athletic training. *Athletic Training.* 20:10–13, 1985.

7 Eickhoff-Shemek, JM, Forbes, FS. The legal significance of standards and guidelines. *The Sports Medicine Standards and Malpractice Reporter.* 9(3):38–43, 1997.

8 Halpin, T, ed. *1999–2000 NCAA sports medicine handbook.* Indianapolis, IN: National Collegiate Athletic Association, 1999.

9 Hawkins, JD. The legal status of athletic trainers. *The Sports, Parks, and Recreation Law Reporter.* 2:6–9, 1988.

10 Herbert, DL. Should athletic trainers be held to the standard of care of physicians? *The Sports, Parks, and Recreation Law Reporter.* 1:56–58, 1988.

11 Herbert, DL. Should sports medicine providers rely on practice parameters? *The Sports Medicine Standards and Malpractice Reporter.* 7(2)25–26, 1995.

12 Herbert, DL, Herbert, WG. Sports medicine and the law, part 1. *The Sports Medicine Standards and Malpractice Reporter.* 11(3):42–44, 1999.

13 Herbert, DL, Herbert, WG. Sports medicine and the law, part 2. *The Sports Medicine Standards and Malpractice Reporter.* 11(4):53–61, 1999.

14 Herbert, DL. *The Sports Medicine Standards Book.* Canton, OH: Professional Reports Corporation. 1992.

15   Lederman, D. 3-judge panel says colleges must provide 'reasonable' emergency care for athletes. *Chronicle of Higher Education.* (April 28):A35–A36, 1993.

16   Litigation Review Topics. URL: *http://usatrainers.com/* 1999.

17   Louisell, DL, Williams, H. *Medical malpractice.* New York: Matthew Bender & Co. 1986, and supplements through 1991.

18   NATA-PEC. *Competencies in athletic training.* Dallas, TX: National Athletic Trainers' Association, 1992.

19   NATA. *Athletic Training Educational Competencies.* Dallas, TX: National Athletic Trainers' Association. 1999.

20   NATABOC. *Role delineation study.* 4th ed. Omaha, NE: National Athletic Trainers' Association Board of Certification, Inc., 1999.

21   NATABOC. Standards for the practice of athletic training. In *Credentialing information and professional practice and discipline standards for the practice of athletic training.* Omaha, NE: National Athletic Trainers' Association Board of Certification, Inc., 1998.

22   Scott, RW. *Health care malpractice.* Thorofare, NJ: SLACK; Inc., 1990.

23   Starkey, C. Legal issues for modalities. Presented to the National Athletic Trainers' Association Annual Meeting and Clinical Symposium, Kansas City, June 19, 1999.

24   Webster, DL, Mason, JC, Keating, TM. *Guidelines for professional practice in athletic training.* Canton, OH: Professional Reports Corporation, 1992.

CHAPTER 16

Risk Management

After reading this chapter, you should be able to:

- Explain various ways to reduce risk of exposure to liability.

- Describe the limitations of assumption of risk, waivers, and statutes of limitations.

- Describe the requirements of informed consent.

- Explain major cases in which athletic trainers have been sued.

Key Terms

risk management
contributory negligence
comparative negligence
statute of limitations
assumption of risk
informed consent
Good Samaritan laws
immunity
waiver

FOR CRITICAL THOUGHT:
1995 WL 739820 (Tenn. Ct. App.)

"In August 1984 a college football player, Michael P, reported for practice and passed his physical examination. On August 25, 1984, the player suffered a blow to the head during practice. He walked to the sidelines, reported that he had been "kicked in the head," and collapsed unconscious.

During the time the player was unconscious, the athletic trainer, James L, examined the athlete. The athletic trainer's notes from the day of the injury show that he found palsy on the left side of Michael's face, no control of the left side of his body, unequal pupils and no response to pain, sound, or movement. These notes show that he remained unconscious for a period of 10 minutes.

After examining Michael, Mr. L summoned an ambulance which transported the athlete to the Volunteer General Hospital. The athletic trainer did not personally go with the athlete, but had a student athletic trainer go with the ambulance. The athletic trainer did not give any information to the student athletic trainer to give to the emergency room physician. Hospital records

---

show the student athletic trainer informed the physician that the athlete lost consciousness for about two minutes. Shortly after Michael arrived at the emergency room, Mr. L arrived, but did not speak to the physician about the neurological signs he had observed on the practice field.

At the hospital, Michael's head was x-rayed and found to be normal. No CT-scan was ever done. The athlete was assigned to Dr. S for follow-up care and was admitted to the hospital for observation. Although all neurological checks were normal, hospital records show the athlete complained of headaches to the hospital staff. The athlete complained that one of these headaches was so severe that it made him sick to his stomach.

On August 26, 1984, Dr. S telephoned the athletic trainer and told him that Michael should not participate in football for a week and that, if further trouble arose, the athlete should return to Dr. S or another physician. On that same day, Dr. S released Michael to Mr. L, who transported the athlete from the hospital to the university.

When Mr. L picked up Michael, he complained to the athletic trainer of a headache. Mr. L did not record this headache in university records. On August 27, 1984, Michael complained of a headache and was given Empirin #4 by Mr. L. On August 28, 1984, Michael told the athletic trainer that he had a headache, but that it was milder than the one he had on the previous day. Mr. L's notes of August 30, 1984, which refer to the athlete, contain the statement "Headache!"

On September 3, 1984, Mr. L contacted the team physician, Dr. P. The athletic trainer told the physician that Michael was asymptomatic for a concussion on September 3. Mr. L did not tell the doctor about the athlete's headaches on the 26th, 27th, 28th, or 30th. Relying on Mr. L's report of Michael's condition, Dr. P concurred with Dr. S's prior advice that the athlete could return to practice if there were no further problems.

On September 3, 1984, Michael returned to practice. He participated in practice, traveled as a member of the team and played in at least two games. Testimony from the athlete's mother, roommate, and girlfriend, indicated that the athlete suffered headaches and complained of dizziness, nausea, and blurred vision throughout the three-week period from September 3 to September 24. Mr. L did not report any of these symptoms to the team physician. On September 24, the athlete stated that he had been "kicked in the head" and collapsed unconscious.

The athlete was eventually taken to Jackson-Madison County General Hospital, where he underwent brain surgery. Surgeons there found that the athlete had sustained a chronic subdural hematoma of three to four weeks duration of several hundred cubic centimeters and an acute subdural hematoma of approximately 25–30 cubic centimeters and a shift of mid-line structures of almost 1.5 centimeters. Michael remained in a coma for several weeks and was transferred to the Lamar Unit of Baptist Hospital in Memphis for intensive rehabilitative treatment. As a result of his injuries, the athlete suffered severe and permanent neurological damage.

Michael brought an action for negligence against the State before the State Claims Commission. A trial on the merits was held before a Claims Commissioner.

At the time of the trial, Michael was a hemiparetic. He had no use of his left arm and very little use of his left leg. He had a shunt to relieve fluid build-up in his brain. He also suffered from severe cognitive problems and frequent seizures. These maladies rendered him unable to hold a job. Additionally, Michael and his mother had incurred approximately $200,000 in medical bills due to this injury. (Paraphrased from 1995 WL 738920 *1 [Tenn. Ct. App.])

Expert testimony at trial indicated that had the athletic trainer informed the emergency room physician of the "lucid interval" and duration of unconsciousness, that a CT-scan would have been ordered which should have identified the subdural *hematoma. Surgery at that time would have been performed, but the patient would most likely have had a normal life. The athletic trainer responded that under Tennessee law, there was no duty to inform emergency room personnel of information that they did not request. Judgment was entered against the athletic trainer and university for $1,500,000. The commissioner noted the athlete was suing others and held the university liable for 30 percent, or $450,000, which was reduced to $300,000.*

ELEMENTS OF RISK MANAGEMENT

To decrease exposure to negligence and possibly other malpractice claims, a **risk management** strategy must be employed. A risk is an exposure to the chance of injury or financial loss.[21] Injuries result in financial loss when healthcare providers and their employers are sued. Damage awards can be based on permitting injured or unfit persons to play; failing to employ competent personnel; failing to provide competent training, instructions, or supervision; and negligently moving an injured player.[2] Risk management can be thought of as the achievement of two interrelated tasks. The first task is to recognize primary risks and take all reasonable steps to eliminate or reduce them. Since not all risks can be eliminated, establishing the defense of suits that are filed is the second task.[5]

There are three ways to decrease risk. The first is to eliminate the risk by eliminating the conditions that cause the risk. This, however, is not possible. Giving required medical care opens the provider up to a variety of injury-causing situations. The second is to share the risk with others, which is the basis for liability or malpractice insurance, and which can be very expensive if there is no active plan to reduce risk exposure. The third is to reduce the risk by looking at all aspects of the activity.

In establishing the duty to act, courts rely on standards of care from national norms as established in state practice acts. Athletic training is singularly lacking as a national medical profession in the provision of such standards. There is a great deal of variability in what constitutes the standard of care from state to state. Without a consistent standard of care, the courts have broad authority to define duty and breach of duty.

Is an athletic trainer, when under the direct supervision of a licensed physician, able to perform all procedures for which the athlete has had course work and clinical experience? This is clearly the case in many clinical settings. Standard first aid also teaches recognition of medical conditions such as hyperthermia, hypothermia, and diabetic coma. Currently, the documentation of competency development for first aid and emergency care of injuries is good, but in the area of illnesses, athletic training is poorly defined.

In states with licensure, courts have a conceptualization of the profession. However, in those states without credentialing, the professional association's documentation standards may have a major influence. With the advent of the new NATA publication, *Athletic Training Educational Competencies*,[19] and the fourth edition of the NATABOC *Role Delineation Study*,[20] the courts have new documentation for establishing standards that include, for the first time, a separate domain in pathology of injuries and illnesses.

While the case law involving athletic trainers can be loosely divided into specific areas, it is important to understand that there are often overlapping areas in deciding standard of care. These cases have all reached the level of federal or state appeals courts before being published in legal literature. Broadly, using negligence as the standard, cases may be divided into diagnoses and treatment, failure to refer, injury prevention, willful and wanton misconduct, and injury prevention.

Risk Reduction

The first place to begin with risk management is with the prevention of injury. This involves preparticipation physical examination of the athletes (see chapter 13). It also involves assessing the level of fitness and the methods used to increase the fitness level to the point necessary to conduct the activity. In addition, assessing the field conditions for dangerous playing areas, lack of space, environmental hazards such as extreme heat and humidity, and lack of water all play a role in reducing the chance of injury.

There have been a number of cases where preparticipation examination findings have led to legal action. For a discussion of four specific cases related to the prevention of injuries, see box 16-1.

The second area to evaluate is the conduct of the activity. Is the equipment adequate for the level of play? Is it safe, undamaged, and the best that may be obtained for the money available? It may be that the equipment is unsafe, but finances dictate that no other equipment purchases are possible. In that case, the activity may have to be eliminated. How the coaches present the material is important as well. There are cases on record alleging improper technique taught by coaches, such as spearing, that

---

■ **Cases Relating to Prevention** *Box 16-1*

In *Elnora S v. Boyd K, et al.*, (673 F. Supp.817 U.S. District Court SD Mississippi, 849 F.2d 960 US Court of Appeals, Fifth Circuit) a black football player, who suffered from sickle-cell trait, became ill and collapsed during football practice at the USM. He was taken to the student health center but transferred to a local hospital, where he died. Suit was filed by his mother, acting for herself and his estate, against USM, the board of trustees, and the head coach, athletic trainer, and team physician, charging that the athletic trainer and physician were unable "to recognize, diagnose, or treat a case of sickle-cell crisis . . . common among black athletes." Trial court dismissed all claims against the institution and the board of trustees. The U.S. Court of Appeals, Fifth Circuit, later dismissed the wrongful death, negligence, and breach of contract claims against the physician, athletic trainer, and coach on the grounds of state sovereign immunity. The case calls into question what should be done in screening black athletes for sickle-cell trait as part of a preparticipation examination. In addition this suit brings up the questions of what duty does an athletic trainer owe to an athlete separate from the physician and can an athletic trainer be jointly and severally liable for allegedly negligent acts or omissions in the overall management of player health care as well as alleged failures in preparticipation screening.[15]

●

The case of Earnest K (*State of Or. v. Superior Court [Lillard]*, 29 Cal. Rptr. 2, 909, [Cal. App.2 Dist. 1994]) is another with a tragic outcome.[13] K entered Oregon State University in the fall of 1990 ineligible to compete in basketball. He suffered a mild stroke in July 1991, resulting in exploratory surgery and his being placed on an anticoagulant. On his return for the 1991–1992 season, the university initially disqualified him from participation. Apparently an assistant basketball coach visited the cardiologist at Oregon Health Sciences University. The cardiologist wrote the team physician on December 17 about allowing Earnest to participate should he desire after he was made fully aware of the potential dangers, including death. The cardiologist also stated that "We are all aware that there are many physicians who would review all this information and simply prohibit Earnest from playing."[22] The athlete

(continued)

■ **Cases Relating to Prevention**   *Box 16-1 (continued)*

was allowed to reduce his level of anticoagulant and he played in seven games. While on a road trip in Los Angeles, he suffered a massive stroke, went into a coma and died. The family has questioned the propriety of a coach influencing physicians charged with an athlete's care.

●

Environmental conditions play far too great a role in sudden death, particularly tragic because heat-related deaths are preventable. In *Donald R and Tammy R, individually and on behalf of the Estate of Donald R, Jr., v. Pasadena Independent School District, et al.,* (981 F. Suppl. 1013 U.S. District Court SD Texas) the plaintiffs allege their son's death was caused by the defendant's conduct of football practice, which went over four hours on a hot, humid summer day in Harris County, Texas. There was no attempt to acclimatize the players to this extensive hot weather exercise, there was no opportunity to rest during the practice, and the players were not given enough water and the chance to drink to avoid dehydration. At the end of the practice the players were required to perform "gasser" conditioning drills, which were 200-yard sprints within 45 seconds as punishment for poor team performance during the practice. Donald complained of discomfort and showed signs of heat exhaustion, heat stroke, and dehydration, but was made to continue the drills. He collapsed and received no medical attention. The coaches completed the drill and then held a team meeting while Donald was still on the ground. The athletic trainer working with the football team was not present at the site during the practice. Defendants moved for summary dismissal, which was denied. The result was upheld, in part, on appeal. The senior administration of the school district, board of trustees members, athletic director, and head athletic trainer were dismissed. The coaches and football athletic trainer were held to remain parties to the action for trial.

●

Terrie C was also the victim of a heat stroke death during conditioning as part of the first practice in summer heat while a member of the soccer team at the University of California at Irvine.[23] The players had to complete a six-mile run within an hour in heat that was extreme enough to move the time trial from 4:00 P.M. to 6:00 P.M. There were no athletic trainers present and no water stations along the route. Terrie collapsed in the last mile. An assistant coach and student athletic trainer arrived afterward, and neither gave any treatment to the downed athlete. The student athletic trainer did not even recognize she was suffering from heat stroke. The assistant coach had to use a phone at a preschool some distance away. The 911 call was recorded at 6:58, possibly as long as 18 minutes after she collapsed. Paramedics arrived on the scene at 7:14, arriving after a fire unit, which arrived at 7:03. Her body temperature was 107 degrees, and she died three days later after multiple organ failure. The case was settled out of court before trial.

have resulted in catastrophic injury. Coaching methods also involve the length of work intervals, timing of rest intervals, timing of water breaks, and water availability. These are factors that can cause injury or promote safe participation.

If there is an injury, there must be in place a demarcation of who is responsible for deciding questions such as return to play. Physicians are not always present at practices or competitions; therefore it is vital that the coaches understand that the athletic trainer is the physician's representative and will make decisions based on what is best for the athlete, not the team. It is best to have this in writing and approved by the athletic director well before play begins. For a discussion of two cases related to the conduct of the activity, see box 16-2.

A third area is the treatment of injuries. Proper evaluation by the athletic trainer, documented in full and transmitted to the physician in charge, is crucial. There must be adequate equipment and supplies to perform emergency first aid and to carry out the physician's orders for follow-up treatment of injured athletes. The equipment must be inspected and recalibrated regularly. Proper referral procedures must be observed.

Direct supervision of the athletic training staff by licensed physicians is also crucial. Whether the physicians are volunteer or paid, written contracts should be executed between the physicians and the athletic department to delineate responsibilities.[7] There must be adequate professional staff to supervise student athletic trainers. The actions of student athletic trainers may well expose the staff supervisor to vicarious liability as the person who should have controlled the improper actions of the student athletic trainer. In postpractice time, environmental factors can be evaluated. In summer athletics, players should be weighed when going out to practice and weighed again after practice. This allows the staff to pinpoint those who may be susceptible to

---

■ Cases Relating to the Conduct of the Activity   *Box 16-2*

In *Mark H v. Gale S, et al.*, (552 F. Suppl. 685 U.S. District Court SD Illinois) the plaintiff alleged that the athletic director, football coach, and the athletic trainer provided the football player with a football helmet that was defective and in unreasonably dangerous condition for use as protective headwear for football games in that it suddenly and unexpectedly failed to protect the player's cervical spine when put to the use intended. Mark further alleged that the dangerous helmet was in the same condition at the time of injury as when it had been sold to SIU. Defendants petitioned for summary dismissal under the Eleventh Amendment to the U.S. Constitution. Mark additionally asserted breach of warranty claims against these defendants and Riddell Corporation, manufacturer of the helmet. All defendants were dismissed from the warranty claims, but defendants (athletic director), (coach) and (athletic trainer) were not dismissed due to the Eleventh Amendment and the case was sent back for trial.

●

In *Tara Joan H v. Wayne V, et al.*, (133 Ill.2d 295, 549 N.E.2d 1240, 140 Ill.Dec. 368) the plaintiff charged that the defendants were negligent in performing their duties as university employees, while making no claim that the defendants acted in violation of the law or in excess of their authority. She alleged that the athletic directors failed to supervise the training and conditioning techniques of the gymnasts, failed to supervise the rehabilitation of injured athletes, and failed to warn the plaintiff that gymnastics was dangerous. She alleged that V failed to get the necessary medical clearance to allow her to perform normal gymnastics activity and failed to properly train, supervise, and care for her during her rehabilitation. Ms. H was attempting to get the suit heard in the circuit court, but the State Supreme Court held the suit was properly in the Court of Claims, hence the case was not tried on its merits. The case was remanded to circuit court for action on the motion to dismiss. On remand, the Supreme Court left the matter to the circuit court to decide whether the dismissal was to be with or without prejudice (leave to refile).

heat illness. See box 16-3 for a discussion of four cases dealing with the treatment of athletic injuries.

The fourth area of risk management is record keeping (see chapter 8). Written records are the best way to establish that duties have been met in order to minimize the risk of injury. The information that is most important (in the legal sense) on an injury evaluation includes: (1) the physician's orders, (2) the treatment plan, (3) the treatment record, and (4) progress reports that evaluate the progression of the treatment plan and prove what care was given and when. For a discussion of a case that deals primarily with the treatment of athletic injuries, but deals at least in part with inadequate record keeping relating to prescription medications, see box 16-4.

■ **Cases Dealing with the Treatment of Injury**   *Box 16-3*

In the case of *Rickey Gillespie and Ghislaine Gillespie v. Southern Utah State College* (669 P.2d 861 [Utah 1983]), Rickey Gillespie sustained a sprained ankle during a basketball scrimmage. The defendant, a student athletic trainer, initiated cold treatment and applied a supportive taping to the injured ankle. The next morning, the student athletic trainer referred Mr. Gillespie to a physician for X rays. The physician ordered the cold and taping support to be continued for seventy-two hours. While continuing under the care of the athletic trainer, Rickey also began his own ice immersion treatments with intervals lasting up to several hours. The athletic trainer notified the physician of these self-treatments who ordered the cold treatments to cease immediately. Six days after the injury Rickey was diagnosed as having thrombophlebitis in his foot, and his fifth toe and other foot tissue was amputated due to gangrene. The plaintiff sought to recover damages, but trial and appellate courts found Rickey's actions were the proximate cause of his injuries. The defendant athletic trainer was held to the standard of a physician in the trial court's instructions to the jury, which was the basis for Rickey's appeal. The appellate court held that even at the standard of a physician, the athletic trainer's conduct met the standard of care.

●

The case of *O'Brien v. Township High School District* (214, 415 N.E.2d 1015 [Ill. 1980]) hinged on the delegation to a student athletic trainer the provision of medical care for which neither the athletic trainer nor the student were qualified. Apparently Mr. O'Brien, a high school student, had received an abrasion in a public pool locker area. During football practice the abrasion began to bleed. The wound was bandaged and the athlete returned to practice. After a few days a boil formed at the injury site. The athletic trainer directed the student to heat the wound area, open the boil, cleanse it and apply a new dressing. Central to *O'Brien* is that no "athletic injury" had taken place (it happened in a municipal pool). The athletic trainer and the student were found negligent because they were outside the state-defined scope of practice. Dissenting opinion in the case examined the issue of athletes bringing medical problems to the athletic trainer that began outside the defined system.

●

In *Darrin J v. Orleans Parish School Board et al.* (600 So.2d 1389) the primary issue was the failure to refer and obtain medical treatment when J injured his wrist. The injury happened when he struck his wrist against a helmet. It may have been aggravated by participation in practice and games, but neither the

■ **Cases Dealing with the Treatment of Injury**   *Box 16-3 (continued)*

coach, Michael S, nor the athletic trainer, Henry D, removed him from playing until the injury was seen by a physician. At the end of the season at J's request, D referred him to Dr. Michael B, an orthopedic surgeon at Tulane Medical center. Dr. B ordered X rays to confirm a suspected scaphoid fracture. The X rays verified a nonunion fracture as well as cystic changes, indicating that either the fracture formed through a cyst or the cyst formed because of collapse. Dr. B indicated that the delay in treatment extended the period of recovery and limited the success of the treatment. After two surgeries and extensive rehabilitation, Dr. B concluded that J had permanent limitations with wrist movement that would prevent vigorous manual labor. The trial court found the coach and athletic trainer were negligent and awarded $50,000 for "past, present, and future pain and suffering, disability, and mental anguish" and $12,725 for past medical expenses. The court further found the school district liable and awarded J an additional $80,000 in general damages and $12,725 for past medical expenses. On appeal, the court found that J had reached the age of majority before the injury, did not request referral after the initial injury until the season was over, and held him one-third responsible, reducing the total award from $80,000 plus past medical expenses to $61,816.91.

•

The case of *Vernon O v. BYU* (960 F. Supp. 1522 US District Court, D. Utah, Central Division and 108 F.3d 1388, 1997 WL 143600 10th Cir. [Utah]) alleges negligence by athletic trainers diagnosing and treating his medical injuries. Vernon O enrolled at BYU after two years in a junior college. In August he felt a pain in his back during a practice drill. After practice, O was examined by associate head athletic trainer Marv R. The athletic trainer concluded that O had probable SI joint immobilization, which he started to treat with heat, massage, and electric stimulation. O's position coach harassed him for missing practice. After being treated the next morning, O practiced. His position coach told him the injury might loosen up during practice. The back was progressively getting better and at the afternoon practice, O told the coach it was better. After receiving five or six treatments, O stopped seeing the athletic trainers. About six weeks later another episode happened, which quickly resolved itself after O saw the athletic trainers. O missed no game time and played without pain during games that year. In 1989 O had pain and stiffness during spring practice. O sought treatment from the athletic trainer and the pain and stiffness resolved itself quickly. O had pain during the fall season, but did not see the athletic trainers as directed by the position coach. For the rest of the season O had repeated episodes of back pain, but does not remember reporting them to the coach or medical staff. In the last game of the season he was examined by an orthopedic specialist, who said he had a trigger point, which the specialist injected with a local anaesthetic. During practice for a bowl game, O had another back injury. He was referred to the medical staff, where he presented with a reticular pain and was sent for radiological imaging, which showed three herniated disks. These were immediately repaired surgically. O then left BYU and played professional football in Finland.

O asserted sixteen separate grounds for negligence (among other claims), including "conditioning payment for medical services on an athletic trainer's determination of medical need; employing

■ **Cases Dealing with the Treatment of Injury**   *Box 16-3 (continued)*

unqualified persons to diagnose and treat football related injuries; allowing unqualified personnel to evaluate his medical fitness to play football; failure of the athletic trainers to refer him to a team physician for diagnosis and treatment; and failing to hire a full-time team physician responsible for diagnoses and treatment in lieu of unqualified athletic trainers." (960 F.Supp. 1522) The university was granted summary judgment on all claims involving the athletic training staff and was held to trial only on a claim of the team physicians violating the standard of care. When O's expert refused to testify against the team physician, the case was withdrawn with prejudice.

■ **Cases Relating to Improper Records**   *Box 16-4*

The case of *Jacqueline W. individually and as Administrator for the Estate of Larry Shannon W v. J. F. B, et al.,* (332 Ark. 189, 961 S.W.2d 712) alleged failure of adequate records as a portion of the claim. Shannon W was a football player at the University of Arkansas who suffered a severe shoulder injury during a game in 1993. He was given the scheduled controlled substance Darvocet, which he took in large quantities during rehabilitation. There was a suggestion in the media at the time that Shannon was clinically depressed. The defendants claimed that he had no Darvocet in his system, but he had consumed large quantities of alcohol, and while under its influence committed suicide. The complaint further states that the university athletic department obtained prescription medications, including scheduled controlled substances in distribution quantities, and allowed athletic trainers to dispense the medications. Shortly after Shannon's death, the Arkansas State Police and the DEA conducted an audit of the controlled substances purchased by the athletic department. Their audit revealed that 13,079 doses had been purchased but only 3,352 dosage units could be accounted for through documentation. W further claimed that the drugs were kept in an unlocked cabinet and that university personnel obtained controlled substances without prescriptions, labels, instructions, or warnings as to dangers or side effects.

There was a criminal prosecution concerning this case in which multiple defendants were found guilty of drug law violations. Two University of Arkansas athletic trainers were sentenced to probation and community service and fined $3,500 and $2,500, respectively.[12] The W case is a civil action that is still active as of this writing.

BASIC DEFENSES

There are several justifications for an athletic trainer's actions that may excuse the resulting damages to an athlete.

Contributory Negligence

Contributory negligence arises when the plaintiff's own negligence contributed to the proximate cause of the injury.[3] In this situation the plaintiff is barred from recovery of damages. The plaintiff has the duty to protect himself or herself from being injured. When Bob, a scholarship football player in season, suffered a first-degree ankle sprain at the student recreation center on Thursday evening playing basketball, and then sprained the ankle again during a game due to the negligent action of sideline personnel, there is a question of contributory negligence. This is not to be confused with failure to mitigate damages, which generally occurs after the fact, while contributory negligence generally occurs before the fact.[3]

Comparative Negligence

Comparative negligence was developed as a reaction to the all-or-none principle of contributory negligence. Nationally, the majority opinion is that only a plaintiff who is equally or less negligent than the defendant may recover damages.[3] Theoretically, defendants are more careful with a comparative negligence system, since the plaintiff's participation does not affect the awarding of damages.

Statute of Limitations

A **statute of limitations** is a state law that sets the length of time that persons may sue for damages under either negligence or malpractice laws. In the states where athletic training is licensed, the statute of limitations probably extends to cover athletic trainers. Where athletic trainers are covered by malpractice laws, the statute specifies from one to three years (depending on the state) to initiate action.[18] Where athletic training is not regulated, there may be no statute of limitations to cover the actions of the athletic trainer. It is also important to note that in most states the statute of limitations is *tolled* for a minor (that is, the time factor is postponed until that person reaches either 18 years old or an age set in the statute). An athlete injured at age 7 can start the statute of limitations at 18. Records, therefore, need to be kept until there is no further exposure to the time limit. In all but seven states, the statute of limitations is also tolled for fraudulent concealment of information that would have caused the patient to consider his or her options for suing the professional.[18] It is an open question whether damage that appears later in life (e.g., traumatic arthritis, degenerative diseases that may require joint replacement) can still fall under the time limits of these laws. There is a case on record (*Jane Doe v. St. G School*, 1989 WL 125283 9 [D.R.I.]) in which a student was sexually assaulted by an athletic trainer and suffered, among other things, post-traumatic stress disorder, dissociative disorder, anorexia, bulimia, and major depression, all induced by the abuse. She did not recall the incident until in therapy ten years later, at which time she filed suit against the school for failing to protect her from the abuse. The school tried to cite the statute of limitations, but the courts found that the statute did not begin to run until the victim was aware of the injuries that had happened to her.

Assumption of Risk

In an **assumption of risk** defense, the athletic trainer will assert that the plaintiff knew before commencing an activity that the activity was dangerous and chose to participate anyway. There are two types of assumption of risk, express assumption of risk and implied assumption of risk. In express assumption of risk, the plaintiff agrees not to hold the defendant liable in advance of possible injury. Even if an act is perpetrated outside the normal playing time, as long as it is no more dangerous than that found during play, the risk is assumed by the participants.[6] This line of thought has long legal standing, but has been narrowed considerably in recent years as courts assess whether the agreement is contrary to public policy. Implied assumption of risk is shown when a person has witnessed an event before, including possible hazards to participants or spectators, yet willingly becomes part of the event. For assumption of risk to be valid, the athlete must "fully appreciate" all of the potential risks and possible outcomes from exposure to these risks. In addition, the athlete must "knowingly, voluntarily, and unequivocally" decide to participate in the face of these risks.[24]

For an athlete to fully appreciate the risks, many courts are stating that the athlete must be informed of *all* possible risks and outcomes. In the case of *Krueger v. Bert Bell NFL Player Retirement Fund* (234 Cal. Rptr. 579 [Cal. App. 1 Dist. 1987]), the court found that not informing the plaintiff of all aspects of his medical condition constituted fraud in that Mr. Krueger was not given the opportunity to make a different decision concerning his return to play after knee surgery. The plaintiff was a professional football player for the San Francisco 49ers from 1958 to 1973. He suffered "innumerable" injuries, the most serious of which involved his left knee. He had a torn meniscus while in college, an MCL repaired in 1963 (including an operative note from the surgeon that the ACL was missing), rehabilitation, and knee bracing for the next four years. Bloody fluid was aspirated from the knee a number of times, and corticosteroids were injected to relieve the inflammation and pain. Mr. Krueger testified he had fifty such treatments during 1964 and an average of fourteen to twenty in succeeding years until he retired. The physician's records indicated a total of seven such treatments. In 1971, loose bodies were removed from the area around the patella due to chondromalacia, which the court found was consistent with known side effects of chronic steroid use. The focus of the trial was the disclosure of information to the plaintiff. He testified he had never been told that he did not have an ACL, he was never told of the dangers of repeated corticosteroid use, and he was never told that the condition causing the operation for the removal of loose bodies in the left knee was consistent with long-term steroid use. The trial court found for the defense, stating that the plaintiff would have continued to play even if he had known all of the factors, thus negating causation. The appellate court found for the plaintiff, stating that the defendant's claim of no concealment could not substitute for professional warnings to which the plaintiff was legally entitled. The appellate court remanded the case to trial court for retrial on the issue of damages alone.[14]

Informed Consent

In physician-patient relations, it has been standard practice for a number of years to explain an entire procedure to the patient, the risks, and the projected outcome, and then have the patient sign an **informed consent** document agreeing that the explanations have been given, that an opportunity to ask questions was offered, and that the patient still wants to proceed. This is also being done more and more in the athletic training room in relation to rehabilitation programs and postinjury prevention programs. It is necessary to inform the athlete of all foreseeable problems and complications. The law does not usually mandate the disclosure of all improbable or extremely remote possibilities.[15] A consent-to-engage-in-treatment form that spells out the treatment, the possible complications, and the

expected duration (rough estimate of days and the requirements to return to play) is probably becoming a necessity. This is a general form, not a diagnosis from a physician.[15]

Good Samaritan Laws

Good Samaritan laws state that those who come to the aid of an injured person and act within their standard of care are immune from actions for damages. These laws do not cover negligent conduct. There is an assumption that no compensation to the athletic trainer was provided. The most common use of these laws occurs when covering state games and charitable events.

Sovereign or Governmental Immunity

At common law, "the king could do no wrong" and was immune from tort actions unless he consented to being sued.[3] The rule was modified at the federal level in 1946 by the Federal Tort Claims Act, which allows the government to be considered liable in the same way as private individuals with the exception of intentional tort or discretionary acts. This latter exception is most often the defense used by public employees in the medical area. As long as protocols are followed, there is no liability, because the procedures were produced through planning and the application of standards. Many athletic trainers are employed by governmental units (public colleges or universities and secondary schools), and use discretionary actions in the conduct of their duties, a situation that gives the athletic trainer sovereign **immunity**. (This was the basis of dismissing the claims in *Sorrey v. Kellet, et al.*) In the recent past, many state governmental units have decreased the individual's claim of immunity due to the prevalence of liability insurance and the inappropriateness of the idea that "the king can do no wrong."[3] States have maintained the governing body's immunity.

Waivers

A **waiver** is a legal contract[4] in which the signatories give up the right to sue for damages in exchange for services performed for them. Contract law carries some standard requirements.[4] First, the participant signing the waiver must be competent and of majority. A second element is the exchange of adequate "consideration" (e.g., allowing participation, use of facilities). Another essential element is mutual assent or a "meeting of the minds." This involves an offer by the first party and acceptance by the second party. If the offer is clear and obvious, then this element is present. Failure to read an otherwise valid release is not viewed as an acceptable defense to enforcing the contract.

It is important to remember that when a parent signs a waiver, it only means the parent gives up the right to sue (in theory, after injury the parent may claim duress and many other things to void the waiver). A minor has been found to be unable to waive the right to sue by parental signature. Minors are also held in court to be incapable of signing a waiver because they cannot legally enter into a binding contract.[4] This situation may be changing, however, as courts in California, Arizona, and Mississippi have all upheld waivers signed by parents or by parents and children as binding.[25]

The courts may also declare that it is not in the public interest to recognize a waiver, so that even though one is signed, it is null and void. In addition, married athletes present another problem when the spouse does not also sign a waiver. The spouse may sue for loss of consortium (loss of consortium by a spouse which is defined as interference with and injury to the marital relationship, including companionship, conversation, comfort, sexual relations, and other aspects of life attributable to marriage[8]) due to the injury. An action brought for loss of consortium is viewed in court as a separate and distinct cause of action that may not be avoided because the injured athlete has signed a release of liability waiver.[4]

It is possible to transfer some of the risk to the athletes by using the informed consent procedures and assumption of risk. It is important to remember that an athlete cannot sign a waiver for willful or wanton misconduct, only unforeseeable acts.[4] In addition, these waivers should inform the athletes of their responsibilities under the provision of services. These would include a responsibility to inform the athletic trainer when they are injured and to follow the written and oral directions of the team physician and the athletic trainer. It is still the athletic trainer's responsibility to follow up and see that the instructions are being carried out.

There are federal and state laws that grant a right to privacy of medical and student records. In the medical arena, there are circumstances that dictate an outside party's need to evaluate the records. These would include insurance company adjustors having access to adjudicate a claim, professional teams having access for the purpose of evaluating an athlete for future employment, and so forth. In these conditions, the athlete needs to sign a waiver allowing the outside party access to the records. Each time the records are to be released, a new form should be signed. The form should specify that the athlete gives consent for the athletic medical staff of the institution to release the medical record to a specific person, representative, or entity. Unlimited use of release forms is potentially damaging to the athlete and should be avoided if possible. The athlete should also be informed that although the records will be released in good faith, once they have left institutional control, the athletic medical staff and the institution no longer has any control over them, who gets them, or what uses are made of them. The athlete should also be informed that in the case of professional teams the complete record will be turned over, and that this record may be viewed by the team in either a positive or a negative light. If these records are stored on a computer, security is a consideration at the storage site. This may mean the installation of a password entry system or other security measure to prevent unauthorized use of confidential medical records.

Another type of waiver is one signed by an athlete when he or she has been told not to participate due to a preexisting or new injury that renders further competition dangerous. This waiver needs to inform the athlete of all possible complications (including death, persistent vegetative coma, and all other lesser maladies). It also needs to state that the physicians and the medical staff have told the athlete not to continue but the athlete is going against these orders at his or her own risk. (Obviously parents and/or spouses need to sign similar waivers as well.) (See chapter 8, "Medical Records," for sample waiver forms.)

It is perhaps a viable point of view if the team physicians have disqualified an athlete who wishes to participate anyway to have the athlete sue for the right to participate.[8] In this way a court makes the decision and the athletic medicine staff is obeying a court order. If the athlete obtains a court order allowing him or her to play, a waiver should still be obtained from all interested parties. Attach a copy of the court order to the waiver and include these in the athlete's medical file.

This procedure was followed by Northwestern University (*Knapp v. Northwestern University et al.,* 95 C 6454 United States District Court, Northern District of Illinois, Eastern Division) when a basketball player, Nicolas Knapp, presented with significant risk for primary ventricular fibrillation and cardiac arrest. Knapp had previously suffered a cardiac arrest that required the use of a defibrillator three times to stabilize irregularities in his heart. The team physicians declined to authorize participation, even knowing the athlete had a cardioverter-defibrillator implanted in his abdomen. After this disqualification, Knapp filed suit under the Federal Rehabilitation Act. Northwestern's attorneys pointed out that the plaintiff's own cardiologist had advised the athlete there was a 25 to 50 percent risk of cardiac arrest and if he played that risk would increase.[11] The trial court found for the plaintiff, but that decision was overturned on appeal (*Knapp v. Northwestern University,* 101 F.3d 473 U.S. Court of Appeals, 7th Cir. 1996), in which the court declined to "define the major life activity of learning in such a way that the Act applies whenever someone wants to play intercollegiate athletics."[10]

Communication

Communication between the sports medicine team and athlete about the comprehensive nature of the athlete's health status is vital to the athlete being able to make an informed decision. A basic problem with poor communications is the interference with informed consent. Sports institutions need to develop policies that acknowledge the independence of

their medical staff from team management. Accurate and complete records of all discussions and information provided to an athlete must be made part of the permanent medical record and maintained by the team physician and/or athletic trainer.

Herbert raises the following questions for discussion and evaluation:

"1. What is the duty of the team physician/athletic trainer/administrative team personnel (and the team itself as the employing entity) to provide accurate and complete medical/health information to a player as to his own medical condition or state of well being?; and, what is the scope of that duty?

2. Is there a conflict between the physician/athletic trainer's duty to the team which employs him and the player who relies upon his professional services and advice?; and, if there is such a conflict, how can it be resolved?

3. What policies, procedures, guidelines and forms should be considered to fulfill physician/athletic trainer duties toward players while at the same time minimizing the risks of claims like that occurring in fraudulent or intentional concealment of medical information cases?"[15]

Laurence Graham[9] described various ways to avoid malpractice. Among these is to have a written contract (at the least, a position description) in writing in the athletic department's policies and procedures manual. These authors informally surveyed twenty college and university athletic trainers from NCAA Division I, II, III, and NAIA Division I schools and found only two with written job descriptions. Having this job description may well establish what the athletic trainer must do and cannot do within his or her job. If this document had been in place at an Ohio Division I institution, the athletic trainer may not have been charged in criminal court with practicing medicine without a license for evaluating athletic injuries (which the prosecution tried to state was diagnosing injuries).

Graham also points out the need to participate in continuing education. It is a requirement of the

NATABOC to participate in continuing education to maintain the certified athletic trainer credential. By not following this standard, an athletic trainer may be sued for practicing out-of-date procedures.

A dissertation study by Zylks[26] surveyed the perceptions of selected certified athletic trainers, selected clinical instructors, and the NATA-approved athletic training education program directors about the degree to which they felt each of the competencies of the role delineation study should be stressed in the education programs. Zylks found that sixteen of thirty-five competencies in the area of "prevention of athletic injuries or illnesses" were rated in the twenty-fifth percentile or lower. Conversely, a study published in 1990 by Leverenz and Helms[17] found that of the thirteen cases in appellate law between 1960 and 1989 dealing with athletic trainers, five of them dealt specifically (four exclusively) with the prevention domain. Leverenz[16] also found that athletic trainers in colleges and universities were more at risk than other athletic trainers, but that athletic trainers were possibly sued less often due to the relative lack of financial incentives.

It is necessary to remember that anyone can sue someone else at any time and for any reason. Lawsuits happen with more regularity today than even three years ago. According to Gallup,[10] when a lawsuit is filed, 60 percent of the time the suit is dropped, 30 percent of the time the suit is settled out of court, and 10 percent of the time the suit will actually go to trial. Only 2 percent of filed lawsuits will be adjudicated in favor of the plaintiff.

To protect themselves, a thorough examination of the risks that can be managed, reduced, eliminated, or shared must be an ongoing and daily part of athletic trainers' routine existence.

Summary

1. There are three ways to decrease risk: eliminate the activity, share the risk, or evaluate the activity.
2. Standards, whether state, regional, or national, affect the standard of care.
3. Case law is based on those cases that reach the appellate courts.
4. The first place to reduce risk is injury prevention.
5. The manner of conduct of each activity must be evaluated.
6. Treatment of injuries includes the entire sports medicine team.
7. Record keeping is of central importance.
8. Contributory negligence on the part of the plaintiff removes a defendant for cause.
9. Comparative negligence assesses what part of the responsibility rests with the plaintiff.
10. A statute of limitations limits the amount of time to file a claim.
11. Assumption of risk requires full disclosure of risks.
12. Informed consent is granted when the patient has been informed of all possible outcomes.
13. Good Samaritan laws protect volunteers assisting the injured.
14. Sovereign immunity is a waiver of liability because of one's status as a government employee.
15. Waivers are legal contracts in which each side gives something of value.
16. Waivers should be used for informed consent, disqualification due to preexisting conditions, release of medical information, and loss of consortium.
17. Medical disqualification should be the province of the team physician. If an athlete is determined to play against a physician's order, he or she should obtain court permission.
18. Communication is vital to minimize interference with informed consent procedures.

For Critical Thought

What should an athletic trainer have done in this situation? Why is this situation possible? Could low staffing levels have led to this breach in the standard of care? When there is a suit filed against an athletic trainer, what steps should he or she take?

Websites

http://www.law.cornell.edu/
  Cornell Law School Legal Information Institute
http://westlaw.com/
  Westlaw legal search engine (fee for public use)
http://www.fastsearch.com/law/index.html

Information about a wide variety of topics in the legal and other arenas

http://www.rmf.org/homepage.html
  Risk Management Foundation from the Harvard Medical School

Applications for Consideration

1. A scholarship female basketball player enrolls at Northern State University. During the PPE it is determined she has a cardiac anomaly. She says she knows all about the problem and is under the care of a cardiologist. The team physicians consult with the cardiologist and reluctantly allow her to play. During the season she falls unconscious during practice. Her blood pressure is 80/40. Her pulse is rapid and weak. The emergency medical service has been summoned. What legal problems are there with this case? What should have been done to minimize the risk involved? Was special equipment necessary?

2. Fran Terrell, an athletic trainer at George Washington High School, is asked by an athlete to give him four Advil tablets. Fran knows this is equivalent to an 800 mg Motrin, a prescription medication. She refuses to give the over-the-counter medication. Why is this a wise course of action? What does Fran not know about this case? What potential problems could Fran have faced if she gave the medication?

3. Sports Medicine Clinic has been seeing Rashid Phillips for the past three weeks for low back pain when weightlifting. After this time, Robert Jones, a certified athletic trainer newly employed at the clinic, notices moderate atrophy to the medial head of Rashid's left gastrocnemius. He informs the physician in charge, who refers Rashid to a neurosurgeon for evaluation. Ten months after back surgery for a ruptured disc that impinged several spinal nerve segments, Rashid sues the clinic, the medical director, the physical therapist, and the athletic trainer who worked on his case. What could have been done differently? What should be in the daily progress notes? What defense does the clinic have against this claim?

References

1 An athletic trainer's standard of care can be elevated: A look at Gillespie v. Southern Utah State College. *The Sports, Parks, & Recreation Law Reporter.* 2:62–63, 1989.

2 Baley, JA, Mathews, DL. *Law and liability in athletics, physical education and recreation.* Boston: Allyn and Bacon, 1984.

3 Blond, NC. *Blond's torts.* New York: Sulzburger and Graham Publishing, Ltd., 1993.

4 Comodeca, JA. Release and waiver of liability forms: The most powerful player on the field. *The Sports, Parks, & Recreation Law Reporter.* 6:17, 20–23, 1992.

5 Dougherty, NJ. Risk management in sports medicine programs. *The Sports Medicine Standards and Malpractice Reporter.* 1(3):47, 50–54, 1989.

6 Drowatzky, JN. Assumption of risk in sport. *Journal of Legal Aspects of Sport.* 2:92–100, 1992.

7 Drowatzky, JN. Legal duties and liability in athletic training *Athletic Training.* 20:10–13, 1985.

8 Gallup, E. Sport and the courts. Presented to the 1994 American College of Sports Medicine National Meeting, June 2, Indianapolis, IN, 1994.

9   Graham, LS. Ten ways to dodge the malpractice bullet. *Athletic Training.* 20:117–119, 1985.

10   Herbert, DL. Sports medicine physician has "final say" in exclusion of athlete from participation. *The Sports Medicine Standards and Malpractice Reporter.* 9(2):17, 20–23, 1997.

11   Herbert, DL. Bethesda conference statement again cited in litigation. *The Sports Medicine Standards and Malpractice Reporter.* 8(2):26–27, 1996.

12   Herbert, DL. Drug dispensing in the athletic training room: Criminal prosecution and penalties. *The Sports Medicine Standards and Malpractice Reporter.* 7(1):7, 1995.

13   Herbert, DL. Another basketball star dies. *The Sports Medicine Standards and Malpractice Reporter.* 5(2):17, 19–20, 1993.

14   Herbert, DL. Proof of fraudulent concealment of medical information requires finding in favor of professional football player. *The Sports, Parks, and Recreation Law Reporter.* 1:23–25, 1987.

15   Herbert, DL. *Legal aspects of sports medicine.* 2d ed. Canton, OH: Professional Reports Corporation, 1995.

16   Leverenz, LJ, Helms, LB. Suing athletic trainers: Part I. *Athletic Training.* 25:212–216, 1990.

17   Leverenz LJ, Helms, LB. Suing athletic trainers: Part II. *Athletic Training.* 25:219–226, 1990.

18   Louisell, DL, Williams, H. *Medical malpractice.* New York: Matthew Bender & Co., Inc., 1986, and supplements through 1991.

19   NATA. *Athletic training educational competencies.* Dallas: National Athletic Trainers' Association, 1999.

20   NATABOC. *Role delineation study.* 4th ed. Omaha: National Athletic Trainers' Association Board of Certification, Inc., 1999.

21   Richards, EP, Rathbun, KC. *Medical risk management: Preventive legal strategies for health care providers.* New York: Aspen, 1983.

22   Rock, S. Athlete died after being allowed to play. *Kansas City Star,* October 8, 1997.

23   Rock, S. Risking players' safety: NCAA doesn't require medical supervision. *Kansas City Star,* October 8, 1997.

24   Scott, RW. *Health care malpractice.* Thorofare, NJ: Slack, Inc., 1990.

25   Waivers and minors: three states where a waiver may work with minors. *The Sports Medicine Standards and Malpractice Reporter.* 10(4):58–60, 1998.

26   Zylks, D. The importance of educational competencies in athletic training as perceived by selected athletic trainers. College Station, TX: Texas A & M University; Unpublished doctoral dissertation, 1988.

PART FIVE

Information Technology

CHAPTER 17

Computer Hardware

After reading this chapter, you should be able to:

- Identify advantages and disadvantages of different computer systems.

- Assess computer needs for optimal athletic training facility operation.

- Evaluate and select computer hardware that will allow optimal athletic training facility operation.

- Develop and implement a plan for buying computer equipment for use in an athletic training facility.

Key Terms

operating system
software
graphical user interface
motherboard
CPU
floppy disk (drive)
hard drive
CD
DVD

FOR CRITICAL THOUGHT:
To Upgrade or to Buy New?

Melissa and Steve are co-head athletic trainers in a university setting. It has come to their attention that the athletic department wants to seek reimbursement for athletic training services provided. Their initial reaction was one of concern. They questioned the athletic training program's readiness to submit medical records for review. Steve and Melissa are not concerned with the quality of care provided to the athletes; they simply question the appropriateness of undergraduate students signing SOAP notes while they are still learning. After consulting with several colleagues, Steve realized that record keeping, his largest concern, could be significantly improved with the use of several computer software packages. The only problem is that the computer in the athletic training room is older than the building itself. Steve does not claim to be a computer expert, but he realizes there are a couple of possibilities for this old system. Steve could upgrade the components of the computer, hopefully getting it up to speed with today's models, or he could purchase a new system. Steve investigates possible funding solutions, as he does not have budget money for this. The local hospital has grant money available for medical technology upgrades in the community, and Steve decides to apply.

Melissa takes the responsibility for investigating upgrading or purchasing a new model. After careful examination, she learns that the computer they currently have contains a 386 processor. The hard drive is 80 MB and the system has 4 megabytes of RAM. Additionally, the monitor has a black-and-white fifteen-inch screen. Melissa determines that the best possible hardware she could install in this system is a 25 MHz Pentium processor. She could manage to upgrade the hard drive to 500 MB and the RAM to 8 MB. The monitor, video, and sound cards, while not requiring replacement, could use some upgrading. These upgrades would cost about $1000. Melissa's other option is purchasing a new system. She cringes that the industry standard systems cost around $2000, twice that of the upgrade price. The exciting part is that the new systems are equipped with processors ten times as powerful as their old computer. The hard drives are in the 20 to 50 gigabyte range, and they all come with speakers for surround sound.

Melissa and Steve confer about the selection of a machine. They consider their needs for the present and the future. The upgrade would be adequate, but future considerations indicate additional need.

The computer has become as commonplace as a desk lamp in recent years. Yet its full potential has not even come close to being realized. The age of information in which we live would not be possible without the computer. The computer is as frustrating as it is useful for most people. The Apollo moon missions in the 1960s and 1970s used Commodore 64 technology, which was a closely guarded military secret. Considering the Apple II computer came into prominence around 1980, by today's standards it is obsolete. The personal computer is still in its infancy. That brand-new computer purchased today will approach obsolescence tomorrow. The super-fast, memory-loaded machine recommended by a friend turns out to be compatible with only one other machine in the world. With a basic understanding of computers and some careful planning, the frustration level can be reduced and the benefits can be maximized.

In this chapter, the various computer systems used in athletic training settings, the specific needs of a computer system in an athletic training setting, pertinent software packages, current issues in computer technology as they relate to athletic training settings, and a plan for purchasing a computer system will be discussed.

COMPUTER SYSTEMS

Personal computers come in various platforms, or **operating systems** (software that controls the computer's operations): Windows-based computers, Apple Computer's Macintosh series, and UNIX-based systems such as Ultra SPARC by Sun Microsystems. To a much lesser degree, mainframe computers are also used in athletic training settings. One or any combination of these systems may be present in, or accessible to, an athletic training facility. Of these various computer systems, athletic trainers are most likely to operate a Windows-based or Apple Macintosh machine. Because computers today have a graphical user interface, the multitude of systems now available is becoming more similar than different. Although older systems utilizing a command line interface (MS-DOS) are a thing of the past, a small percentage of these systems are still in use with limited application.

Windows-Based Computers

Windows-based computers comprise the largest percentage of machines used today. Currently, they dominate the personal computer market due to the widespread use of the Microsoft Windows operating systems (Windows 95, Windows 98, Windows NT, etc.). In response to this, many vendors produce Windows-based machines and software in an effort to find their niche in the technology marketplace. Consequently, experts are easy to find (self-proclaimed or otherwise) who can help to select, set up, or repair a Windows-based machine.

Software for these types of machines is abundant and comes with either a **graphical user interface** or a command line (MS-DOS) interface. In most cases, graphically oriented software packages (basic word processors, databases, presentation software) are used in which the user "points and clicks" to navigate through the program. This type of software has distinct advantages in that it is user-friendly and is quite powerful. With MS-DOS-based or command line–oriented software, the user needs to understand the language associated with typing commands to operate software. Although this type of software (custom or commercially available) is still used today, it is quickly phasing out. Since there are so many companies producing Windows-based machines, the cost of hardware and software is generally quite reasonable. Warranties and technical support also tend to be good due to the competition among vendors. See chapter 18 for more information on software.

Macintosh Computers

Macintosh computers operate using a graphical interface. This means that many of the applications designed for the Macintosh rely heavily on using a mouse or other pointing device similar to Windows-based applications. Macintosh computers are known for their ease of use and powerful graphics features. Software applications are very user-friendly, and these programs are well integrated. The Macintosh has been the system of choice for desktop publishing and graphic-intensive applications.

Macintosh's newer line of computers, the Power Mac G4 and the iMac, are competitively priced, very powerful, and have the ability to run MS-DOS and Windows applications. These systems are gaining great popularity primarily for multimedia and desktop publishing applications. Furthermore, these machines are directed toward competing with Windows users with scientific or other intensive computer needs.

Generally speaking, Macintosh systems are somewhat more expensive than Windows-based machines. Although this trend seems to be diminishing over time, it is primarily the result of the broad competition among PC manufacturers. One of the early criticisms of Apple computers was the lack of software available for these systems compared to PCs. However, at present this is no longer a limiting

factor, as most of the applications used by athletic trainers are available in both Macintosh and Windows versions. Additionally, many CD installation programs have both Macintosh and Windows formats on them.

UNIX-Based Computers

The introduction and development of the UNIX operating system for computers is not new at all. In fact, the use of this operating system first began in the early 1970s for minicomputers. UNIX is a multiuser, multitasking operating system that can be used on Mac or PC platforms. UNIX is very similar to other operating systems in that it allows for basic integration and functioning of the hardware and software used by the computer; furthermore, these systems can perform the same functions as a Mac or PC.

There are a few companies that market and produce UNIX-driven systems. Although different versions of this operating system exist, they are used on power computers called workstations. Popular workstations that use a UNIX operating system include Sun Microsystems' Ultra SPARC and Silicon Graphics' SGI-O2. These workstations are primarily used for scientific applications that require intensive mathematical calculations. Cost and limited general software prevent them from becoming widely used in the personal computing environment. However, if advanced scientific computing is needed such as in biomechanics research, this type of system should be considered.

Mainframe Computers

Mainframe computers are available in most collegiate settings and some secondary school and private settings. Many people can access and use a mainframe computer at once. For instance, many universities operate multiple servers for networking capabilities. In this situation, mainframes could be used as a central storage device for multiple systems that feed into it. Mainframe computers are useful for some applications but are not ideal for many personal applications. By comparison with most microcomputers, mainframes are quite slow, since their value lies in accommodating volume and network accessibility rather than speed.

If there is access to a mainframe computer and a desire to use it for personal computing needs, contact a member of the information technology or computer center staff to learn about the available software and computing policies and procedures.

HARDWARE NEEDS

Different computers have different configurations. Some are fast, some have a lot of memory, some have good graphics displays, others have few redeeming values. Understanding the different options available on computer systems is important for several reasons: (1) the relative ease of use, (2) the power needed for the software to be run, and (3) cost, among others. Generally, the following should be considered when selecting a computer system: motherboard, CPU, memory, floppy disk drives, fixed hard drive, CD/DVD drive, display adapters, sound adapters, monitors, printers/plotters, scanners, and modems/fax boards/network cards.

Motherboard

The **motherboard** is what every device in the computer connects to (CPU, RAM, video card, hard drive, sound card, etc.). It is analogous to being the traffic cop of the computer. Data runs between the CPU and the program while images are processed in the CPU and sent to the video card via the motherboard for display. The same occurs for sound to be heard through the computer. As the traffic cop it contributes to how fast the computer is. If too much information is being passed around, a traffic jam occurs, and the system slows down. Motherboard speed is also measured in MHz, but this feature is usually standardized based on available technology. When considering a new computer, make sure to have the newest motherboard (chipset) available to insure future compliance.

CPU

The **CPU** (central processing unit) essentially represents the processor used by the computer to execute its many functions. The CPU can also be thought of as the brains of the computer. There are currently many processors available in computers. All are rated according to speed, regardless of brand. The speed at which a computer processes information is expressed in units of million cycles per second or megahertz (MHz). Generally, the higher the rating or speed of the processor or "chip," the faster the system will perform. The rate at which the computer processes information may or may not be important. The faster the speed, the faster the computer will accomplish the tasks requested. Speed becomes particularly important when using graphical environments. If a computer is relatively slow (90 MHz, such as an older Pentium II system), a lot of time is spent waiting for the computer to run software. If a computer is relatively fast (500 to 600 MHz, such as a Pentium III system), software commands are processed almost instantaneously.

Memory

Memory refers to the computer's ability to store information. Because software runs the computer, and the software occupies space, memory must be allocated within the computer's hardware for storage purposes. There are two basic types of memory: random access memory (RAM) and read-only memory (ROM). Information stored in RAM is represented by electrical impulses within a chip. The amount of RAM a system has a marker of how much data the computer can store while applications are in use, as well as current computer functions (scanning hard drive, floppy drive, etc.). When the computer is turned off, the information stored in RAM is lost. Access to RAM is much faster than access to a disk drive, hence, information can be retrieved considerably faster. More RAM in a system translates directly into increased performance. Read-only memory (ROM) contains programs built into the computer that are read-only and cannot be changed. All memory, whether it is RAM or ROM, is quantified in megabytes (MB).

Floppy Disk Drives

Traditional disk drives accommodate **floppy disks** that are 3.5 inches in diameter. These disks can store between 320 kilobytes (KB) and 2.0 MB of data, depending on their density. One of the newer drives at this time is the LS 120 Super Disk, which has a storage capacity of 120 MB on a slightly larger and thicker disk than the traditional 3.5-inch disk. The LS 120 disk drive can also run the older 3.5-inch floppy disks.

Other forms of storage are also entering the mainstream. These types of units can interface to the computer through various types of connectors or ports (serial, parallel). Generally, such devices represent larger floppy disks, where each single disk can store between 100 MB and 2 GB of data (depending on product). Different types of these devices have become popular in an attempt to expand the storage capacity of the traditional floppy disk. Tapes, similar to a music cassette tape, are also used. Tapes were commonly used in the early days of computing, but are relegated to more mundane functions these days (serving as backups to hard disks).

Fixed Hard Drives

Size does matter. This is where the operating system and any applications installed (operating system, programs, files) will go. **Hard drive** capacity is measured in megabytes or gigabytes. In simple terms, 1000 MB equals 1 GB. 1000 GB equals 1 terabyte (TB). The larger the hard disk, the more applications that can be installed. Applications are progressively getting larger. Recommend the largest hard drive available in order to prevent obsolescence. This is especially important for those who are active on the Internet and transfer files. Multimedia files are large, also.

CD/DVD Disc Drives

These are high-capacity removable discs. Compact discs hold 650 MB of data and DVDs have a theoretical maximum of 18 GB. This medium is the preferred medium of software distribution. Multimedia applications usually come in **CD** or **DVD** format due to their high storage capacity. The hardware for using them is different. DVD ROMs are the newest and are backward compatible with CD—that is, DVD players will play CDs, but not the other way around. Another reason this is important to mention is because there are writeable CD-ROM disks (CD-Rs) and DVD-RAMs, which are used to back up records and files in athletic training. CD-ROM disks hold large amounts of data and are practically indestructible. The technology to write to these disks is still quite expensive, but as costs go down, their usage will inevitably increase.

Display Adapters

Modern computers need to have a display adapter (graphics card). Its sole job is to transfer the visual images from computer form to a viewable monitor. These should come with a computer package. They can allow the user to connect the computer directly to a television if the correct type is installed. Characteristics of a video card include resolution (number of dots on the screen) and colors or color depth (thousands or millions of colors displayed).

Sound Adapters

Sound adapters (sound cards) convert the digital computer language for sounds into the audible sounds we hear. Without them the computer would not be able to produce sound. Sound cards allow for speakers or outside amplifiers to be connected to a computer. Different sound cards can process different sound effects, and some are entirely digital. For the most part any sound card is capable of reproducing every sound a computer program or operating system creates. A large segment of the education software produced today requires a sound interface.

Monitors

Monitors come in various sizes. The most common sizes are 14, 15, 17, 19, and 21 inches. Monitors are rated in a couple of areas. Dot pitch refers to the space between the individual phosphor spots that create the viewable image (too small to see). A common dot pitch is .26 mm. Along with the video card, the monitor determines how many pixels (individual picture elements that make up the images displayed in the monitor) it can display. Common display resolutions are 640 × 480, 800 × 600, or 1024 × 768 pixels. Obviously the more pixels available on a screen, the more space there is available for displaying. At the same time, the higher the resolution, the smaller each element (icon, font, picture, etc.). For example, more of a web page can be seen when viewing an image that is 1024×768 pixels than one that is 640×480 pixels. At the same time if the monitor is only 15 inches, 1024×768 pixels are going to be squeezed into a small area, making it difficult to view elements. In this case a larger 17- or 22-inch monitor would more adequately display all of the pixels.

Printers/Plotters

If a paper copy of a letter or a picture is wanted, a printer and maybe a plotter will be needed. Printers are common peripheral devices. They come in two basic styles: typeset quality and dot matrix. If you want publication-quality documents, either a laser-type printer or an ink-jet printer will meet the need. Dot matrix printers come either with 9-pin, 11-pin, or 24-pin configurations. They produce documents with relatively grainy text or graphics. Forms generated by dot matrix printers are the ones that can easily be seen to have been generated on a computer. Some dot matrix printers (24-pin) can produce near publication-quality documents. In the past, laser-type printers were much more expensive than dot matrix printers, but the cost of laser-type printers has fallen tremendously.

If it is necessary to print a graphic image, a plotter may be purchased. A plotter "draws" the picture with a robotic arm. Consequently, the output looks more hand-drawn than output from a printer. Plotters are more expensive than most printers, and their output is not much better than that of a quality laser printer.

Color printers and plotters are available for a break from the drab world of black-and-white and shades of gray. As might be expected, color costs more.

Scanners

Scanners can be used to "copy" graphics or text into a format that can be handled by the computer. Scanning graphic images (photographs, line drawings, cartoons, etc.) will allow incorporation of these images into word processing or other documents.

Scanning text can be helpful when transferring paper documents to computer. The document is simply scanned using optical character recognition (OCR) software to transform the document into a word processing file. It can then be used as any other word processing file. This technology eliminates the need to reenter information from paper documents.

Modems/Fax Boards/Network Cards

Modems allow documents (in electronic form) to be sent through telephone lines. They allow the sending and receiving of information to or from other computers. Many people connect to Internet service providers (ISPs) such as America Online or Prodigy through modems. This allows access to e-mail.

A fax board allows the sending or receiving of faxes from a computer. A note can be typed and simply sent to someone's fax machine. Computer fax boards are compatible with most fax machines. They are recognized and stored as graphical images by the computer. If both of these capabilities are desired, fax/modem boards are available and relatively inexpensive.

Network cards allow connection to a network. In order to use a network card, access to a server is a must. Network cards allow a much faster connection to the Internet. Check with the network administrator to purchase the correct type of network card.

BUYING CONSIDERATIONS

Warranties and cost should be considered when purchasing a computer system. A warranty covers the costs of repair or replacement of faulty parts on the computer. The hardware covered by the warranty and the duration of coverage are important aspects to consider. You need to know whether faulty equipment needs to be shipped back to the factory or can be serviced at a local dealer or distribution center. Does technical support cost money, or is it free via an 800 number? Is the purchase of a service contract needed to extend the warranty? Because the market is very competitive, it is not difficult to find an adequate warranty.

Cost is also an important factor when purchasing a computer. Make sure to purchase a computer that will meet all of the athletic training facility's needs without spending too much money. Plan on paying anywhere from less than $1,000 for computers with older technology or network computers to several thousand dollars for a top-of-the-line system. Again, competition among vendors results in very attractive prices. Avoid walking into a mall and purchasing the first computer that appears

to meet the needs. Mail order is an option to consider. If using mail order, make sure the company the computer is purchased from is reputable. If this is not done, it is possible to get stuck with a defective computer from a fly-by-night manufacturer.

Summary

1. The first choice is the operating system. This dictates the hardware to be purchased.
2. Microsoft Windows is the most popular PC-based system.
3. Apple Macintosh is a viable graphical interface computer.
4. Unix-based systems are good for complex calculations.
5. Mainframe computers are slower but accommodate large volume and network access.
6. The motherboard is the central piece of the computer.
7. The central processing unit runs programs.
8. Memory is divided into random access (RAM) and read only (ROM).
9. Floppy disks are convenient forms of storage for data.
10. Fixed hard drives have large capacities and are convenient for programs.
11. CD/DVD drives are excellent for storage and utilization of educational software.
12. Sound adapters are needed to run most educational software.
13. Monitors come in different sizes and different dot pitch.
14. Printers are either publication quality (laser and ink-jet) or dot matrix.
15. Other peripherals are useful productivity tools.

For Critical Thought

When it is all said and done, Melissa and Steve opt to purchase a new system. The computer they purchased is well equipped to handle modern software packages and has the space to store records well into the future. Would you do the same? Is the

extra money they spent worth the investment? Even the system they purchased will soon become obsolete. Is this a reason to avoid purchasing new systems? How upgradable are upgradable computers?

Websites

Windows 98 requirements:
http://www.microsoft.com/windows98/guide/Win98/SysReq/default.asp

Windows 95 requirements:
http://support.microsoft.com/support/kb/articles/q138/3/49.asp

Apple OS 8.6 System Requirements:
http://til.info.apple.com/techinfo.nsf/artnum/n60200

http://www.mkdata.dk/click/

 A huge site that explains everything to do with a computer (Illustrated)

http://www.sysopt.com/

 System upgrade information

http://www.tomshardware.com/

 Hardware reviews and information

http://computers.yahoo.com/computers/review/

 Computer reviews likely to stay current and online

Applications for Consideration

1. Mary Elizabeth has been allotted $1500 in her budget to purchase a new computer. Using computer trade magazines or electronics store prices, identify the hardware she should purchase. At a minimum she needs a computer, monitor, and printer. She needs a modem to connect to an ISP if she wants Internet access. Find the best deal!

2. In order to maximize the efforts in computerizing the athletic training room's record keeping, it was decided to network the three athletic training facility computers so data can be entered from multiple computers. Explore the hardware available for building a network. How much will it cost? What are the options? Explain the pros and cons for each solution.

CHAPTER 18

Computer Software

After reading this chapter, you should be able to:

- Evaluate and select computer software that will allow optimal athletic training facility operation.

- Evaluate and select software that fosters better personal productivity.

- Understand the purchasing and licensing options for software.

Key Terms

word processor
spreadsheet
database
hypertext markup language (HTML)
computer virus
freeware
shareware

FOR CRITICAL THOUGHT:
The Trouble with Software

Melissa and Steve now have their new system and are nearly ready to begin logging records. Before they can officially begin computerized record keeping, they need appropriate software. Fortunately, as is usually the case when new computers are purchased, software packages were preloaded on the system. The athletic training department computer already has a word processing suite, Internet software, printing software, and various CD-ROMs. Melissa and Steve need to purchase the specific record keeping software they will use for their athletes. The word processing suite allows the staff to type in the word processor. The other components of the package allow the staff to maintain databases and produce spreadsheets. Graphical presentations can be produced for classroom use using this package. Overall, this may be the most important piece of software they use. Steve and Melissa appreciate the other components that add functionality to the computer, allowing them to "surf the Web" and print documents, but they are still lacking the meat and potatoes for their intended use. They investigate several corporations' packages. The variety of features is nearly endless. Some software packages allow the athletic training staff to print out visual pictures of exercises, while others allow for take-home medication instructions. Overall, they are *satisfied with the choices but a little apprehensive considering how much they will have to learn before being able to use the software. The staff settles on a package that does nearly everything and contains only a few bells and whistles. The total cost of the software is $500. When the staff becomes proficient with the new software they will have complete medical histories, demographic information, injury evaluations, rehabilitation notes, referrals, and discharges all on the computer using this software package.*

Computers are of little value to most people without software applications. Software is available for nearly every task imaginable. Those that apply to athletic training facilities include word processing, spreadsheets, databases, scheduling, financial, e-mail clients, record keeping, educational, web authoring software, web browsing, and virus scanning software. Many other types of software exist and may be useful in particular situations. The most basic types of software will be reviewed.

Software can be purchased in retail stores, through instructional or technical media departments in local institutions, or through mail-order companies. Software prices tend to be higher at retail stores. Substantial discounts can often be realized when ordering through an institution. Many software companies offer reduced prices for educational institutions. Mail-order companies generally have reasonable prices and can often deliver an order in less than forty-eight hours.

Software may also be obtained through an institution by having the institution purchase a site license. Site licenses are much cheaper per copy than purchasing the software retail and may come without thorough documentation, but they are the full working software package.

Office suites—software packages that include several software applications such as a word processor, spreadsheet, and database—are sometimes more cost-effective than purchasing applications separately. There are two primary office suites, one by Microsoft and the other by Corel.

SOFTWARE APPLICATIONS

Word Processors

Word processor programs have evolved to an amazing level of sophistication. They are no longer simply substitutes for typewriters; they are actually desktop publishing tools.

Word processing applications in the athletic training room are quite varied. They can be used to simply write letters and reports to coaches or physicians, produce newsletters for alumni or patients, prepare flyers to advertise upcoming events, or even serve as an e-mail client. Essentially, if there is a need to produce something that has text or text and graphics, then it can most likely be done with a word processor.

Popular word processing packages include Microsoft Word, Corel WordPerfect, and WordPro.

Spreadsheets

Spreadsheets are software packages that provide sizable rows and columns in which numbers or text can be entered. These packages also provide mathematical functions that allow manipulation of the rows or columns of numbers that are entered. They also allow convenient table functions, especially where there may be some tabulation within columns or rows. Three-dimensional environments allow the user to create second-level spreadsheets in single cells of the first-level spreadsheet. Spreadsheets are extremely useful tools for creating and maintaining inventory records, traffic flow patterns, types of treatments given, and scheduling therapy appointments.

Spreadsheets are particularly useful for inventory maintenance and supplies purchasing. Consider the example inventory in figure 18-1. If all items generally purchased for the athletic training facility have been included, the quantity for each item can be edited as necessary and the subtotal for that item will automatically be adjusted. Likewise, if the unit price changes for an item, simply change it

	A	B	C	D	E
1	Item No.	Description	Qty.	Cost	Total
2	27450	Triadine, P-1 whirlpool cleaner	2	25.28	50.56
3	71660	Ultrasound Gel	6	30.00	180.00
4	81351	Stethoscope/single head	2	10.50	21.00
5	75200	Bandage scissors	3	11.25	33.75
6	75321	Filled instrument case	1	34.95	34.95
7	23120	Equipment utility cart	1	152.15	152.15

Figure 18-1   Sample spreadsheet application

on the spreadsheet and all subtotals and totals will automatically reflect the change.

Popular spreadsheet packages include Lotus 1-2-3, Microsoft Excel, and Corel Quattro Pro.

Databases

Database software is used to organize, coordinate, and relate data. Records can be stored in fields, linked to other records, and searched. Database software behaves much like a card file, except finding things goes much faster when the search is completed electronically.

Database software has tremendous flexibility and can be used to keep track of almost anything. Some programming skills are necessary to make the best use of a database. Once mastered, however, a database can be made to do anything, including keeping athletic training room records.

Popular database packages include dBase IV, Microsoft Access, and Microsoft FoxPro.

Financial

Financial software enables an athletic trainer to maintain the budget. Packages range from powerful applications designed for large businesses to user-friendly applications for small businesses or personal use. The small business/personal packages are generally sufficient for athletic training applications.

Popular financial packages include Microsoft Money, MoneyCounts, Peachtree Accounting, and Quicken.

E-mail Clients

E-mail has become an essential communication tool. In many ways, it has replaced both the telephone and regular mail. It is fast and efficient. There are many e-mail software packages available. Many word processors, web browsers, and office suites have e-mail built in. The most popular e-mail clients include Microsoft Outlook, Netscape Messenger, ccMail, Pegasus Mail, and Eudora.

Record Keeping

Computerized records can be an extremely powerful tool for the athletic trainer if used properly. The mundane task of shuffling paper and manually completing and filing medical records can be made less time consuming, and the information contained in the records can easily be used for tasks such as personnel justification and injury trends (see chapter 8 for more information on record keeping).

Several record-keeping software packages are available for both Windows and Macintosh systems. Database software or integrated software packages can also be used for record keeping, but they require a more extensive knowledge of computing.

There are several commercial record-keeping software packages that are designed specifically for athletic training such as *Athletic Injury Management (AIM)* from Cramer Products, Inc., *SportsWare Injury Tracking Software* from Computer Sports Medicine, Inc., and *SIMS/SIRS* from Med Sports Systems, Ltd. These packages vary in user-friendliness and power.

The package used will depend upon the record-keeping functions that would be computerized. We recommend requesting a demonstration disk from the manufacturer to evaluate each package.

Educational Software

Educational software is useful where clinicians have student supervision responsibilities. Software is available to demonstrate anatomy and physiology, provide problem-solving scenarios, and almost anything else that can be thought of. There are few applications specifically designed for athletic training, but software from other fields is abundant and many times quite applicable.

Lectures can be significantly enhanced through computer instruction. Laboratory experiences of students can be altered by a system that offers a teaching-learning interaction not possible through human/animal dissection (eliminate unnecessary time spent dissecting, space, expendable supplies that must be replaced, etc). This could be accomplished using Animated Dissection of Anatomy for Medicine (ADAM), for example, which allows viewing and dissection of regions of the human body. ADAM is an interactive multimedia atlas of the human anatomy that integrates detailed graphics with intuitive operation to enhance the knowledge and communication capability not possible with other forms of learning. Because cadavers are unavailable at many institutions, ADAM would allow the development of the laboratory components of anatomy and physiology or injury evaluation classes.

Clinical topics can be presented using printed text and interactive computer software. This type of software can include tutorials, case studies, and decision support tools. Together, the printed text and software present an integrated, systematic approach to learning the evaluation and treatment of an injury. As with any allied health profession, clinical exposure to all types of injuries and illnesses is not possible. Computer simulations allow a broader introduction to clinical situations that could reasonably occur on the job.

Web Authoring Software

Being able to produce a website for a facility (regardless of the type of setting) is becoming a necessity. Advertising and sharing of information are being accomplished with the World Wide Web. E-mail, calendaring, and many other applications may be delivered through a web page. Therefore, the availability of web authoring software is very important. Web pages are written in the **hypertext markup language (HTML)**. Modern HTML authoring software packages require little or no knowledge of HTML. Most now use a graphical, WYSIWYG (What You See Is What You Get) interface. There are a number of popular HTML editors, including Microsoft Front Page, Claris Home Page, Adobe Page Mill, HomeSite, HTML-pad, WebScripter, Webber32, Arachnophilia, and Macromedia Dream Weaver. In fact, many popular word processors can also produce HTML documents, including Corel WordPerfect and Microsoft Word.

Web Browsers

Web browsers are used to surf the Internet (see chapter 19). They are used to see personal and commercial websites and even to serve software, slideshows, and other multimedia presentations. There are two major web browsers available commercially: Microsoft Internet Explorer and Netscape Communicator. These require a connection with an Internet service provider, usually a private company accessed through local phone lines. Additionally there are commercial sites such as AOL (America Online), Compuserve, and Prodigy, which combine the web browser with the service provider. These types of services tend to be more limited in their Internet access than a service provider accessed through MIE or Netscape.

Virus Scanning Software

Virus scanning software has become a necessity. **Computer viruses** can permanently damage computer files if not removed. Virus scanning software detects and removes viruses before they cause damage. They require constant upgrading as new viruses are introduced almost daily. The most popular virus scanners are Dr. Solomon's, McAfee ViruScan, and Norton AntiVirus.

PURCHASING OPTIONS FOR SOFTWARE

Software may be purchased at a manufacturer's recommended price or it may be provided as freeware or shareware. **Freeware** is provided to users at no cost, but authors usually ask that the product not be modified or that the author is given credit. **Shareware** is provided as a "demo." If the user likes the software, he or she is asked to send the author money to use it. Often, shareware is disabled (not fully functional), time-bombed (stops working after

a period of time), or contains nag screens (windows that pop up reminding the user to register or pay for the product).

Shareware and freeware are usually cheaper than products made by larger software companies but are generally not as well supported. Shareware or freeware authors may be willing to modify their product for a clinician if there is a specific application that would be beneficial. Some authors make a living doing just that. E-mail addresses are often provided for authors, so contacting them is often easy. Shareware and freeware do not typically come with manuals or fancy packaging. They also tend not to be as well tested as commercially available packages. Table 18-1 contains URLs (Universal Resource Locator—the Web address) for several popular shareware/freeware sites.

Shareware is not free. Labeling software "shareware" is a licensing decision made by the company or individual who wrote the software. In order to have a fully functional copy of the software, a fee must be paid. The cost of shareware is usually less than that of software sold through retail outlets.

■ **TABLE 18-1**   Shareware and Freeware Download Sites

Name	Type	Description	URL*
TUCOWS.com	Shareware/freeware	The ultimate collection of Winsock software	www.tucows.com
TUDOGS.com	Freeware/shareware	The ultimate collection of gratis software	www.tudogs.com
JUMBO.com	Shareware/freeware	Contains over 300,000 shareware and freeware programs	www.jumbo.com
FILEMINE.com	Shareware	Collection of shareware downloads	www.filemine.com
WinFiles.com	Shareware/freeware	Windows shareware, drivers, bug fixes, etc.	www.winfiles.com
SOFTSEEK.com	Freeware/shareware	Collection of shareware and freeware programs	www.softseek.com
TheFreeSite.com	Freeware	Collection of freeware, some shareware	www.thefreesite.com

*URL may bring the viewer to a main page where a local server is selected.

Summary

1. Software is required to make a computer perform.
2. Word processors are communications tools used for applications from desktop publishing to simple letter writing.
3. Spreadsheets allow calculations in a tabular format.
4. Databases allow the categorization of data and access to any part or all of the data at any point in time.
5. Financial software helps track budgets.
6. E-mail software allows electronic mail communication.
7. Record-keeping software is in use throughout the medical arena, with some specifically designed injury tracking software available for athletic training.
8. Educational software helps with teaching, research, and review for students.
9. Web authoring software allows connection of a program or person to the Internet.
10. Web browsers access the Internet.
11. Virus scan software protects a computer from malicious programs that damage the contents.
12. Software may be purchased from manufacturers, or downloaded as shareware or freeware.

For Critical Thought

Steve and Melissa decided to purchase commercially available record-keeping software because they did not feel comfortable developing their own application. With minimal programming knowledge, they could have chosen to use database software to develop their own record keeping system. How could they go about doing this? Could they develop the software so they could access records over the web? What are the concerns they should consider if they integrate the records into web documents? What are the advantages?

Websites

(see also table 18-1)

www.microsoft.com

Microsoft's web page. Includes information on all of their products.

www.corel.com

Corel's web page. Includes information on all of their products, including Corel Office Suite and WordPerfect.

Applications for Consideration

1. Select a spreadsheet software package and prepare a budget for a sports medicine clinical site. Construct the file so that it can be used to generate purchase orders and serve as an inventory.
2. Using the Web, research the different office suites and determine the one that will best meet the needs for the clinical site in application 1. At minimum, consider the user-friendliness of the package, integration capabilities, institutional support for the software, and price. Prepare a list of advantages and disadvantages for all packages.

CHAPTER 19

The Internet

After reading this chapter, you should be able to:

- Use the Internet to locate information.
- Understand Internet tools such as e-mail, electronic discussion lists, and newsgroups.
- Demonstrate how to subscribe to an electronic discussion list.

Key Terms

Internet
World Wide Web
hypertext markup language (HTML)
electronic mail
search engines
electronic discussion lists
newsgroups
chatting
e-commerce
telemedicine

FOR CRITICAL THOUGHT:
Reaching Across the State

Cindy is an athletic trainer at a small Division III college. Her team physician practices in a city ninety miles away. The physician comes to town for games and at least once a week to see patients. Although the physician comes as often as she can, there are many instances when Cindy needs to consult with her but cannot because of distance. Transporting athletes to the city in order to see the physician is very time-consuming and expensive. College vehicles must be rented in order to drive to the city, and it is impractical for her to make the trip as it inevitably uses up at least half a day. She tries to find a local physician who is interested in helping out but is unable to do so. Being a bit of a technology maven, she begins thinking about using the Internet to communicate with the physician. The physician has Internet access in her office. Cindy has Internet access in the athletic training facility. She began to wonder if she could use voice and video delivered across the Internet to accomplish at least some physician visitations. She discusses this idea with the physician. Both are willing to look into the possibilities.

WHAT IS THE INTERNET?

The **Internet** began in the mid-1960s when government officials felt that a bombproof communications system was needed. They decided to link computers together throughout the country. Having information spread out over large areas would allow the system to weather a nuclear attack without hindering the ability for messages to get out.

In the early phases, only government think tanks and a few universities were linked. Basically the Internet was an emergency military communications system operated by the Department of Defense's Advanced Research Project Agency (ARPA). The whole operation was referred to as ARPANET.

ARPANET computers were installed at every university in the United States with defense-related funding. The Internet gradually evolved from a military pipeline to a communications tool for scientists. As more scholars came online, the system transferred from ARPA to the National Science Foundation.

Eventually, businesses, and later private citizens, began using the Internet, and the administrative responsibilities were once again transferred. Currently, no single party "operates" the Internet; there are several entities that "oversee" the system and the protocols that are involved.

WHAT IS THE WORLD WIDE WEB?

The **World Wide Web** is a graphical interface (or illustrated) version of the Internet. It began in the late 1980s when a physicist wrote a small computer program for his own personal use. This program allowed pages within his computer to be linked together using keywords. It soon became possible to link documents in different computers, as long as they were connected to the Internet. The document formatting language used to link documents is called **HTML (Hypertext Markup Language)**.

The Web remained primarily text based until 1992, when the first graphical web browser, NCSA (National Center for Supercomputing Applications) Mosaic, was written. This program was provided to interested users for free. The browser made it easier to access the different websites that had started to appear. Soon websites contained graphics, sound, and video as well as text.

ELECTRONIC MAIL

Electronic mail (or e-mail) has begun to replace more traditional methods of communication, such as the telephone and written or typed communications sent through U.S. mail. E-mail can be used to send text messages as well as any other type of computer file by means of attachments. There are specific e-mail programs (e.g., GroupWise, Microsoft Outlook) or the major web browsers all have e-mail capability (Netscape, Microsoft Internet Explorer, AOL, Prodigy).

SEARCH ENGINES

Search engines are important tools for the World Wide Web. Search engines are used to find information. Key words are typed in and the search engine software finds sites that include the key words. Some search engines have premade folders for popular topics. There are many search engines available. Often, sites will have their own built-in search engine so their pages can be searched.

Some of the more popular search engines include (alphabetical order):

- Altavista.com
- Excite.com
- Google.com
- GoTo.com
- HotBot.com
- Infoseek.com
- Lycos.com
- Northernlight.com
- Yahoo.com

ELECTRONIC DISCUSSION LISTS

The **electronic discussion list** is the tool most frequently used by athletic trainers to communicate, en masse, with each other (table 19-1). Electronic discussion lists are run by software that receives e-mail messages and distributes them to a list of subscribers. Subscribers can send questions or

■ **TABLE 19-1** Example Electronic Discussion Lists

LISTSERV Lists

AMSSMNET@LIST.MSU.EDU
American Medical Society of Sports Medicine

YUSTA@YORKU.CA
York University Sport Therapy Association

SPORTSMEDNEWS-L@WEBBER.OUP.CO.UK
Oxford Medical Publications: Sports Medicine and Sports
   Science News

CECSTALK@LISTSERV.DARTMOUTH.EDU
Outcomes research & CQI of health care

FINAN-HC@WUVMD.WUSTL.EDU
Health Care Financial Matters Discussion List

HEALTHRE@LSV.UKY.EDU
Health Care Reform Discussion List

HEALTHPOL@HOME.EASE.LSOFT.COM
Health care policy discussion list

AT-EDUC@RAZZLE.ETSU.EDU
Athletic Training Education; sports medicine; teaching
   and learning

MHCARE-L@LISTS.MISSOURI.EDU
Managed Health Care Discussion Forum

HS-ATC@LAWRENCEVILLE.ORG
High School Athletic Training Listserv

LISTPROC Lists

ATHTRN-L@LISTS.INDSTATE.EDU
Discussion list for athletic trainers

SPORTSCIENCE@STONEBOW.OTAGO.AC.NZ
The science of sport and exercise

WISHPERD@LISTPROC.SJSU.EDU
Women in Sport, Health, Physical Education, Recreation
   and Dance

HESTA-L@SCU.EDU.AU
Health and Exercise Science Technologists' Association

ERGOMED@UCDAVIS.EDU
Ergonomics and human factors in medicine

SPTSINJ-L@GALAXY.CSUCHICO.EDU
Sports medicine

MAJORDOMO Lists

HEALTH-FIN@VICNET.NET.AU
The Health Care Financing Email list

comments to the list and other subscribers may answer the question or respond to the comment. There are three major software packages that run these lists: LISTSERV, LISTPROC, and MAJORDOMO.

ATHTRN-L is the most popular electronic discussion list for athletic trainers. Important tips for using ATHTRN-L follow. Many of these same tips can apply to any electronic discussion. Information specific to ATHTRN-L will be used.

Subscribe/Unsubscribe

SUBSCRIBE and UNSUBSCRIBE allow subscribers to join or leave a list. To join ATHTRN-L, send an e-mail message like this:

TO: LISTPROC@LISTS.INDSTATE.EDU
SUBJ:
MESSAGE: SUBSCRIBE ATHTRN-L Firstname
Lastname

Note that the subject line is left blank. Of course, actual first name and last names should be used rather than Firstname Lastname in the MESSAGE field. This is a command that is sent to the computer that runs the list. Any message sent to the LISTPROC@LISTS.INDSTATE.EDU address is a command that will automatically be executed by the computer. Messages sent to the LISTPROC@ address will be returned in the form of an error message. Some common errors with this command are putting last name first and first name last, using someone else's first and last name, placing first and last name in quotes, placing first and last names between the less than and greater than symbols (<and>), and sending the SUBSCRIBE command to the ATHTRN-L@LISTS.INDSTATE.EDU address. Some mail software packages do not allow the sender to leave the SUBJ field blank. If text is included in the SUBJ field, it is still possible to successfully subscribe, but an error message might be generated. To leave ATHTRN-L, send the following e-mail message:

TO: LISTPROC@LISTS.INDSTATE.EDU
SUBJ:
MESSAGE: UNSUBSCRIBE ATHTRN-L

Mail/Mail Postpone/Digest

LISTSERV mail lists, such as ATHTRN-L, allow customization of the way mail is received. Postings from ATHTRN-L can be received as they are distributed (the default), one mailing per day including all messages posted that day, or no mail at all. To no longer receive mail from ATHTRN-L without using UNSUBSCRIBE, send the following e-mail message:

TO: LISTPROC@LISTS.INDSTATE.EDU
SUBJ:
MESSAGE: SET ATHTRN-L MAIL POSTPONE

Mail will not be received from ATHTRN- L until the MAIL command is sent as follows:

TO: LISTPROC@LISTS.INDSTATE.EDU
SUBJ:
MESSAGE: SET ATHTRN-L MAIL

If receiving mail in bulk is preferred rather than several times per day, use the DIGEST command:

TO: LISTPROC@LISTS.INDSTATE.EDU
SUBJ:
MESSAGE: SET ATHTRN-L MAIL DIGEST

Review

Send away for a file listing the names and e-mail addresses of all ATHTRN-L subscribers by sending the following e-mail message:

TO: LISTPROC@LISTS.INDSTATE.EDU
SUBJ:
MESSAGE: REVIEW ATHTRN-L

The REVIEW command should be used before sending a post requesting the e-mail address of an individual.

Conceal

CONCEAL allows removal of a subscriber's name from the REVIEW list. This is accomplished by sending the following message:

TO: LISTPROC@LISTS.INDSTATE.EDU
SUBJ:
MESSAGE: SET ATHTRN-L CONCEAL YES

Mail is still received. To unCONCEAL, send the following message:

TO: LISTPROC@LISTS.INDSTATE.EDU
SUBJ:
MESSAGE: SET ATHTRN-L CONCEAL NO

Athtrn-L Notebook

Every posting ever distributed by ATHTRN-L has been archived. This collection of archived postings is called a NOTEBOOK. The NOTEBOOK is divided into files that can be sent away for using the GET filename filetype command. Each file is called a LOG. ATHTRN-L used monthly LOGs until the last week of February 1995. After that, LOGs are separated by week. LOGs are descriptively named for easy retrieval. For example, LOG9406 is the LOG for June 1994. Since LOGs are now weekly, the log for the first week of August 1999 would be LOG9908A. "A" means the first week of the month. To send away for LOG9908A, send the following message:

TO: LISTPROC@LISTS.INDSTATE.EDU
SUBJ:
MESSAGE: GET ATHTRN-L LOG9908A

Searching ATHTRN-L's NOTEBOOK. Searching ATHTRN-L's NOTEBOOK is done through a web interface. Visit http://lists.indstate.edu:81/ and register for access. Once registered, this page is used to enter as a registered user. Once in, click on ATHTRN-L. The web page provides instructions to help.

Lists

While ATHTRN-L is the only discussion list specifically for athletic trainers, there are many other lists that may be of interest. Lists can be discovered by word of mouth or a list of lists can be sent away for. These instructions refer only to LISTPROC lists. There are other types of lists (e.g., LISTSERV, Mailbase, Mailserv, and Majordomo), but they will not be specifically addressed. To obtain a list of lists maintained by the ATHTRN-L server, send the following message:

TO: LISTPROC@LISTS.INDSTATE.EDU
SUBJ:
MESSAGE: LISTS

For a list of all known LISTPROC lists, send this message:

TO: LISTPROC@LISTS.INDSTATE.EDU
SUBJ:
MESSAGE: LISTS GLOBAL

This will return a very large file. A better solution is to search lists using keywords. For example, to search for all lists with the word SPORT in them, send the following message:

TO: LISTPROC@LISTS.INDSTATE.EDU
SUBJ:
MESSAGE: LISTS GLOBAL SPORT

Other Archived Materials

There are other useful documents archived by ATHTRN-L. Send the following message:

TO: LISTPROC@LISTS.INDSTATE.EDU
SUBJ:
MESSAGE: HELP {topic}

Topics include: add, afd, alias, approve, archive, configuration, configure, delete, discard, edit, fax, free, fui, general, get, hold, ignore, index, information, initialize, join, lists, listproc, live, lock, new-list, purge, put, query, recipients, review, release, reports, run, search, sendme, set, signoff, statistics, subscribe, system, unlock, unsubscribe, version, view, which, which-owned. The names are descriptive of the type of help that will be received. Not all are of interest to the casual user.

Postings

The primary purpose of ATHTRN-L is to foster discussion relating to athletic training. These discussions occur by sending electronic mail messages called postings. Subscribers submit lines in mailer software, paraphrase or type the quoted

material in. Also, if the original subject line was "Volunteers needed for Empire State Games" make sure the subject says "Re: Volunteers needed for Empire State Games." Some Reply functions do this automatically. Often, lines from an original posting are preceded by > (greater-than signs). Some mail editors do this automatically, others require it to be done manually or set the "indent character" to >.

Use normal capitalization and separate paragraphs with blank lines. This makes the message easier to read and more inviting to potential readers. Read the "To:" and "Cc:" lines in the message before it is sent. This gives all locations where the mail will be received. If a posting is found from a friend and the response is to be directed only to him or her, be careful not to use the Reply function. This will send the note to ATHTRN-L, not the person that is intended. ATHTRN-L is edited, so chances are the posting will not be distributed. The editor sends postings to the computer that runs the list (server). The server sends the posting to the editor. The editor reviews the posting and returns it to the server or the sender. If returned to the server, the posting is then distributed to all subscribers of the list.

Postings must:

- Be addressed to the whole list. If an individual response is desired, send it to that individual and not the whole list.
- Be professional and relevant to athletic training.
- The sender should include his or her name and e-mail address, usually at the end of the message. Many mail software packages include name and e-mail address in the FROM field, some do not. Please show courtesy to those who cannot ascertain a poster's identity from the FROM field. Many mail software packages allow the automatic inclusion of a signature file. A signature file is a file containing the sender's name, address, e-mail address, or whatever else he or she would like to include that is automatically tagged on the end of each message that is sent.
- Include information relevant to the posting in the subject line. Messages with blank subject lines are sent back to authors.

- Postings should not:
  - Degrade or personally attack anyone.
  - Include the entire contents of a message being responded to. The Reply key is very easy to use and is often misused. If the contents of the message are important, edit out unnecessary parts. No one wants to read the whole message again. Besides, it makes LOGs unnecessarily large. Postings that include whole parts of previous messages (i.e., not appropriately edited) are sent back to authors.

Netiquette

Netiquette means network etiquette. Proper netiquette reduces (but never eliminates) the possibility of a flame (a violent verbal expression of disapproval). When a discussion turns into a flame session, learning and sharing on the list decreases. Here is a suggested list of do's and don'ts:

Do:

- Leave just enough of a message to indicate what is being responded to. Eliminate mail headers with the possible exception of the "From:" line. If you can't figure out how to delete lines in a mailer's software, paraphrase or type the quoted material in.
- Use normal capitalization and separate paragraphs with blank lines. This makes messages easier to read and more inviting to potential readers.
- Read the "To:" and "Cc:" lines before the message is sent. If posting a reply to a friend, be careful not to use the Reply function. This will send the note to ATHTRN-L. ATHTRN-L is edited, so chances are the posting will not be distributed. The editor will read it, however. This is embarrassing to the editor and the person who inadvertently sent the personal message to the list.
- Posters should treat every post as though they were sending a copy to their boss, their minister, and their worst enemy. Although ATHTRN-L is more informal than a scientific journal, posters still want to be represented in a positive manner.

- Remember that no one can hear tone of voice intended by the poster. The nuances of verbal communication are not always apparent in text. Use emoticons (or smilies) like :-) or :(to represent intentions. CAPITAL LETTERS can be used for emphasis or net conventions used for "italics" and *underlines*.
- Remember that sometimes silence is more effective than words. If a discussion turns into a flame session, it is not necessary for every subscriber to voice their disapproval. The sooner a flame session is over, the sooner the list can return to productive discussions.

Don't:

- Include the entire contents of a previous posting in a reply. Never include mail headers except maybe the "From:" field. If deleting lines can't be figured out, paraphrase or manually type in the quoted material.
- Reply to a point in a posting without quoting or paraphrasing what is being responded to and who said it. Numerous postings may occur between the original message and the next reply. In some instances, the reply may get there before the original.
- Send a message like "Why doesn't anybody say anything about ultrasound and cold?" or "Who wants to talk about combining ultrasound and cold?" If someone wants to initiate a discussion on this topic, they should say something like "I read an article in the Journal of Athletic Training that says that cooling before ultrasound does not enhance the heating effects of ultrasound. I have found it to work exceptionally well clinically. I think it is because the combination of cold and ultrasound triggers an otherwise unknown temperature regulation reflex. Does anyone have an opinion on this matter?"
- Send lines longer than 70 characters. This is a courtesy to people whose mail gateways truncate extra characters. As might be expected, sentences that end in the middle are hard to follow.
- SEND A MESSAGE IN ALL CAPITAL LETTERS. CAPITALIZED MESSAGES ARE HARDER TO

READ THAN LOWERCASE OR MIXED CASE. BESIDES, ALL CAPS MEANS THAT SOMEONE IS YELLING. No one would stand up in the middle of a room and yell "Does anyone have a list of supplies to keep in a kit for a diabetic athlete?"

- Assume that readers can tell the difference between serious statements and satire or sarcasm. Use emoticons :∧)
- Send a posting that says nothing but "Me, too" "I don't know" "Good question" or the like. These one-liners are particularly annoying when the whole message that being responded to is included.

Network Abbreviations

Posting may include unfamiliar abbreviations. Internet users have begun to abbreviate commonly used phrases. Some of the more popular abbreviations include:

> BTW (by the way)
> FWIW (for what it's worth)
> IMHO (in my humble opinion)
> YMMV (your mileage may vary)

The purpose of an abbreviation is to shorten a frequently used phrase or word. In medical and allied medical fields, we use *LOTS* of abbreviations: ROM, bid, Hx, PRE, etc. These abbreviations are universally known and decrease note-taking time. In general, these are good abbreviations.

Abbreviations can become burdensome when it takes the reader an extended time to figure out what the abbreviation means, or worse yet, when the reader cannot figure out what the abbreviation means. Some abbreviations have become universally understood (like the ones listed above).

Use abbreviations only when they are considered the first-degree term. For example, consider IBM and International Business Machines. If one reads International Business Machines, his/her brain automatically translates that to IBM. In this case the abbreviation, IBM, is the first-degree term. Conversely, consider BTW and "by the way." When one reads BTW, his/her brain translates this to "by the way." Therefore, "by the way" is the first-degree term.

ATHTRN-L is not a scientific journal, so postings are not rejected if they use abbreviations. However, out of courtesy to the list and to help communicate ideas more clearly, keep abbreviations to a minimum.

NEWSGROUPS

Newsgroups are electronic bulletin boards. Items are posted and can be responded to by e-mail. Depending upon the online service or Internet service provider (ISP), a reader should have access to about 12,000 newsgroups (currently there are nearly 26,000). With this many newsgroups there is probably at least one out there for everyone. USENET, the international newsgroup network, is much like the Internet itself in that no single agency is in charge. The system connects computers from around the world. The system administrators decide which newsgroups to supply. Very few systems supply all of the newsgroups.

CHAT

Chatting in chat rooms is one of the most popular activities on the Internet. It is one of the big selling features of the online services. In fact, at one time the online services were the only place most people could go to chat in real time.

Chatting is done using "user names" or "nicknames." No real names are used. Chatrooms and IRC channels may seem a little intimidating at first due to the jargon often used. Taking time to see how the chat room runs and the language used is valuable before jumping in.

E-COMMERCE

E-commerce (electronic commerce) is the selling of products online. This is accomplished using web pages that allow visitors to view pictures and descriptions of the products they are interested in purchasing and ordering them, using credit cards, over the Internet. Special encryption techniques are used to protect the transmission of credit card numbers to protect against theft. Online ordering of products ranging from computer software to collectible sports cards is available. Doing business electronically has become a necessity. Products delivered may be goods or services. Athletic training facilities and sports medicine clinics may begin delivering information and advice, for a fee, to interested visitors to their web pages.

TELEMEDICINE

Telemedicine can be defined as the use of modern information technology, especially two-way interactive audio/video telecommunications, computers, and telemetry, to deliver health services to remote patients and to facilitate information exchange between healthcare providers. It can include the transfer of basic patient information over computer networks, the transfer of images such as radiographs, CT scans, MRIs, ultrasound studies, pathology images, video images of endoscopic or other procedures, patient interviews and examinations, consultations with medical specialists, and healthcare educational activities.

Summary

1. The Internet is an international communications network.
2. The World Wide Web is the graphical interface with the Internet.
3. The primary WWW communications interface is HTML.
4. Electronic mail is a major communications method.
5. Search engines allow users to seek specific information on the Web.
6. Electronic discussion lists are e-mail groups that enable others to respond.
7. ATHTRN-L is one of the most popular electronic mail groups.
8. Usenet News newsgroups are another form of electronic mail communications.
9. Chat and chat rooms enable instantaneous e-mail communications.
10. E-commerce enables people to purchase goods and services over the Web.
11. Telemedicine is a form of multimedia that includes both visual and audio real-time communications.

For Critical Thought

Cindy and her team physician experiment with Net-Meeting, a software package that delivers video and voice over the Internet. Although the video is a bit choppy and the voice is sometimes garbled, for some things it was much easier than driving a 180-mile round trip. Both computers were connected to the Internet using 33.3 baud modems. They began looking into the possibility of getting T1 connections into both offices. Their feeling was that the faster connection would improve both video and voice performance. They began to do a cost analysis for two T1 connections as compared to driving back and forth between the two sites. They were also realistic in the number of trips that would actually be replaced with technology. Although T1 connections appear to be cost prohibitive at this time, they continue to keep their eyes open for technologies to improve this process. They continue to use NetMeeting whenever possible.

Websites

http://www.atmeda.org/
    American Telemedicine Association
http://www.telemedtoday.com/
    Telemedicine Today
http://www.telemedmag.com/

Telehealth Magazine
http://www.ctl.org/
    Telemedicine Law
http://www.nttc.edu/telemed.html
    NASA Telemedicine technologies gateway

http://www.stevegrossman.com/jargpge.htm

Chatter's Jargon Dictionary

http://www.access.digex.net/~ikind/babel.html

BABEL: A Glossary of Computer Oriented Abbreviations and Acronyms

Applications for Consideration

1. Join an electronic discussion list, such as ATHTRN-L, and collect the following information:
   - archived postings from the list on a specific topic
   - a list of all subscribers to the list and their e-mail addresses
   - send for help information from the list
   - send a posting to the list regarding a topic of interest, being sure to follow proper netiquette.

2. Design a web page for your current clinical site. Be sure to include all of the information needed to inform a visitor about the purpose of the facility. Are there other features that can be included to improve the functioning of the facility?

Glossary

A

accident an unforeseen event or circumstance that often results in personal injury to the person(s) involved.

allied health professional person who has limited scope of medical practice within the healthcare system.

Americans with Disabilities Act the law designed to eliminate discrimination against persons with disabilities.

assumption of risk a legal concept for defense against a liability claim in which the plaintiff knew before taking part in an activity that the activity was potentially dangerous, but chose to take part regardless.

athletic trainer an allied health professional who works under the direction of a supervising physician and who provides a variety of services, including injury prevention, evaluation, immediate care, treatment, and rehabilitation of injuries and illnesses in physically active individuals.

athletic training the allied health profession dealing with the prevention, care, and rehabilitation and reconditioning of athletic injuries and injuries to those engaged in physical activity.

athletic training services practicing the profession of athletic training in diverse settings in accordance within applicable state laws and the standard of care.

B

basic medical insurance insurance that covers injuries sustained during competition, supervised practice, and/or team travel.

benefits remuneration beyond salary or wages such as vacation time, health insurance, or retirement funds.

bid written request for dollar amounts to be placed on goods.

breach of duty a condition in which the standard of care has been violated.

budget a financial plan of operation for a program that specifies the services to be provided and the resources that must be expended to achieve the appropriate level of service.

burnout condition encompassing emotional exhaustion, depersonalization, and reduced personal accomplishment that can occur in people who deal with other people.

C

catastrophic insurance insurance that provides coverage in the event that an injury is so severe that activities of daily living are permanently compromised.

causation the determination that the actions led to damage and to what extent the individual was responsible for the damage caused.

central processing unit (CPU) the processing chip used by computers to execute its functions.

certification means the individual has submitted minimum credentials of eligibility and then taken some form of state-administered examination.

Certified Athletic Trainer (ATC) an athletic trainer who has passed the NATABOC certification examination.

chain of command identification of the person responsible for the health care of patients and the direction of subordinates.

chatting conversation via a keyboard through a central open computer network.

clinical evaluation evaluation of objectives to be demonstrated and reinforced in psychomotor and affective domains for the major tasks a student has completed in the classroom.

coalition a group that is large enough to sustain its position on a particular issue but has differing viewpoints on other issues.

communications (medical records) written records that enhance the understanding of diagnoses and treatments.

compact disk (CD) high capacity removable disk for storage of programs and data.

comparative negligence developed as a reaction to the all-or-none principle of contributory negligence.

computer virus a program that attached to files and may cause damage to files or the computer.

concept planning document a document that defines the philosophy of the facility and the intended allocation of space.

conflict a disagreement in which the parties are aware of the directly opposite nature of their respective positions and in which each side wishes to maintain its position.

conflict resolution modification of the positions of opposing parties using imposition, withdrawal, inaction, yielding, compromise, and/or problem solving.

consent agreeing to a particular course of action.

content theories theories that focus internally on needs and how they can be satisfied.

contract written or oral document that binds an employer to an employee.

contributory negligence arises when the plaintiff's own negligence contributed to the proximate cause of the injury.

corridor deductibles occur when the secondary coverage has a deductible that is not affected by the primary coverage payments.

cover letter letter explaining why a potential employee is writing to the employer and what the employer should pay attention to in his or her résumé.

CPT Codes (*Physicians Current Procedural Terminology*, 1994 edition) identifies the procedure performed—used in conjunction with diagnostic codes for billing purposes.

D

damage component of negligence, specifying the injury caused to another.

database software used to organize, coordinate, and relate data.

deductible a set amount of money not covered by an insurance plan.

direct video disk (DVD) higher capacity than a CD, used to store video, audio and data.

disappearing deductibles the deductible that must be paid when the primary insurance carrier does not reimburse enough money to cover the cost of the deductible, whereas if the primary reimbursement is greater than the deductible amount, the deductible is waived.

disqualification decision based on valid medical reasons that the athlete is at risk of injury if allowed to compete.

documentation for reimbursement records establishing the interaction of a patient with the healthcare system, including the procedures performed and the diagnosis that required these procedures.

duty responsibility of a healthcare provider.

E

e-commerce (electronic commerce) the selling of products online.

electronic discussion lists discussion threads run by software that receives e-mail messages and distributes them to a list of subscribers.

electronic mail electronic messages sent over a network.

emergency care plan a written document that defines the standard of care required in every conceivable event during an emergency situation.

exclusion a situation that is specifically not covered by the insurance policy, such as overuse injuries.

exclusive provider organization (EPO) a group of providers that has a contract with an insurer, employer, third-party administrator, or other sponsor.

exemption the process of identifying a specific profession or group of practitioners and allowing that group to utilize the methods of a licensed profession.

expanded coverage package deals that include riders for common and significant athletic medical problems falling outside basic medical insurance.

F

feedback communication that is positive, negative, or problem-centered; feedback keeps workers informed regarding where they stand and what the future may hold.

fee-for-service arrangement in which healthcare services are paid directly by the healthcare recipient.

floor plan architectural drawing to scale showing actual space utilization.

floppy disk portable storage unit for data and programs.

freeware computer software provided to users at no cost, but authors usually ask that the product not be modified or that the author is given credit.

fund raising raising monies outside the normal budgeting process.

G

gatekeeper healthcare provider who controls access into the healthcare system.

Good Samaritan laws laws stating that those who come to the aid of an injured person and act within their standard of care are immune from legal actions or damages.

graphical user interface software interface that allows users to point and click to elicit commands to the computer.

H

hard drive a fixed drive that uses an internal disk to store data and programs.

health appraisal update process used for returning athletes in which the athletic trainer is required to identify and document all conditions or injuries that have developed since the last PPE or health appraisal update.

health insurance insurance that covers all that medical insurance does and, in addition, includes preventive care, which medical insurance does not.

health maintenance organization (HMO) organization that provides health care to plan participants through hired or contracted healthcare providers.

human relations management (or democratic administration) a style of management based on reaction to scientific management that incorporated the behavioral sciences.

human resources management a series of decisions about the employment relationship that influence the effectiveness of employees and organizations by assessing conditions, setting objectives, and evaluating the results.

hypertext markup language (HTML) the document formatting language used to develop web pages.

I

immunity condition indicating that an athletic trainer may not be sued if found liable for actions because of employment by a government agency, such as a public education institution.

informed consent document that explains a procedure to the patient, including the risks and the projected outcome, and presents an opportunity to ask questions, determining whether the patient still wants to go on with the procedure.

intergroup conflict in the workplace, if limited resources are fought over, when one side wins the other must lose, so that not only reaching goals but also controlling access for the other group become a focus.

International Classification of Disease (ICD) codes codes used to communicate diagnoses to insurance companies.

Internet a worldwide network of computers.

interview a potential employee's contact with an employer to determine if he or she is appropriate for the job.

intrinsic and extrinsic factors conditions of a job that lead to job satisfaction or dissatisfaction.

inventory listing of supplies and equipment on hand.

J

job description a detailed advertisement that describes a position and sets out the conditions of employment for that position.

L

Leadership (Managerial) Grid a system integrating concern for production with concern for people.

Leadership studies a series of management studies during the 1940s that described characteristics of people centered management.

legal (use of records) medical records establish what was done and told to patients.

liability responsibility for actions that cause harm to others and for which the courts routinely award damages.

liability insurance insurance that covers athletic trainers who are practicing their profession legally against liability awards to an injured party.

licensed refers to a person who meets qualifying standards and passes an examination.

life-threatening emergency situation in which the victim's life is in immediate danger (e.g., failure of the cardiovascular or respiratory systems, shock or severe hemorrhaging).

line-item budget budget system in which expenditures are itemized by categories such as expendable supplies, professional expenses, operations, and capital outlays.

M

malpractice a liability by which there is an unfavorable outcome of patient-athletic trainer interaction due to any number of reasons, among them negligence, failure to inform, breach of contract, or assault and battery.

managed care type of care provision where arrangements are made with selected providers to deliver comprehensive healthcare services.

managed care organization organization that arranges delivery of healthcare services.

Management by Objectives a participative system integrating personnel needs with those of the association.

maturity in an athletic medical context, biological development compared with chronological age.

McGregor's Theory X and Theory Y a complementary pairing of scientific management and human relations management incorporating the psychological variables omitted by these two methods.

mediation third-party intervention that brings together parties of a dispute and tries to direct negotiations to common ground allowing settlement of the problem.

medical examination evaluation of the various body regions and systems, including head, eyes, ears, nose, throat, chest, abdomen, skin conditions, and genitalia, including hernia evaluation, designed to identify the presence of common medical conditions.

medical history information about the past relating to an athlete's family background, personal involvement with the medical system, and personal orthopedic background.

medical insurance a policy that will reimburse the policyholder a fixed percentage of the cost of medical services related to illness or injury.

medical record storage and retrieval of information from a specific location containing personal, financial, and medical data; contents may be prescribed by law.

medical record software computer software used to store and retrieve information from a specific location containing personal, financial, and medical data.

motherboard what every device in the computer connects to (CPU, RAM, video card, hard drive, sound card, etc.).

motivation the provision of the opportunity to work, through which the workers will meet their individual needs.

multisite communication when multiple sites are used for practice and competition, a method of communications is necessary to link the field site with emergency medical personnel.

N

needs missing elements that people seek to gain in order to reach physical and mental homeostasis.

negligence conduct that can either be an act of commission that invades the interests of another or an act of omission where another is injured by one's failing to act when there was a duty to act.

negotiation a process of communication in which all competing sides to a disagreement examine the issues, give their positions, and exchange proposals and counterproposals.

networking using a computer interconnected to other computers or interacting with professional peers.

newsgroups electronic bulletin boards.

non–life-threatening emergency situation in which the victim's life is not in immediate danger, yet requires the intervention of the emergency medical system and/or transportation to a hospital emergency room for treatment (e.g., fractures).

O

open accounts accounts that exist to purchase supplies in smaller quantities.

operant conditioning theory that a rewarded behavior will be repeated while a punished behavior will be extinguished.

operating system software that controls a computers operations.

P

performance evaluation a measurement and communications process describing the extent to which an employee is meeting job performance objectives.

personnel athletic trainers, therapists, physicians, and other persons who work in athletic, medical, or sports medicine clinic settings.

personnel scheduling various ways of assigning athletic trainers and other persons to cover practice, competition, and reconditioning of athletic injuries.

point-of-service (POS) plan healthcare plan in which members receive care provided by network participating providers, but have the option of obtaining care outside the network.

policies the basic framework of principles and rules used to govern and expedite decision making.

practice setting location or place where a healthcare professional provides service.

preferred provider organization (PPO) purchasers of health care services who choose organizations of providers to provide health care services for their covered individuals.

premium the amount of money that the policyholder pays to the insurance company to execute the insurance policy.

preparticipation physical examination (PPE) an examination designed to collect medical information about athletes to ensure their readiness to participate in their chosen sports.

primary coverage all expenses related to an injury that are paid by the insurance policy.

procedures description of the process by which something is done; there may be some overlap in the written definitions of the what and why (policy) and how (procedure).

process theories theories that look at how individual behavior is directed and maintained.

profession membership in a group that signifies having a duty to exercise skills and knowledge normally employed by others to prevent unreasonable risk of harm to others.

program area subunits that house similar activities, such as electrotherapy or hydrotherapy, manual exercise, or team preparation, that exist within some budget systems.

program budgets functional categories within an overall budget that include all of the costs of a particular program.

public relations presentation of information about and points-of-view concerning a particular topic.

public relations plan a formal plan to advance the public's knowledge in a particular area.

purchase plans methods used to purchase equipment and supplies, usually either competitive bid, direct purchase, or open account.

R

recruiting advertising a position in an athletic training setting to find prospective employees.

registration refers to a professional who meets standards of eligibility and pays a fee.

research in athletic training, using medical records to document numbers and types of injuries, traffic flow patterns at different times of day or in different athletic training rooms, and so on.

résumé a document that is the initial contact when applying for a job; it allows individuals to present their education, work experience, and career objectives to potential employers.

rider a clause in which the insurance carrier agrees to add previously excluded situations for an additional premium.

risk management policies that strive to either eliminate, share, or modify and reduce the risk associated with a particular activity.

role definition whether roles are within the mandatory, allowable, or forbidden realm of work responsibilities.

S

scientific management concept that management could be reduced to a mathematical model in which money was the incentive to motivate people to perform jobs.

screening utilizing the available information to select those applicants who will be interviewed for an athletic training position.

search engines software used to find information on the Internet.

searching the process of locating professionals for posted jobs.

secondary coverage coverage whereby all remaining expenses after the use of a primary coverage plan are paid by the policy.

self-insurance a type of primary coverage plan in which an institution places the amount of money normally paid as a premium into an escrow account and pays medical expenses directly from that account.

shareware computer software that is provided as a demo. If the user likes the software, he/she is asked to send the author money to use it.

situational leadership model containing elements from the leadership studies relating task-oriented and relationship-oriented variables.

SOAP progress-note writing system that has four parts: subjective, objective, assessment, and plan.

software computer programs written for a specific purpose, such as medical record keeping.

space allocation the assignment of available square footage to various tasks in an athletic training room.

sport-specific test designed to assess readiness to participate in a specific sport rather than to assess overall athletic ability or aerobic conditioning.

spreadsheet software packages that provide rows and columns in which to enter numbers or text.

standard of care the level of medical sophistication and competency that must be demonstrated by a person who has similar education and training to other persons in that particular group.

standard operating procedures agreed-upon procedures that are carried out during the execution of an emergency care plan.

statute of limitations state law that gives the length of time in years that a person has to file a claim (between one and eight, depending on the state).

straight deductible a fixed dollar amount that must be paid out of pocket for each contact or procedure.

strategies for change various methods of orchestrating change in an organization.

student athletic trainer organizations student athletic trainer run groups that promote the common interests of student athletic trainers.

T

telemedicine the use of modern information technology, especially two-way interactive audio/video telecommunications, computers, and telemetry to deliver health services to remote patients and to facilitate information exchange between healthcare providers.

tort legal wrong other than breach of contract for which the courts provide some remedy, usually in the form of monetary damages.

Total Quality Management (TQM) a customer-/consumer-oriented philosophy that strives to always meet or exceed the needs and expectations of the consumer in an ongoing, planned system.

U

Universal Billing (UB) codes codes used in hospitals to bill for health care services provided.

W

waiver a legal contract in which the signatories give up the right to sue for damages in exchange for services performed for them.

word processor software that can operate in a simple manner, such as a typewriter, or in a complex manner, such as a desktop publishing facility.

World Wide Web (www) a graphical interface (or illustrated) version of the Internet.

Z

zero-based budgets refinements of performance budgets in which the organization constructs a new performance budget each year independent of performance in past years, as if it were brand new.

zone of indifference opinions of directives that are expected by workers from what they know of their organization.

Index